Lecture Notes
in Business Information Processing 158

Series Editors

Wil van der Aalst
Eindhoven Technical University, The Netherlands

John Mylopoulos
University of Trento, Italy

Michael Rosemann
Queensland University of Technology, Brisbane, Qld, Australia

Michael J. Shaw
University of Illinois, Urbana-Champaign, IL, USA

Clemens Szyperski
Microsoft Research, Redmond, WA, USA

Andrzej Kobyliński
Andrzej Sobczak (Eds.)

Perspectives in Business Informatics Research

12th International Conference, BIR 2013
Warsaw, Poland, September 23-25, 2013
Proceedings

 Springer

Volume Editors

Andrzej Kobyliński
Warsaw School of Economics
Department of Business Informatics
Warsaw, Poland
E-mail: andrzej.kobylinski@sgh.waw.pl

Andrzej Sobczak
Warsaw School of Economics
Department of Business Informatics   ·
Warsaw, Poland
E-mail: andrzej.sobczak@sgh.waw.pl

ISSN 1865-1348   e-ISSN 1865-1356
ISBN 978-3-642-40822-9   e-ISBN 978-3-642-40823-6
DOI 10.1007/978-3-642-40823-6
Springer Heidelberg New York Dordrecht London

Library of Congress Control Number: 2013947536

Typesetting: Camera-ready by author, data conversion by Scientific Publishing Services, Chennai, India

Printed on acid-free paper

Springer is part of Springer Science+Business Media (www.springer.com)

Preface

Business Informatics is a discipline that combines Information and Communication Technology (ICT) with the knowledge of management. It is concerned with the development, use, application, and the role of management information systems and other ICT solutions. It is an established academic and research discipline. This is evidenced by the fact that many universities offer degrees in business informatics. The academic teaching programs are not detached from the research. The area of research that lies in the focus of business informatics is constantly evolving. It is clearly visible when you look at the topics of subsequent conferences under the eternal name Perspectives in Business Informatics Research (BIR). The BIR conference series was established 13 years ago as the result of a collaboration of researchers from Swedish and German universities. The goal was to create a forum where researchers in business informatics, both senior and junior, could meet and discuss with each other. The conference series has a Steering Committee, to which one or two persons from every appointed organizer are invited. So far, BIR conferences were held in: Rostock (Germany – in 2000, 2004, 2010), Berlin (Germany – 2003), Skövde (Sweden – 2005), Kaunas (Lithuania – 2006), Tampere (Finland – 2007), Gdańsk (Poland – 2008), Kristianstad (Sweden – 2009), Riga (Latvia – 2011) and Nizhny Novgorod (Russia – 2012). This year's 12th International Conference on Perspectives in Business Informatics Research (BIR) was held in Warsaw (Poland), during September 23rd and 25th, 2013, at the Warsaw School of Economics (SGH), the oldest and most prestigious Polish university of economics and business.

This year the BIR conference attracted 54 submissions from 14 countries: ranging from Taiwan to Peru, and from Sweden to Israel. They were rigorously reviewed by 41 members of the Program Committee representing 21 countries. As the result, 19 full papers (presenting novel research results) and 5 short papers (reporting on preliminary results of ongoing research) from 12 countries have been selected for publication in this volume. The volume also includes invited papers by Witold Abramowicz and Bernhard Thalheim. The papers presented at the conference cover many aspects of the business informatics research, and this year there is a particular emphasis on business process management, enterprise and knowledge architecture, information systems and services, organizations and information systems development. Apart from the main conference satellite events: workshops and a doctoral consortium took place during the first day of the conference.

We would like to thank everyone who contributed to the BIR 2013 conference. First of all we thank the authors for presenting their research, we appreciate invaluable contributions from the members of the Program Committee and external reviewers and we thank all the members of the local organization team from the Department of Business Informatics at the Warsaw School of Economics for their help in the organization of the conference. We acknowledge the EasyChair development team for providing a convenient tool for preparing the proceedings and the Springer publishing team for their collaboration. Last but not least, we thank the Steering Committee and we hope that BIR 2013 will be a memorable link in the BIR conference series.

July 2013

Andrzej Kobyliński
Andrzej Sobczak

Conference Organization

Program Co-chairs

Andrzej Kobyliński	Warsaw School of Economics, Poland
Andrzej Sobczak	Warsaw School of Economics, Poland

Program Committee

Jan Aidemark	Linneaus University, Sweden
Esma Aïmeur	University of Montreal, Canada
Eduard Babkin	Higher School of Economics (Nizhny Novgorod), Russia
Per Backlund	University of Skövde, Sweden
Janis Barzdins	University of Latvia, Latvia
Rimantas Butleris	Kaunas University of Technology, Lithuania
Sven Carlsson	Lund University, Sweden
Witold Chmielarz	Warsaw University, Poland
Cristian Ciurea	Bucharest University of Economic Studies, Romania
Horatiu Dragomirescu	Bucharest University of Economic Studies, Romania
Peter Forbrig	University of Rostock, Germany
Bogdan Ghilic-Micu	Bucharest University of Economic Studies, Romania
Jānis Grabis	Riga Technical University, Latvia
Michal Gregus	Comenius Unniversity, Slovakia
Horst Günther	University of Rostock, Germany
Markus Helfert	Dublin City University, Ireland
Björn Johansson	Lund University, Sweden
Kalinka Kaloyanova	University of Sofia – FMI, Bulgaria
Valeriy Kalyagin	Higher School of Economics (Nizhny Novgorod), Russia
Dimitris Karagiannis	University of Vienna, Austria
Mārīte Kirikova	Riga Technical University, Latvia
Vladimir Krylov	MeraLabs, Russia
Yannis Manolopoulos	Aristotle University of Thessaloniki, Greece
Lina Nemuraite	Kaunas University of Technology, Lithuania
Jacob Nørbjerg	Copenhagen Business School, Denmark
Jyrki Nummenmaa	University of Tampere, Finland
Enn Õunapuu	Tallinn University of Technology, Estonia
Tomáš Pitner	Masaryk University, Brno, Czech Republic
Nava Pliskin	Ben-Gurion University of the Negev, Israel

Václav Řepa	University of Economics, Czech Republic
Narcyz Roztocki	State University of New York at New Paltz, USA
Alessandro Ruggieri	University of Tuscia, Italy
Kurt Sandkuhl	University of Rostock, Germany
Chris Stary	Johannes Kepler University, Austria
Janis Stirna	Stockholm University, Sweden
Bernhard Thalheim	Christian Albrechts University, Germany
Benkt Wangler	University of Skövde, Sweden
Stanisław Wrycza	University of Gdańsk, Poland
Jelena Zdravkovic	Stockholm University, Sweden
Iryna Zolotaryova	Kharkiv National University of Economics, Ukraine

BIR Steering Committee

Kurt Sandkuhl	University of Rostock, Germany (Chair)
Eduard Babkin	State University - HSE, Nizhny Novgorod, Russia
Per Backlund	University of Skövde, Sweden
Rimantas Butleris	Kaunas University of Technology, Lithuania
Sven Carlsson	Lund University, Sweden
Peter Forbrig	University of Rostock, Germany
Horst Günther	University of Rostock, Germany
Mārīte Kirikova	Riga Technical University, Latvia
Harald Kjellin	Kristianstad University College, Sweden
Andrzej Kobyliński	Warsaw School of Economics, Poland
Lina Nemuraite	Kaunas University of Technology, Lithuania
Jyrki Nummenmaa	University of Tampere, Finland
Eva Söderström	University of Skövde, Sweden
Bernd Viehweger	Humboldt University, Germany
Benkt Wangler	University of Skövde, Sweden
Stanisław Wrycza	University of Gdańsk, Poland

Additional Reviewers

Kestutis Kapocius, Lithuania
Sergejs Kozlovics, Latvia
Edgars Rencis, Latvia
Edvinas Sinkevicius, Lithuania Tomas

Skersys, Lithuania
Dirk Stamer, Germany
Serhii Znakhur, Ukraine

Table of Contents

Organisations and Information Systems Development

Information Systems and Services

Applications

Should Business Informatics Care about Linked Open Data?

Witold Abramowicz[1] and Krzysztof Węcel[1,2]

[1] Poznań University of Economics,
Al. Niepodległości 10, 61-875 Poznań, Poland
{witold.abramowicz,krzysztof.wecel}@ue.poznan.pl
[2] Business Information Systems Institute Ltd., Poland

Abstract. In this paper the current situation in organisations regarding the reuse of information is discussed. Problems of both information publishers and consumers are presented. Many of them can be avoided by adopting the new paradigm for sharing information, namely linked open data. Although this paradigm is getting on importance, being promoted by public administration, still it has not achieved a critical mass satisfactory for enterprises. Future research challenges for business informatics with respect to linked data on the Web are sketched in the conclusions.

Keywords: linked open data, information reuse, ontological foundations of business, research directions, challenges.

1 Introduction

In today's world enterprises need to access, retrieve and integrate information from external sources. In order to achieve this they have to overcome many technical barriers like various data formats, frameworks, and interfaces. Virtually in every company there are departments responsible for acquisition and publishing of information. Some of them also aggregate information streams from different external sources that are relevant for their area of responsibility. Managing the heterogeneous environment is burdensome and costly. Various solutions are then target of business informatics research.

One can expect that information of the highest credibility is published by public bodies. The mission to make data open is very often imposed by law, e.g. the US Open Government Directive of December 8, 2009[1], or European Directive on the re-use of public sector information (PSI Directive, 2003)[2]. General economy data as well as data concerning operations of specific institutions is made available today by various public bodies. They analyse relevant sectors of economy, public life or governmental processes. In the end information is often published on the organisations' web pages. The exemplary topics of published data include:

---

[1] http://www.whitehouse.gov/omb/assets/memoranda_2010/m10-06.pdf
[2] http://ec.europa.eu/information_society/policy/psi/rules/eu/index_en.htm

A. Kobyliński and A. Sobczak (Eds.): BIR 2013, LNBIP 158, pp. 1–9, 2013.

- statistical reports on the state of the economy
- the reports on banking sector delivered by national banks
- the legal system (including courts and prisons)
- public procurement data
- the local government budgets.

2 Motivation

In the following sections we briefly analyse the situation regarding reuse of information both from publishers' and consumers' points of view.

2.1 Publishing – The Supply Side

An important source of data in each country is the statistical office. There is usually an on-line system which offers access to data. For example, EUROSTAT's system offers powerful data browsing functions with ability to slice the data geographically, temporally and according to different measures relevant for the particular subject. It is very valuable for various economic, demographical and social analyses. However, it only allows to export some of the data in the form of spreadsheets. The rest is available as tables on the web pages or in PDF documents, which are intended for people to read, but are hardly digestible by programs.

Similar approach is adopted by many national statistical offices. Fig. 1 present an example of Central Statistical Office in Poland. Data can be located by navigation in a specifically designed structure (left). Data itself is available as Excel files (right).

Excel spreadsheet is considered as a proprietary format. Moreover, it does not allow to represent deeper structure than just rows and columns. Therefore, institutions possessing more complex data migrate towards more advanced solutions.

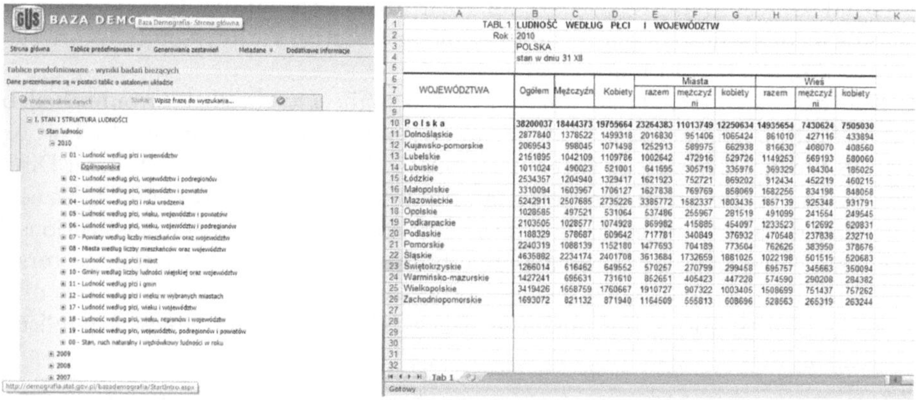

Fig. 1. Statistical data available as spreadsheet

Data originates from a database that is maintained internally in the organisation. Usually it is published by creating a custom built script, that exports the desired portion of data, then formats it according to Web standards and outputs the Web page. The problem with such process is that the script is custom, i.e. each time the decision what should be the outcome of the publication depends largely on an author of the script. This discourages standardisation of the format of the published data, as script authors are not always familiar with the state-of-the-art solutions in this area. Moreover, it is not always their mission to deliver data in the programmatically accessible form – they only care about human recipients of their data.

Another problem is that such publication process prevents important description of data from being published – metadata is either not delivered, or provided as textual, human-readable annotations. This does not assure further use of data. To some extent, the solution is provided by XML files. They usually reflect what is otherwise available on the Web in human-readable form as regular tabular data. Although data is well structured in such form, it is usually not described in enough details to make it directly accessible for programmatic consumption. Another problem is that the format adopted usually does not follow open standards correctly. An example of XML data offered by Polish National Bank is presented in Fig. 2. Knowledge of language is the prerequisite to make good use of this data.

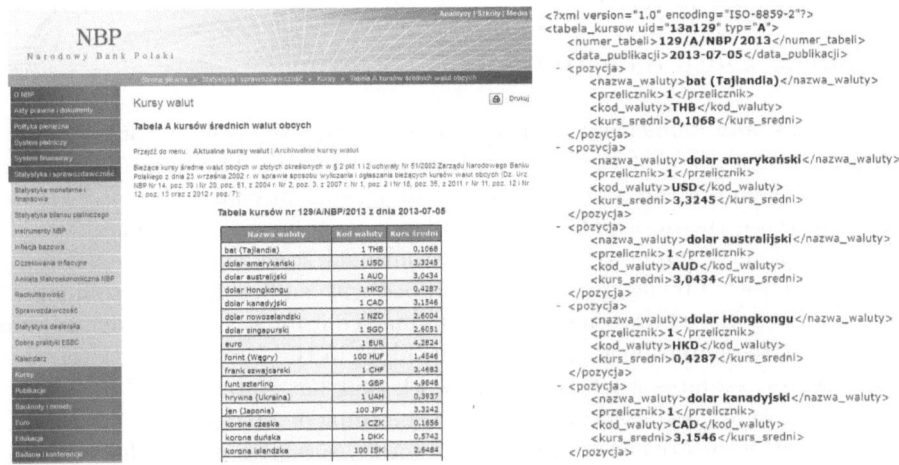

Fig. 2. Financial data serialised in XML

2.2 Consumption – The Demand Side

One of the most important challenges in the data consumption process is identification of relevant datasets on the Web. Major search engines offer little support in identifying data sources and searching for particular values of a given measure is virtually impossible. Furthermore, even though one manages to identify the sources, it is not straightforward to retrieve data since it is not available in formats easily digestible by programs. Custom built export formats, lack of description and lack of metadata and linking between different datasets prevents reasoning over the data that cross a single dataset. Data once extracted has to be cleansed and integrated, which require heavy technologies and expensive software, as well as large amounts of consulting work to do it accurately. These factors especially impact smaller companies, which can hardly afford such burdens, and therefore are banned from using the data that is in theory "made public and available". All in all, the automatic interpretation and processing of data is still a problem because of deficiencies in the publishing process and data formats.

This discrepancy between publishers and consumers is a root of worse than optimal efficiency of information flow. **Information gap** means in fact that a decision maker does not have appropriate information to take a wise decision. On one hand, more and more data is available on the Web and in internal repositories. On the other hand, it is not always the data needed for personal and business decisions. Such data has to be identified. Increasing amount of data makes this task even more difficult.

There are, however, some technologies on the horizon that can help in this situation. For example, semantic web technologies may facilitate data description and search. A more advanced Linked Open Data initiative goes even further with data integration.

3   Linked Data as a Remedy

As it was initially defined by Berners-Lee, the Semantic Web is not a separate Web but an extension of the Web we know and see [1]. The only difference is that information is given a well-defined meaning, so that computers have greater chances to reuse the information in accordance with human intentions.

In his visionary paper [1] Berners-Lee outlined some possibilities. Our life might be supported by agents, which, equipped with sufficient contextual knowledge, could negotiate between each other to make our life easier. In order to fulfill this vision data should be accessible to machines in the form easily processable. This, however, requires a lot of manual work that has to be carried out. Sadly, the idea is over 10 years old and has not been implemented yet.

As a result of unsatisfactory progress, several years after initial idea emerged, the vision was redefined and the scope of the Semantic Web was restricted to the proper representation of data [2]. As the vision of the Semantic Web proved to be too ambitious, more and more people started talking about an intermediate state – linked data. Not formally annotated documents or web pages, but just data. It still bases on RDF, a very simple model where each fact is represented as a triple: subject, predicate and object [3].

Linked Data (LD) is a set of principles applied for publishing of structured data one the Web in the form of RDF graphs. These principles are as follows [4]: Universal Resource Identifiers (URIs) are used as names of things, URIs are based on HTTP, URIs return useful information, and URIs are interlinked allowing the navigation.

Linked Open Data (LOD) is a linked data paradigm applied for public open data in order to make data available to anybody. The trend is already take followed by many countries worldwide. In October 2007, 30 open government advocates met in Sebastopol, California to discuss how government could open up electronically-stored government data for public use. An effect of their work are 10 principles for Opening Up Government Information. Among these principles are[3]: completeness, primacy, timeliness, ease of physical and electronic access, machine readability, non-discrimination, use of commonly owned standards, licensing, permanence and usage costs.

Linked data is currently considered a solution to remedy the information gap. It makes it easier for developers to connect information from different sources. The simplicity of representation and interpretation of meaning proved to be very attractive. Extraction of simple facts provide ground for big datasets. It bases on exploitation of Web 2.0 trend where people voluntarily provide a lot of data.

We can further distinguish two important components that form linked data: vocabulary and data.

3.1 Vocabularies

Core concepts can be defined as "simplified, reusable, and extensible data models that capture the fundamental characteristics of an entity in a context-neutral and language-neutral fashion" [5]. Then, core vocabulary is "a core concept, represented in a particular representation language, such as an RDF or XML schema" [5].

Organisations base on common vocabularies to allow cooperation and interchange of data. Commonly referred vocabularies are in fact available in plethora of formats. The majority is available in proprietary formats, and many still needs to be converted to semantic representation.

Relatively good situation is in core vocabularies, e.g. Dublin Core (DC), and in the case of metadata specifications and schemas, e.g. Simple Knowledge Organisation System (SKOS), Vocabulary of Interlinked Datasets (VoID). For external reporting companies heavily use code lists for activities (e.g. NACE), countries (e.g. ISO 3166), languages (e.g. ISO 639), regions (e.g. NUTS), etc. More detailed geographical vocabularies are an important assets, like references to geographic locations and jurisdictions, e.g. cadastre, spatial planning, map information. There are also controlled vocabularies or taxonomies, which are more domain-specific, e.g. Eurovoc, Agrovoc. Proper functioning of economy is not possible without reference collections of organisations and people, e.g. registers of government agencies, business registers, citizen databases, social networks.

A good collection of vocabularies is available at Linked Open Vocabularies (LOV) site[4].

---

[3] http://sunlightfoundation.com/policy/documents/ten-open-data-principles
[4] http://lov.okfn.org/dataset/lov/

3.2   Data

A lot of data is available in multitude of datasets. We no more deal with islands of datasets, earlier called data silos – the data is already somehow related. This phenomenon was first investigated in May 2007 by Linked Open Data community. The well known picture of LOD cloud by Richard Cyganiak and Anja Jentzsch presents main sources contributing data (`http://lod-cloud.net`). The contribution of the authors of this LOD cloud diagram was an inventory of existing datasets and links between them. Each year the cloud is significantly extended – the "global data base" is growing.

The real explosion is observed only recently. There are several initiatives that are trying to organise a list of sources in a form of catalogues that additionally offer the possibility to search by keywords, domain, licence, or just browse the data. One example is Publicdata.eu[5], a pan-European data portal, which provides access to datasets opened by European public bodies, from local, through regional to national level. It is developed by Open Knowledge Foundation (OKFN) and supported by LOD2 project.

Such an effort requires a solid technological foundation. Publicdata.eu is based on CKAN (Comprehensive Knowledge Archive Network), the world's leading open-source data portal platform. CKAN has many official instances[6] for countries like Argentina, Austria, Brazil, Czech Republic, Finland, Germany, Greece, Italy, Netherlands, Norway, Serbia, Spain, UK, Uruguay, and USA. Besides, 16 cities have its own CKAN instances. The installation allows registration of datasets conforming to linked data regime, making counting and linking dataset more convenient. As of June 2013 there are over 6400 datasets in the Datahub catalogue[7].

The most prominent example, the flagship of linked data initiative is DBpedia. It contains extracted facts from the Wikipedia. As it is often used as a reference point for other datasets, it is put in the centre of LOD cloud diagram. The English version of the DBpedia currently describes almost 4 million things. It describes 764,000 people, 573,000 places, and 192,000 organisations. The localized versions of DBpedia are available in over 100 languages. The whole DBpedia consists of 1.9 billion triples, of which 400 million are from English version.

4   Directions of Research in Enterprise Linked Data

The state of the art concerning linked open data being made available changes constantly. At the beginning we had just two portals – one in Great Britain and the other in the United States – that made their data accessible and available using linked data standards. Number of linked data portals is flourishing now. There are still numerous data sources that exist in EU or national databases that are waiting to be made available to the general public as Linked Open

---

[5] `http://publicdata.eu`
[6] `http://ckan.org/instances`
[7] `http://datahub.io/dataset`

Data. This includes for example data of the European Central Bank or Tenders Electronic daily. Each enterprise can identify own datasets worth converting.

Advantages of making data open are visible both for government, society, and also for companies:

- transparency and control of governments
- new or improved products and services combining open and company data
- improved efficiency and effectiveness of government services
- measuring impact of policies
- knowledge from combined data sources and patterns in large data volumes.

We have identified two main obstacles that prevent wider adoption of linked data in enterprises: scope and integrity.

4.1 Scope

Most of the dataset available today contain general-knowledge facts. Bigger focus on business is needed to involve bigger players and achieve a critical mass. For example, data about companies is not easily available and complete but would facilitate business greatly. There are fortunately some interesting initiatives regarding this issue. One of the biggest business registries available as linked data is OpenCorporates[8]: it holds 55,096,325 companies (as of 2013.07.06) in 65 jurisdictions, including 393,491 from Poland. Other relevant datasets include: product catalogues, public procurement contracts, profiles of experts, information about labour market, environmental and energy-related data.

4.2 Integrity

It is a fact that more and more datasets are converted into triples [6]. Paradoxically, it does not improve the situation of data reuse. Let us analyse a simple example with triplification of NACE (*Nomenclature statistique des activités économiques dans la Communauté européenne*), one of the most important vocabularies regarding economic classification. NACE rev. 2 is available in RDF from at least two sources.

The first is offered by LATC project[9]. They have decided to leverage the W3C recommendation – this triplification uses SKOS to represent taxonomy. The standard properties like `skos:broader` and `skos:narrower` model relations between NACE concepts. Unfortunately, it uses hash for fragments i.e. to separate local concept name from the namespace. This can be problematic for some applications[10].

The second one is available from Eurostat's RAMON[11]. It defines own classes named after NACE nomenclature, for example it uses property `inSection` to show relation between two levels. Additionally, it uses slash for fragments.

---

[8] http://opencorporates.com
[9] http://eurostat.linked-statistics.org/dic/nace_r2.rdf
[10] Current trend is to use slashes, it also makes more efficient use of HTTP.
[11] http://ec.europa.eu/eurostat/ramon/rdfdata/nace_r2.rdf

There are further differences in URI patterns. "Agriculture, forestry and fishing" is represented as `<http://eurostat.linked-statistics.org/dic/nace_r2#A>` in the first and as `<http://ec.europa.eu/eurostat/ramon/rdfdata/nace_r2/A>` in the latter case. Discovery of links is hindered when we go to third level – the naming convention differs even more: `<http://eurostat.linked-statistics.org/dic/nace_r2#A011>` vs. `<http://ec.europa.eu/eurostat/ramon/rdf-data/nace_r2/01.1>`. Problem of too many identifiers has already been observed by business informatics society. It has been addressed by EU-funded Okkam project, which stated "Identifiers should not be multiplied beyond necessity" [7].

4.3   Access and Use of Data in Applications

New or improved products and services combining open and internal data delivered by companies may increase the quality of life of citizens. The crucial asset here is data. A lot of research effort is required for developing methods for acquisition of datasets. While links between datasets and common identifiers make navigation easier, search is not properly addressed yet. In fact, we need a breakthrough similar to what Google was for Web pages.

Having data in the standardised form facilitates using multiple tools that enable to process this data. Reusability of this kind of data greatly contributes to making all services more efficient and effective. Currently, data may be processed only by tools developed with this purpose in mind. With the unified format more processing facilities will be available. Analysis of large data sources, using reasoning combined with data mining techniques enables to generate extra knowledge, previously not available for companies.

The Internet tomorrow should have another layer in addition to what we have today. This layer may be defined as the Web of data in which the data is available to everyone and where one dataset refers another one. Data in standardised formats that enable machine querying and assure data reusability – this is the challenge for business informatics. Business informatics research should definitely care about linked open data.

Acknowledgement. This work was supported by a grant from the European Union's 7th Framework Programme provided for the project LOD2 Creating Knowledge out of Interlinked Data (GA no. 288176).

References

1. Berners-Lee, T., Hendler, J., Lassila, O.: The Semantic Web. Scientific American 284(5), 28–37 (2001)
2. Feigenbaum, L., Herman, I., Hongsermeier, T., Neumann, E., Stephens, S.: The Semantic Web In Action. Scientific American Magazine 297(6), 90–97 (2007)
3. Brickley, D., Guha, R.V.: RDF Vocabulary Description Language 1.0: RDF Schema (2004), http://www.w3.org/TR/rdf-schema/

4. Berners-Lee, T.: Linked Data - Design Issues (2006)
5. ISA Program: D3.1 Process and Methodology for Core Vocabularies. Technical report, European Commission (2011)
6. Ermilov, I., Auer, S., Stadler, C.: Crowd-Sourcing the Large-Scale Semantic Mapping of Tabular Data. In: Proceeding of the ACM Web Science (2013)
7. Bouquet, P., Stoermer, H., Niederee, C., Maa, A.: Entity name system: The backbone of an open and scalable web of data (2008)

Open Problems
of Information Systems
Research and Technology

Bernhard Thalheim

Christian Albrechts University Kiel, Department of Computer Science, D-24098 Kiel, Germany
thalheim@is.informatik.uni-kiel.de

Abstract. Computer science and technology is an area of very intensive research and development. It is estimated that the half-life period of knowledge in this area is about 12 to 18 months. No other branch of science has such short half-life period. Therefore new problems have to solved. At the same time some of the old open problems must be solved. This invited talk aims at a systematic survey of open problems and proposes a number of solutions to their solution. We structure these open problems in structuring problems, into size or more generally complexity problems, functionality problems, interactivity problems, distribution problems, and general problems.

1 Computer Science and Technology

Let us first consider the primary sources for open problems of information systems research and technology. They are mainly caused by the technology itself and stream of research in this area. They are also caused by the evolution of information systems. Another obstacle are the notions we use differently in different settings. Computer Science and Technology (CS&T) is a young branch of science and technology. It took hundred if not thousands of years for other sciences to become matured. Mathematics, for instance, can be based on three main principles: topology, order, and algebra. Social sciences use the principles individual, development, and society. CS&T may however also be based on four main principles in Figure 1: structuring, evolution, collaboration and modelling. Each of these principles has a number of aspects. Structuring is either structuring in the large, i.e., architecture, or in the small that is based on the notion of the state. Evolution

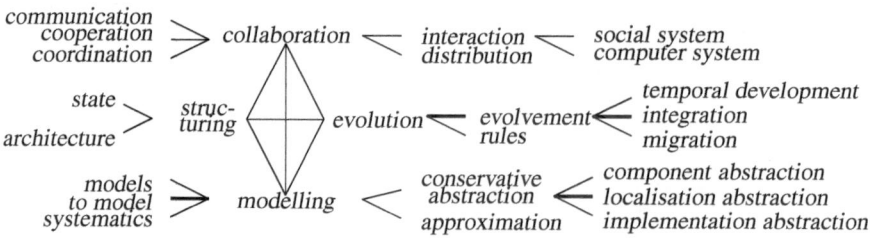

Fig. 1. The four principles of Computer Science and Technology

A. Kobyliński and A. Sobczak (Eds.): BIR 2013, LNBIP 158, pp. 10–18, 2013.

can also be either evolution in the small which is based on rules for state transformation or evolution in the large with its temporal, integration or migration aspects aspects. Collaboration is far less well understood. Collaboration services can be build based on the 3C framework [5] that separates supporting services into communication services, coordination services, and cooperation services. It is either on interaction between social systems and computer systems or on distribution among systems. Modelling is far less well understood although more than 50 different kinds of models are known for CS&T [12]. It is however possible to develop a general notion of the model [10], of the activity of model development [8] and systematic methodology backed modelling [9].

Information, data and knowledge are often used as synonyms. The separation into data, information and knowledge is displayed in Figure 2. For the definition of notion of knowledge we refer to [11]. There are several definitions for information. Information is defined in [2]. as raw data that is well-formed and meaningful data and that has been verified to be accurate and timely relative to its context, is specific and organised for a purpose, is presented within a context that gives it meaning and relevance, and which leads to increase in understanding and decrease in uncertainty. The second definitions is based on the mathematical notion of entropy. The third definition bases information on the data a user has currently in his data space and on the computational and reasoning abilities of the user. Business information systems understand information as data that have been shaped into a form that is meaningful, significant and useful for human beings. If we consider information systems as an element of social systems

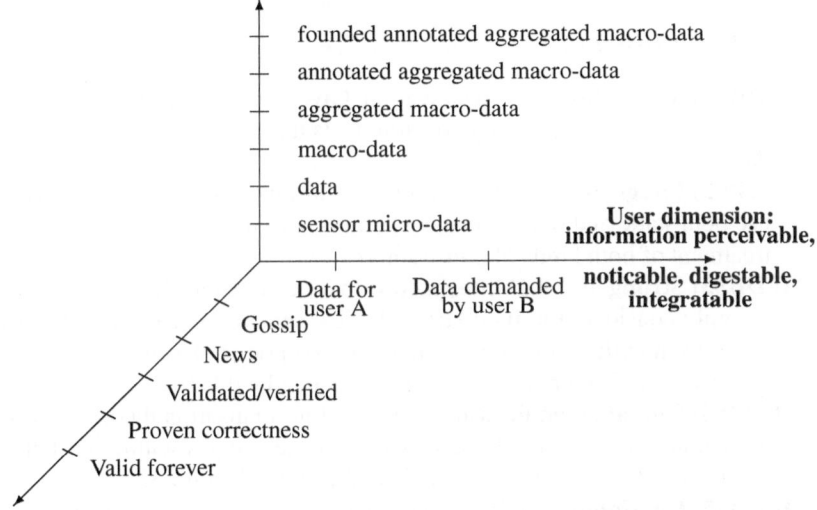

Data dimension: correct, complete, in right format, at right moment of time, in a form requested, in right size and structuring

Knowledge dimension: quality, validation/verification, sustainable, grounded, on consensus

Fig. 2. Three dimensions of semiotics: Syntax by data, semantics by knowledge, and pragmatics by information

then we can use the anthroposophic form: Information as processed by humans, is carried by data that is perceived or noticed, selected and organised by its receiver, because of his subjective human interests, originating from his instincts, feelings, experience, intuition, common sense, values, beliefs, personal knowledge, or wisdom, simultaneously processed by his cognitive and mental processes, and seamlessly integrated in his recallable knowledge. The separation into data, information and knowledge is displayed in Figure 2.

Computer science and technology has four sources: mathematics, electronics, engineering and applications. The first two sources are well acknowledged. The scientist adds to the store of verified, systematised knowledge of the physical or virtual world. The engineer brings this knowledge to bear on practical problems[1]. The software engineering triptych [3,1] consists of the application domain description, the requirements prescriptions, and finally the systems specifications. Requirements must be reasonably well understood before software can be designed, programmed, and coded. The application domain must be reasonable understood in all its dependencies, weak and sufficient properties before requirements can be expressed properly. Software engineering classically considers only the second and the third dimension. Application domain engineering has not yet got its foundations.

2   Open Problems

In the sequel we list main open problems. The suggestions, hypotheses and proposals for their solution are given in the lecture and in an extended variant of this paper. We first start with a list of problems that is now over 25 years old [6,7].

2.1   The MFDBS List

(MFDBS1) Satisfiability of specification: Given a structure specification of a database, e.g., a schema with integrity constraints. Is this specification by a finite, non-empty database.

(MFDBS2) Integration of static and operational constraints: Information systems use both static and operational constraints. Are there systems that allow a coherent treatment of both kinds of constraints?

(MFDBS3) Strong and soft interpretation of constraints: Integrity constraints are often only considered in their strong logical semantics. We might however use also natural semantics and allow systematic exceptions of validity of these constraints in a database. Is there any theory that can handle this?

(MFDBS4) Global normalisation: Classical normalisation theory treats each type in a separate form despite the association of these types within a schema. Is there a mechanism to integrate normalisation for global handling?

(MFDBS5) Continuous engineering and consistent extensions: Database systems are constantly evolving, are extended, are integrated with other systems. How we may support this kind of evolution?

---

[1] "Scientists look at things that are and ask 'why'; engineers dream of things that never were and ask 'why not'." (Theodore von Karman) [4].

(MFDBS6) Integration of quality requirements into specification: Software engineering knows more than 40 different characteristics of quality of a software product. The same applies to information systems. How these quality characteristics can be given in a coherent and manageable form?

(MFDBS7) Complexity of constraint sets: Constraint set complexity has so far mainly considered only for simple classes of constraints. Develop an approach for complexity characterisation of constraint sets!

(MFDBS8) Enforcement of integrity constraint sets: Constraints are declared within a formal language. They must be enforced within a database system in both declarative and procedural way. Develop a formal theory of enforcement of integrity constraints that allows to enforce constraints either procedurally or at the interface level!

(MFDBS9) Implication problems on the level of kinds of constraints: The logical handling of integrity constraints is still based on a strict separation of these constraints according to their kind. Practical applications are however using functional, inclusion, join, exclusion, cardinality etc. constraints all together. Develop an approach that allows to manage constraints without a separation into kinds of constraints!

(MFDBS10) Treatment of semantics by views: Database technology uses still a local-as-view approach and specifies views on top of the logical or conceptual schemata. Applications use however views and onyl in very rare cases the global schema. Develop an approach for management of semantics at the view level!

(MFDBS11) Distributed integrity management: Is there any mechanism to manage integrity constraints in distributed environments?

(MFDBS12) Integration of vertical, horizontal and deductive normalisation: Classics considers only vertical normalisation. how to incorporate horizontal and deductive normalisation in this management?

(MFDBS13) Treatment of incomplete specifications: Specifications are normally incomplete. How to handle this incompleteness?

2.2   Open Problems: Technology

(TT1) Partial identifiability: Objects can be partially depending on the profile and portfolio of their utilisation. Develop a treatment of this identification!

(TT2) Query optimisation considers so far relational algebra. Develop an extension that allows aggregation, grouping, ordering!

(TT3) Inheritance is defined at design, code, or decision layers. Develop a layer-independent approach to inheritance.

(TT4) Maintenance optimisation: Systems provide their own mechanism for maintenance, e.g. time/mode/strictness of integrity maintenance. Develop a general approach to maintenance optimisation!

(TT5) View towers: Typical information system applications based on the local-as-view approach use towers of views. Develop a technology for view tower handling, e.g., with partial local enforcement!

(TT6) Component systems support industrial production-line development of information systems. Their technology needs sophisticated collaboration support.

(TT7) Quality management for distributed information systems: Information systems are often not entirely correct or complete or up-to-date. We need however a supporting quality management for these systems.

2.3   Open Problems: Co-design

Modern information systems development is based on development of structuring, on functionality development, and on development of interaction features. Additionally, systems are distributed. Therefore, co-design and co-evolution of systems becomes a major feature.
Co-design is still under development. The current state of the art is challenging. Without conceptual models we face late specification, inflexibility, and un-maintainability of systems. Extension, change management and integration become a nightmare.

(C1) Coherence of models: Co-design can be based a separation of concern and on representation by various models. A model suite must however be based on coherence conditions and associations.

(C2) Compiler-based transformation of conceptual schemata: Conceptual schemata are often directly mapped by an interpreter. The logical schema is later optimised. We may however develop a compiler approach beyond the interpretation or rule-based approach.

(C3) Semantics treatment: Classical semantics of databases and information systems uses the strict approach of mathematical logics. It is often inappropriate. Therefore, we need a flexible treatment of semantics, e.g., depending on the kind of constraints or sets of constraints.

(C4) Global-as-view schemata: The classical information system architecture is based on a local-as-view approach. Develop new approaches opposite to classical local-as-view 2/3-layer architectures!

(C5) Object-relational design starts with an OR-schema (e.g., HERM-schema) and ending with a object-relational schema of modern DBMS. Develop novel design methods for OR logical schemata.

(C6) Content services: Information services are becoming one of the major technologies in the web. They are based on content delivery to different users and content extraction from various resources. Develop a faithful content service on top of database systems.

(C7) Faithful mapping from and to UML: UML is becoming a communication language for systems development. It does however not provide a holistic semantics for its diagrams. Brute-force interpretation of diagrams is the current state of art. Develop a faithful mapping that allows to use collections of diagrams of different kinds.

2.4   Open Problems for Structuring

(S1) Conceptual modelling in the large is partially as extension of conceptual modelling in the small. Develop additional solutions for modelling in the large.

(S2) List semantics for (extended) entity-relationship modelling: ER models are typically interpreted based on set semantics. Sometimes ER schemata are also mapped to XML schemata. We need however an approach that supports mapping to list-based languages.

(S3) Centre-periphery integration into schemata: Classical information system modelling treat the schema as a holistic solution. Schemata have however an inner structure. Especially they have central or kernel types and peripheric types. This separation is based on overlay techniques. Develop a technique for centre-periphery separation within a schema.

(S4) Level of locality and globality: Beside global as view and local as view models we might also look for compromises between local-centric or global-centric schemata. Develop structuring with the best globality.

(S5) Null marker logics: Null markers (inappropriately called values) carry a variety of different application semantics. Develop techniques for management of these markers beyond the existence, non-applicability and unknown.

(S6) Pattern of structures: Information system development can be based on experience and skills of developers. They use general solutions and pattern for their work. Develop pattern beyond the small patterns of Blaha.

(S7) Redundant schemata: Schemata need redundant types. Develop an approach for explicit maintenance of redundancy of types and data in information systems.

2.5 Open Problems: Constraints

(TIC1) Complexity: The complexity of constraint sets is only known for some basis kinds of constraints. Develop a complexity theory for real life constraint sets! Develop an approach to average complexity of such constraint sets!

(TIC2) Incomplete constraint sets: Normalisation requires complete constraint knowledge. Develop an approach for incomplete knowledge.

(TIC3) Denormalisation: Normalisation is lucky break. Typical applications need however well-settled denormalisation as well. Develop a definition, treatment, algorithmics for denormalisation.

(TIC4) Global normalisation: Develop an approach to global schema normalisation beyond classical local vertical normalisation.

(TIC5) Partial axiomatisation: Incomplete constraint sets are the normal case for specification. Therefore we need an approach for deductive systems that provide a partial axiomatisation.

(TIC6) Graphical reasoning has shown to be useful for handling, reasoning and management of functional and multivalued dependencies. Develop graphical reasoning systems for other constraint sets.

(TIC7) Real-life constraint sets: Constraints cannot be handled only within its specific kind. We need techniques for constraint handling outside the orientation to kinds.

2.6 Open Problems: Functionality

(F1) (e)ER-SQL: SQL is becoming the main database language and is currently going to be combined with NoSQL features. (e)ER-SQL can be graphically developed based on VisualSQL. Develop an integration of VisualSQL with NoSQL features!

(F2) Holistic functionality description: Functionality specification is often using different languages for the application domain, for business processes and for conceptual functionality specification. We need however a holistic specification technique.

(F3) Dynamic semantics is still a step-child of integrity constraint handling. Develop an appraoch to dynamic semantics beyond transition rules that reflect static semantics.

(F4) Robust workflows: Workflows often use exception handling and try to reflect any potential case. This technique is infeasible for most processes. Instead develop an engineering approach that handles errors and failures without requesting a complete specification.

(F5) Flexible workflows: Workflows typically specify a hard-coded control flow. Life is however more flexible. Develop techniques for controllable deviations from flow and coherent finalisation.

(F6) Information systems functions: Information systems are often entirely based on database techniques. Users need however also functions on their own beyond retrieval and state change operations.

(F7) Generic views: View tower development may result in hundreds of almost unmanageable views. Develop a view derivation technique similar to generic functions.

2.7 Open Problems: Algebra

(TA1) Transaction semantics for higher SQL: SQL:1999, SQL:2003, and SQL: 2007 provide extended and sophisticated techniques for transaction handling. We need a holistic management for such transactions.

(TA2) Spatial operations have been for more advanced spatial data structures. We need however an algebra that allows to compute also spatial data.

(TA3) Program transformation: Database programs can be specified at the conceptual level. We lack however program transformation techniques.

(TA4) Greatest consistent specialisation: The GCS approach allows to derive specialisations of operations that internally maintain integrity constraints. Develop GCS techniques beyond functional and inclusion constraints!

(TA5) Trigger assembly creation: Triggers are currently linear static programs. They need very sophisticated development techniques and a deep understanding of their impact. Develop techniques for trigger assemblies.

(TA6) Transformation of expressions: Queries can be simplified if we know integrity constraints. We need a systematic transformation of expressions in the presence of IC.

(TA7) Extension of structural recursion: Structural recursion is the main definition technique for algebraic operations. We need however also structural recursion for holistic expressions.

2.8 Open Problems: Distribution

(D1) Partial consistency of databases: Distributed databases and information systems follow a variety of consistency paradigms. We need however also techniques that support collaboration of systems based on specific contracts and protocols.

(D2) Recharging of partner databases: Databases may collaborate based on pattern such as publish-subscribe. Develop a data integration technique depending on subscription mode of partner databases.

(D3) Coordination: The 3C approach to collaboration uses coordination as a central conception. Develop techniques for coordination beyond contracts.

(D4) General model of services: One of the most overused notions in CS&T is the service as specific software with support and with compliance. Develop a general model for services.

(D5) Exchange frames: The 3C framework uses techniques of communication similar to protocol engineering. It depends on the chosen architecture. Exchange frames are typical supporting means. They are given in a very technical way and thus depend on the underlying firmware. Develop a general technique for exchange frames.

(D6) Component database systems: with specific coupling facilities, collaboration contracts

(D7) Pattern of distributed systems: Pattern have been developed for specific integration in software engineering research. Information systems are more specific. Therefore, we need a specialisation of these pattern to information and database systems and specific pattern for these systems.

2.9   Open Problems: Interactivity

Interactivity is nowadays the main concern for web information systems. Their technology, their specification and their theory are not yet systematised. They will however have the same fate as classical information systems: they will stay with us longer than it has been expected when they have been developed. At the same time they face the same problems as we have already observed for human-computer interfaces.

(I1) Edutainment stories: One main kind of web information systems are edutainment systems (often called e-learning systems). Develop techniques and solutions for edutainment beyond classical blended learning and towards collaboration and true interaction.

(I2) New stories: In the app age we face a large variety of solutions based on small components. Their integration and coherent deployment is still a challenge to the user. It seems that they are partially arbitrarily combinable and thus only integrate-able by a human user. There are however main deployment pathes based on ministories with data coherence. Develop a technology for such systematic treatment of new stories.

(I3) Screenography is a generalisation of scenography and dramaturgy. It supports systematic development of screens and allows an adaptation to the user. Develop an approach integration of screenography into conceptual modelling.

(I4) Life case bakery: System development is still based on packages that provide a fully fledged solution to a collection of application problems. Real life is however based on life event and life situations. Life cases may reflect both. They can be mapped to business use cases and business stories which are the basis for requirements prescription. We need techniques for continuous adaptation to the specific life event or life situation.

(I5) I^*-generalisation: The I^* model allows to model the intentions, desires, beliefs and goals of users. Goals can also be soft goals. These specification techniques for (Soft)Goals ∪ Tasks ∪ Actors ∪ Resources can be generalised to the story spaces, obligations and life cases.

(I6) Privacy of users: Privacy of users becomes a major bottleneck of the 21st century. We currently lack techniques privacy profile, controlled opening of shared data, flexible protection etc.

(I7) Workspace integration of users: Users have their own systems with their own workrooms, workspace and libraries. These systems vary a lot and cannot be generalised to some holistic system environment. Instead we need techniques for flexible integration of user workspaces into current information systems.

References

1. Bjørner, D.: Software Engineering 3: Domains, requirements, and software design. Springer, Berlin (2006)
2. Greco, G.M., Paronitti, G., Turilli, M., Floridi, L.: The philosophy of information: A methodological point of view. In: Wissensmanagmeent, pp. 563–570. DFKI, Kaiserslautern (2005)
3. Heinrich, L.J.: Informationsmanagement: Planung, Überwachung und Steuerung der Informationsinfrastruktur. Oldenbourg Verlag, München (1996)
4. Samuel, A., Weir, J.: Introduction to Engineering: Modelling, Synthesis and Problem Solving Strategies. Elsevier, Amsterdam (2000)
5. Schewe, K.-D., Thalheim, B.: Development of collaboration frameworks for web information systems. In: IJCAI 2007 (20th Int. Joint Conf on Artificial Intelligence), Section EMC 2007 (Evolutionary Models of Collaboration), Hyderabad, pp. 27–32 (2007)
6. Thalheim, B.: Open problems in relational database theory. Bull. EATCS 32, 336–337 (1987)
7. Thalheim, B.: Entity-relationship modeling – Foundations of database technology. Springer, Berlin (2000)
8. Thalheim, B.: The art of conceptual modelling. In: Information Modelling and Knowledge Bases XXII. Frontiers in Artificial Intelligence and Applications, vol. 237, pp. 149–168. IOS Press (2012)
9. Thalheim, B.: The science and art of conceptual modelling. In: Hameurlain, A., Küng, J., Wagner, R., Liddle, S.W., Schewe, K.-D., Zhou, X. (eds.) TLDKS VI. LNCS, vol. 7600, pp. 76–105. Springer, Heidelberg (2012)
10. Thalheim, B.: The conception of the model. In: Abramowicz, W. (ed.) BIS 2013. LNBIP, vol. 157, pp. 113–124. Springer, Heidelberg (2013)
11. Thalheim, B., Kitawara, Y., Karttunen, E., Jaakkola, H.: Future directions of knowledge systems environments for web 3.0. In: Information Modelling and Knowledge Bases. Frontiers in Artificial Intelligence and Applications, vol. 225, pp. 413–446. IOS Press (2011)
12. Thomas, M.: Modelle in der Fachsprache der Informatik. Untersuchung von Vorlesungsskripten aus der Kerninformatik. In: DDI. LNI, vol. 22, pp. 99–108. GI (2002)

Requirements Definition for Domain-Specific Modelling Languages: The ComVantage Case

Robert Andrei Buchmann, Dimitris Karagiannis, and Niksa Visic

University of Vienna, Faculty of Computer Science, Knowledge Engineering Research Group,
Währinger str. 29, A-1090, Vienna, Austria
{rbuchmann,dk,niksa}@dke.univie.ac.at

Abstract. The goal of this paper is to investigate the challenge of defining and answering modelling language requirements with domain specificity in the instance case of the ComVantage EU research project, which provides a multi-faceted domain, with subdomains identified along two dimensions: a) the application dimension, where subdomains are defined by the application areas providing use cases: mobile maintenance, customer-oriented production and production line commissioning; b) the technical dimension, where subdomains are derived from a grouping of the encountered technical problems - supply chain definition in virtual enterprises, business process-driven mobile app and data requirements, business process management considering the execution environment and control of access to its resources/artefacts, design of products and services, or incident escalation management. The paper describes the requirements sources, their definition methodology and an initial derivation of modelling method building blocks from the identified requirements.

Keywords: modelling requirements, metamodelling, business process, knowledge acquisition.

1   Introduction

The paper addresses the challenge of conceptually modelling a multifaceted domain and of identifying requirements for realizing a modelling method that can answer this challenge. The content is mainly targeted to the conceptual modelling community.

From a conceptual modelling perspective, The ComVantage research project [1] tackles a domain encompassing three application areas from which both distinguishing and overlapping concepts emerge. The application areas are symbolically depicted in Fig. 1 (derived from [1], public deliverable D311):

1. For production line commissioning, two key phases can be identified: the pre-deployment phase - from the design of a production line (based on its output specification) to its deployment, and the post-deployment phase - focused on cycle time monitoring and process control;

A. Kobyliński and A. Sobczak (Eds.): BIR 2013, LNBIP 158, pp. 19–33, 2013.
© Springer-Verlag Berlin Heidelberg 2013

2. The customer-oriented production refers to the on-demand production of shirts based on customization requests, and the triggering of a production process to fulfill the required customization;
3. The mobile maintenance refers to a requirement for remotely monitoring machine sensors and running test cases in order to diagnose defects and initiate repair requests.

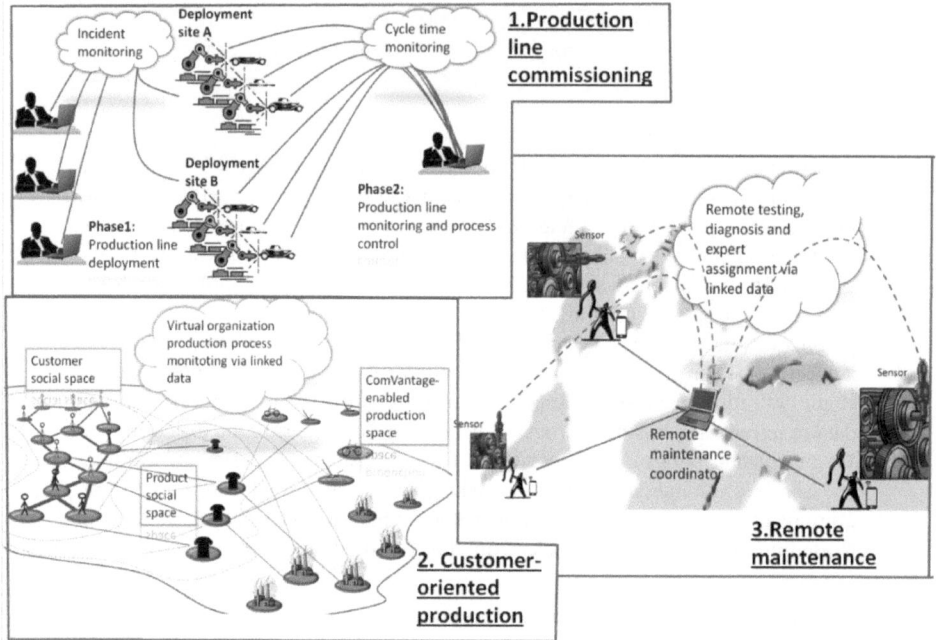

Fig. 1. Overview of the ComVantage application areas

The core focus of ComVantage is to propose a run-time information system architecture to cover these application areas, based on mobile app front-end consuming a Linked Data-based back-end. Our main task, reflected in the current paper, is to complement the run-time component with design-time support in the form of a modelling method that can help future businesses adopting the ComVantage technological specificity to structure and analyse their business and map its IT requirements in a process-centric and holistic manner.

A modelling method for ComVantage needs to deal with this domain heterogeneity, thus the result must be a hybrid method covering multiple layers of abstraction, from domain-specificity to concepts that are generic enough to be reusable over the three application areas (to capture their overlapping aspects). Thus, we can state that the paper describes a knowledge acquisition effort, enveloped by the requirements elicitation phase for the run-time information system, and an initial structuring of the resulted knowledge in the form of a modelling stack. An overview of the abstraction layers and views supported by the modelling method is also provided.

The content is structured as follows: Section 2 describes the problem statement, the technological and methodological context and provides related works references, while section 3 details the developments and results of the work. The paper ends with a conclusive SWOT analysis and outlook to future work.

2   Problem Statement and Background

2.1   Motivation, Framework and Related Works

We consider, as state of the art for our approach, knowledge elicitation methodologies such as the Soft Systems Methodology [2], but we lower the abstraction level with a metamodelling approach driven by a) the building blocks of our metamodelling framework and b) the knowledge captured in the requirements elicitation and data design processes for the run-time prototype.

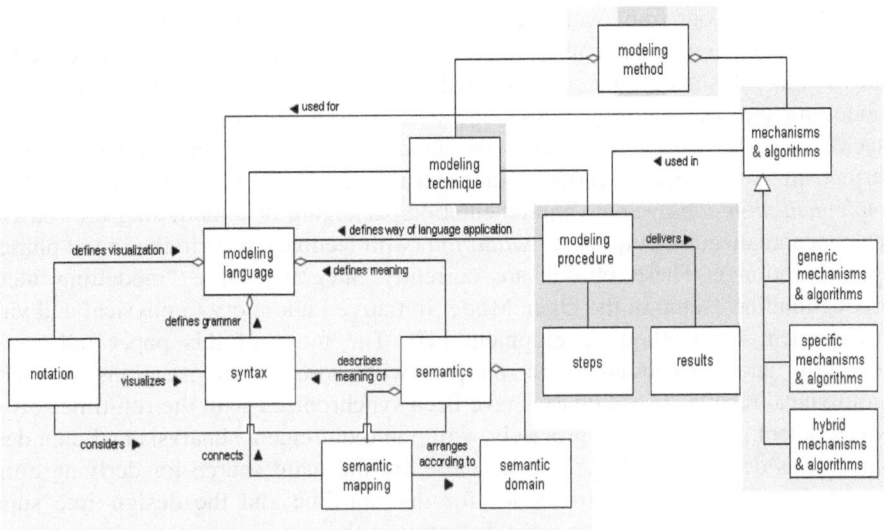

Fig. 2. The structure of a modelling method [3]

The framework under which the modelling method is being developed has been previously described in [3]. According to this, the method building blocks are *the modelling language* (modelling constructs, their properties and constraints), *the modelling procedure* (steps to be followed by the modeller) and *the functionality* (mechanisms and algorithms that take as input structures and properties found in models, for various purposes, usually for evaluation) – see Fig. 2. During the ComVantage development, we identified the following dependencies between this framework and modelling requirements:

- Modelling requirements can be captured as a "to-be" modelling procedure – high level steps that are envisioned to reach the modelling goals; this maps closely to the notions of "use case" and "goal" from traditional requirements engineering, while being more procedure-oriented;
- The "to-be" modelling procedure suggests scenarios that are weakly structured but still capable of providing an initial structure of the modelling language, called "the modelling stack". The stack is a decomposition of the domain in abstraction layers and subproblems that are usually tackled with different, specialized, model types. A "model type" is a subset of the modelling language and it groups constructs (concepts and relations) that are relevant to a particular subproblem encountered during the modelling procedure. The model stack must integrate all model types from multiple abstraction / detail layers – in order to achieve this, inter-model linking opportunities must be identified;
- The functionality can be approached by identifying opportunities for automating steps of the modelling procedure, their required inputs and necessary outputs. The required inputs suggest additional properties and constructs that must be available in the modelling language.

Additionally, our framework defines a method engineering cycle that includes the phases of a) *cognition* (acquisition of user stories and weakly structured domain knowledge – this should be synchronized), b) *conceptualization* (identification of the modelling method building blocks and a structured specification of the modelling stack), c) *formalization* (capturing the modelling relations and constraints with a formalism to support further theoretical development and evaluation), d) *implementation/deployment* (implementation/packaging of a modelling tool based on the conceptualization output), e) *validation* (with feedback loop to the initial phase for agile iterations). These phases are currently integrated in a "modelling method production line" setup in the Open Model Initiative Laboratory (a physical and virtual environment for method development [4]). The focus of this paper falls on the cognition and conceptualization phases, with some brief mentions of current prototypical results. These phases have been synchronized with the run-time software development process (more precisely, with the requirements analysis and data design phases), as depicted by Fig. 3, since these are the main source for deriving domain knowledge. However, the lifecycles for the run-time and the design-time support diverge after this, as goals are very different: in the run-time system, the domain can be described by class diagram, ER diagram or ontological schema with the purpose of guiding code development and anchoring data querying in the data structure; in the modelling method, the domain is captured in a metamodel to be implemented by a metamodelling platform and to become "the model of future models".

Reference [5] gives an overview of available metamodelling platforms, advocates hybrid modelling and discusses some of its challenges. It also distinguishes between domain specific modelling languages (exemplified by [6]) and general purpose modelling languages (placing UML in this latter category). The ComVantage modelling method has a domain-specific focus, but needs to also integrate overlapping concepts that are abstract enough to be relevant to each of the three application areas. The main commonality is a requirement for business process modelling, as a primary requirement for the method is to be process-centric.

Another work related to knowledge elicitation for modelling purposes is [7] (with additional lessons learned presented in [8]), where the authors describe their team-based elicitation process for information demand modelling. The commonality with our work is that it also involves both "requirements modelling" (how to model a specific type of requirements) and "modelling requirements" (what is required to be modelled). The distinction is that it focuses on role-based enterprise information requirements, while we follow the technological specificity of ComVantage – Linked Data and mobile apps required for business process execution (also role-driven). The view that our work is a knowledge acquisition effort is supported by papers such as [9], where the knowledge dimension of business process models is discussed. A comprehensive coverage of knowledge elicitation methods is given by [10]. Specific methods, frameworks and works that have been involved in our work will be referred in Section 3, as direct input to the modelling requirements definition process.

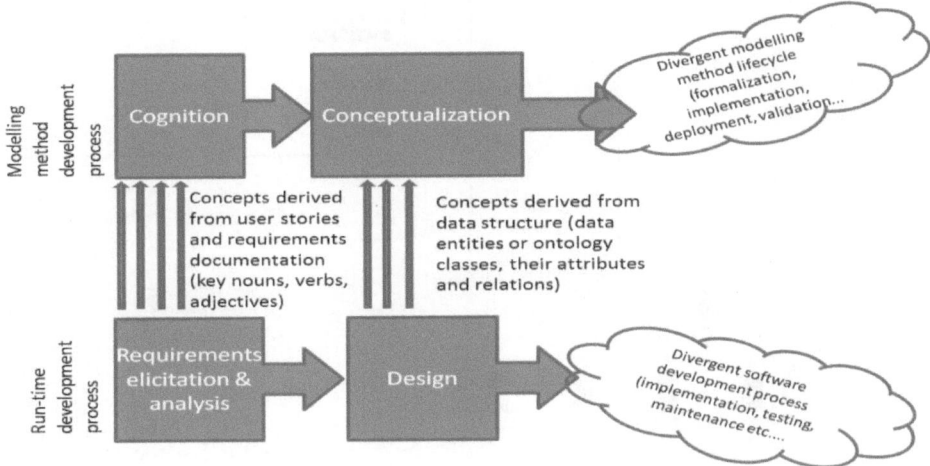

Fig. 3. The initial synchronization of the run-time and the modelling method development processes

2.2   Technological Context

The project as a whole aims to create proof-of-concept prototypes for supporting collaborative businesses using mobile apps as the front-end. Linked Data [11] is chosen as the data integration concept for improving interoperability, by replacing data silos with data networks that can be easily navigated by federated or orchestrated SPARQL queries [12]. Ontologies are employed to give structure to the cloud of Linked Data and to anchor cross-organizational queries. Mobile apps are aimed to improve mobility of actors and decision makers, and to expose Linked Data to them on a trustful basis.

As previously mentioned, this run-time architecture is complemented by the design-time modelling support addressed by the current paper. The hybrid domain-specific modelling language is designed to cover process-based requirements for these technological specificities. It is being implemented on the ADOxx metamodelling platform [13], under the metamodelling framework described in section 2.1. An initial implementation, covering strictly the process-based app requirements modelling aspects is available as an Open Model Initiative Laboratory project, at [4] (accessible to registered modelling community members). Fig. 4 gives a screenshot of the tool, showing a business process model fragment (left), an app usage flow derived from this process (bottom) and an app mockup assigned to one of the apps (right). However, the focus of this paper is not on the implementation or the models themselves, but the definition of requirements and their coverage by the hybrid modelling language.

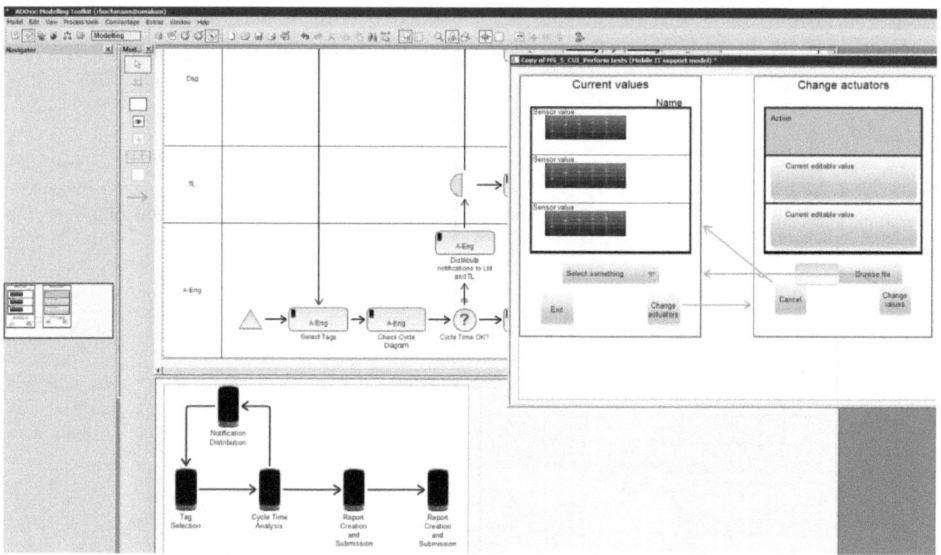

Fig. 4. Screen capture of the OMILab modelling tool implementation

3   Development

3.1   Modelling Requirements Sources and Approach

The software development process for the run-time ComVantage prototypes was extended with complementary ways of deriving the modelling requirements, thus the source of these requirements is manifold:

1. The functional and technological requirements elicitation approach was based on workshops and techniques suggested by the Volere [14] and Persona [15] methodologies. The collaborative workshops relied mainly on the Volere template as a structuring tool, interviews, protocol analysis (based on user stories structured as activity diagrams) and goal decomposition. This effort captured user roles, user

stories, use cases, operating environment constraints and development goals for use case partners. Since the ComVantage use case partners act in the role that will be taken by future users of the modelling method (businesses trying to deploy and align to the ComVantage generic technology), their input was also relevant for modelling, as it helped identifying the subdomains along the technical dimension and the scenarios that can potentially be structured on modelling level. We describe the identified facets of the modelling domain in Table 1:

Table 1. Facets concerning each application area

Concerns grouped by application area	Technical subdomains (facets)
Overlapping concerns	App and data requirements
	Collaborative business process management
	Access control requirements
	Human resources requirements
	Business modelling
	Geographical distribution modelling
Concerns for production line commissioning	Production line structuring
	Incident management
Concerns for customer-oriented production	Supply chain design for virtual enterprises
	Product design
	Market structuring
Concerns for mobile maintenance	Defect modelling
	Skill requirements
	Service Level Agreement structuring

Table 2. Knowledge externalization requirements

Required knowledge categories (and steps)	Customer oriented production	Production line commissioning	Mobile maintenance
Step1. to know what are the domain-specific triggers of my business processes	The structure of requested customized product	The structure of a requested production line	The sensor configuration and thresholds of a machine defect/state, with a valid service level agreement
Step2. to know what are my business processes	A structured „make to order" supply chain and its business actors	A structured "engineer to order" supply chain and its business actors	A maintenance service delivery process and its business actors
Step3. to know how my business processes run	Manufacturing business processes	Engineering business processes, automated production processes	Testing, repair and maintenance business processes
Step4. to know what my business processes need in order to run	Apps, data, humans	Apps, data, humans, robots	Apps, data, humans
Step5. to constrain the access to needed resources	Access rules	Access rules	Access rules

2. The to-be modelling procedure has been derived, with every step suggesting the knowledge externalization requirements from Table 2 (we consider that modelling helps a modeller to externalize his knowledge in a structured manner, in order to facilitate a better understanding and communication through visualization):

3. The metamodelling framework (Fig. 2) and technology used to implement the modelling method as a tool imposed additional requirements and constraints, mainly with respect to how the language has to be specified. As the modelling tool is being implemented on the ADOxx metamodelling platform, this imposes some constraints on how to describe the conceptualization output as a **metamodel,** and make it available for implementation. This is aligned with an already published formalism, in terms of set theory – FDMM [16]. A detailed specification of the metamodel is being developed iteratively in a series of public deliverables ([1], deliverables D311, D621, D721, D821);

4. Once the subdomains have been identified and delimited with a sufficient granularity, literature, best practices (on one hand) and the users stories (on the other hand) helped to identify keywords, which in turn suggested key concepts/relations/properties for each application area and subdomain. For example, literature on maintenance frameworks [17] suggested a classification with corrective, predictive and preventive approaches based on sensor value thresholds. Best practices in supply chain management indicated SCOR [18] as a key framework for structuring processes, also applicable in virtual enterprises. As supply chain is one of the facets of the ComVantage domain, we also took inspiration for SCOR-driven requirements for information systems [19].

The elicitation for runtime requirements suggested features and competency questions to be addressed by queries on the runtime prototypes. Usually such questions refer to the properties of a certain entity and have a certain goal that can be fit in the Table 2 knowledge categories. For example, from a runtime query (for the maintenance subdomain) like *give me current sensor values for a machine*, and by inquiring the goal of this query - *to decide what maintenance process to perform*, it is possible to derive modelling concepts (*machine*), properties (*sensor values* and *diagnosis thresholds*) and a conceptual link between a trigger (*the machine state*) and its consequence (*the maintenance process*). On this basis, model types have been designed for the machine state (covering the concepts/properties of machine, sensors and diagnosis thresholds), for the maintenance process (as a control flow-based business process with swimlanes, roles and resource requirements attached), and a navigable link has been defined between them.

4. Further on, the data design phase provided valuable conceptual information. As previously mentioned, class diagrams, ER diagrams and ontologies are particular types of conceptualizations, a key commonality with the metamodel necessary to describe the modelling language. ComVantage relies on ontologies to structure a cloud of Linked Data and these ontologies are domain-specific (for each application area). However, ontologies are aimed to support run-time queries and processing on instance level, so not all their concepts are relevant on a modelling level; and viceversa, additional concepts can be necessary in visual models, but irrelevant to run-time queries and instance data manipulation. For example, in the maintenance ontology, the fact that machines are described in terms of their sensors and actuators (rather than in terms of what they do) provided valuable input to the machine state visual modelling, while aspects like test configuration and test case result fields are meaningful rather in execution time, for returning data at instance level. From the other side, machine state models are linked to business (maintenance) processes that

must be communicated between stakeholders, but are not present in the run-time system ontology. Thus, replicating run-time data structures in the metamodels for design-time is not a solution, but design documentation analysis proved to be an important source for deriving modelling constructs.

This approach is also justified by the fact that both data schemas/ontologies and modelling tools have a key goal of answering competency questions, which usually mean querying concept attributes and relations conforming to some constraints. The usage is, again, different – in the first case the focus is on getting instance data or generating reports at run-time, in the second case the focus is on model analysis or evaluation. But there is a new requirement that derives from this: conceptual linking is necessary for both querying approaches. ComVantage relies on Linked Data for this, while the metamodel of the modelling method uses several type of conceptual references that must be navigable in the modelling tool, and must support cross-model querying. We identified several types of such conceptual links:

- **Model-to-model:** relevant when two different models are conceptually related, for example they express two facets on the same problem, or a link between a trigger and its effect; a typical case is the link from a machine state model to its corresponding maintenance process model;
- **Object-to-model:** relevant when a model further describes the semantics of an object (on a new level of abstraction/with additional details that are too complex to be described in the object properties); a typical case is when a process step (activity) is itself a process – for example in the SCOR process taxonomy;
- **Object-to-object:** relevant when two objects are conceptually related and creating a visual connection between them would overload the model; typically, it is used between objects from different models, for example a feature of a product (from a product model) linked to a goal of a customer segment (from a market structure model);
- **Reused object:** this is implicit linking derived from the fact that the same object identity is reused in multiple models; it avoids the necessity of creating two separate objects and connecting them explicitly with a relation stating their equivalence (like in the "sameAs" linking from the Linked Data paradigm); this is typically used in the pool of resources, a repository of reusable "process resource" objects.

6. The existing market of domain-specific modelling tools and frameworks (Fig.5) suggested some already validated approaches that inspired a hybridization of solutions across the multiple facets of the ComVantage domain, integrating concepts from languages and paradigms with narrower scopes: e3 value [20] for high level business models, feature-oriented domain analysis [21] for product design, ADONIS BPMS [22] for business process management, the Cameleon Framework [23] for mobile app modelling, the existing SCOR tools for supply chain modelling [24] and XACML [25] for structuring access control policies. The metamodel integrates concepts from these languages with inter-model linking - a key requirement to support navigation between related models expressed with different language subsets ("model types") and cross-model querying.

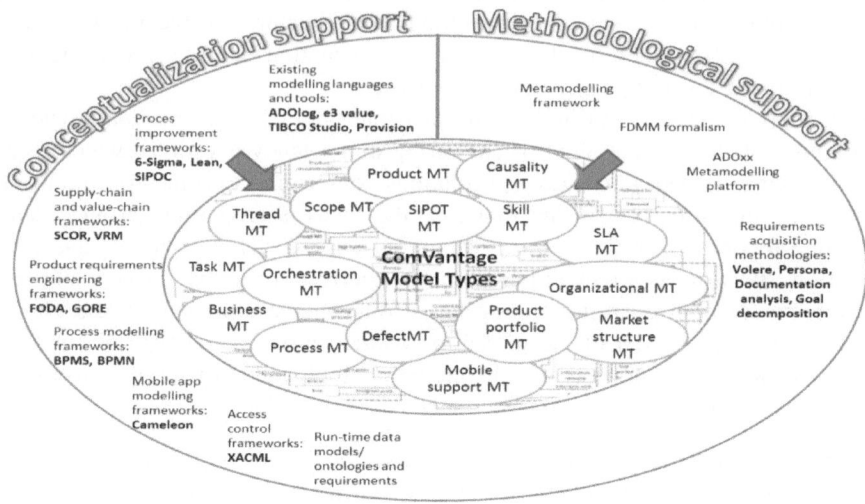

Fig. 5. Sources for defining the ComVantage modelling requirements

3.2   Resulted Modelling Stack

The modelling stack derived during the conceptualization phase of the ComVantage method covers, in the current iteration, the following layers, each with specific model types interlinked by the navigable link types mentioned in the previous section:

The Business Modelling Layer. Here the e3 value modelling language [20] is employed for the highest abstraction view on the modelled business, to depict abstract value exchanges between business entities (Fig.6).

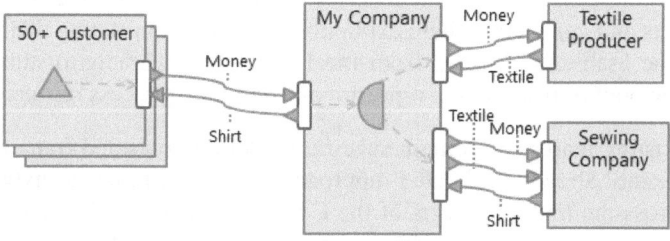

Fig. 6. The business modelling layer

The strategic layer covers several strategic aspects: the market structure captures the market segments, their needs and goals that have been identified by existing marketing research results; a product decomposition inspired by feature oriented analysis [21] combined with Kano's feature classification [26] has its structure mapped on the identified market needs/goals. Multiple product configurations are derived by activating various product features; each product configuration is linked to a supply chain process modelled according to a variation on the thread diagrams from the SCOR framework, then the production roles are further linked to the scope model (also suggested by SCOR) that describes the logistical distribution of the business partners. Just as with the product models, a global scope depicting all partners that can fulfil each production role is the base for deriving scope configurations for each product configuration, based on customization requests (Fig. 7).

Current work is being developed in order to extend the product structure models to also include maintenance services (whose "features" are service level agreement "terms"). For the maintenance domain, the product structure is replaced with a machine state/defect model (depicting diagnosis variables and their threshold) which triggers, instead of a supply chain, a maintenance service delivery process. For the production line commissioning, the trigger is a plant structure model linked to its supply chain (for production line deployment) and its automated production process. Thus, this is the layer where domain specificity suggested by Table 2 is most prevalent.

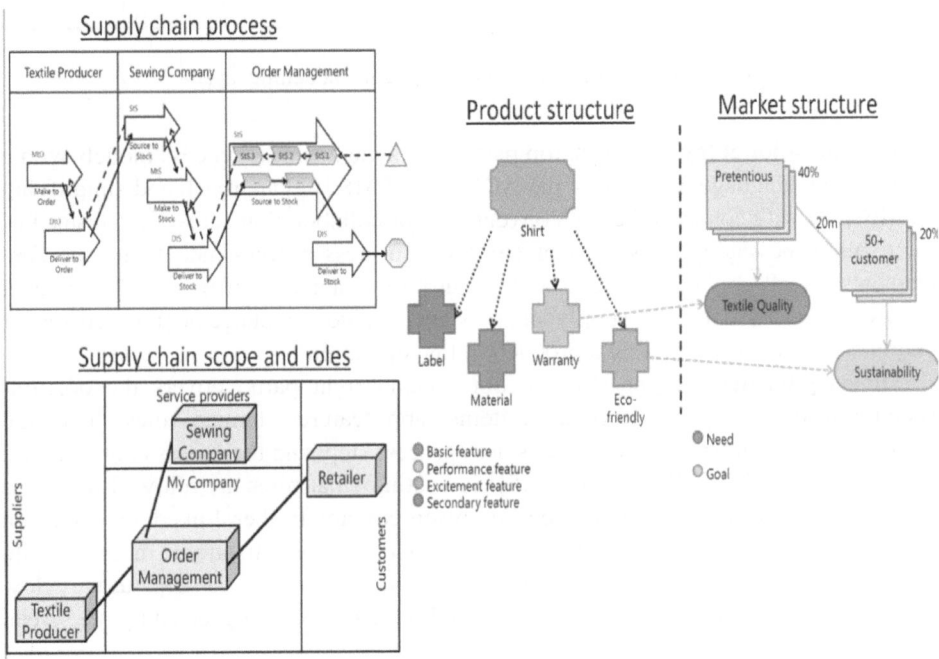

Fig. 7. The strategic modelling layer

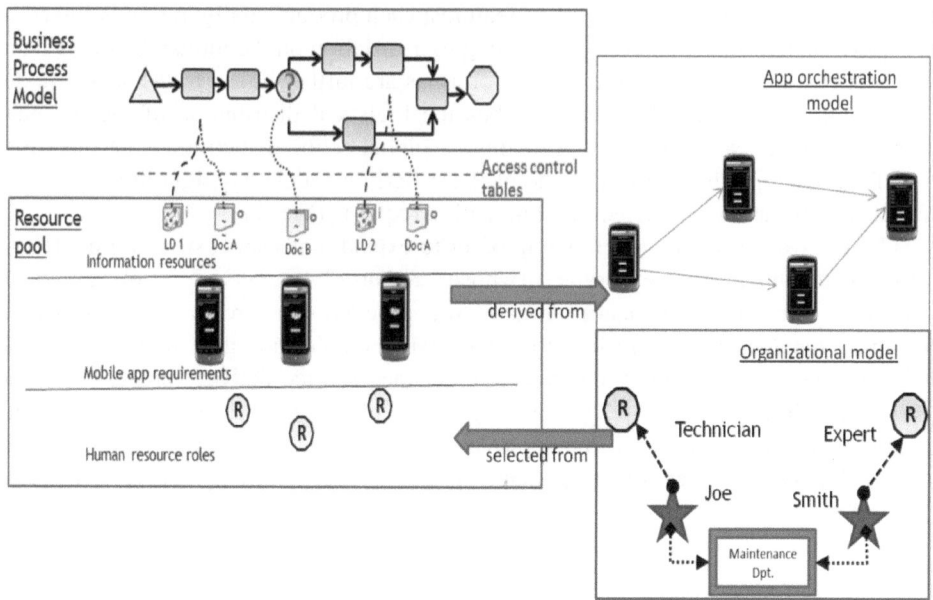

Fig. 8. The operational and requirements modelling layers

The operational layer (Fig. 8, top part) covers the business process models with a control flow language inspired by the ADONIS BPMS [22] approach and simplifying BPMN [27] with some modelling conventions for collaboration semantics (instead of the explicit messaging constructs of BPMN). Business process models are the core elements for all application areas – they can be maintenance processes, lower level SCOR processes detailing supply chain steps, incident management processes or automated processes depicting a production line operation.

The requirements layer (Fig. 8, bottom and right parts) covers the domain-specific resource types (information items, app features, human roles, hardware resources) that can be mapped to a business process step, and the access control tables (inspired by the XACML structure [25]) indicating what roles are allowed to access certain resource objects. Some types of resources are further linked to extension models – for example, the human roles are selected from organizational models, while the app features are the basis for automated derivation of app usage flow requirements. Each app can further be detailed in mockups as suggested by the screen capture from Fig.4).

We provide in Table 3 a mapping of model type coverage for the identified domain facets (from Table 1):

Table 3. Modelling coverage of the domain facets

Domain facets	Modelling coverage	Goal
App and data requirements	The resource pool, app interaction and app orchestration model types, SIPOT model type	To describe, in a business process, what app functionality and data objects are required at each process step
Collaborative business process management	Business process model type (with swimlanes) Task model type (hierarchical decomposition of an activity)	To describe a business process and its decomposition in subpprocesses
Access control requirements	Permission tables in resources from the resource pool	To describe the access policies for each resource
Human resources requirements	Organizational model type	To describe the organizational structure and roles to be involved in business processes
Business modelling	E3 value model type	To describe the abstract business model
Geographical distribution modelling	Scope model type (SCOR-based)	To describe the collaboration network involved in a virtual enterprise
Production line structuring	Plant structure model type (under development)	To describe the production line components
Incident management	Business process model type (with swimlanes and events)	To describe event handling business processes
Supply chain design for virtual enterprises	Thread model type (SCOR-based)	To describe the high level supply chain process for delivering a service or creating a product
Product design	Product configuration, product portfolio model types	To describe and classify the features of a product and a product portfolio overview
Market structuring	Voice of the customer model type	To describe the needs for which the product features are created
Defect modelling	Machine state model type	To describe the sensor configuration for which a certain maintenance process is designed
Skill requirements	Skill model type	To describe the skills required for performing a maintenance process
Service Level Agreement structuring	SLA model type	To describe the features/terms of a service level agreement (for maintenance mainly)

3.3   Business Benefits

Conceptual modelling benefits have to do, first of all, with knowledge externalization, thus with understanding and communication [28]. A modelling language educates its users to structure descriptions of situations from reality with a limited and abstract set of visual constructs that facilitate knowledge sharing and query-based analysis. Additionally, in our modelling method, model analysis, transformation and simulation can add value to the conceptual models in several ways. These are only briefly mentioned, as their technical description is out of this paper's scope:

- all models can be queried within the modelling tool with constraints applicable on the properties of each modelling objects (e.g. "give me all activities with a certain property or a link to a certain resource");

- all models can be exported in an RDF serialization format that converts the navigable links to Linked Data, and enables SPARQL-based querying and processing of models outside the modelling tool, opening possibilities for process-aware information systems implementation;
- business process models can be simulated using an interaction stepper that guides the user through each process step, highlighting its properties and requirements; this facilitates process assimilation for employees, and also validation of the mobile app support (derived from mobile app requirements) and resource assignment to activities.

4   Conclusions

We present here a conclusive SWOT analysis of the modelling requirements definition approach employed in the ComVantage research project. Its main *strength* is the multiview integration of technological constraints and concepts derived from use case and design documentation. As a *weakness*, we indicate the difficulty of validating against end-users whose knowledge of the domain may not include some of the practices suggested by the literature and the market (e.g. SCOR). We identify the *opportunity* of defining a fully-fledged conceptualization methodology, as a particular approach to knowledge acquisition, for knowledge to be described in diagrammatic models; and the *threat* that our approach can be overridden by more structured practices of knowledge acquisition from fields such as expert systems engineering - although the scope and goal significantly differs, and their applicability need to be further investigated.

The project has an agile iterative approach and it is currently at the middle of its development. Further refinements will be done towards the final iteration of the modelling method, including a list of domain-specific queries that each model type will be capable of answering. The mentioned OMILab implementation is still subject to adaptations based on lessons learned from its application in concrete use cases.

Acknowledgment. The research leading to these results was funded by the European Community's Seventh Framework Programme under grant agreement no. FP7-284928 ComVantage.

References

1. The ComVantage Project Public Deliverables, http://www.comvantage.eu/results-publications/public-deriverables/
2. Checkland, P.B., Poulter, J.: Learning for Action: A short definitive account of Soft Systems Methodology and its use for Practitioners, teachers and Students. Wiley (2006)
3. Karagiannis, D., Kühn, H.: Metamodelling platforms. In: Bauknecht, K., Tjoa, A.M., Quirchmayr, G. (eds.) EC-Web 2002. LNCS, vol. 2455, p. 182. Springer, Heidelberg (2002)
4. OMILab, the ComVantage experimentation space, http://www.openmodels.at/web/comvantage/home

5. Karagiannis, D., Visic, N.: Next Generation of Modelling Platforms. In: Grabis, J., Kirikova, M. (eds.) BIR 2011. LNBIP, vol. 90, pp. 19–28. Springer, Heidelberg (2011)
6. Hrgovic, V., Utz, W., Karagiannis, D.: Service Modelling: A Model Based Approach for Business and IT Alignment. In: The 5th Int. IEEE Workshop on Requirements Engineering for Services (COMPSAC Workshops), pp. 422–427. IEEE Computer Society (2011)
7. Lundqvist, M., Sandkuhl, K., Seigerroth, U.: Enterprise Modelling in Distributed Teams-Lessons Learned from Information Demand Modelling. In: Kirikova, N., Stirna, J. (eds.) Proceedings of the CAISE Forum 2012. CEUR Proceedings, vol. 855, pp. 139-146, CEUR-WS.org (2012)
8. Lundqvist, M., Sandkuhl, K., Seigerroth, U.: Transfer of Method Knowledge and Modelling in Distributed Teams – Lessons Learned. In: Aseeva, N., Babkin, E., Kozyrev, O. (eds.) BIR 2012. LNBIP, vol. 128, pp. 26–40. Springer, Heidelberg (2012)
9. Businska, L., Kirikova, M.: Knowledge Dimension in Business Process Modeling. In: Nurcan, S. (ed.) CAiSE Forum 2011. LNBIP, vol. 107, pp. 186–201. Springer, Heidelberg (2012)
10. Burge, J.E.: Knowledge Elicitation Tool Classification, http://web.cs.wpi.edu/~jburge/thesis/kematrix.html#_Toc417957413
11. The Linked Data Design Issues, http://www.w3.org/DesignIssues/LinkedData.html
12. SPARQL Query Language, the official web page, http://www.w3.org/TR/sparql11-query/
13. ADOxx – the official product page, http://www.adoxx.org/live/
14. Website of Volere Requirements Specification Template, http://www.volere.co.uk/
15. Pruitt, K., Adlin, T.: The Persona Lifecycle. Morgan Kaufmann (2006)
16. Fill, H.-G., Redmond, T., Karagiannis, D.: FDMM: A Formalism for Describing ADOxx Meta Models and Models. In: Maciaszek, L.A., Cuzzocrea, A., Cordeiro, J. (eds.) Proceedings of ICEIS, pp. 133–144. SciTePress (2012)
17. Márquez, A.C.: The Maintenance Management Framework. Springer (2010)
18. The Supply Chain Operations Reference, http://supply-chain.org/scor
19. Liepina, L., Kirikova, M.: SCOR based ISS Requirements Identification. In: Abramowicz, W., Maciaszek, L., Węcel, K. (eds.) BIS 2011 Workshops. LNBIP, vol. 97, pp. 232–243. Springer, Heidelberg (2011)
20. Gordijn, J., Akkermans, H.: E3-value: design and evaluation of e-Business models. IEEE Intelligent Systems 16(4), 11–17 (2001)
21. Kang, K., Cohen, S., Hess, J., Novak, W., Peterson, A.: Feature-Oriented Domain Analysis (FODA) Feasibility Study, http://www.sei.cmu.edu/reports/90tr021.pdf
22. ADONIS – Community Edition, the official website, http://www.adonis-community.com/
23. Calvary, G., Coutaz, J., Thevenin, D., Limbourg, Q., Bouillon, L., Vanderdonckt, J.: A Unifying Reference Framework for Multi-Target User Interfaces. Interacting with Computers 15(3), 289–308 (2003)
24. Software supporting the SCOR framework, http://supply-chain.org/scor/software
25. XACML specification, the official website, https://www.oasis-open.org/committees/tc_home.php?wg_abbrev=xacml#CURRENT
26. Kano, N., Nobuhiku, S., Fumio, T., Shinichi, T.: Attractive quality and must-be quality. Journal of the Japanese Society for Quality Control 14(2), 39–48 (1984)
27. BPMN, the official website, http://www.bpmn.org/
28. Mylopoulos, J.: Conceptual modeling and Telos1. In: Loucopoulos, P., Zicari, R. (eds.) Conceptual Modeling, Databases, and Case An Integrated View of Information Systems Development, pp. 49–68. Wiley (1992)

Using Process Variants in Design of Flow Management Systems

Jānis Grabis

Institute of Information Technology, Riga Technical University
Kalku 1, LV-1658, Latvia
grabis@rtu.lv

Abstract. Customer flow management (CFM) systems integrated hardware, sensing, software and data analysis technologies to delivery customer service processes. While the traditional CFM systems focus of managing customer queues independently of the service provided, this paper investigates business processes where flow management is an integral part of the business processes delivered. A method for design of the CFM systems is elaborated. The method focuses on identification and evaluation of business process delivery variants providing the best customer flow management performance. The evaluation is performed using static analysis and simulation, and run-time adjustment algorithms are used to alter process delivery according to the current execution context. The design method is applied in a case study exploring development of interactive museum expositions.

Keywords: Flow management, business process variants, run-time adjustment.

1 Introduction

Customer flow management (CFM) systems [1] are used to organize customer service processes and to ensure that the service level is maintained regardless of the flow intensity. Commercial CFM systems focus on customer queuing solutions. However the novel concept of sensing enterprise [2], rapid expansion of Internet of Things and context awareness provide new opportunities for enhancing the CFM systems. The modern CFM systems integrate hardware, software, communication and data processing technologies to maximize the customer flow throughput and customer experience. They implement the underlying customer flow management business process involving both manual and electronic activities.

The queuing theory and simulation [3] provides basis for quantitative analysis and improvement of the customer flow management processes. Business process management [4] techniques provide the general framework for improving the CFM business processes. Workflow management systems are used to implement high frequency business processes, and methods for optimization of workflow's throughput are available [5]. Context aware workflows [6] are a type of workflows dealing with changing operation circumstances (e.g., increasing customer flow). The queuing theory, simulation and business process management deal with business level

A. Kobyliński, A. Sobczak (Eds.): BIR 2013, LNBIP 158, pp. 34–47, 2013.

optimization of CFM processes while workflow management systems concern with the process execution software. However, the existing research provides limited guidelines for designing integrated CFM systems.

In this paper it is argued that usually there are multiple alternative solutions for implementing CFM business processes. These multiple solutions can be represented as process variants. Static and simulation based analysis is used to determine the most efficient process variants. Additionally, multiple process variants giving the best result in different circumstances can be implemented, and during the execution, the CFM system switches from one process variant to another depending upon the context. Thus, the objective of this paper is to elaborate a process variants based method for designing CFM systems. The paper formulates the overall design method, describes representation and analysis of process variants and demonstrates application of the proposed method.

The contribution of the paper to existing research is threefold: 1) extension of the concept of flow management systems by moving from queuing solutions to integrated flow management systems; 2) elaboration of the process variants based method for design of flow management systems; and 3) simulation based evaluation of the process variants.

The rest of the paper is organized as follows. Section 2 defines integrated flow management systems and reviews related research. The method for designing flow management systems is presented in Section 3. The evaluation of process variants is discussed in Section 4. Section 5 evaluates the proposed method by its application in a case study, and Section 6 concludes.

2   Flow Management System

Flow management problems occur in business process management as well in operations management. This section defines the proposed concept of flow management as well as reviews the related work.

2.1   Definition

Traditional customer flow management systems focus on organization and optimization of customer queues. In these systems, flow management is viewed independently from the service provided. In this paper, the concept of customer flow management is expanded by considering, systems where flow management is an integral part of the service provided, and the system is responsible for delivery of the whole service rather than just providing the queuing functions. Examples of such flow management systems can be observed in trade fairs and museums, where customers interact with different digital objects or use other interactive features as they traverse through the exhibition.

The main characteristic of flow management systems is integrated utilization of software, hardware, sensing and data processing technologies. Fig. 1 shows a graphical representation of the general flow management system. There is a continuous flow of customers who receive a service consisting of multiple steps forming the flow management process. The flow management process has a limited capacity. The service is provided using both electronic and physical means. The customers use interactive hardware devices such as touch screens and virtual assistants to consume software based services such as information services and games. Some of the devices and services can be used for service delivery purposes while others are primarily intended for flow management purposes. Data about customer flow intensity, other customer characteristics and general context information is provided by sensing services. These data are required to alter the service delivery according the current context. Flow management services are responsible for evaluation of the impact of flow intensity on the service level and for determination of appropriate measures to improve the service level. The flow management engine integrates together all components of the flow management system. The flow management system should ensure that customers receive the required service and that the desired service level expressed in customer waiting time or related parameters is achieved. It is also important that the systems provide a high customer throughput at a reasonable cost.

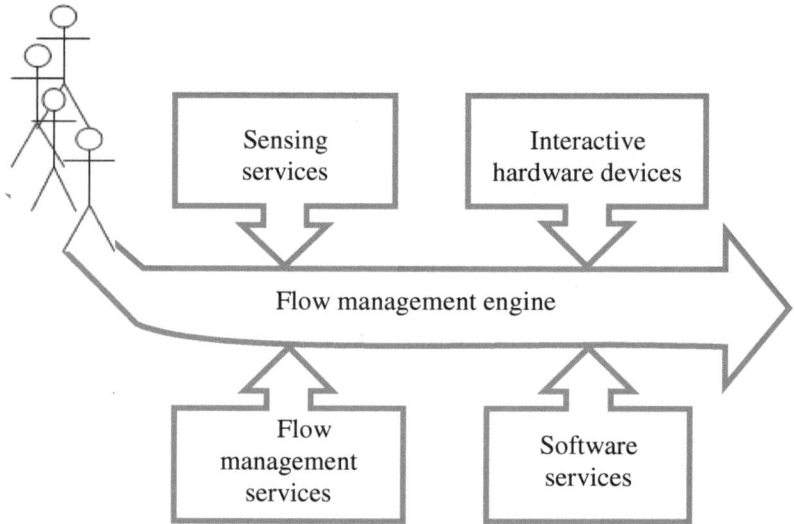

Fig. 1. The main components of the flow management system

2.2   Related Work

The related work to flow management can be divided in three large groups: business process management research, optimization of industrial systems and research on workflow management systems.

Business process management deals with continuous improvement of business processes and a number of business process management methodologies and methods have been developed [7]. Best practices [8] and patterns [9] are used for qualitative business process improvement, while evolutionary optimization techniques are used for quantitative optimization of business process structure [10]. Liman Mansar et al. [11] elaborate an AHP based methodology for selection of appropriate process improvement methods. These investigations focus on the structural aspects of business process improvement.

Glykas [12] defines multiple perspectives of business process management. Out of these, the performance measurement perspective is the most relevant for the customer flow management processes. Tan et al. [13] elaborate a methodology for process performance evaluation. The methodology includes definitions of performance measurements based on Activity Based Costing and Activity Based Management as well as tools for evaluation of these measures. Simulation is one of the tools used. Kamrani et al. [14] evaluate business process performance with emphasis on evaluation of efficiency of human agents involved in the process. Their business processes is modeled using BPMN. Damij et al. [15] propose a Tabular Activities Development methodology, which addresses both business process improvement and implementation of information system supporting the improved business processes. Process simulation is used to determine the process cycle time and related measurements is one of the key parts of the methodology. Oliveira et al. [16] use Petri nets to analyze business process performance both analytically and using simulation.

Business process analysis and improvement often results in multiple alternative process designs also referred as to process variants [17]. Methods for representing and managing the process variants have been elaborated [18, 19, 20].

The flow optimization is a traditional problem investigated in operations management and optimization of manufacturing systems in particular [21]. Scheduling, resource allocation and flexible manufacturing systems are among methods used to optimized throughput in such systems. Simulation modeling is also frequently used to investigate queuing problems in healthcare applications (e.g., [22]).

Workflow management systems are used to implement business processes, especially, if there are high requirements towards system's throughput. Reijers & Aalst [5] show that organizations achieve significant processing cycle time improvements after implementation of workflow management systems. Adaptive workflows [23] are used to handle exceptions and changes occurring during the workflow execution. Rule and template based approaches are often used to provide adaptation [24]. Smanchat et al. [6] reviews these and other methods used in workflow adaptation.

3   Design Approach

The CFM systems integrate software, hardware, communication and data analysis technologies to deal with the varying customer flow and execution context. The CFM system design method covers both the system's design and execution phases (Fig. 2). During the design phase, variants for implementing the CFM process are evaluated and mechanisms for run-time adjustment of CFM processes are implemented. During the execution phase, the flow management context is monitored and process execution is automatically adjusted according to changes in the context.

The design phase starts with definition of the general customer flow management process. Different process execution alternatives are identified during the next step. That includes identification of multiple alternative process execution paths as well as identification of software or hardware solutions for implementing the process activities. Each of the identified process execution variants is evaluated using the static analysis. The main evaluation criteria are process implementation and execution cost as well as the process throughput. These criteria capture technical characteristics of the process design and execution. The customer experience is also affected by user satisfaction with interactions with the CFM system. User-centric design and systems' acceptance testing methods could be applied to addresses these aspects of the customer experience. A more detailed dynamic analysis is conducted using simulation. The objective of the static and dynamic analysis is identification of the most efficient process variants for implementation as well as definition of switching rules. The switching rules are used to specify when the flow management system should switch from one process execution variant to another (e.g., if the customer flow increase breaks a certain threshold the system switches to an expedite service delivery node). The most efficient process variants are implemented along with the switching rules and mechanisms for process adjustment during their execution. Mechanisms for capturing the customer flow and other context data are also implemented.

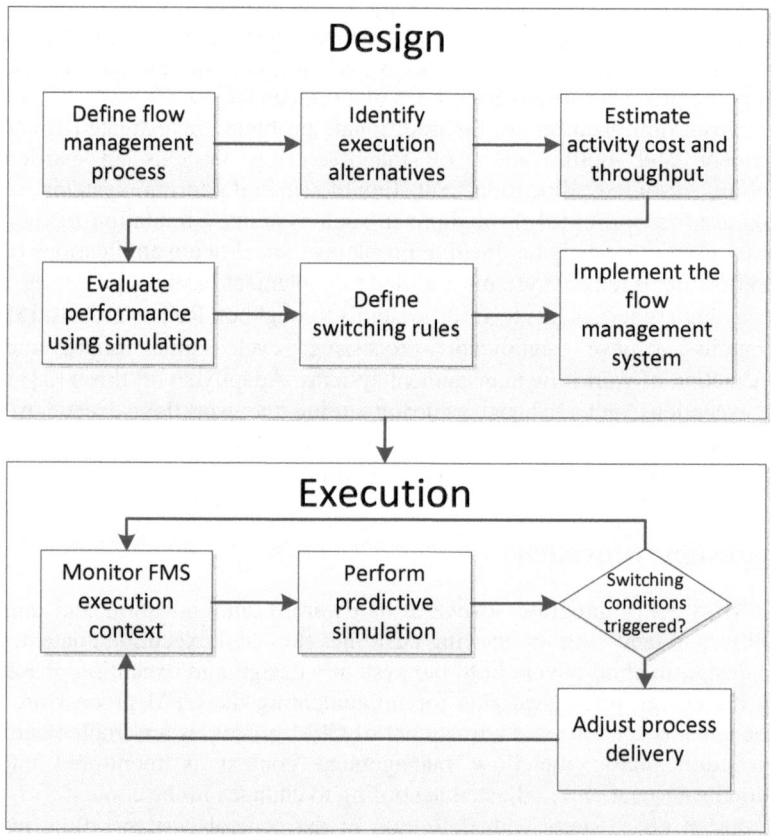

Fig. 2. The customer flow management system's design method

During the execution phase, the customer flow and other context data are continuously monitored and compared with targeted customer service requirements. Given that the current customer flow affects the system's performance with time delay, a real-time simulation can be performed to proactively identify potential performance deterioration. Both actual observations and predictions made by simulation are used to trigger the switching rules, and the customer flow management processes execution is adjusted accordingly.

4   Process Variants

The flow management general process, which is a starting point of designing the customer flow management system, is modeled using a business process modeling language of the choice, e.g., BPMN. It represents the key activities of the flow management process. Similarly as in Dijkman et al. [25], the general process is expressed as

$$BP = (N, E, G, C), \tag{1}$$

where N is the set of tasks in the process, E is the set of events, G is the set of gateways and $C: N \times E \times G$ is the set of connectors.

The general process is enriched by specifying alternatives for execution of each task:

$$BP^* = (N, E, G, C, \alpha), \tag{2}$$

where $\alpha: N \to A$ associates alternatives with tasks and A is the set of alternatives.

The enriched model can be expanded into a business process explicitly showing all alternative tasks and execution paths

$$BP^E = (N', E', G', C', \Phi, R), \tag{3}$$

where function $\Phi = (\phi_1, \phi_2, \phi_3, \phi_4)$ defines transformation from BP^* to BP^E applied to tasks, events, gateways and connectors, respectively. For example, $\phi_1: N \cup A \to N'$ defines transformation of initial nodes and their execution alternatives into the set of tasks in the expanded model. The expanded model is used to generate process execution variants, and in order to ensure their consistency, the set of restrictions R is also added to the extended model. The restrictions specify logical and temporal dependencies between elements of the business process model. These dependencies are specified in a form of rules as proposed in [19]. The flow management process execution variants $BP_1, \dots, BP_M$ are generated by either selecting or excluding particular elements of the process and compliance with the dependencies is determined for each process variant.

Quantitative attributes are assigned to all elements in each process variant. The total costs and execution time for the process can be determined in the static analysis using expressions provided in [26]. Simulation is used for more detailed evaluation of the process variants.

5   Case Study

The proposed approach for designing flow management systems is evaluated in a case study. In this case study, a flow management system is designed for a museum. The museum offers to visitors several digital expositions and interactive services as a part of the overall exhibition. One of these interactive services is a photo corner where the visitors can make retro styled pictures of themselves and take away the pictures as memorabilia. During the design stage of the photo corner service, one of the main concerns was to avoid excessive queuing to get access to the service because that would significantly affect the overall visitor experience. Therefore, different alternatives for providing the service and keeping visitors satisfied are investigated.

5.1   Process Design

Initially, the general photo corner process BP showing its core activities is developed (Fig. 3). The visitors receive instruction about using the photo corner upon entering the exhibition. The Start photo session task initiates the photo session. The task may include different setup or registration procedures. The visitor dresses-up for the photo scene and takes photos. The photos made are displayed to the visitor who can add different visual effects to the photos and send the photos to selected outlets (e.g., printing center, photo sharing websites, e-mail). The task also includes represents the final delivery of the photos to the visitor at the museum printing center. The general process only defines the main tasks of the business process without providing specific details on task execution. The flow management system implementing the business process implementation includes hardware (touchscreen displays, camera), software and sensing devices (used to monitor the visitor arrival flow).

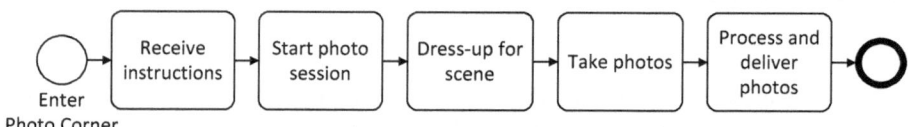

Fig. 3. The general business process model

In order to provide the execution details, execution alternatives for each task are identified and are represented in the expanded business process model BP^E (Fig. 4). The expanded business process model, for instance, shows that the Receive instructions task can be executed using on-screen instructions, giving oral instruction by a museum assistant or using a virtual assistant. To perform the Start photo session task, the visitor is requested to scan her ticket, the ticket is checked manually by the museum assistant or no specific initiation activities are performed. Similarly, there are multiple ways for processing and sending photos starting from simple direct routing to the photo delivery till advanced photo editing and sharing.

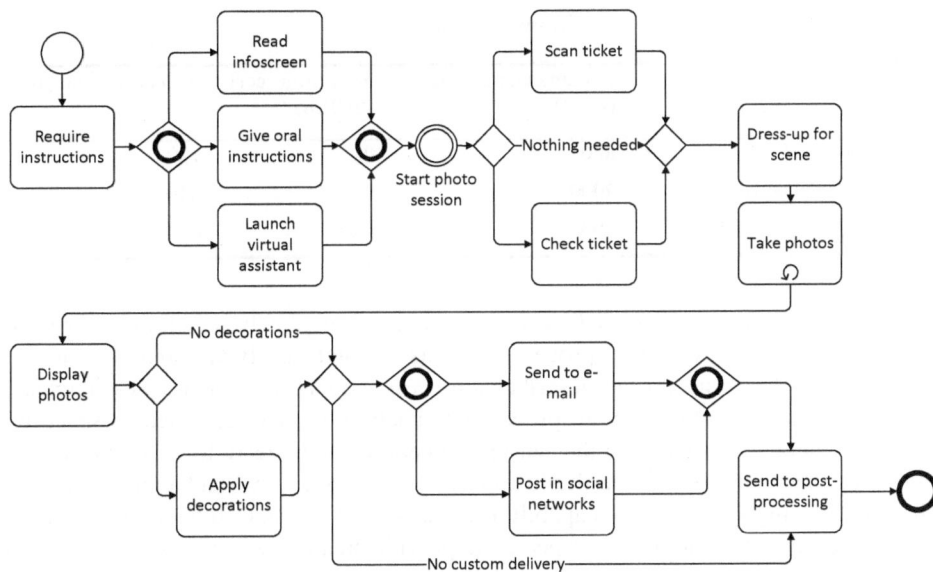

Fig. 4. The expanded business process model for the Photo Corner process

The quantitative attributes are assigned to each task in the expanded process (Table 1). The implementation cost represents costs associated with developing particularfunctions in the flow management system including hardware installation and software development cost. The execution cost represents maintenance cost of the system's components and labor cost for manual tasks. The execution time represents the average time for performing the task by the visitors. The values listed in the table are based on expert evaluation and are not obtained by actual measurements.

Table 1. Cost and time attributes characterizing the Photo Corner process

Task	Implementation Cost (EUR)	Execution cost (EUR/h)	Execution times(s)
Require instructions	0	0	0
Read infoscreen	1000	0.01	120
Give oral instructions	100	10	60
Launch virtual assistant	30000	0.1	60
Scan ticket	1000	0.01	60
Check ticket	50	8	10
Dressup for scene	0	0	120
Take photos	700	0.01	45
Display photos	1200	0.01	30
Apply decorations	800	0.01	180

Table 2. (*continued*)

Task	Implementation Cost (EUR)	Execution cost (EUR/h)	Execution time (s)
Send to e-mail	800	0.1	120
Post in social networks	2000	0.1	240
Send to post-processing	800	0.01	0

Different process variants BP_i can be generated on the basis of the expanded process. Fig. 5 shows two process variants named as Basic and Advanced, respectively. The Basic variant describes a process without any specific session start-up procedures and without photo processing capabilities. It is designed to speed-up the flow though the lack of the set-up procedures may lead to a single visitor repeating the photo session multiple times. The Advanced variant emphasizes the photo processing and delivery capabilities. The virtual assistant though significantly more expensive to implement is expected to provide clearer instructions to the visitors and thus to reduce the process execution time and variability. Additionally, it

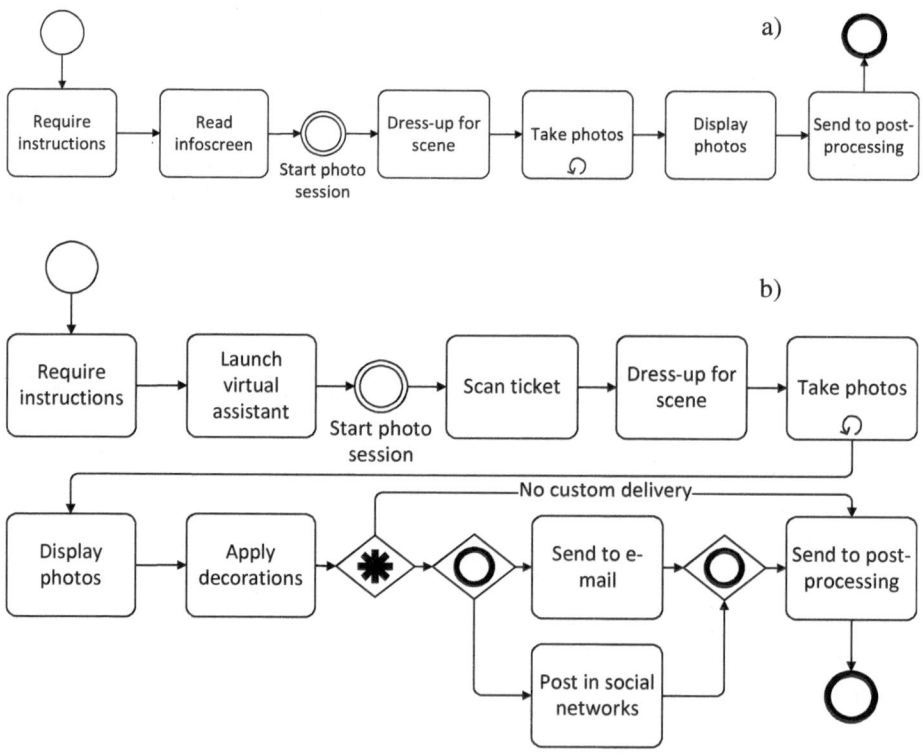

Fig. 5. Business process variant of the Photo Corner process: a) Basic variant; and b) Advanced variant

improves the overall customer experience. There is a complex gateway after the Apply decorations task. The process execution path can be determined by the visitor or by a run-time adjustment algorithm. The algorithm uses the current number of visitors waiting at the photo corner to determine whether the visitor can use the advanced delivery capabilities or the photos are sent directly to post-processing at the printing center.

5.2   Process Evaluation

The process variants designed are evaluated using both static analysis and simulation. The implementation and maintenance costs as well as deterministic process execution cycle time are determined using the static analysis (Table 2). The execution cost is determined over two year period. The Advanced variant is significantly more expensive than the Basic variant and results in longer execution time. However, it also provides more functions than the Basic variant. The deterministic cycle time does not take into account visitor arrival and task execution time uncertainty.

Table 3. Static Evaluation of the Photo Corner process

Process variant	Implementation cost (EUR)	Execution cost (EUR)	Total cost (EUR)	Execution time (min)
Advanced	37300	2046	39346	12.25
Basic	3700	186	3886	5.25

In order to account for the uncertainty, the process performance is also evaluated using simulation. Two scenarios are considered: 1) low visitor flow scenario – visitors arrive every 25 minutes; and 2) high low visitor flow scenario – visitors arrive every 13 minutes. The customer arrival interval is modeled using an exponential distribution. The task execution uncertainty is represented using a lognormal distribution.

Initially, the variants are compared if visitors are allowed and choose to use the advanced delivery functions (Table 3). The cycle time increases significantly comparatively to the static evaluation due to the impact of queuing. The advanced variant shows unacceptably long cycle time, especially in the case of the high flow. The increase of the number of visitors in the system is a particular concern because the museum wants to eliminate crowding. However, the performance of the Advanced variant can be improved by using run-time adjustment. A simple switching rule is defined. It implies that if the number of visitors in the system exceeds a certain threshold the custom delivery functions are not offered to the visitors. Fig. 6 shows the cycle time depending upon the threshold value.

Table 4. Simulation based evaluation of the photo corner process

Process variant	Low flow		High flow	
	Cycle time (min)	Vistors in the system	Cycle time (min)	Vistors in the system
Basic	12	0.5	15	1.3
Advanced	32	1.8	72	8.6

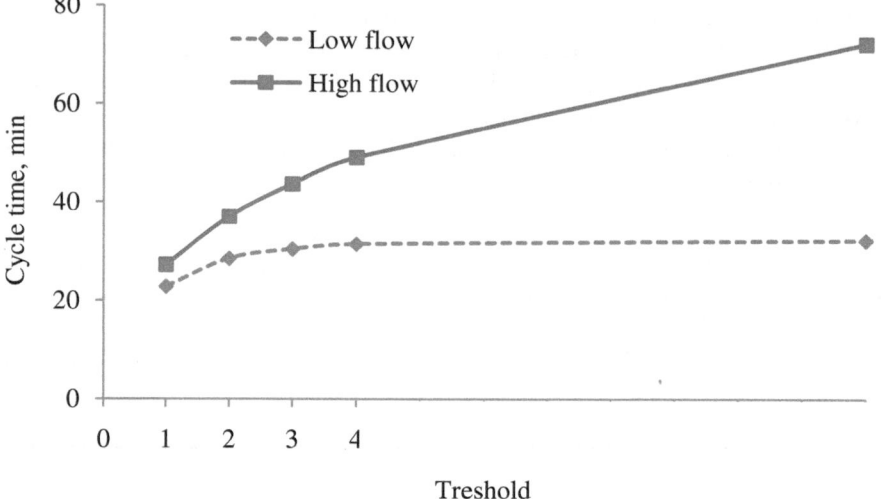

Fig. 6. Impact of adjustment on the simulated performance. The last data item represents the Advanced process variant without adjustment.

In flow management systems, visitors are concerned not only with the average cycle time but also with the promised maximum cycle time. The cycle time distribution is given in Fig. 7. The histogram suggests a bimodal distribution. That is caused by application of the switching rules. The first mode is characteristic to visitors not using the custom delivery while the second mode is characteristic to visitors using the custom delivery.

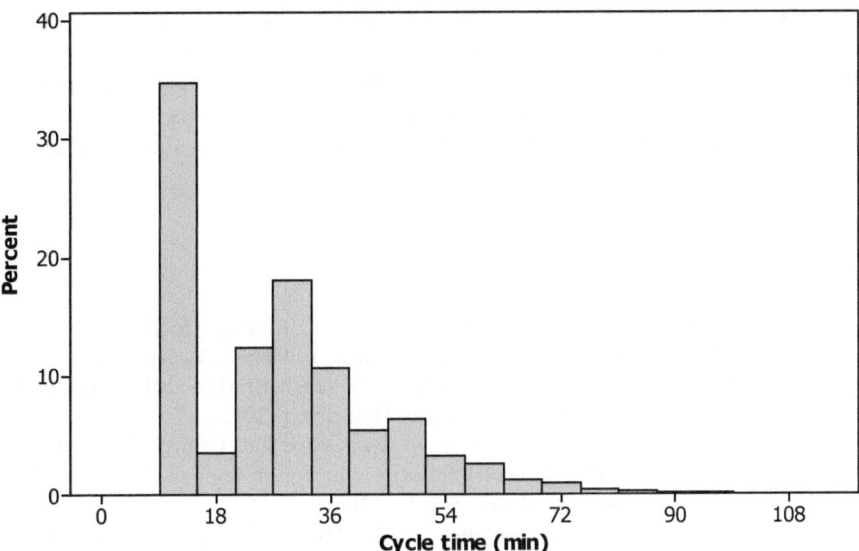

Fig. 7. Cycle time distribution for the Advanced variant, low customer flow and the threshold equals to 2

6   Conclusion

The method for designing customer flow management systems has been proposed in the paper. It is intended for business processes where flow management is naturally intervened with the service delivered to customers. Hardware, software, sensing and data processing technologies are integrated to implement these kinds of business processes. The paper has described the overall design approach and application of process variants is elaborated into more details. Elaboration of technical issues of implementing the proposed customer flow management system and solutions for predictive simulation considered in the execution phase are subject to further research.

The application of process variants allows to identify the most appropriate and efficient way of delivery customer flow management business processes what is of major important to deal with high intensity customer flows. The expanded business process is proposed as a way for representing all business process delivery alternatives. The static analysis and simulation are used to evaluate performance of the business process variants during the design phase. The simulation based analysis yields more comprehensive evaluation results. The static analysis is useful in practice to obtain initial estimates of the expected performance for each process variant because development of the simulation model requires extra effort not always available in the development projects. The experimental studies using the museum digital exposition case show that the run-time adjustment is an effective solution for maintaining the required customer throughput level. However, that is achieved by limiting the number of services available to visitors. That is not possible for many businesses processes and should be weighted with regards to the overall customer experience. The same applies to evaluation of the process variants. In this paper, the process implementation and execution cost as well as the business process execution cycle time are used as main evaluation criteria. The customer satisfaction also should be taken into account.

References

1. Paschou, M., Sakkopoulos, E., Sourla, E., Tsakalidis, A.: MobiQ: Mobile Based Processes for Efficient Customer Flow Management. In: Bider, I., Halpin, T., Krogstie, J., Nurcan, S., Proper, E., Schmidt, R., Soffer, P., Wrycza, S. (eds.) BPMDS 2012 and EMMSAD 2012. LNBIP, vol. 113, pp. 211–225. Springer, Heidelberg (2012)
2. Lampathaki, F., Vlad-Câlcic, D.: Translating Knowledge into Growth: Views from ICT Research to Support Future Business Innovation. In: Future Internet Enterprise Systems (FInES) Workshop, Aalborg, Denmark, May 9 (2012)
3. Nyhuis, P., Von Cieminski, G., Fischer, A., Feldmann, K.: Applying simulation and analytical models for logistic performance prediction. CIRP Annals - Manufacturing Technology 54, 417–422 (2005)
4. Van der Aalst, W.M.P., ter Hofstede, A.H.M., Weske, M.: Business process management: A survey. In: van der Aalst, W.M.P., ter Hofstede, A.H.M., Weske, M. (eds.) BPM 2003. LNCS, vol. 2678, pp. 1–12. Springer, Heidelberg (2003)
5. Reijers, H.A., Van der Aalst, W.M.P.: The effectiveness of workflow management systems: Predictions and lessons learned. International Journal of Information Management 25, 458–472 (2005)
6. Smanchat, S., Ling, S., Indrawan, M.: A survey on context-aware workflow adaptations. In: 6th International Conference on Advances in Mobile Computing and Multimedia, MoMM 2008. Linz, Austria, pp. 414–417 (2008)
7. Elzinga, D.J., Horak, T., Lee, C., Bruner, C.: Business process management: Survey and methodology. IEEE Transactions on Engineering Management 42, 119–128 (1995)
8. Reijers, H.A., Liman Mansar, S.: Best practices in business process redesign: An overview and qualitative evaluation of successful redesign heuristics. Omega 33, 283–306 (2005)
9. Barros, O.: Business process patterns and frameworks: Reusing knowledge in process innovation. Business Process Management Journal 13, 47–69 (2007)
10. Vergidis, K., Saxena, D., Tiwari, A.: An evolutionary multi-objective framework for business process optimization. Applied Soft Computing Journal 12, 2638–2653 (2012)
11. Limam Mansar, S., Reijers, H.A., Ounnar, F.: Development of a decision-making strategy to improve the efficiency of BPR. Expert Systems with Applications 36, 3248–3262 (2009)
12. Glykas, M.M.: Effort based performance measurement in business process management. Knowledge and Process Management 18, 10–33 (2011)
13. Tan, W., Shen, W., Zhao, J.: A methodology for dynamic enterprise process performance evaluation. Computers in Industry 58, 474–485 (2007)
14. Kamrani, F., Ayani, R., Moradi, F.: A framework for simulation-based optimization of business process models. Simulation 88, 852–869 (2012)

15. Damij, N., Damij, T., Grad, J., Jelenc, F.: A methodology for business process improvement and IS development. Information and Software Technology 50, 1127–1141 (2008)
16. Oliveira, C.A.L., Lima, R.M.F., Reijers, H.A., Ribeiro, J.T.S.: Quantitative analysis of resource-constrained business processes. IEEE Transactions on Systems, Man, and Cybernetics Part A: Systems and Humans 42, 669–684 (2012)
17. Hallerbach, A., Bauer, T., Reichert, M.: Capturing variability in business process models: The Provop approach. Journal of Software Maintenance and Evolution 22, 519–546 (2010)
18. Lu, R., Sadiq, S., Governatori, G.: On managing business processes variants. Data and Knowledge Engineering 68, 642–664 (2009)
19. Becker, M., Klingner, S.: Towards Customer-Individual Configurations of Business Process Models. In: Bider, I., Halpin, T., Krogstie, J., Nurcan, S., Proper, E., Schmidt, R., Soffer, P., Wrycza, S. (eds.) BPMDS 2012 and EMMSAD 2012. LNBIP, vol. 113, pp. 121–135. Springer, Heidelberg (2012)
20. Kumar, A., Yao, W.: Design and management of flexible process variants using templates and rules. Computers in Industry 63, 112–130 (2012)
21. Anupindi, R., Chopra, S., Deshmukh, S.D., Van Mieghem, J.A., Zemel, E.: Managing Business Process Flows Principles of Operations Management. Pearson Prentice Hall, Upper Saddle River (2011)
22. Su, Q., Yao, X., Su, P., Shi, J., Zhu, Y., Xue, L.: Hospital registration process reengineering using simulation method. Journal of Healthcare Engineering 1, 67–82 (2010)
23. Muller, R., Greiner, U., Rahm, E.: AGENT WORK: a workflow system supporting rule-based workflow adaptation. Data Knowledge Engineering 51, 223–256 (2004)
24. Weber, B., Reichert, M., Rinderle-Ma, S.: Change patterns and change support features - Enhancing flexibility in process-aware information systems. Data and Knowledge Engineering 66, 438–466 (2008)
25. Dijkman, R.M., Dumas, M., van Dongen, B.F., Käärik, R., Mendling, J.: Similarity of business process models: Metrics and evaluation. Information Systems 36, 498–516 (2011)
26. Canfora, G., Di Penta, M., Esposito, R., Villani, M.L.: A framework for QoS-aware binding and re-binding of composite web services. Journal of Systems and Software 81, 1754–1769 (2005)

Visual Simulation
for the BPM-Based Process Automation

Silke Holzmüller-Laue[1], Paul Schubert[2], Bernd Göde[2], and Kerstin Thurow[1]

Center for Life Science Automation at the University of Rostock, F.-Barnewitz-Str. 8,
18119 Rostock, Germany
{Silke.Holzmueller-Laue,Kerstin.Thurow}@celisca.de,
{Paul.Schubert,Bernd.Goede}@uni-rostock.de

Abstract. A graphical standard notation for the analysis and execution of operational business processes is available since 2011 the Business Process Model and Notation (BPMN) 2.0. A new possibility is now established to automate complex, longer-than-average, interdisciplinary process chains including a powerful human task management cost-efficiently. The end-to-end process automation in life science automation demands comprehensive systems integration in heterogeneous, hybrid automation environments. Already at the early stages of the development of such solutions exists a great need for simulations of process execution. The presented simulation solution, interesting also for other target industries, is an important tool to an early staged quality assurance, to a definition of the components related automation demand and a validation of the process model. This visual simulation system shows the potentials of a BPMS-based automation using an animated process model, application simulations of the distributed automation and information systems, controlled video sequences or application screenshots and corresponding detailed information. It supports the argumentation for process-controlled, model-based applications, which transform the currently autonomous sub-systems and isolated applications into an overall system with a comprehensive, reproducible process control and monitoring. This article explains the solution and the impact of the BPM-oriented process simulation.

Keywords: Business Process Simulation, Business Process Automation, Model-Driven Automation, Life Science Automation, Laboratory Automation.

1 Introduction

Nowadays, laboratory processes in the life sciences are often dominated by high throughput applications. In the field of drug discovery for example substance libraries containing hundreds of thousands or millions of substances are tested for their biological activity against chosen targets. This screening results in less than 1% of potential therapeutic candidates for further investigations. Such high throughput applications require a high degree of automation. In the laboratories so called islands of automation are established today, which are able to execute special, but often isolated subprocesses. Extensive preparatory and accompanying subprocesses, like

A. Kobyliński and A. Sobczak (Eds.): BIR 2013, LNBIP 158, pp. 48–62, 2013.

method development, storage, maintenance, analytical preparation, evaluation, interpretation and knowledge extraction are usually time-consuming manual tasks, which are insufficiently integrated into the automated processes. Different software systems are applied in each subprocess to control and monitor the process (process control systems - PCS) as well as to capture, manage and process data (Laboratory Information Management Systems - LIMS, Spectroscopy / Chromatography Data Systems - SDS/CMS, Electronic Laboratory Notebooks - ELN, spreadsheets, data visualization and analysis systems, etc.). This situation results in many different interfaces to exchange data.

As an interdisciplinary research institute the Center for Life Science Automation (celisca) at the University of Rostock (Germany) develops high throughput applications for key processes of the life sciences, for example, in the fields of screening technologies and analytical measurement. The high-end system solutions consist of necessary equipment systems, the controlling software, and the professional applications. Innovative solutions are created for more and more complex processes by using modern technologies. Thereby new areas of application are opened up.

The objective of the BPM-based automation approach is a flexible end-to-end automation to control and monitor processes with technologies of modern business process management (BPM). The core component is a specific kind of technology that is particularly suitable to achieve process automation, co-called Business Process Management Systems (BPMS) [1]. This is a new approach in the application field of life sciences. All tasks or subprocesses, which influence the process result, will be integrated regardless of their degree of automation. Fig. 1 shows typical examples of such process components and puts the corresponding devices and systems into the hierarchically structured laboratory automation. Such end-to-end processes are performed across the islands of automation, across the disciplines and organizations. They integrate manual tasks as well as all needed automation and IT systems. Thereby an important challenge is to consider the dataflow in the automation. This is especially significant for the quality assurance and its obligation to prove the compliance with regulations, which is particularly relevant in this field of application.

The model-driven automation approach is based on the standardized business process modeling. For the definition of such business processes the graphical notation standard BPMN (Business Process Model and Notation) has been established in the recent years, which pursues the goal to overcome the understanding gap between IT-specialists, automation engineers and business users [2],[3],[4]. With the BPMN 2.0 published in 2011 a direct executable notation is available. The fact, that the notation is an executable end-to-end integration language as well, is especially helpful to the objective of automation efficiency in R&D laboratories as it allows understandable and easy adaptable complex process models for the immediate process control. The concept presented in [5] has been positively validated over the past two years. During this evaluation the idea of an animated and media supported simulation to demonstrate the potential of the process-oriented approach has been created.

This article describes the developed web-based workflow simulation as a supplementary tool for the development process of the innovative BPM-based process automation. The simulation solution takes into account characteristics of life science applications as well as requirements of automation engineering.

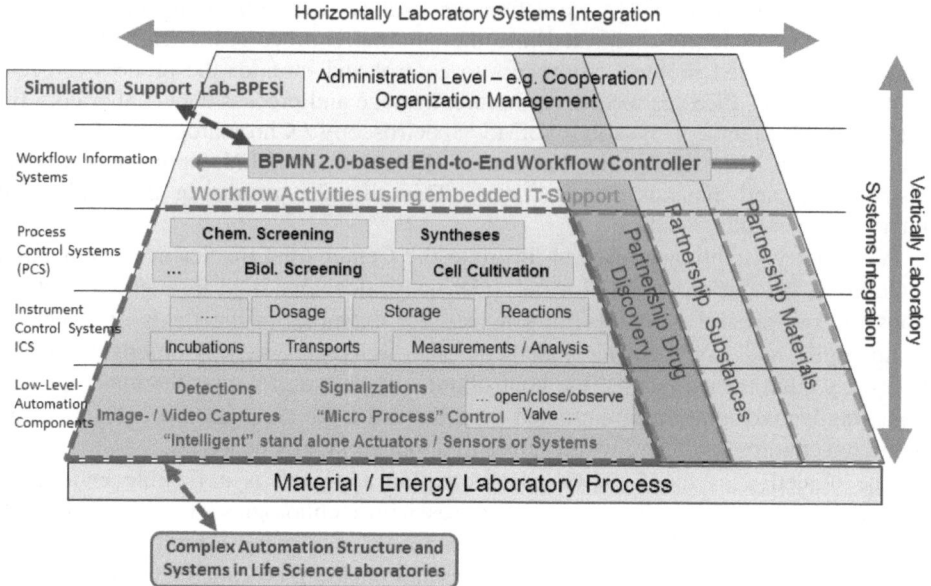

Fig. 1. Application background of the model-driven end-to-end process automation in the life sciences

1.1   Business Process Simulation

Often a simulation component is a substantial part of BPMS [6], [7] either as embedded tool within the modeler or through third-party integration [8], [9]. The second option requires an additional mapping of process model and simulation model as well as simulation skills of people or proper training in simulation analysis [7].

For example, in [8] a mapping algorithm is presented to simulate the flows generated by the BPM tool Netflow in the simulation environment of Arena. Januszczak [9] describes a standard for defining business process simulation scenarios (Sim4BPM), which combine the business process definition and the set of scenario parameters. Simulation models are just one possible consumer of these business process scenario definitions. Therefore, this standard is not based on BPMN. In contrast, the simulation engine L-SIM [10] developed by the Lanner Group uses BPMN diagrams for animated visualizations and quantitative statistics. Waller et al. suggest in [10] resource-related extensions to BPMN. The behavior of resources is often modeled in a simplified manner [7].

A comparison of embedded simulation components of current tools on the market can be found, e.g., in [11], [12]. The pursued objectives of business process simulation within the scope of workflow management are [13], [14], [15], [16], [17]:

- Identification of critical paths and bottlenecks in the resource allocation (prevention of bottlenecks / optimization of cycle times / prediction of resource utilization),
- Determination of the predicted execution time (cycle time, waiting time), e.g., for dimensioning of resources,
- Testing the executable model before deployment on servers to validate the ability of execution of process models (formal correctness and consistency),
- Comparison and evaluation of alternative process configurations, and
- Graphically visualized validation of process models using an animated simulation.

The stochastic, discrete event simulation is most prevalent. It allows an analysis of the dynamic behavior [17]. Often the simulation model is based on the respective system specific meta-model of the BPMS. To simulate a business process more than just a business process definition is needed. It needs also real-time, historical and estimated data values [6]. Such simulation relevant information including times, costs and quantities for single tasks are requirements for the determination of process variables related to the flow and the resources as an answer to the above-mentioned objectives.

1.2   Requirements

The success of the new methods and technologies of BPM as an innovative standardized and at the same time cross-disciplinary approach for workflow automation and systems integration is depending on the acceptance achieved on early stages of process development. During the process development phase the process simulation should be utilized to visualize potentials of the process-oriented and BPM-based automation approach as well as to support the argumentation for process controlled applications. As a result there is the demand for a graphically visualized and media supported validation of the process model using an animated simulation. A helping tool should be provided for a team of developers and professional users to define the specific process behavior and the automation demand. It can be used as a basis for discussions on the support of operational decision processes.

The animated simulation can focus different specific scenarios (e.g., human task support, task-related IT-support, full automation, integration of islands of automation with differentiated degree of integration, quality assurance procedures, etc.) to be optimally adjusted accordingly to the current objective of a presentation. This requires an easy configuration of the underlying simulation model as well as a suitable comprehensible definition language.

The dataflow is not visible in executable process models. Process variables represent data. During the process development phase, however, decisions have to be made regarding the automation of the dataflow, e.g.:

- Who requires which data?
- How has data to be transformed using which kind of resources?

- At which places and when has data to be provided?
- How are data transmitted in respective stages of the process progress?
- Which data are to be captured and in which scope to be protected and archived?

Therefore the integration of the dataflow into the visualization is an essential requirement. Usually a simulation is an execution of a process without any calls of real services or external applications. Thereby return values of the integrated services are predefined. This way an analysis of the dynamic process behavior is only possible if errors of external systems can be ruled out. This is a useful option in the case of testing. Regarding the intended discussion on an automation concept, however, it is beneficial to have the possibility to interactively trigger a reaction of an external system and define its return value. Effects on the further process execution can thus be observed.

2   Procedure Model for Business Process Automation with Simulation

A typical development process of the end-to-end automation of life science processes complemented by the process simulation could be described as follows:

Analysis of Existing or Planned Workflows. The flow of existing or newly to be developed workflows will be analyzed in detail. Thereby also subprocesses are considered, which will not be controlled in detail by a BPMS later, but already are automated by an island of automation. The analysis of those subprocesses is crucial to the determination of the demand for automation. Often the control systems of these automation systems do not consider the dataflow. The not executable BPMN model, the result of this step, also serves as part of the end-to-end process documentation. Thus methods and workflow descriptions of integrated subprocesses, which have usually been vendor-specific and only been locally accessible, are available in a common standardized notation now. In this way long-term knowledge management is possible.

Identification of the Demand for Automation. The BPM-based workflow automation allows an improved level of documentation of the current process instance by an automated IT-based recording, e.g., of manually executed process steps, without increasing the personnel effort. IT systems are integrated and adequately provided to the user at the right moment. At this step the identification takes place of how and what is documented during the process and of how the dataflow and the data provision could be automated. The resulting basically executable BPMN model lacks programming-intensive components like interfaces towards external systems. Roles and resources are being assigned to activities and notifications as well as dialogs are being implemented. The incomplete but executable process model acts as the basis of the simulation model. Furthermore it supports further discussions involving professional users to proceed with the requirement analysis.

Simulation. The simulation model is based on the BPMN process model developed in step two. It is expanded with important data objects, input and output data of activities, as well as screenshots, screencasts and videos to visualize activities. Relevant activities are being identified and relevant process paths are being determined considering the objective of the simulation. Parallel process paths can be visualized in a sequentialized manner.

By the animated process flow professional users as end users of life science applications can realistically examine and understand the process, review the fulfillment of their requirements and discuss implementation alternatives and already achieved solution effects. This is especially supported by the PCS simulation component. As a result there is a final description of requirements.

Process Development and Deployment. The implementation of the final executable process model requires adjustments to new requirements as well as the implementation of interfaces towards external systems including data transformation and error handling. In the course of this the development of reusable components is aimed.

Utilization of the Process Model and Optimization. During utilization of the process model adjustments to changed boundary conditions or optimization of the process model are often needed at some point. This especially applies to the flexible, quickly changing processes of the life science research and development. This effort is expected to decrease using visual simulation at the development stage.

3 Visual Simulation System Lab-BPESi

The simulation components of business process management systems are insufficient related to the above-mentioned objectives, which are most relevant to the LSA, because their focuses are different ones (section 1.1). Furthermore no human interaction is usually wanted in the BPMS-embedded simulation. This, however, can be helpful in the LSA development process to discuss different scenarios and process paths. For these reasons, the visual simulation described below has been developed. It takes into account the complex automation objectives and typical automation structures of life science laboratories. The intended visualization for the standard driven workflow automation cannot be limited to a simple BPMN control flow visualization, but must integrate the components aspect and therefore the partial solution aspect corresponding to the Fig. 1. In this sense it is an industry-oriented business process execution simulation for laboratories of life sciences (Lab-BPESi).

3.1 Architecture Overview

The web based simulation tool consists of three functional, configurable modules (Fig. 2):

Business Process Execution Simulator (BPESi). This module is responsible for industry independent presentation of the process model, the marking of the current BPMN 2.0 element and the display of respective detailed data like a description or in-/output data. The control flow is visualized using an animated process model. The BPESi allows a time-controlled process flow and a single step mode.

Task Visualization. This module visualizes operations belonging to the current activity using graphics, images, animated images, and/or videos.

Lab Robot Simulation. This module represents many different typical automation systems like transport robots or various islands of automation, which are usually controlled by vendor-specific process control systems (PCS). It provides an automated as well as an interactive access to reflect the different degrees of automation of the provided interfaces of these systems for an external control. This module can also be used separately.

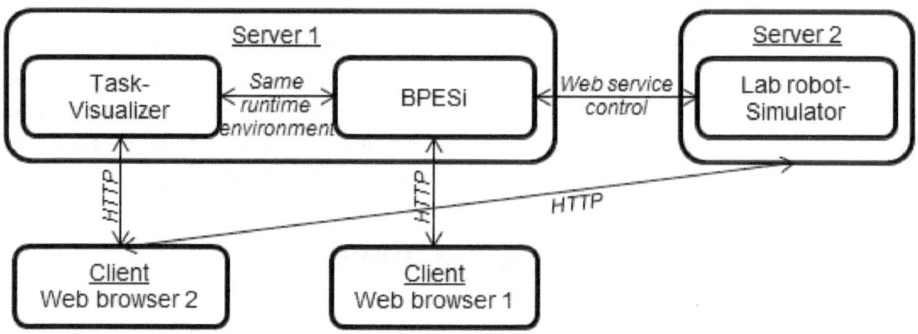

Fig. 2. Architecture of the simulation solution Lab-BPESi

3.2   Business Process Execution Simulator

The BPMN process diagrams are the basis of the process simulation component as they provide a descriptive, well interpretable and at the same time informative representation. Due to complexity and length of a typical end-to-end process chain in the field of application the animated presentation is divided into an overview diagram (1) and the detailed process diagram (2), which contains all relevant activities (Fig. 3).

An animation of the diagrams allows a transparent presentation of the control flow. A color highlighting (yellowish background) is used to relate the different subprocesses in the overview diagram with the current process model. A further differentiation can be achieved by a color coding of the current subprocess element in the overview diagram (green), which allows a better orientation any time. The current activity or gateway (or any other BPMN 2.0 element) is visually marked by a token (red circle) in the detailed process diagram (2), which facilitates an intuitive understanding of the control flow. Furthermore an automated scrolling function has been implemented to ensure readability of large activity networks.

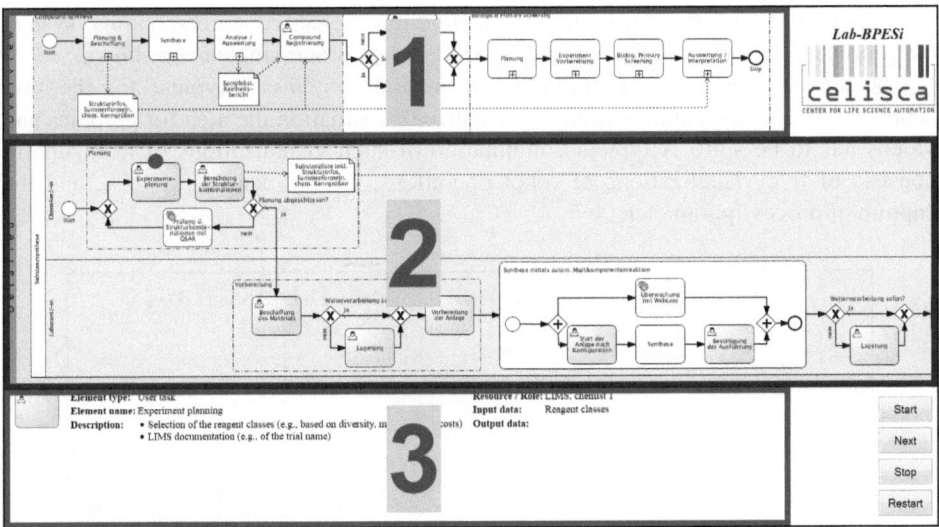

Fig. 3. The user interface of the BPESi with its three areas: (1) overview, (2) animated process diagram and (3) data on the current activity

The structured information area (3) provides details about the current activity:

- Label and type (user task, service task, etc.),
- Description stating the effect on the overall objective of the process,
- Involved process roles and resources,
- Dataflow (input/output).

The animation is controlled by a time-based fixed order and can be broken at any time. Activities or elements can be early terminated (and thereby also skipped) while being in the single step mode. Besides breaking the simulation it can also be restarted. The time-based process progress is preconfigured in the simulation model or interactively determined in the single step mode. The simulation model, containing all important data on the animation, is the basis of the simulation and is described below. The BPESi component communicates with the other two components "Task Visualization" and "Lab Robot Simulation" to check the status or call functions.

3.3   Task Visualization

This module visualizes the operations and the "just-in-time IT-support", which belong to the current activity, using graphics, screenshots or videos (Fig. 4). Those activities are especially user tasks, meaning activities, in which humans are directly involved. Additionally, the reference to all involved information systems, utilized during the task execution, will be shown. This points out the resolved or yet unsolved task-related systems integration. The effect of the task visualization allows evaluating the respectively targeted and actually achieved degree of automation. Specifically, e.g., alternatives of the information transmission, selective corresponding system calls, process data visualization or the controlled data processing can be shown.

The simultaneous use of multiple information systems is typical for the task support in life science automation. To visualize this situation the area for graphics and videos has to be split. A typical combination of such visualizations of task support consists of live visualizations of robot operations, remote access for PCS, and the capture of process parameter.

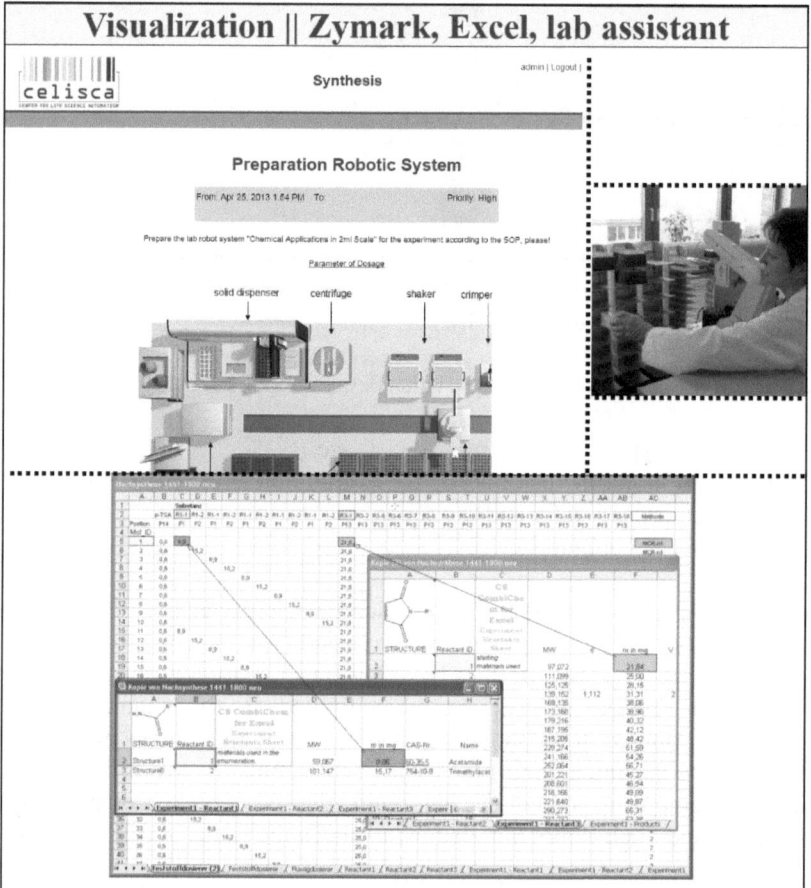

Fig. 4. The user interface of the Task Visualization being just one big area for graphics or video

3.4   The Lab Robot Simulation

As opposed to the BPM-method application in the commercial-administrative workflow automation the integration of structured, often hierarchical automation systems is essential in life science applications. The general automation system will be represented by a set of process control systems and device controls such as method controller for analytical systems, controls for transport robots or automated islands with a different degree of automation of the integration interface (Fig. 1). Additional automation components, e.g., at the intelligent sensor level, can be solved by the Task Visualization. Largely independent of the purpose and the complexity of integrated islands of automation some basic functionalities for a sufficient abstraction of process control systems in life science applications can be found. This abstraction approach of the simulation objective for PCS is limited to the following features:

- Naming the PCS and the device / automation system,
- Visualization of the user interface of the PCS (in parts, visualizations of workflow as well),
- Display and input options for important process variables (method, run duration, current status, file interface for parameterization),
- Triggering of errors with an error message, e.g., by defining time from start,
- Interactive control options: start, stop, error, reset,
- Automated control via web service,
- Sufficient interaction between PCS and BPMS or BPESi regarding the workflow control flow (status, error, process variables).

Fig. 5 shows the features realized in the graphical user interface. The Lab Robot Simulation is configured in a file. This allows multiple preconfigured alternatives of this module to simulate different automation systems simultaneous.

The Lab Robot Simulation has been developed as a completely independent module with a web service interface. This enables the usage in executable BPMN models as alternative to external systems (like real PCS) regardless of the availability of such systems. Furthermore this allows the usage of the process model at an early stage at which there are no interfaces to the final backend system yet or if a real automation system is occupied by experiments. Using the web service interface the Lab Robot Simulation module is controllable and relevant data (e.g., the current status) are retrievable for the BPMN-defined flow control.

3.5   Simulation Model

Considering the requirement for easy exchanging and modifying possibilities the Extensible Markup Language (XML) has been chosen as notation of the simulation model.

The underlying grammar in form of an XML schema describes two main elements. The element having the tag *bpmProcess* represents one process or subprocess. It contains any desired number of elements having the tag *bpmElem*. These elements represent the single BPMN 2.0 elements within the process including activities or

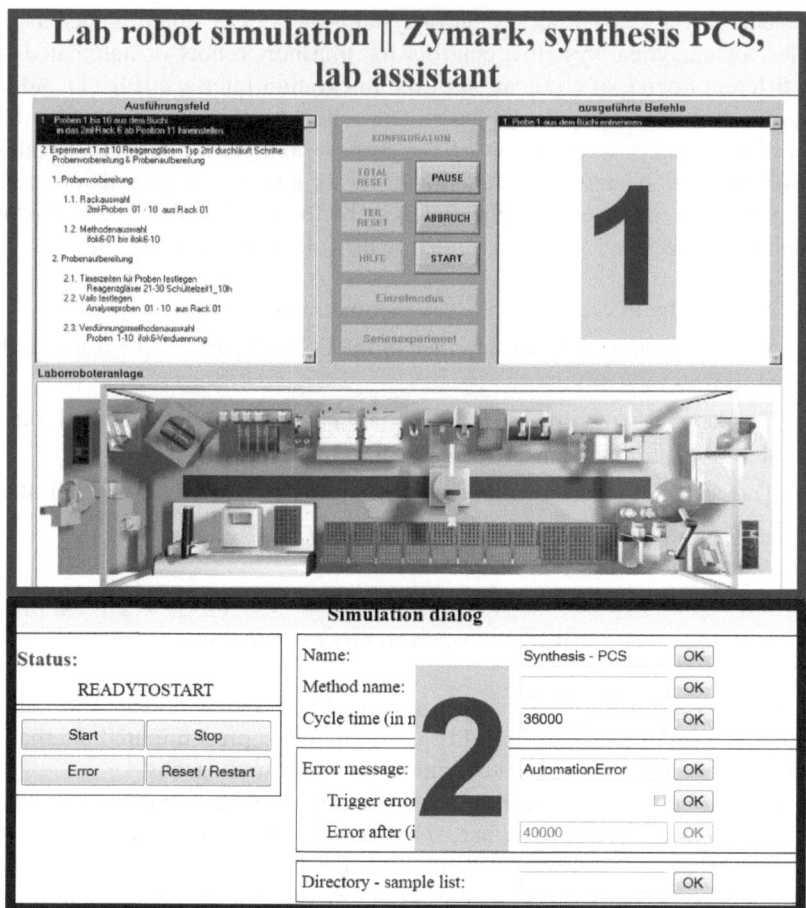

Fig. 5. The user interface of the Lab Robot Simulation with the areas System Presentation (1) and Simulation Dialog (2)

gateways. Subordinated elements describe all relevant data for the simulation. The start element contains details on the overview diagram and the detailed process model to be displayed, among others. Thereby multiple detailed process models can be used for single subprocesses.

Task-related Configuration of BPESi. The sub-elements of each *bpmElem* element contain all the data necessary for the animated simulation and the area for the details:

• *name*   *(Type: String)*
    Name of the task.

• *desc*   *(Type: String)*
    Detailed description.

- *resource (Type: String)*
  All in the task involved resources (e.g., devices or humans).

- *posX und posY (Type: int)*
  Position of the token marking the current task.

- *runtime (Type: int)*
  Execution time in seconds, which will be simulated.

- *inputData und outputData (Type: String)*
  Required input data and generated output data.

Task-related Configuration of the Lab Robot Simulation. As the BPESi has the ability to control multiple instances of the lab robot simulation simultaneous, the simulation model needs to provide information on whether the current element requires such activities. Whether the control of the lab robot module is fully automated or has to be done manually is stored in sub-elements as well:

- *robotXMLPath (Type: String)*
  Relative path to the configuration file of the special version of the PCS.

- *isRobotSimulatorStart   (Type: boolean)*
  Start the lab robot simulation.

- *isRobotSimulatorAutoStart   (Type: boolean)*
  Automated start of the lab robot simulation.

- *isRobotSimulatorStop   (Type: boolean)*
  Wait for the execution of the lab robot simulation to finish.

Task-related Configuration of the Task Visualization. A graphic or a video inclusively its viewing time can be defined for each simulated BPMN 2.0 element. It is also possible to specify multiple graphics or videos, which then will be consecutively shown. All graphic formats supported by the utilized web browser (like PNG, JPG or GIF) or video formats supported by the HTML5 element *<video>* (like MP4, WebM and Ogg) can be used.

```
<media>
        <mediaElem time="25">Grafic.jpg</mediaElem>
        <mediaElem time="240" video="true">Video.ogg</mediaElem>
</media>
```

3.6   Technologies

The simulation is implemented object-oriented on the server side. As many BPM tools are developed in Java this simulation component is also programmed in Java (version 7) to ease subsequent integration. On the client side simulation parts are implemented using HTML5, JavaScript and Cascading Style Sheets (CSS). The user interface is generated on the server using servlets and Java Server Pages (JPS). These servlets are also endpoints to dynamic requests by the client to the server.

3.7   Application of the Process Simulation

The developed BPM-based process execution simulation has been tested using an above-average complex life science application. The representative end-to-end process in the field of drug discovery includes subprocesses on multiple islands of automation with differentiated external access possibilities, manual activities and several integrated IT systems.

Aspects, to be especially emphasized, which are only now realizable by the BPM based workflow automation without any additional personnel effort, are:

- The integration of manual activities into the central process control by notifications using work lists of BPMS human task management or e-mails,
- The coordination of automated and manual subprocesses and activities,
- The usage of digital signatures for the purpose of archiving documents created during the process (relevant to the quality assurance),
- The automation of the data and file transfer (including transformation) for provision for other involved components or for archiving,
- The time-controlled process monitoring and triggering of notifications in the case of timeouts,
- The provision of selective data,
- The automated recording of activities in a central documentation system,
- The integration of an information system common in the targeted industry (that is e.g. a LIMS in life science laboratories) as a central source of information, a documentation system, a middleware for the device system level, a visualization tool and a data processing engine.

During the simulation the stated aspects are shown by utilizing application simulations of the distributed automation and information systems, controlled video sequences or screenshots and the respective corresponding detailed data. In this way it is possible to visualize to which extent and using which new possibilities a BPM based workflow automation could support and automate the process execution in the life science automation.

4   Conclusions

For the first time a graphical standardized automation language of the workflow layer is available with the BPMN 2.0 across all industries. Therefore BPMS can act as a new high level integration platform of the process automation. The new automation approach of BPMN 2.0-based BPMS allows extremely flexible and unlimited process control. Manual subprocesses and any heterogeneous hybrid information and automation systems can be combined in one integration platform for controlled end-to-end processes. An executable BPMN 2.0 process model is an interesting basis for cross-disciplinary teamwork. Often automation objectives are only realizable while closely cooperating. Equally important is, however, an early process simulation, which focuses on the controlled cooperation of all information and automation components without forestall in detail the achieved or purposed degree of automation. The addition of the BPM approach and an accompanying preview simulation offers an extensive solution and efficiency potential in the future life science automation. Procedures with higher complexity in research laboratories, increasing numbers of analysis as well as strict regulatory requirements demand higher degrees of automation and/or human task support, which also effects data management and data processing. The presented process oriented end-to-end automation supports this in a manner, which meets the special flexibility requirements of fast moving research applications. Compliance with the different regulations is an important topic in all fields of application of the life science engineering. The BPM based workflow automation serves that purpose by integrating manually executed tasks into the time- and state-controlled end-to-end process control including of automating their recording and safe documentation.

The combination of BPMS development environment and the presented laboratory process execution simulation (Lab-BPESi) allows shortening the life cycle of the standard based workflow automation. In contrast to the commercial administrative fields of application this especially applies to the special requirements of the structured laboratory automation including numerous information systems. The web based simulation platform ensures an open integration concept for the simulation components and a high availability in cooperation networks of involved application and automation developers. At the same moment the presented simulation explains the benefits of BPM-based process automation. In this way it can operate as a basis for motivation, a descriptive basis for discussions on the project development, and, therefore, effectively support operative decisions.

To reduce the development effort for further simulations it is pursued to directly use the BPMN 2.0 process model as the basis of the simulation model and to extend it by the simulation specific attributes in the future.

References

1. Dumas, M., La Rosa, M., Mendling, J., Reijers, H.A.: Fundamentals of Business Process Management. Springer, Heidelberg (2013)
2. OMG: Business Process Model and Notation (BPMN) Version 2.0 (formal/2011-01-03), http://www.omg.org/spec/BPMN/2.0
3. Allweyer, T.: BPMN 2.0. Introduction to the standard for business process modeling. Books on Demand, Norderstedt (2010)
4. Silver, B.: BPMN method and style. With BPMN implementer's guide, 2nd edn. Cody-Cassidy Press, Aptos (2011)
5. Holzmüller-Laue, S., Göde, B.: B.: Agile Business Process Management in Research Projects of Life Sciences. In: Grabis, J., Kirikova, M. (eds.) BIR 2011. LNBIP, vol. 90, pp. 336–344. Springer, Heidelberg (2011)
6. Hill, J.B., Cantara, M., Deitert, E., Kerremans, M.: Magic quadrant for business process management suites. Gartner Core Research Note G00152906, Gartner, Inc., Stamford (2007)
7. van der Aalst, W.M.P.: Business process simulation revisited. In: Barjis, J. (ed.) EOMAS 2010. LNBIP, vol. 63, pp. 1–14. Springer, Heidelberg (2010)

8. Kanalici, I., Erdem, A.S., Ozturan, M.: Integration of a simulation platform into a business process management tool. In: Proceedings of the European and Mediterranean Conference on Information Systems, EMCIS (2009)
9. Januszczak, J., Hook, G.: Simulation standard for business process management. In: Proceedings - Winter Simulation Conference, art. no. 6147801, pp. 741–751 (2011)
10. Waller, A., Clark, M., Enstone, L.: L-SIM: Simulating BPMN Diagrams with a Purpose Built-in Engine. In: Proceedings of the 2006 Winter Simulation Conference (2006)
11. Mühlbauer, K., Bartmann, D.: Marktübersicht über moderne Werkzeuge zur Simulation von Geschäftsprozessen-forFLEX Report: forFLEX-2011-002, Bamberg, Erlangen-Nürnberg, Regensburg (2011)
12. Jansen-Vullers, M., Netjes, M.: Business process simulation - a tool survey. In: Workshop and Tutorial on Practical Use of Coloured Petri Nets and the CPN Tools, Aarhus, Denmark (October 2006)
13. Becker, J., Kugeler, M., Rosemann, M.: Prozessmanagement-Ein Leitfaden zur prozessorientierten Organisationsgestaltung. Springer, Berlin (2005)
14. Gadatsch, A.: Entwicklung eines Konzeptes zur Modellierung und Evaluation von Workflows. Lang, Frankfurt am Main, Hagen (2000)
15. Gadatsch, A.: Grundkurs Geschäftsprozess-Management-Methoden und Werkzeuge für die IT-Praxis: eine Einführung für Studenten und Praktiker. Vieweg+Teubner Verlag, Wiesbaden (2010)
16. Liem, S., Blecher, G., Gehr, F.: Simulation in der Geschäftsprozessoptimierung: Konzepte und Weiterentwicklungen. In: Information Management, Sonderausgabe 1997, pp. 64–68 (1997)
17. Rücker, B.: Business Process Simulation selbstgemacht. JavaMagazin, 20–25 (2011)

Towards Completeness and Lawfulness
of Business Process Models

Ludmila Penicina and Marite Kirikova

Institute of Applied Computer Systems, Riga Technical University, 1 Kalku, Riga,
LV-1658, Latvia
{ludmila.penicina,marite.kirikova}@rtu.lv

Abstract. We address the existing gaps between business process models, enterprise architecture (EA) models and, external regulations that hinder completeness and lawfulness of business process models. As a solution we propose
a high-level architecture for business process knowledge management that
bridges the identified gaps. We use de-facto industry standards for modelling
business processes and EA - BPMN and ArchiMate. We propose to use Bunge-
Wand-Weber (BWW) model as a theoretical foundation for storing business
process knowledge represented in BPMN and ArchiMate models and storing
elements that address lawfulness of the models. BWW model provides a
framework for systematically storing internally maintained process knowledge
(models) and externally maintained knowledge (regulations), and supporting
completeness and lawfulness of the models. Thus, the main contributions of our
approach is supporting completeness and lawfulness of business process models
and supporting the creation of information services to increase efficiency in the
business process modelling context.

Keywords: Business process modelling, BPMN, ArchiMate, BWW.

1 Introduction

Business processes are valuable assets of any organization as they contain vital
organizational know-how knowledge. According to [1] knowledge is the most strate-
gically important resource of the firm and primary role of any organization is application of knowledge in its everyday activities. However, the application of existing
business process knowledge has always been a sophisticated task. Business process
knowledge must be reusable and applicable across many business processes [2]. The
need for business process knowledge reuse is driven (1) by the challenge to build
accurate, complete and compliant with regulations business process models, (2) by the
need to facilitate common understanding of processes, and (3) by intention to save the
time and resources for business process modelling and analysis. Business process
knowledge can be stored in internal artefacts of enterprise (e.g., business process
models and enterprise architecture models) and externally maintained documents
(e.g., legislation, regulations). One of the most important issues in business process
modelling is to create models that are consistent with legislative and regulatory

A. Kobyliński and A. Sobczak (Eds.): BIR 2013, LNBIP 158, pp. 63–77, 2013.

documents (for simplicity further in the text we call these documents "regulations") and to provide valuable information services for monitoring of changes in regulations.

Nowadays organizations employ industry modelling standards like BPMN [3] to understand and improve business processes. However, BPMN models are only one component of business modelling required for a holistic view of end-to-end business processes. More information is needed to build information systems supporting organizational business processes [2]. To create complete business process models additionally to the process flow aspect it is necessary to consider the following aspects of organizations:

- Structural aspects such as actors, data objects, existing application landscape, network infrastructure, etc. Therefore Enterprise Architecture (EA) models that can reflect these aspects are an essential component of creating accurate and complete business process models and must be linked with business process models.
- Vital process knowledge (like lawful states and events) reflected in externally maintained regulations. Therefore real-time linkage with regulations is essential to support lawfulness of the models and monitoring of changes.

The aforementioned requirements were acquired empirically during the joint research project (contract No. 5/7-2012) with Ltd "Komerccentrs DATI grupa", Latvia. During the project the case study creating an enterprise model process patterns for the Latvian Accounting Law was carried out (published in [4]). The obtained results showed the limitations of BPMN concerning structural modeling and modeling of lawful aspects of the system.

Thus, building complete and accurate business process models requires maintaining the relationships with EA models and externally maintained regulations related to business process models. A growing number of different initiatives and projects (like [5] and [6]) that support implementation of a machine-readable set of technology-neutral electronic representations (in XML format) of regulations show that regulations maintenance moves forward to making open and "visible" the structure and semantic components of regulations so as to support the creation of high value information services to increase efficiency in different every-day contexts. Making regulation structure "visible" and machine-readable opens a potential for linking external regulations with internal artefacts like business process models and, namely, with BPMN 2.0 process models. The new BPMN 2.0 specification [3] allows integration with third party components using XML-based representation languages (e.g., OWL, RDF) [2]. We envision that initiatives to make regulations machine-readable and "visible" will grow world-wide in coming years.

BPMN standard itself does not allow to link business process model with other models of enterprise architecture, however, many so-called Business Process Analysis (BPA) suites allow to do it [2]. ArchiMate enterprise architecture modelling language has been developed to provide a uniform representation for diagrams that describe enterprise architectures [7]. Here the existence of business processes model is depicted. However, ArchiMate does not prescribe to list the flow of activities in detail. Linkage between business process models and EA models would allow to look at the business processes at different layers of the enterprise in detail and to describe artefacts and actors related to the business process at different enterprise layers. However, unlike BPMN 2.0 standard ArchiMate 2.0 specification does not describe elements that support integration with externally defined third party artefacts.

This paper presents an on-going research which aims to propose architecture for business process knowledge management providing linkage of business process models, EA models and externally maintained regulations for efficient business process modelling supporting completeness and lawfulness of the models. To provide an efficient environment for business process modelling that allows (1) linking process models with EA models and external regulations and (2) systematically storing and retrieving business process knowledge represented in BPMN and ArchiMate models - we propose to use a meta-structure as the foundation for business process knowledge storage. We propose to use Bunge-Wand-Weber (BWW) model [8] as the meta-structure for business process knowledge and its management. BWW model consists of constructs that are present in the real world and must be represented in information system [9], including lawful and unlawful states and events that are an important issue in regulations.

The potential practical implications of the proposed approach can be summarized as follows:

- It allows systematically storing and reusing the knowledge contained in BPMN, ArchiMate models and externally defined regulations.
- It provide the frame for complete and regulations complaint representations of the system being modeled.
- It allows describing lawful and unlawful aspects of information systems not addressed in BPMN and ArchiMate models.
- It allows describing conceivable event and state space of information systems reducing the possibility to include non-existing ("unconceivable") states in the models.

The paper is structured as follows. In Section 2 the related work is outlined. In Section 3 existing gaps in providing completeness and lawfulness of business process models are discussed. Section 4 describes the proposed solution. In section 5 an example of the proposed solution is discussed. Brief conclusions and future work are presented in Section 6.

2   Related Works

BWW model [7] extends the systems ontology presented by Mario Bunge [10]. Wand and Weber developed it as a formal foundation for modelling information systems consisting of the constructs present in the real world that must be represented in information system [8]. BWW model is an upper level ontology containing general concepts that are necessary for description of information systems [9]. Elements in BWW model can be grouped in the following groups (adapted from [9]; the elements of BWW model are shown in italics):

1. *Things* - including *Properties, Classes* and *Kinds* of *Things*. *Thing* is an elementary unit in BWW. *Things* possess *Properties*, which defines *States* of a *Thing*. *Things* can belong to *Classes* or *Kinds* depending on a number of common *Properties*. A *Thing* can act on another *Thing* if its existence affects the *History* of the other *Thing*. *Things* are coupled if one *Things* acts on another.

2. *States of Things - Properties* of *Things* define their *States*. *State Law* restricts *Values* of *Properties* of *Things*. *Conceivable State Space* is a set of all *States* a *Thing* can assume. *Lawful State Space* defines *States* that comply with *State Law*. *Stable State* is a *State* in which a *Thing* or a *System* will remain unless forced to change by a *Thing* in the *System Environment*. *Unstable state* is a *State* that will be changed into another *State* by the *Transformations* in the *System*. *History* is the chronologically-ordered *States* of a *Thing*.

3. *Transformations* – transformation between *States of Things*. *Transformation* is a mapping from one *State* to another. *Lawful Transformation* defines which *Events* in a *Thing* are lawful.

4. *Events* - event is a change in *State* of a *Thing*. *Conceivable Event Space* is a set of all *Events* that can occur to a *Thing*. *Lawful Event Space* is a set of all *Events* that are lawful to a *Thing*. *Events* can be *Internal Events* and *External Events*. *Events* can be *Well-Defined* - an *Event* in which the subsequent *State* can be predicted - or *Poorly-Defined* - an *Event* in which the subsequent *State* cannot be predicted.

5. *Systems* – a set of coupled *Things*. *System Composition* are *Things* in the *System*. *System Environment* are *Things* outside the *System* interacting with the *System*. *System Structure* is a set of couplings that exists among *Things*. *Subsystem* is a *System* whose composition and structure is a subset of the composition and structure of another *System*. *System Decomposition* is a set of *Subsystems*. *Level Structure* is an alignment of the subsystems.

The BWW model has been used in a number of studies for evaluation of modelling techniques. The authors of [9] report on the outcomes of an ontological analysis of BPMN and explore identified issues by reporting on interviews conducted with BPMN users in Australia. As a result [9] defines few potential shortcomings in BPMN - such as existence of some ambiguous elements in its specification. The authors of [11] propose a comprehensive Conceptual Modelling Quality Framework based on BWW model bringing together and organizing the various quality cornerstones and then defining many quality dimensions that connect one to another. The authors of [12] examine how process modelling techniques have developed and compare modelling techniques using BWW model as a benchmark used for the analysis of grammars that purport to model, the real world, and the interactions within it. The authors of [13] propose an approach for developing a conceptual model that represents the structural, relational and behavioural elements of the computing systems based on the BWW model. The authors of [14] use of the BWW model to compare the representation capabilities of two business rule modelling languages. We selected the BWW model for this study for the following reasons (a) BWW model was created for Information Systems discipline, (b) because of BWW foundational quality - BWW model is an upper ontology describing generic elements that must be present in every information system, (c) there is a significant research track record of using BWW.

Authors of [15] present a framework for business process repositories that assists in managing large collections of process models. The authors emphasize that BPMN models repository should be stored in XML format and ontologies must be stored in repository that will facilitate integration of processes from multiple parties.

A number of initiatives and researches exist for presenting legislative and judiciary documents in machine readable format to support automatic retrieval interoperability. AKOMA NTOSO schema [6] is a set of XML machine-readable descriptions of official documents such as legislation, debate record, minutes, etc. that allow exchanging and reusing parliamentary, legislative, and judiciary documents more efficiently enabling addition of descriptive structure (markup) to the content of parliamentary and legislative documents [6].

Authors of [16] provide a high-level architecture of the document analysis and change detection system which is used for the retrieval of regulations and document analysis and preparation for their linkage to business processes. Authors of [4] report on enterprise modeling experiment that is based on representation of regulations as reusable business process model parts. Their experiment showed that for proper positioning of the parts it is necessary to represent in models not only the process per se, but also other related information available in regulations [4]. Authors of [17] envision an approach where regulations are translated into business process model "spare parts" or raw materials that can be used by designers of business processes at several enterprises (or several units in one enterprise).

Related works have encouraged this research and showed that BWW model can be used for the analysis of the completeness of knowledge about the enterprise and its information systems, in general, as well as of business processes, in particular.

3   Existing Gaps in Providing Completeness and Lawfulness of Business Process Models

This section presents shortcomings of existing standards and methods in relation to abilities to present a complete business process description compliant with regulations and store business process knowledge contained in business process models.

Figure 1 depicts existing gaps in supporting completeness and lawfulness of business process models in different domains of business process knowledge, namely, the lack of standardized linkage between BPMN models and ArchiMate models and the lack of linkage between BPMN, ArchiMate, and regulations to provide lawfulness of the models. These gaps hinder completeness and lawfulness of business process and EA models – without such linkage lawful and unlawful aspects of the system are not depicted in the models and thus models may contain meaningless states and events, since a set of conceivable states and events also are not depicted. Without a meaningful coupling between EA, business process models, and regulations, the models are isolated, potentially not compliant with regulations, inconsistent, and conflicting.

Some tools like ARIS [18] allow augmenting BPMN and ArchiMate models in their modelling environments, however, these are just tool vendor initiatives and there exist no standardized linkage between BPMN and ArchiMate. Linkage between BPMN and regulations is still a challenge. However the new BPMN 2.0 specification [3] allows integration with third party components using XML-based representation languages (e.g., OWL, RDF) [2]. This new BPMN 2.0 "plug-and-play" feature opens the potential for linking external resources represented as XML structures with

BPMN 2.0 models. But, to utilize it, it is necessary to provide a foundation for such linking - a consistent meta-structure for storing and reusing business process knowledge contained in business process models, enterprise architecture models, and external documents such as XML-based regulations. In ArchiMate 2.0 specification there is no description of how ArchiMate 2.0 models can be linked with external resources.

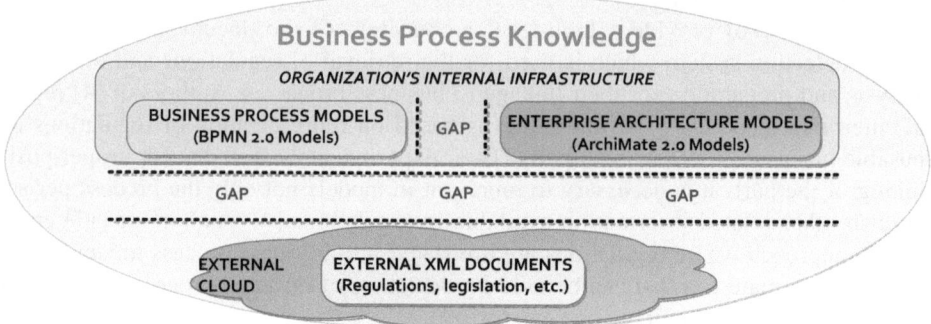

Fig. 1. Existing gaps between BPMN, ArchiMate and externally maintained regulations

To best of our knowledge there is no research papers available that close the gap in linking BPMN, ArchiMate and externally maintained XML-based regulations and managing business process knowledge based on BWW model. Since BWW model describes the elements that must be addressed in every system, including lawful and unlawful states and events of the system; we propose to use BWW as a meta-structure for storing business process knowledge depicted in EA models, BPMN models, and regulations.

3.1   BPMN Limitations

Business Process Model and Notation (BPMN) [3] is the de-facto standard for representing in a very expressive graphical way the processes occurring in virtually every kind of organizations [19]. However BPMN has its limitations when it comes to modelling other aspects of organizations such as organizational structure and roles, functional breakdowns, data, strategy, business rules, and technical systems [2]. Thus BPMN alone cannot provide complete business process descriptions.

Research presented in [9] describes which BPMN elements correspond to BWW model. There are 6 BWW model elements that are not supported by BPMN notation, namely, *State law, Conceivable State Space, Lawful State Space, History, Conceivable Event Space,* and *Lawful Event Space*. Since BWW model describes aspects that are important for building information systems [9], these six elements are to be taken into consideration to define a complete, lawful and consistent description of business processes.

3.2   ArchiMate Limitations

Architecture descriptions are formal descriptions organized in a way that supports reasoning about the structural and behavioural properties of the system and its evolution [7]. To provide a uniform representation for diagrams that describe enterprise architectures, the ArchiMate enterprise architecture modelling language has been developed [7]. It offers an integrated architectural approach that describes and visualizes the different architecture domains and their underlying relations and dependencies [7]. ArchiMate 2.0 is a modelling language that provides graphical representations of enterprise architecture based on TOGAF standard [20].

ArchiMate 2.0 language defines 3 layers of an enterprise architecture [7]:

1.   Business layer offers products and services to external customers.
2.   Application layer supports the business layer with application services.
3.   Technology layer offers infrastructure services needed to run applications.

In an ArchiMate model, the existence of business processes is depicted. However, it does not prompt to represent the flow of activities in detail. During business process modelling, a business process can be expanded using a business process design language; e.g., BPMN [3].

ArchiMate modelling language does not support 11 concepts of BWW model, namely, *State, Conceivable state space, Lawful state space, State law, Stable state, Unstable state, History, Conceivable event space, Lawful event space, Well-defined event, Lawful transformation.* Unlike in BPMN, ArchiMate does not define specific event types in which subsequent *State* can always be predicted. Although the ArchiMate modelling language does not support the description of 11 BWW elements, which is more than 6 BWW elements missing in BPMN, the ArchiMate allows defining structural components of an information system at all three levels of the enterprise architecture in much greater detail than BPMN.

3.3   Business Process Repositories Limitations

Most business process management platforms provide business process repositories for managing knowledge contained in business process models.

Based on literature analysis we have identified the following shortcomings of existing business process repositories:

–   Most of existing repositories for storing business process models and related knowledge are based on Relational DBMS, however in case of storing knowledge contained within BPMN models it is preferable to use XML based structures for storing, e.g., XQuery, since BPMN formal meta-model is defined using XML [3].
–   The authors of [15] state that BPMN Repository based on XML database and ontologies is rather an architecture than a practical implementation.

Existing methods for storing knowledge of business process models do not address the issue of linking business process models with EA models, linking business process models with externally maintained XML based regulations, and structuring the knowledge flexibly according to various systems of the enterprise. We propose to use BWW model as the foundation for business process repository and build business process repository using XML based structures to support process models linkage with external structures.

4   Proposed Solution

This section describes proposed solution to bridge existing gaps in business process knowledge management by using BWW model as a meta-structure for storing business process knowledge. We employ BWW model as a foundation for linking BPMN, ArchiMate and externally (to business process repository) maintained XML-based regulations.

Figure 2 depicts a high-level architecture for the proposed solution. Our approach provides the following:

– Linking externally maintained XML structured regulations with BPMN 2.0 models - using the new BPMN 2.0 "plug-and-play" functionality to integrate with the third party XML based documents.
– Proposing an extension for ArchiMate 2.0 standard to enable linking ArchiMate 2.0 models with the third party XML based documents.
– Using existing research (e.g., [21]) to enhance BPMN 2.0 and ArchiMate 2.0 integration to provide a valuable mapping and linkage between these two complementary standards.
– Storing in BWW based XML structured repository business process knowledge from BPMN and ArchiMate models with descriptions of lawful and unlawful aspects of the system depicted from regulations as a result of the linkage.

ArchiMate models complement BPMN models with different layers of enterprise architecture. External regulations complement BPMN and ArchiMate models with lawful and unlawful states and events of the system. A meta-structure (background knowledge) is necessary to maintain the relationships between BPMN models, EA models, and external regulations. If BWW model is used as a meta-structure for storing knowledge about the business process, and if BPMN and ArchiMate are used as languages of representation of this knowledge; it is necessary to identify which elements from BWW model are supported by BPMN and ArchiMate models. BWW model defines elements of the information system that are supported by BPMN and ArchiMate standards as well as a set of elements that are not supported by these standards but are depicted in regulations and must be addressed in models to support lawfulness of the system (e.g., lawful states, lawful events). Majority of BPMN and ArchiMate core elements can be mapped to BWW constructs. However BPMN models do not cover 6 BWW elements and ArchiMate models do not cover 11 BWW elements. BPMN provides elements that support BWW model elements that are not supported by ArchiMate modelling language. Linked BPMN models with ArchiMate models cover more BWW elements than ArchiMate models can cover separately.

Still there exist six elements that cannot be represented using interlinked BPMN and ArchiMate modelling languages, namely, *State Law (SL), Conceivable State Space (CSS), Lawful State Space (LSS), History (H), Conceivable Event Space (CES), and Lawful Event Space (LES)*. It is necessary to address these missing elements in order to support the lawfulness of the system and eliminate non-existing ("unconceivable") states from the models. Using BWW model based business process knowledge repository will allow to describe these elements and to support creating ArchiMate and BPMN models compliant with regulations.

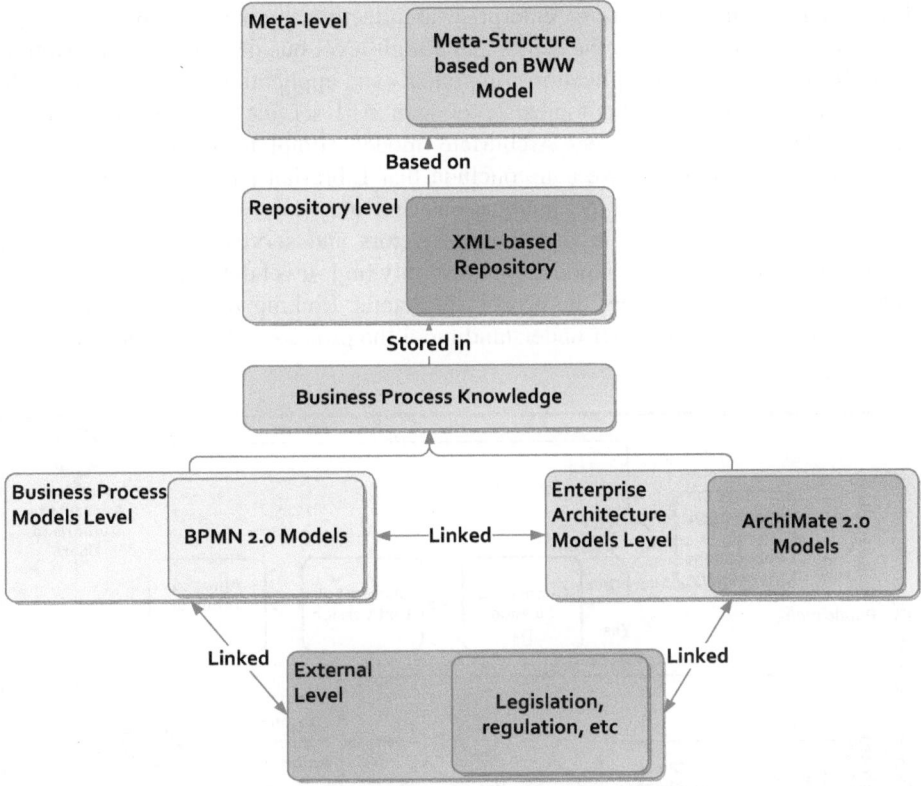

Fig. 2. The proposed high-level architecture for closing existing gaps between BPMN, ArchiMate and externally maintained regulations

5   Example

Figure 3 shows a BPMN model of publication self-archiving process (or Green Open Access) at University. This process provides a possibility for researchers to publish their works as full texts in Open Access online repository. Two of the most important steps of this process are:

- Researchers must choose a licence under which they wish to publish their publication (activity "Choose CC Licence"). For this process we use a set of ready licences provided by Creative Commons (CC) organization [22]. CC licences are available online and in a machine-readable format which unlocks possibilities to use these licences in web-services.
- Researchers must choose a version of the full text which the publisher permits to archive in the institutional repository. The possible versions of the publication's full texts are: Pre-print, Post-print or Published version.

Figure 4 shows ArchiMate 2.0 model for a self-archiving process at University. This model contains 3 layers of enterprise architecture, namely, (1) business layer with actors, assigned roles to the actors and a high-level business process description, (2) application level with application components and application services used by the business level, and (3) technological level with API service and systems software used by the application layer. ArchiMate model complements BPMN business process model with actors: we can conclude that Librarian has the role of Systems Administrator that manages the publications and also we can see application and technological services used in the process. Actors and services are not present in BPMN model. ArchiMate 2.0 model contains only high-level definition of the process while BPMN model describes the process in details. Linking BPMN and ArchiMate models will contribute to better understanding of the process and its components.

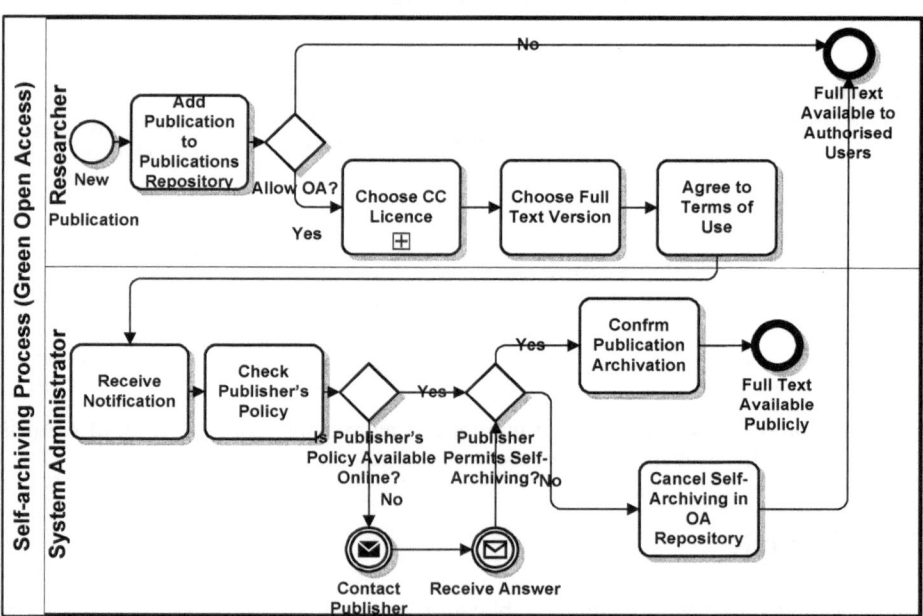

Fig. 3. BPMN 2.0 model of the self-archiving business process

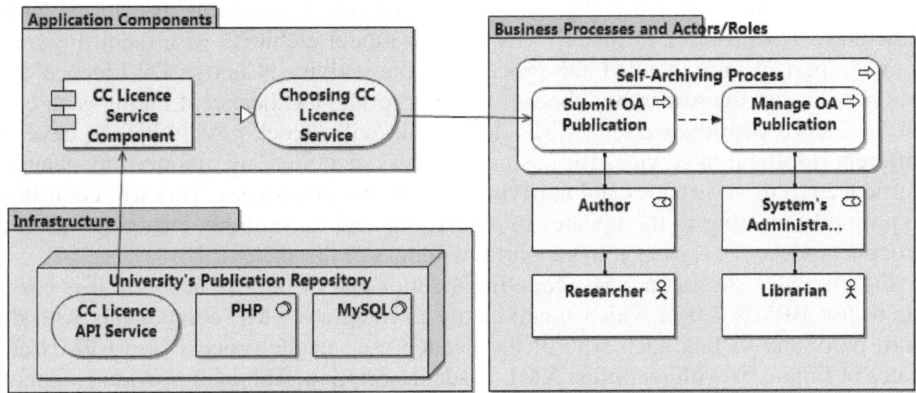

Fig. 4. ArchiMate 2.0 model of the self-archiving process

ArchiMate model supplements BPMN model with business, application and technology layers of the enterprise, still these models do not include descriptions of:

1. *State Law* – a set of all properties that are lawful to a Publication. We assume that a Publication can have the following properties: Version of the Full Text, Meta-Data, Licence, and Status. Each of the mentioned properties has a set of the values that are lawful, e.g., in this process it is important to understand what version of the full text the Author has submitted so the System Administrator can check if it corresponds to the Publisher's policy. Values for the *Property* "Version of the Full Text" would be {Pre-print, Post-print, Published version}, values for the *Property* "Status" would be {Full Text Available to Authorised Users, Full Text Available Publicly}, etc. However neither BPMN nor ArchiMate allows to define sets of lawful Publication's properties.

2. *Conceivable State Space* for a Publication can correspond to the situation where Publication's full text would be available publicly in case when Publisher's policy does not permit it. For example, Author has submitted post-print version of the full text but Publisher permits publishing only pre-prints – this state is *Conceivable* but it is *Unlawful*.

3. *Lawful State Space* for a Publication would correspond to the situation when the availability of the version of the full text of Publication publicly conforms to Publisher's policy.

4. *History* of states for a Publication would include all states of the publication in the process, e.g., including the past state Full Text Available to Authorised Users and the present state Full Text Available Publicly.

5. *Conceivable Event Space* can correspond to the situation when Systems Administrator does not receive a notification about a new Publication or the notification is sent out to the wrong employee, another *Conceivable* but *Unlawful* event might be when a Publisher does not reply to the System's Administrator request to permit publishing.

6. *Lawful Event Space* can correspond to the following events: Author submits a Publication, System's Administrator receives a notification about a new Publication, and the Publisher replies to the System's Administrator request.

If the regulations to which the models must comply are available as external XML structures, it is possible to link BPMN process model elements with them. Figure 5 shows a part of an expanded sub-process for the activity "Choose CC Licence". In this sub-process the researcher chooses the appropriate CC licence. Linking each type of the licence with their online XML description will unlock possibilities to develop different information services for business process modeller, e.g., monitoring changes introduced to these licences and notifying responsible employees. This will contribute to promptly reacting to the updates in regulations and accordingly changing business process models, if necessary, to support lawfulness of the system.

Figure 5 also shows an XML code fragment of one of the CC licences. It is possible to use BPMN 2.0 provided functionality to integrate XML components with the third party and to link each type of the licence used in the process (see BPMN end states in Figure 5) with its online XML based description. This will provide an opportunity for a business process modeller to access the licence using the model and developing a service for monitoring changes.

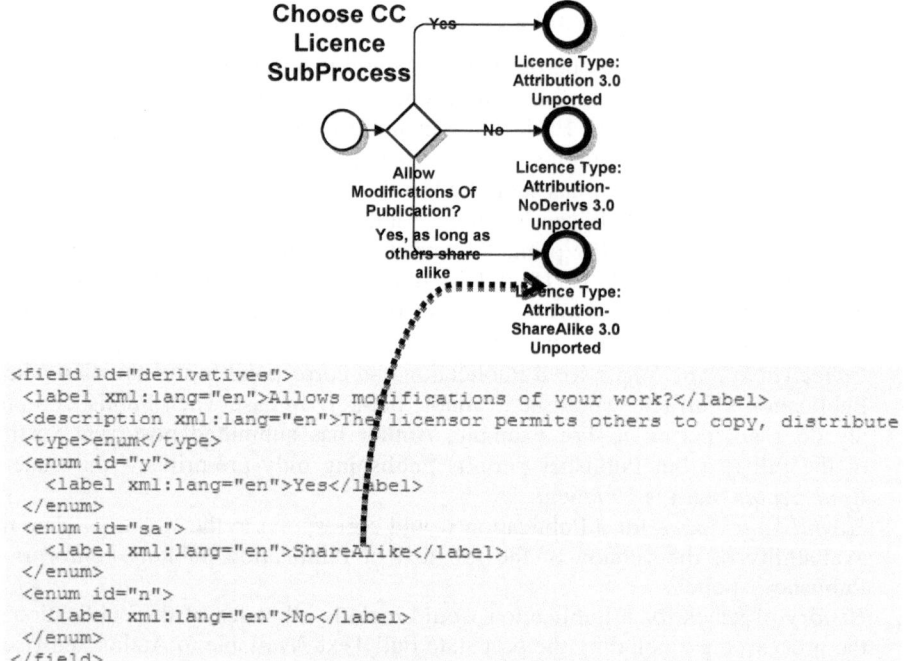

```
<field id="derivatives">
  <label xml:lang="en">Allows modifications of your work?</label>
  <description xml:lang="en">The licensor permits others to copy, distribute
  <type>enum</type>
  <enum id="y">
    <label xml:lang="en">Yes</label>
  </enum>
  <enum id="sa">
    <label xml:lang="en">ShareAlike</label>
  </enum>
  <enum id="n">
    <label xml:lang="en">No</label>
  </enum>
</field>
```

Fig. 5. "Choose CC Licence" sub-process and an XML fragment of CC licence, taken from [23]

Using the solution proposed in this paper it is possible to improve the process described in Figure 3 by automating the "Check Publisher's Policy" task that a System's Administrator must perform manually. SHERPA/ROMEO [24] is a searchable database of publisher's policies regarding the self-archiving of journal articles on the web and in Open Access repositories. SHERPA/ROMEO provides a machine-readable XML descriptions of publishers policies (e.g., [25]). Using the services and API provided by the SHERPA/ROMEO it is possible to automate the task of obtaining the information regarding the version of the full text the publisher permits to self-archive in institutional Open Access repository (*Lawful State* of the full text). After obtaining this information it is necessary to store it as a *Lawful State* of the Publication's full text and all other possible states of the Publication's full texts as *Conceivable States*. In Figure 6 we illustrate obtaining *Lawful State* (lawful version of publication's full text) from external XML structure (SHERPA/ROMEO XML [25]). As mentioned in this paper, BPMN and ArchiMate do not allow describing lawful aspects of the system, so using the proposed process models linkage with XML structures that allows obtaining lawful aspects of the systems and using BWW based business process knowledge repository for storing identified lawful aspects will contribute to supporting lawfulness of business process models and developing services that monitor changes in external XML documents in the real time supporting the compliance of the business process models with the newest versions of XML based regulations.

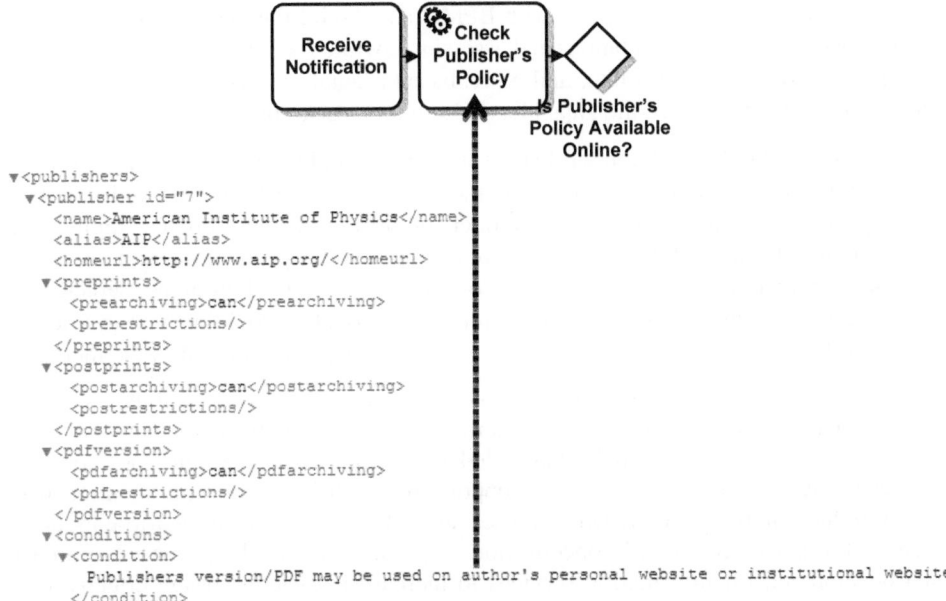

Fig. 6. Linkage between service "Check Publisher's Policy" and an XML fragment of SHERPA/ROMEO publisher's policy licence (a fragment of XML is taken from [25])

First experiments with the proposed approach show that it can contribute to the emergent challenges that organizations face in order to maintain relationships between business process, EA models, and external regulations.

6   Conclusions and Future Work

This paper presented a research towards creating an efficient business process modelling environment using BWW model as the foundation for systematically storing and retrieving business process knowledge contained in interlinked BPMN models, ArchiMate models, and external XML based documents. The advantage of proposed approach resides in the following:

- BWW allows straightforwardly addressing the lawful and unlawful events and states of systems.
- BWW allows straightforwardly addressing conceivable event and state space of the system reducing the risk of including non-existing states ("unconceivable") states in the models.

BPMN and ArchiMate languages do not have elements that support identifying and storing information about lawful and unlawful states and events of the system and describing a set of conceivable states. Thus providing meaningful and accountable BPMN and ArchiMate linkage with regulations is out of the scope of these standards. BWW model provides a set of elements that can be used to store lawful and unlawful aspects of the system and link these aspects with BPMN and ArchiMate models thus providing a valuable coupling with regulations and assessing lawfulness of the system.

Therefore BPMN, ArchiMate, and XML based regulation linkage based on BWW model has capacity to close the gaps identified in this research:

1. Describing lawful and unlawful states and lawful and unlawful events of systems - neither BPMN nor ArchiMate has the ability to describe lawful and unlawful aspects of systems. Using BWW model for storing business process knowledge will provide capacity for storing lawful and unlawful aspects of the system.
2. Describing conceivable states and conceivable events of systems depicted in regulations, business process and ArchiMate models, providing possibilities to identify non-existing "unconceivable" states that might be present in the models.

BWW model based business process knowledge management contributes to creating complete and lawful business process models and systematically storing and reusing the associated business process knowledge. The presented example does not fully illustrate how the proposed approach supports the high-level concepts mentioned in the introduction (e.g., "knowledge reuse" and "holistic view of end-to-end processes"). Further research will concern more experiments with the proposed approach and development of information services to increase knowledge usage effectiveness and efficiency in business process modelling context. Also the ArchiMate 2.0 viewpoints will be analysed with regard to addressing regulations.

References

1. Grant, R.M.: Toward a Knowledge-based Theory of the Firm. Strategic Management Journal 17, 109–122 (1996)
2. Silver, B.: BPMN Method and Style with Implementer's Guide. Cody-Cassidy Press (2011)

3. OMG: Business Process Model and Notation 2.0, http://www.bpmn.org
4. Businska, L., Kirikova, M., Penicina, L., Buksa, I., Rudzajs, P.: Enterprise Modeling for Respecting Regulations. PoEM Short Papers 2012. In: Emerging Topics in the Practice of Enterprise Modelling: The 5th IFIP WG8.1 Working Conference on the Practice of Enterprise Modelling (PoEM 2012), CEUR Workshop Proceedings, pp. 106–118 (2012)
5. An Official Web Site of the United States Government, http://www.data.gov/
6. Akoma NTOSO: XML for Parliamentary, Legislative and Juridiciary Documents, http://www.akomantoso.org/
7. The Open Group: ArchiMate 2.0 Specification, http://goo.gl/7gC5B
8. Wand, Y., Weber, R.: On the ontological expressiveness of information systems analysis and design grammars. Information Systems Journal 3, 217–237 (1993)
9. Recker, J., Indulska, M., Rosemann, M., Green, P.: Do Process Modelling Techniques Get Better? A Comparative Ontological Analysis of BPMN. In: Campbell, B., Underwood, J., Bunker, D. (eds.) 16th Australasian Conference on Information Systems (2005)
10. Bunge, M.: Treatise on Basic Philosophy. Ontology II: A World of Systems, vol. 4 (1979)
11. Nelson, H.J., Poels, G., Genero, M., Piattini, M.: A conceptual modeling quality framework. Software Quality Journal 20, 201–228 (2011)
12. Rosemann, M., Recker, J., Indulska, M., Green, P.: A study of the evolution of the representational capabilities of process modeling grammars. In: Martinez, F.H., Pohl, K. (eds.) CAiSE 2006. LNCS, vol. 4001, pp. 447–461. Springer, Heidelberg (2006)
13. Goumopoulos, C., Kameas, A.: Theory and Applications of Ontology: Computer Applications. Springer, Netherlands (2010)
14. zur Muehlen, M., Indulska, M., Kamp, G.: Business Process and Business Rule Modeling: A Representational Analysis. In: 2007 Eleventh International IEEE EDOC Conference Workshop, pp. 189–196. IEEE (2007)
15. Yan, Z., Dijkman, R., Grefen, P.: Business process model repositories – Framework and survey. Information and Software Technology 54, 380–395 (2012)
16. Rudzajs, P., Buksa, I.: Business Process and Regulations: Approach to Linkage and Change Management. In: Grabis, J., Kirikova, M. (eds.) BIR 2011. LNBIP, vol. 90, pp. 96–109. Springer, Heidelberg (2011)
17. Kirikova, M., Buksa, I., Penicina, L.: Raw Materials for Business Processes in Cloud. In: Bider, I., Halpin, T., Krogstie, J., Nurcan, S., Proper, E., Schmidt, R., Soffer, P., Wrycza, S. (eds.) BPMDS 2012 and EMMSAD 2012. LNBIP, vol. 113, pp. 241–254. Springer, Heidelberg (2012)
18. Softwareag: ARIS ArchiMate Modeler, http://goo.gl/WI76E
19. Chinosi, M., Trombetta, A.: BPMN: An introduction to the standard. Computer Standards & Interfaces 34, 124–134 (2012)
20. The Open Group: TOGAF 9.1, https://www2.opengroup.org/ogsys/catalog/g116
21. Van Den Berg, M.: ArchiMate, BPMN and UML: An approach to harmonizing the notations. Orbus software white paper (2012)
22. Creative Commons, http://creativecommons.org/
23. Creative Commons: CC API documentation: Version 1.0, http://goo.gl/I1FNC
24. SHERPA/RoMEO - Publisher copyright policies & self-archiving, http://www.sherpa.ac.uk/romeo/
25. SHERPA/RoMEO: XML schema for Publisher's version/PDF, http://goo.gl/OypG6

Cooperation of Business Processes – A Central Point of the Content, Technical, and Human Aspects of Organization Management

Václav Řepa

Department of Information Technologies, University of Economics, Prague,
W.Churchill sqr. 4, 130 67 Prague, Czech Republic

Abstract. The paper deals with the topic of cooperation of business processes identifying it as a crucial current problem in the area of business process modeling and management. The natural complexity of the management of an organization is discussed and the concept of Service as a common denominator of content, technical, and human aspects of the organization management is found. Cooperation of processes is analyzed from the process MetaModel point of view. Service as a form as well as fundamental meaning of the cooperation of business processes is analyzed in detail and final conclusions about these facts are formulated.

Keywords: business process modeling, process based management, service-orientation.

1 Introduction

This paper introduces the problem of cooperation of business processes as a crucial problem in the area of business process modeling and management. Unfortunately, this problem is still not sufficiently reflected by the current BPM methodologies. It is well visible also as the state of the art of business process modeling languages. For example BPMN (Business Process Modeling & Notation) [1], even if it is established as a worldwide standard in the field of business processes modeling, is still mainly oriented just on the description of internal algorithmic structure of a business process and disregards the global view on the system of mutually cooperating processes. The only way of modeling the cooperation of different processes in BPMN is using "swimming pools and lanes" in the Collaboration Diagram. Unfortunately, the global aspects of the system of business processes cannot be sufficiently described this way nor its completeness ensured. The BPMN primarily views processes as sequences of actions in the time line. But the global model requires seeing processes primarily as objects (relatively independent on the time), distinguishing different kinds of them (especially the key versus supporting ones), describing their global attributes (like the goal, reason, type of customer, etc.), and recognizing their essential relationships to other processes which is obviously impossible to describe as a process flow.

A. Kobyliński and A. Sobczak (Eds.): BIR 2013, LNBIP 158, pp. 78–90, 2013.
© Springer-Verlag Berlin Heidelberg 2013

The object-oriented approach to business processes can be found in the field of "process ontologies". This work is mainly oriented on the methodical aspects (how to model processes) which is not relevant for the problem discussed here (see 3 and 6 for instance). Nevertheless, there are some ontological attempts which are more relevant for our problem connected with the so-called "goal-oriented" business process modeling. In 2 the explanation of this approach can be found: *"While traditional approaches in business process modelling tend to focus on "how" the business processes are performed (adopting a behavioural description in which business processes are described in terms of procedural aspects), in goal-oriented business process modelling the proposals strive to extend traditional business process methodologies by providing a dimension of intentionality to the business processes".* Although this approach clearly distinguishes between the system and the process view of processes it is still focused just on some particular aspects of processes and especially do not take into the account their collaboration.

One of the mostly accepted "de facto" standards which fully supports the system (object-oriented) view of business processes is the Eriksson-Penker Notation [4]. It was created as an extension of the UML [11] which corresponds with the above discussed "object nature" of the global view on processes. This notation distinguishes between the "Business Process View" which illustrates the interaction between different processes and the "Business Behavioral View" which describes the individual behavior of the particular process. This way it respects the important difference between the global object-oriented view of a process system and the detailed process-oriented view of a single process. Therefore the MMABP methodology presented in this paper uses the Eriksson-Penker process diagram as a complement to the BPMN in order to compensate the absence of the global view in this language. Detailed explanation of the methodical need for global model of processes as well as related criticism of the BPMN can be also found in [9].

The problem of cooperation of business processes is seen in this paper from different perspectives: content, technology, and people. As a methodological basis for this view we use the MMABP methodology (Methodology for Modeling and Analysis of Business Processes) (7, 10). MMABP places the basic process management principles presented in this paper in the common context and also explains the above discussed critical need for the global view of processes besides the detailed process description. In the following section the natural complexity of the management of an organization is discussed. Three main areas of crucial management aspects are identified and analyzed in order to find their common denominator. Then the problem of cooperation of processes is analyzed from the process MetaModel point of view and the concept of Service as a form as well as fundamental meaning of the cooperation of business processes is found. This concept as a main subject of interest is analyzed in detail in the fourth section. Finally main conclusions about the service-oriented approach to the analysis and implementation of business processes and its relation to the problem of mutual cooperation of processes are expressed.

2   Complex Nature of the Organization Management

Figure 1 shows different problem areas connected with the process based organization. All three exemplary viewpoints at the figure together address all substantial parts of the organization's life: content, technology, and people. Each particular point of view is characterized by typical questions which should be answered by the methodology in that field.

Process-oriented Management represents the basic idea of process based organization, excellently expressed in [5] and originally called "Business Process Reengineering". This idea argues for the fact that the organization has to build its behavior on objectively valid structure of its business processes to be able to fully exploit the possibilities offered by the technology progress. This condition is typically not fulfilled in traditionally managed organizations where hierarchical organization structure prevents seeing, as well as managing, the crucial process chains which should be the central subject of change due to the technology progress. For achieving the needed ability to fully exploit the technology progress the traditional hierarchical way of management should be rejected and substituted with the management style based on the objective model of business processes of the organization.

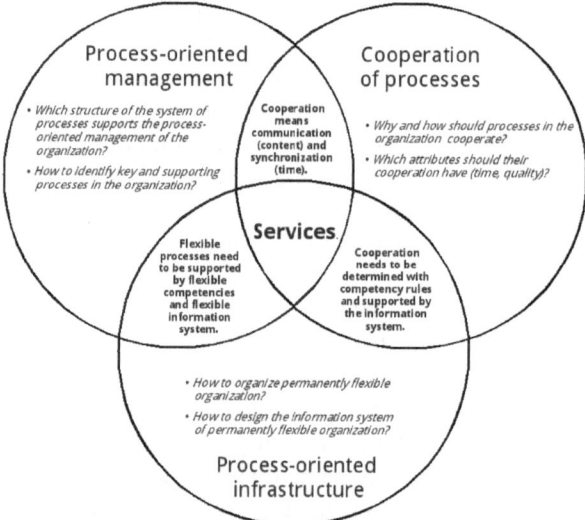

Fig. 1. Service as a common denominator of content, technical, and human aspects of the 73organization management

Realization of such idea nevertheless raises the consequential questions:
- *Which structure of the system of processes supports the process oriented management of the organization?*
- *How to identify key and supporting processes in the organization?*

In order to make the organization flexible enough towards the possibilities of the technology progress one should firstly find the "right" structure of the system of organization's business processes. This means at first to identify the key processes profiling the organization, and according to them then order all necessary supporting activities to so-called supporting processes. Key business process is such a natural process chain which covers all the way from the initial need of a customer until the fulfilling this need with the appropriate product or service. Nevertheless the definition above does not mean that the key process has to include all the activities necessary for the product/service delivery. It has just to cover all the process, i.e. to manage it using the services of supporting processes for ensuring the necessary productive activities on the way to the final delivery. Such a way the key process represents the management side of the workflow while supporting processes represent the production side of it. Basic structure of internal business processes in the organization is created via deciding about the border between the key and supporting processes in terms of services. The concept of Service plays the role of a universal separator which defines the meaning of the management as well as the contents of the production.

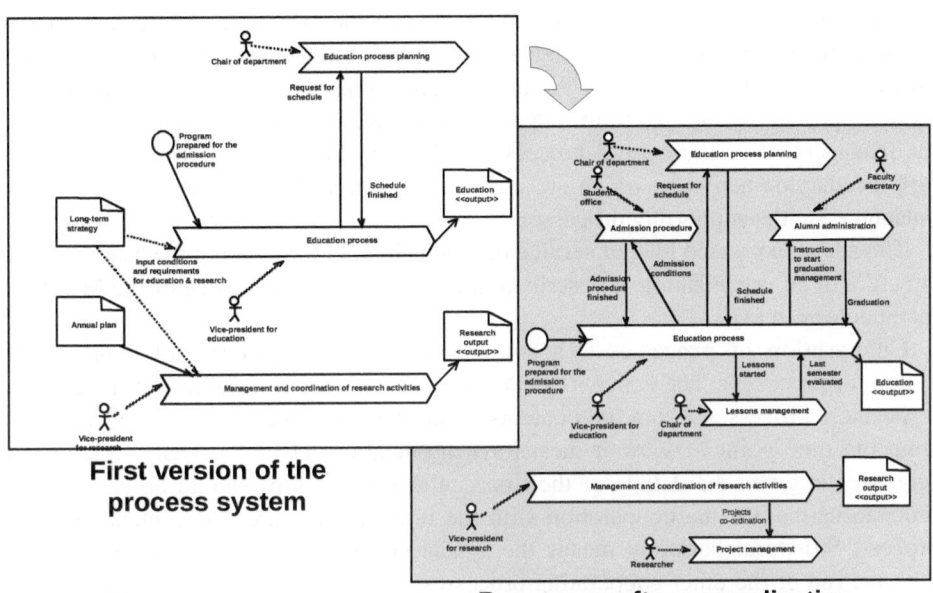

Fig. 2. Evolution of the university process system by the use of MMABP methodology

Figure 2 shows very simplified example of the global process model (in the Eriksson-Penker notation) from the real project aimed on the creation of the conception of the process based university management. The two key processes of the university has been identified: the *Education Process* and the *Management and*

Coordination of Research Activities. These processes correspond to the two main types of products of the university: *Education* and *Research output.* The definition of every key process describes the way of achieving the given product. All other activities in the organization should be subordinated to these main goals. The example also shows the evolution of the process system during the analysis. In the first version of the system just several processes, especially the key ones has been identified. Then the details of both key processes have been analyzed and a number of standalone supporting processes have been discovered in the bodies of key processes by the use of the specific "process normalization" technique called also "process thinning" (see 8 and 10). The "process normalization" technique is an exact step-by-step instruction how to analyze the single process in order to transform it to the structure of several cooperating processes. This technique is similar to the famous technique for normalization of data structures from the database analysis and design methodologies. It uses similar terminology (first, second, and third normal form of processes) and has the similar goal: to uncover the natural structure of universal processes from the purpose-specific single process. The detailed explanation of this technique overcomes the extent of this paper and can be found in 7.

The resulting system (see the second version of the system at Figure 2) contains much more supporting processes together with their relationships to the original key processes where they came from. All these relationships represent the services offered by the supporting processes to the supported ones. Key process then can focus just on the management of the overall process of achieving the product which is its main task. Production activities which are not directly a part of its primary task has been outsourced to the supporting processes.

The above expressed idea of service-driven technique for creating the basic process structure of an organization is described in more detail as a root idea of the MMABP methodology in [8].

Cooperation of processes is a crucial problem in the process of building the system of processes. The concept cooperation has two main meanings in the context of business processes. From the contents point of view it means communication and from the time point of view it means synchronization. Once the basic structure of processes is given the details of their particular relationships should be analyzed in order to harmonize the cooperation with the internal structure and contents of each process. Structural harmony means the synchronization of the internal process run with the run of the other cooperating processes. Content harmony means taking each cooperation point as an act of the communication of both processes. Considering this cooperation point as a *service* one can think about both sides of harmony in one: service always means delivering the right product in right time.

Analysis of details of the cooperation of business processes naturally brings the consequential questions:

- *Why and how should processes in the organization cooperate?*
- *Which attributes should their cooperation have (time, quality)?*

As it is argued above the cooperation of processes always means their communication. The need for the cooperation follows primarily from mutual positions of both processes. According to the MMABP methodology and consistently with the ideas of process based management there are only two correct reasons for the existence of the process:

- purpose of the key process is implicitly undoubted: it is given by the fact that this process represents the direct way of satisfying the need of a customer what is the universal mission of any organization. Key process always represents the direct *service* to customers;
- purpose of the supporting process is given by the *services* by which this process is supporting other processes.

Any cooperation between processes always means providing the service either directly for the customer or indirectly by supporting other processes. MMABP methodology contains the above mentioned "process normalization technique" for the design of the cooperation structure of processes via "internal outsourcing" of producing process chains from the key processes. This natural way the basic supporting processes are created and cooperation as well as the basis of the structure of processes in the organization is established.

Figure 3 shows the internal structure of the first version of the Education process in the BPMN notation. The main process structure is a sequence of the four main parts: *Preparation of the learning process and admission procedure*, *Management of the teaching process*, *Planning and coordination of the alumni administration*, and *Study program evaluation*. The first three activities are signed as compound ones which means that they hide sub-processes (structures of sub-activities). In this first conception of the process all the activities needed by the process of education are regarded as parts of this process. After the normalization of this process (see Figure 2) the production contents of all activities (sub-processes) has been removed to the standalone supporting processes: *Education process planning*, *Admission procedure*, *Lessons management*, and *Alumni administration*. The new contents of the Education process then express the use of services of these supporting processes in order to achieve the key process goal. The main difference between these two versions of the process is the fact that the it delegated the production competence to the supporting processes. The key process now just manages the supplies instead of the control over all production sub-activities which are now performed independently on the key process. In other words the key process decides about which services are to be delivered in the given context but not about how they are performed. Thus the original hard control over all sub-activities has been turned to the cooperation of relatively independent processes where each process can fully focus on its partial competence. The form of the cooperation of processes is their communication about the services (ordering, changing, checking, etc.) using the standard form of SLA (Service Level Agreement).

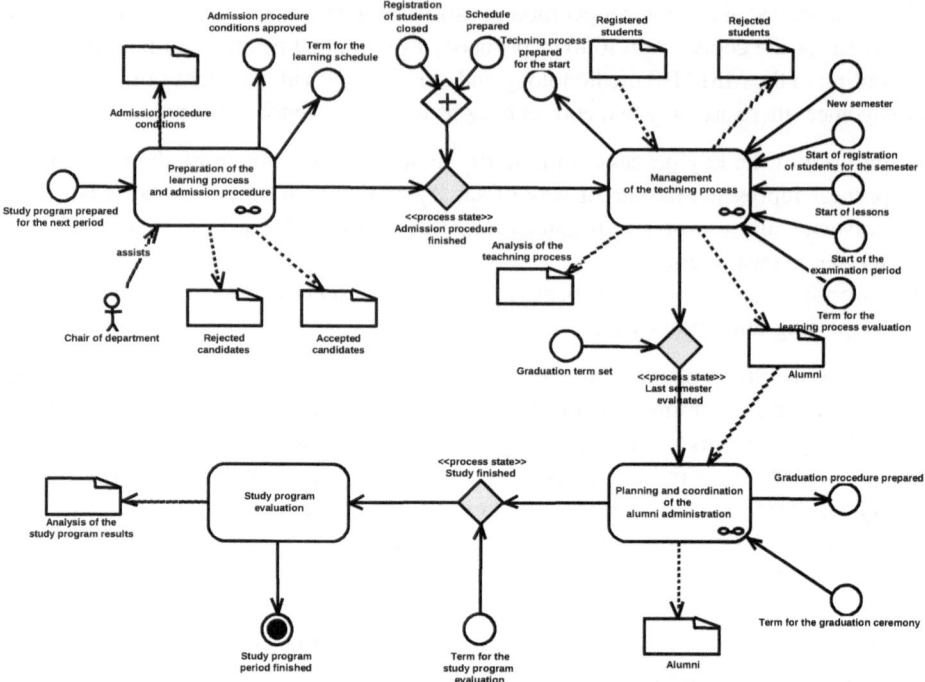

Fig. 3. Internal structure of the Education process

Process-oriented Infrastructure

For putting the system of business processes into the real life it is necessary to create the needed infrastructures. There are two main kinds of infrastructures representing two main resources in the organization: technological infrastructure representing the aspects of automation, and organizational infrastructure representing the people aspects of the organization's behavior. As the main goal of the process based management of the organization is to make it principally and permanently flexible also its infrastructures have to have these attributes. Thus there are two crucial questions to answer regarding the implementation of the process-managed organization:

- *How to organize permanently flexible organization?*
- *How to design the information system of permanently flexible organization?*

In [10] the methodology for design of the process based organization is presented. The last step in the procedure called "Building resulting infrastructures" is based on the work with the structure of services identified in previous steps. Services are identified as a general meaning of the relationships among business processes – their mutual cooperation. Details of every service (alias cooperation act) are described in

the form of Service Level Agreement (SLA) and are used in the last step of the procedure as a common basis for creation of all the needed infrastructures: organization as well as information system. Organization structure of the organization is then built directly on the structure of competencies derived from the mutual competency relationships of processes which are defined in their common SLA. So the rights and responsibilities of managers as well as regular attendees of both processes are directly following from the needs of the processes. This way the organization structure is flexible exactly according to the flexibility of processes.

Comparing both versions of the process system at Figure 2 one can see that dividing the competence among more supporting processes creates the opportunity to personalize the competences at the same time. There are new actor roles added in the second version of the process system: *Students office*, *Faculty secretary*, etc.. The roles are mapped to processes in different types of relations. As there are defined the bilateral competences for all mutually cooperating processes in the form of the SLA definitions these competences at the same time represent the mutual competences of all actors belonging to these processes. This way one of the main outputs of the university project has been created – the exact system of mutual competences of the university actors[1] alias the complete flexible organizational structure of the university in fact[2].

Similarly the structure of the information system is derived from the mutual relationships of processes which are defined in their common SLA. SLA defines all necessary products of the service (alias processes cooperation act) and their quality as well as time attributes which is a perfectly sufficient basis for the decision about the necessary functionality of particular parts of the information system. Particular behavior of the system is then given by the process itself because the basic functionality is principally called by the workflow-management engine as an integral part of the system. Workflow management system is thus the basic condition for making the information system of the organization flexible enough in terms of the main principle of process based organization.

The common intersection of all three viewpoints is characterized by the concept of Service which represents their universal common meaning. The concept of Service as it is discussed above from all three viewpoints represents a common denominator of content, technical, and human aspects of the organization management.

---

[1] Not only employees but the students and other external actors like sponsors of students (mostly their parents) and the Ministry of Education as well.

[2] Some of the traditional roles had to remain for the legislation reasons. Nevertheless, many traditional roles significantly changed their contents thanks to the exact definition of competences based on the system of process. For instance the *Chair of department* is rather a representative of some scientific school and study program than just a formal "managerial position" By the way, this new contents of this role matches the evolutionary original meaning of the concept of "university professor".

3 Cooperation of Processes in the Context of the Business Process MetaModel

Figure 4 shows the Business Process MetaModel which is a part of the Business System Metamodel - a central product of the project OpenSoul [7]. As the MetaModel shows the concept of *Service* represents the fundamental meaning of the cooperation of two processes. Cooperation of two different processes always means the service provided by one process to the other one so that the first process has in this relationship the role of *Supplier* (provider) and the second one has the role of *Customer* (consumer of the service). In order to understand all the crucial meanings of the concept of *Service* it is necessary to look at the interface of two cooperating processes from both sides: customer, and supplier one. In the part of the Business Process Metamodel describing *Service* and immediately connected concept (see the gray area of the model at Figure 4) the *Process Interface* is a couple of two *Interface Sides*. Each *Interface Side* must belong to the particular *Business Process* and represents exactly one of two essential roles in the contract of both processes indicated *Customer*, and *Supplier*. *Supplier* is a producer while *Customer* is a receiver of at least one *Service Product*. Both roles have direct relationship (Supplier's Customer versus Customer's Supplier) represented by the concept of *Process Interface* which is a place of use of particular *Service*.

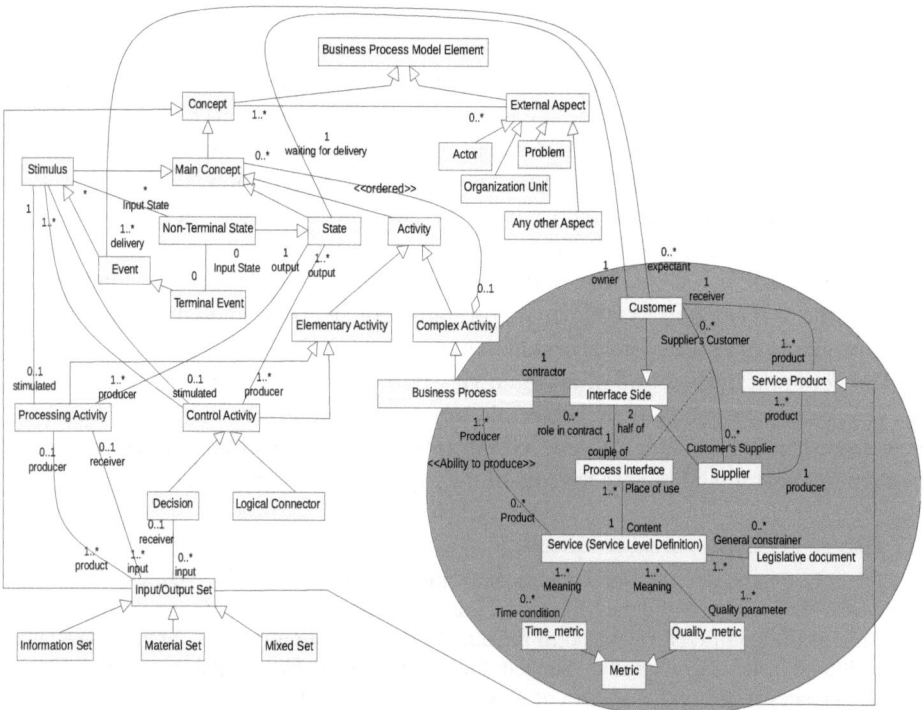

Fig. 4. Service is a form as well as fundamental meaning of the cooperation of business processes

Besides the concept of *Service* and its context the model also describes the concepts of an internal structure of a business process. Details of this metamodel are out of the range of this paper and are explained in [10] for instance. Nevertheless, from the point of view of the cooperation of processes the relationships of the *Service* related concepts to the internal business process concepts are important. Looking at the relationships among the gray area and the rest of the metamodel one can see the substantial consequences of the cooperation of processes and the internal process structure:

- The concept of *Business Process* is a special kind of *Complex Activity* from the process internal point of view. This means that some complex (i.e. non-elementary) activities of the process can be regarded as something more than the activity only – as a standalone business process. Nevertheless the explanation of the meaning of such special kind of the activity is not in the scope of the interest from this – internal – point of view already[3].
- Reciprocally, inputs and outputs of the business process (*Input/Output Set*) as an important concept connected with other essential parts of the process is, from the services point of view, just a special kind of the *Service Product*. This conceptual construction expresses the rule that every input and output of the business process must be the product of some service, i.e. it must have some value for the customer or for some other business process at least. In other words, "an sich"[4] inputs and outputs of processes, without a meaning defined by the relation to some service are inadmissible because they represent just the technical aspects of the process which can never be sufficient in the world of **business** processes.
- *Customer* role has two essential relationships to the internal concepts of a business process:
  - delivery of the *Service Product* always represents the *Event* for the *Customer*. This means that every product delivery stimulates some action of the customer process (as the *Event* is a kind of the *Stimulus* according to the metamodel).
  - It is always necessary to wait for the product delivery. Thus the *Customer* role of the process in the *Process Interface* is always related to the internal *State* of the process. This process state represents waiting for the delivery of the *Service Product*.

The above discussed facts expressed in the metamodel emphasize the necessity to respect both dimensions of a business process: the technical as well as the semantic one. At the same time they show the way which the MMABP methodology supports this necessity. The concept of *Service* plays in the methodology the role of the central point representing both mentioned dimensions. Relationships to the related concepts explains the technical consequences of fulfilling of the business needs and goals, as

---

3   The meaning of this special kind of activity is important from other points of view like the cooperation viewpoint represented by the gray part of the metamodel for instance.

4   Thing-in-itself according to the philosophy of Kant: an object as it is in itself independent of the mind, as opposed to a phenomenon.

well as the business meaning of the technical aspects of the cooperation of processes at the same time.

4   Conclusions

There are many popular misunderstandings and mistakes in the field of processes cooperation. Some of the most popular ones follow:

- Cooperation of processes means *ownership of one process by the other one*. This idea which is in direct contradiction with the main idea of process-oriented management if even supported by most of process modeling languages. In fact, the process based management represents the opposite meaning of relationships among processes: all processes are mutually independent in principle, their collaboration always means mutual supporting with services instead of serving just one process as its part.
- Cooperation of processes means *control of one process over the other one*. This idea is in contradiction with the main idea of process-oriented management as well even if it is widely used as a leading idea for creating the system of competencies over business processes. Unfortunately, such a system of competencies cannot satisfy the needs of processes for services from other processes. In fact, each process should offer its services as independently as possible and for as much potential supported processes as possible. This is an Iron Rule of the service-orientation which follows from the crucial role of standards in this field as well as in the field of the technology development generally. Any system needs standards to develop itself. Even an organization as a system of collaborating processes needs the standards in the form of the definitions of services which allow to evaluate the effectiveness as well as efficiency of processes according to these standards. Moreover, these standards should meet the general standards in order to make the evaluation of processes as objective as possible. As it follows from the above mentioned facts the fatal requirement for the standardization of services offered by the internal processes directly excludes any specificity in the communication of processes. The "control of one process over the other one" is an extreme form of such specificity – tailoring the service for the only consumer.
- Cooperation of processes means *only sharing data among processes*. This idea is typical for database-oriented approaches to the business process modeling and management. The problem connected with this approach is that the other non-technical cooperation aspects like stimulating responsibility are not respected by such an approach. Moreover also the time aspects of the cooperation cannot be sufficiently managed just by the data.

All such misunderstandings and mistakes can be easily identified and overcome with the principal role of the service in business process management in mind.

The methodology for business processes system design, mentioned in this paper, which is based on the "principle of services", has been evaluated in several projects.

Every use of the methodology in the project brought some new experience and positively influenced its content. That way we lastly uncovered the need for elaborating the concept of service in general, for instance. Projects covered fields of university education (some examples are used in this paper), production, finance, and public administration. The main knowledge from this heterogeneous experience is:

- the idea of Process Management is valid in general, for all types of organizations, thus it should not be reduced just to the area of market-oriented organizations,
- thinking in terms of services is relevant for all types of different systems harmonization: coordination of processes as well as harmonization of competencies following from the organization structure with specific process competencies needed, harmonization of the organization specific needs with general technology possibilities, etc.
- the traditional gap between the business conception and the applications development can be overcome by regarding so-called "user requirements" as services of information system required by the nature of processes. This view on the problem also significantly changes the traditional approach to the distribution of tasks among typical roles in the information systems development, and, at the same time, explains the "role of the application user" often discussed nowadays in the communities of applications developers.

Acknowledgments. The work presented in this paper has been supported by the Czech Science Foundation in the grant project No. P403/11/0574 Enterprise Architecture for Cloud Computing Environments.

References

1. Business Process Model and Notation version 2.0, OMG Adopted Beta Specification, OMG Document Number: dtc/2010-06-05, June 21 (2010)
2. Cardoso, E.C.S., Almeida, J.P.A., Guizzardi, G., Guizzardi, R.S.S.: Eliciting Goals for Business Process Models with Non-Functional Requirements Catalogues. In: Halpin, T., Krogstie, J., Nurcan, S., Proper, E., Schmidt, R., Soffer, P., Ukor, R. (eds.) BPMDS 2009 and EMMSAD 2009. LNBIP, vol. 29, pp. 33–45. Springer, Heidelberg (2009)
3. De Nicola, A., Lezoche, M., Missikoff, M.: An Ontological Approach to Business Process Modeling. In: Proceedings of the 3rd Indian International Conference on Artificial Intelligence, December 17-19 (2007)
4. Eriksson, H.E., Penker, M.: Business Modeling with UML: Business Patterns at Work. Wiley (2000) ISBN 978-0-471-29551-8
5. Hammer, M., Champy, J.: Re-engineering the Corporation: A Manifesto for Business Revolution. Harper Business, New York (1993)
6. Cabral, L., Norton, B., Domingue, J.: The business process modelling ontology. In: 4th International Workshop on Semantic Business Process Management (SBPM 2009), Workshop at ESWC 2009, June 1 (2009)
7. OpenSoul Project (2000-2013), http://opensoul.panrepa.org

8. Řepa, V.: Role of the Concept of Service in Business Process Management. In: Information Systems Development, pp. 623–634. Springer, New York (2011) ISBN 978-1-4419-9645-9

9. Repa, V.: Business Process Modelling Notation from the Methodical Perspective. In: Cezon, M., Wolfsthal, Y. (eds.) ServiceWave 2010 Workshops. LNCS, vol. 6569, pp. 160–171. Springer, Heidelberg (2011)

10. Řepa, V.: Information Modelling of Organizations. Bruckner, Prague (2012) ISBN 978-80-904661-3-5

11. Unified Modeling Language Specification, v. 1.5. document ad/03-03-01, OMG (2003)

Pattern Use in Knowledge Architectures:
An Example from Information Logistics

Kurt Sandkuhl

University of Rostock, Chair Business Information Systems
Albert-Einstein-Str. 22, 18059 Rostock, Germany
kurt.sandkuhl@uni-rostock.de

Abstract. The paper aims at contributing to improved information logistics by bringing together experiences from knowledge modeling and pattern-based reuse in information system development. We propose a pattern-based knowledge architecture with several inter-working layers of services for implementing information logistics in networked organizations. The knowledge architecture forms a framework for selecting and configuring suitable resources for a given problem situation. The knowledge architecture principle and three types of knowledge patterns within the architecture framework are discussed: task patterns for representing enterprise knowledge of member organizations in a networked organization, information demand patterns addressing the information demand of typical roles in a networked organization, and ontology design patterns for capturing context information for decision support.

Keywords: Information Logistics, Knowledge Architecture, Knowledge Pattern.

1   Introduction

Accurate and readily available information is a crucial basis for decision making, problem solving, or performing knowledge-intensive work. In networked organizations with geographically distributed work force and processes, like logistics networks or SME-clusters, quickly finding the right information for a given purpose often is a challenge. Some studies show that users spend a lot of time in searching for the right information causing unnecessary delays and costs. An example is [1] showing that 2 out of 3 top or mid-level managers participating in a study among Swedish enterprises perceive an information overload due to "far too much information" (37%) or "too much information" (29%). An improved information supply would contribute significantly to saving time and most likely to improving productivity.

The paper aims at contributing to improved information logistics by bringing together experiences from knowledge modeling and pattern-based reuse in information system development. We propose a pattern-based knowledge architecture with several inter-working layers of services for implementing information logistics in networked organizations. The knowledge architecture forms a framework for selecting and configuring suitable resources for a given problem situation. The contributions of the paper are: (a) it proposes a novel vision of architecting

A. Kobyliński and A. Sobczak (Eds.): BIR 2013, LNBIP 158, pp. 91–103, 2013.

knowledge, which is considered promising for knowledge-based systems and decision support systems, (b) it contains a general review of knowledge architecture and knowledge pattern concepts and (c) it shows the application potential of knowledge architectures for supply networks.

The remaining part of the paper is structured as follows: the next section describes an application case from automotive supplier industries as a motivating scenario for this paper including the lifecycle of supply networks. Afterwards the knowledge architecture principle and several types of knowledge patterns within the architecture framework are discussed. Finally, the supply network scenario is revisited to investigate suitability of the different knowledge pattern types for this scenario. A discussion of achievements and future work concludes the paper.

2   Motivating Scenario: Supply Networks

A flexible supply network includes independent companies based on the principle of cooperation within a defined application domain, which are capable of coordinating their activities for production and delivery of the desired product/service. Organizations of this form use information and communication technologies to extend their boundaries and physical location and form multiple links across the boundaries to work together for a common purpose [9]. Such networks experience different phases, which form the "life-cycle" of a network organization and can be considered as organizational frame for competence supply. The most important phases are [2]:

- Community building: enterprises with joint objectives or interests gather in a community of loosely coupled members. Initial purpose is information exchange and communication within the network in order to prepare collaboration in joint business, load balancing between partners or sharing of production resources.
- Formation: based on specific requirements for a collaboration project (e.g. a joint engineering activity, like product development), the formation of a project team is started based on the capabilities of the members. As a result of this phase, potential partners with respect to the specific requirements have been identified.
- Integration: potential team members have been selected and negotiate the legal and financial conditions for joint project work. Furthermore, a collaboration infrastructure is being implemented for all relevant levels of collaboration. The result of this phase is a project network.
- Operation: the collaboration project is carried out within the project network. This operation is supported by the collaboration infrastructure.
- Discontinuation: the project network discontinues to exist. Dis-integration on all levels of the collaboration infrastructure and with respect to legal and financial issues is carried out.
- Community discontinuation: the joint objectives or interests within the community no longer exist. The network is dissolved.

Figure 1 illustrates the lifecycle of flexible supply networks. Usually it is not fully obvious to the network members, which competence and resources are available from which partner in which quantity to which expenses and how to access them. In this context, efficient support for configuration of collaborations and efficient reuse of existing knowledge is a critical success factor. Configuration includes selection of suitable partners based on their competences and integration of work processes and existing knowledge sources in order to ensure a common level of knowledge and commitment. This also includes providing relevant information for decision making and operations support.

Fig. 1. Lifecycle of flexible supply networks

In order to illustrate the concept of supply networks, this section presents a case from distributed product development in a networked organization from automotive supplier industry, which originates from the MAPPER project [8]. The main partner is the business area "seat comfort components" of a first tier automotive supplier from Scandinavia, working with development and manufacturing of products for the automotive business world-wide. The main products are seat comfort products, like seat heating, seat ventilation, lumber support and head restraint. Development of products in this business area includes identification of system requirements based on customer requirements, functional specification, development of logical and technical architecture, co-design of electrical and mechanical components, integration testing and production planning including production logistics, floor planning and product line planning.

Within the first tier supplier, this process is geographically distributed involving engineers and specialists at several locations and SMEs from the region. A high percentage of seat comfort components are product families, i.e. various versions of the components exist and have to be maintained and further developed for different product models and different customers. In this context, fast and flexible product development and integrated management of concurrently performed forward-development processes is of crucial importance. Smooth collaboration and information sharing is a key success factor to meet these basic needs.

Figure 2 shows a typical collaboration set-up for collaborative design. The customer for a new variant of a seat heating is an Original Equipment Manufacturer (OEM), e.g. for trucks. The first tier supplier receives the order for designing and manufacturing the seat heating and involves several sub-suppliers and partners. These partners are responsible for specific components, like the carrier material or the copper wires, or for specific services, like the controller design or manufacturing of the control unit. The first tier supplier controls the overall design process, contributes own components and services, and performs the system integration.

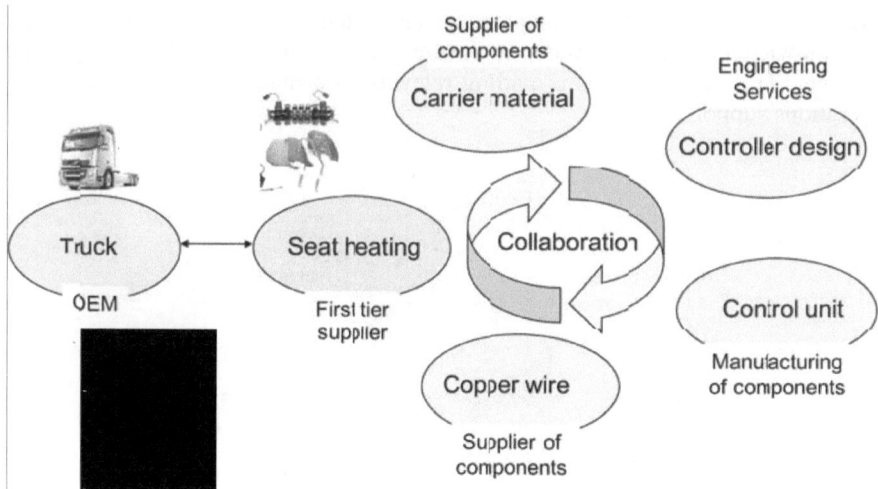

Fig. 2. Example supply network in collaborative product design

3   Knowledge Architecture Approach

The term knowledge architecture originates from knowledge modelling and knowledge representation, which is a well-researched area in computer science and discussed in [20], to take an example. However, the term "knowledge architecture" is less established and needs clarification: Architectures in general identify main building blocks of the system under consideration including their interfaces and structural relationships. Similarly, knowledge architectures focus on the knowledge building blocks needed for a specific application and their relationships. In this paper, an enterprise perspective has to be taken in order to also capture potential dependencies between knowledge building blocks and business models. The term enterprise knowledge architecture will be used and defined as follows: *The enterprise knowledge architecture identifies elements of enterprise knowledge including their structural relationships and their context of use [18].* The main difference in comparison to other architecture perspectives is that the context of knowledge use is modeled explicitly, since the context of use is essential for tailoring the knowledge to the demand at hand. In our case, "context" includes both, the characteristics needed to determine the decision situation in a member company of the supply network and the demands of an individual user. Furthermore, an essential part of the knowledge architecture is the knowledge about the services, which the network members possibly could provide.

The constituents of an enterprise knowledge architecture potentially include business processes, organization structures, products structures, IT-systems or any other perspective relevant for the system under consideration. Established approaches for modeling enterprise knowledge can be divided into at least two major communities: the enterprise engineering community and the artificial intelligence inspired community. Chen et al. [4] provide a detailed account of enterprise modeling and integration approaches from an enterprise engineering perspective. Fox and

Gruninger [7] are prominent representatives of the AI-related approaches favoring ontologies for knowledge representation.

More concrete, the proposed knowledge architecture consists of three main layers:

- Enterprise knowledge of the different member enterprises in the supply network, including process, product and service knowledge,
- Knowledge about the information demand of typical roles in the supply networks, like product design managers, process verifiers, quality managers or production logistics responsible,
- Knowledge about actual situations of these typical roles.

In addition to the above characteristics of knowledge architectures, which are primarily motivated by the application scenario of supply networks, such architectures also need certain technical qualities. A knowledge architecture is supposed to contribute to engineering knowledge-based systems and to capturing and reusing organizational knowledge. In this context, a proper representation is required. General requirements connected to this representation are that the terminology used in the knowledge architecture needs to be shared and made explicit. Furthermore, it must be possible to define the components of the architecture and express them as such with different levels of detail, and to express constraints guiding or limiting the composition of components. Additionally, the representation must also be suitable for discussing with business stakeholders, like in the supply network scenario.

Since so far there are no standards or proven approaches for knowledge architecture representation, related work from other areas might provide relevant technologies:

- In software engineering, architecture description languages have been developed, like ArchC [15], DAOP-ADL [14] or π-ADL [13]. Their focus is on specifying components, services offered by the components, interface to the components and constraints to be applied. However, in practice of software engineering, often block-diagrams or UML specifications are used [19].
- In enterprise modeling, ontology-based approaches and visual models are commonly in use, as already indicated above. From the perspective of knowledge architectures, active knowledge modeling is a promising approach due its combination of visual language and formality [10]. Furthermore, more formalized approaches, like DEMO would provide extensive language support [5].
- In knowledge engineering, architecting knowledge bases recently has been investigated in the context of the semantic web. Examples here are ontology-based techniques and include ontology modules [6] and ontology patterns [1].

Looking back at the general requirements to the knowledge architecture representation, the software engineering approaches seem to be not suitable since component interfaces in terms of services are not a priority in knowledge architectures. But a combination of enterprise modeling (due to the requirement to be suitable for business stakeholders) and knowledge engineering (due to the requirement of formalization) seems appropriate. Since enterprise models and ontologies can be converted into each other, we decided to investigate the use of ontologies. Among the many ontology definitions available, we will use the following definition, which is based on [11]:

An ontology structure is a 5-tuple $O := \{C, R, H^C, rel, A^O\}$, consisting of

- two disjoint sets C and R whose elements are called concepts and relations respectively.

- a concept hierarchy HC: HC is a directed relation $H^C \subseteq C \times C$ which is called concept hierarchy or taxonomy. H (C1,C2) means that C1 is a sub-concept of C2.

- a function $rel : R \rightarrow C \times C$, that relates concepts non-hierarchically (note that this also includes attributes). For rel(R)=(C1,C2) one may also write R(C1,C2).

- a set of ontology axioms AO, expressed in an appropriate logical language.

With this definition as a basis, we will investigate the use of different types of knowledge patterns as components of a knowledge architecture.

4   Knowledge Patterns

In computer science, patterns are considered a promising way to capture proven practices in order to facilitate reuse. Within the knowledge architecture approach, we propose to use task patterns for representing enterprise knowledge, information demand patterns for the typical information demand of roles and ontology design patterns for capturing the actual decision context. These three pattern types, which can be considered as knowledge patterns, will be briefly introduced in the following.

4.1   Task Patterns

The concept of task pattern is a result of the EU-FP6 project MAPPER [8]. In this project, collaborative engineering was supported by adaptable models capturing best practices for reoccurring tasks in networked enterprises. These best practices were represented as active knowledge models using the POPS* perspectives. Active knowledge models are visual models of selected aspects of an enterprise, which cannot only be viewed and analyzed, but also executed and adapted during execution. The POPS* perspectives include the enterprise's processes (P), the organization structure (O), the product developed (P), the IT system used (S) and other aspects deemed relevant when modeling (*). In the context of task patterns, these other aspects were the competences required to fill roles in the organization structure and business requirements attached to different processes.

The term "task patterns" was introduced for these adaptable visual models, as they are not only applicable in a specific company, but are also considered relevant for other enterprises in the application domain under consideration. Task pattern in this context is defined as "self-contained model template with well-defined connectors to application environments capturing knowledge about best practices for a clearly defined task" [16]. In this context, self-contained means that a task pattern includes all POPS* perspectives, model elements and relationships between the model elements required for capturing the knowledge reflecting a best practice. Model template indicates the use of a well-defined modeling language and that no instances are contained in the task patterns. Connectors are model elements representing the adaptation of the task pattern to target application environments.

In order to use task patterns as components in our knowledge architecture, we need to formalize the concept more and match it onto the formalization shown in the previous section, i.e. onto the ontology representation defined for the knowledge architecture.

We define a task pattern as a tuple $TP := \{E, R, sub, fol, resp, \sup, req\}$, consisting of

- Two disjoint sets E and R whose elements are called entity and relations respectively.
- A function $sub : R \mapsto E \times E$ that relates entities and sub-entities. With sub(R) = (E_1, E_2) we define E_2 as a sub-entity of E_1. With this function, it is possible to express hierarchical relationships between processes, organisation units, products and IT-systems in a task pattern.
- A function $fol : R \mapsto E \times E$ that relates entities with following entities. With fol(R) = (E_1, E_2) we define E_2 as following the entity E_1 from a time perspective. This function allows for capturing process chains.
- A function $resp : R \mapsto E \times E$ that relates entities with a responsible entity. With resp(R) = (E_1, E_2) we define E_1 as responsible for E_2. This function is used for expressing the responsibility of an entity of the organisation structure for a process, an IT-system of a product entity or sub-entity.
- A function $req : R \mapsto E \times E$ that relates required entities. With req(R) = (E_1, E_2) we define E_2 as a required entity for E_1. This function is used for expressing the need of a resource (product or IT system entity) for a process.
- A function $\sup : R \mapsto E \times E$ that relates supportive entities. With sup(R) = (E_1, E_2) we define E_2 is supported by E_1. This function is applied for showing the support of a resource (e.g. an IT system entity) for a process or a competence for an organisation structure entity.

The above definitions provide a basic formalization for the POPS* perspectives of task patterns and allow for a rich set of relations between various entities. This formalization could be extended by typing the entities and adding a wider set of functions for reflecting all elements of visual modeling languages. As ontologies have a clearly richer descriptive power than task patterns, the mapping on a notation level does not cause serious technical problems.

Table 1. FM to EM mapping

Task Pattern	Enterprise Ontology	Remark
E	C	Entities are represented as concepts
sub(E1,E2)	H (C1,C2)	Entity hierarchy is represented as concept hierarchy
fol(E1,E2)	fol(C1,C2)	Other entity relations are represented as the same relationship type in the ontology
resp(E1,E2)	resp(C1,C2)	
req(F1,F2)	req(C1,C2)	
sup(F1,F2)	sup(C1,C2)	

The approach proposed in this paper is to preserve existing hierarchies between entities by mapping an entity sub-entity structure to a concept hierarchy in the ontology. The other relationships between entities in the task pattern, i.e. follows, is_responsible_for, is_required_for and is_supporting, are represented in the ontology by creating the respective relationship types in the ontology. **Error! Reference source not found.** summarizes the proposed mapping

4.2   Information Demand Patterns (IDP)

The general idea of information demand patterns is similar to most pattern developments in computer science: to capture knowledge about proven solutions in order to facilitate reuse of this knowledge. In this paper, the term information demand pattern will be defined as follows: *An information demand pattern addresses a recurring information demand problem that arises for specific roles and work situations in an enterprise, and presents a conceptual solution to it.* An information demand pattern consists of a number of essential parts used for describing the pattern [17]:

- A statement about the organizational context where the pattern is useful.
- Problems of a role that the pattern addresses. The tasks and responsibilities a certain role has are described in order to identify and discuss the challenges and problems, which this role usually faces in the defined organizational context.
- The conceptual solution that resolves the problem includes the information demand of the role, quality criteria for the different parts of the information and a timeline indicating the points in time when the different information parts should be available at the latest
- The effects that play in forming a solution. If the needed information part should not be available or arrive too late this might affect the possibility of the role to complete its task and responsibilities.

The above parts of a pattern are described in much detail in the textual description of the pattern. Additionally, a pattern can also be represented as a kind of enterprise model. This model representation can be used to show the link to the relevant task patterns introduced in the previous section, including the relation of the role to co-workers and other roles in the organization, the relation between the different parts of the information demand and IT system in the enterprise, which are potential source of this information; and the relation of tasks and responsibilities to processes in the organization.

In order to use information demand patterns as components in our knowledge architecture, we again need to formalize this pattern concept and match it onto the ontology representation of the knowledge architecture. Since information demand patterns also use an enterprise model representation very similar as to task patterns, we can use the same formalization as introduced for task patterns. However, it has to be emphasized that only if an enterprise model representation exists, an information demand pattern can be used as component in the knowledge architecture. The textual representation alone would not be sufficient, since it is not precise enough for matching to the ontology structure of the knowledge architecture.

4.3   Ontology Design Patterns (ODP)

Ontology design patterns can be defined as a set of ontological elements and construction principles that solve a clearly defined particular ontology engineering problem [3]. Ontology design patterns are considered as encodings of best practices, which help to reduce the need for extensive experience when developing ontologies, i.e. the well-defined solutions encoded in the patterns can be exploited by less experienced engineers when creating ontologies. The two types of ODP probably receiving most attention are logical and content ODP. Logical ODP focus only on the logical structure of the representation, i.e. this pattern type is targeting aspects of language expressivity, common problems and misconceptions. Content ODP often are instantiations of logical ODP offering actual modeling solutions. Due to the fact that these solutions contain actual classes, properties, and axioms, content ODP are considered by many researchers as domain-dependent. For the purpose of representing knowledge about the decision context of an information logistics situation, ODP such as "situation" or "role-actor" can be applied.

Since ODP use the same ontological formalization as the knowledge architecture representation, no transformation of mapping needs to be applied. ODP can be used as components in the knowledge architecture.

5   Knowledge Architecture and Pattern Use in Supply Networks

Based on the lifecycle model for supply networks introduced earlier in this paper, this section will investigate how knowledge architectures in general and the different pattern types in particular can support the lifecycle phases. For this paper, formation phase and integration phase are of specific interest, since these phases are decisive for finding the right partners for a collaborative project and creating a working network. The formation phase requires an efficient way to describe the competences and services required for the joint network activity, e.g. for collaborative product design, completely on a sufficient level of detail. The integration phase adds requirements regarding selection of partners. Table 2 summarizes the requirements from both phases, i.e. what do knowledge architecture and knowledge patterns have to support?

Table 2. Requirements from lifecycle phases to competence demand models

Formation Phase	Integration Phase
Tasks to be completed by the complete supply network or by single partners	Approaches and tools for matching the demand of the collaboration project with the network members' competences
Results to be delivered by the task	Selection of individual team members at the selected member organizations,
Express, store and access competence profiles of organizations and individuals in an information system	Support for integration of IT infrastructure and enterprise systems required for the collaboration.
Capacity needed in terms of machinery or equipment	
Instruments and tools required	

Table 3 uses the requirements from table 2 and shows how the knowledge architecture and the pattern types can support implementation of the requirements.

Table 3. Knowledge architecture and pattern support for requirements of lifecycle phases

Requirement from Formation/Integration	Knowledge Architecture	Knowledge Patterns
Tasks to be completed by complete network or single partners	Defines overall structure how to model tasks in a consistent and inter-related way	TP and IDP: Tasks are common elements of enterprise models (EM) and information demand descriptions. Patterns of tasks can be applied to specify the tasks to be completed by the network. ODP: Task types can be modeled as concepts with appropriate attributes
Results to be delivered by task	Defines controlled vocabulary for specification of resources	TP: Outputs of tasks are common EM elements and can be used to model results IDP: shows dependencies between information demand and results of a task ODP: Result types can be modeled as concepts; relationship type between task and result expresses dependency
Instruments and tools required	Defines controlled vocabulary for specification of instruments and tools	TP: Resources of tasks are common EM elements and can be used to model instruments/tools ODP: Instrument types and tool types can be modeled as concepts; relationship type expresses dependency
Capacity needed in terms of machinery or equipment	No support	TP: Most EM approaches allow for attributes of resource, which can be used for storing capacity ODP: Can be expressed as attribute of the instrument or tools concepts
Express, store and access competence profiles of organisations and individuals in an information system	Contributes to the design of the knowledge base for such an information system	TP: Requires usually a conversion in highly structured format, which is searchable and can easily be processed ODP: Ready for use in knowledge bases
Matching competence demand with the existing competence profiles	No support	ODP: Exact matching possible based on inference; semantic matching is emerging technology
Selection of individual team members at member organization	No support	TP and ODP: possible; depends on granularity level of EM / ontology
Support for integration of IT infrastructure and enterprise systems required for the collaboration.	No support	TP: EM include information required for this purpose on logical level, but usually not all technical information ODP: Can be used as element in interoperability solutions

The first column of table 3 lists the requirements identified for formation and integration phase in table 2. The middle column "knowledge architecture" presents the contribution of the knowledge architecture to implementing the requirement under consideration and the last column presents the contribution of the knowledge pattern. Here, TP is used for task patterns, IDP for information demand pattern and ODP for ontology design pattern.

Table 3 shows that all pattern types and the knowledge architecture contribute to the requirements identified in formation and integration phases. Most promising seems to be the task pattern type, which is contributing to all requirements except the requirement of matching competences. Ontology patterns seem to be a suitable complement to task patterns. This indicates that a knowledge architecture consisting of orchestrated task patterns and an integrated controlled vocabulary as part of it would be most promising. Information demand patterns contribute only marginally to the requirements.

When using patterns and knowledge architecture for a supply network, e.g. for the collaborative product development discussed in section 3, the following steps could be applied:

a) Identify task patterns from the different network partners which are relevant for the purpose of the supply network, i.e. the network partners decide what tasks or services they are willing to provide within the network and describe these tasks using task patterns.

b) Construct an ontology for the supply network which represents the terms and entity types included in the task patterns which were selected in step a). The construction can be based on content and logical ontology design patterns. The ontology represents the terminology implied by the task patterns.

c) Construct the knowledge architecture for the supply network based on the task patterns from step a). The knowledge architecture identifies potential integration scenarios for the patterns and specifies the interfaces for the patterns needed for these scenarios. Integration points between the patterns are identified using the supply network ontology from step b).

d) During formation phase, use the knowledge architecture and the ontology for selecting those task patterns, which are required for completing the tasks to be provided by the network.

e) During integration phase, refine the patterns towards actual solutions, deploy and apply them in supply network operations by using an ontological representation.

6   Summary and Future Work

The paper investigated the use of different pattern types within a knowledge architecture in the context of information logistics. Based on a lifecycle model for networked organizations and an illustrative example, the requirements from the lifecycle phases were contrasted with the characteristics of the pattern types. From an application perspective, the conclusion of the work so far is that a knowledge architecture consisting of orchestrated task patterns and supporting ontology design patterns would be most promising.

From a technical perspective, it was shown that an ontological representation of the knowledge architecture could serve as a technical basis for accommodating both, task patterns transformed to an ontology representation and ontology design patterns. However, when constructing an actual knowledge architecture from task patterns and ODP from different authors or sources, the known problems of integrating heterogeneous information into a homogeneous representation can be expected. Examples are semantic mismatches between concepts from different sources, different levels of granularity or different modeling styles. When exploring the use of the knowledge architecture approach for a logistics application [18], we found it useful to initialize the knowledge architecture with a defined vocabulary, i.e. a domain ontology for the field under consideration, and adjust all knowledge patterns to this vocabulary.

Future work will be of experimental and conceptual nature. From an experimental perspective, the proposed approach has to be implemented and evaluated in controlled environments or real-world cases. This will most likely lead to changes, refinements and improvements of the proposed approach. The conceptual work includes to further elaborate the aspects of knowledge architecture formalization, identifying integration and combination potential between the different pattern types, and adequate software infrastructure for implementation.

References

[1] Blomqvist, E.: Semi-automatic Ontology Construction based on Patterns. PhD thesis, Linköping University, Department of Computer and Information Science (2009)

[2] Blomqvist, E., Levashova, T., Öhgren, A., Sandkuhl, K., Smirnov, A.: Formation of Enterprise Networks for Collaborative Engineering. In: Proceedings CCE 2005, Sopron (Hungary), (April 2005) ISBN 91-975604-1-3

[3] Blomqvist, E., Sandkuhl, K.: Patterns in Ontology Engineering. In: Proc. 7th ICEIS, Miami, USA (May 2005)

[4] Chen, D., Doumeingts, G., Vernadat, F.: Architectures for enterprise integration and interoperability: Past, present and future. Computers in Industry 59(7), 647–659 (2008)

[5] Dietz, J.: Enterprise Ontology – Theory and Methodology. Springer (2006)

[6] Doran, P., Tamma, V., Iannone, L.: Ontology module extraction for ontology reuse: an ontology engineering perspective. In: Proceedings of the Sixteenth ACM Conference on Information and Knowledge Management (CIKM 2007), pp. 61–70. ACM, New York (2007), doi:10.1145/1321440.1321451

[7] Fox, M.S., Gruninger, M.: Enterprise Modelling. AI Magazine 19(3) (1998)

[8] Johnsen, S., Schümmer, T., Haake, J., Pawlak, A., Jorgensen, H., Sandkuhl, K., Stirna, J., Tellioglu, H., Jacucci, G.: Model-based Adaptive Product and Process Engineering. In: Rabe, M., Mihok, P. (eds.) New Technologies for the Intelligent Design and Operation of Manufacturing Networks. Fraunhofer IRB Verlag, Stuttgart (2007)

[9] Laudon, K.C., Laudon, J.P.: Management Information Systems: Organisation and Technology in the Networked Enterprise. Prentice Hall International, New York (2000)

[10] Lillehagen, F., Krogstie, J.: Active Knowledge Modelling of Enterprises. Springer (2009) ISBN: 978-3-540-79415-8

[11] Maedche, A.: Ontology Learning for the Semantic Web. Kluwer Academic Publishers, Norwell (2003)

[12] Öhgren, A., Sandkuhl, K.: Information Overload in Industrial Enterprises - Results of an Empirical Investigation. In: Proceedings ECIME 2008, London, UK (2008)

[13] Oquendo, F.: π -ADL: an Architecture Description Language based on the higher-order typed π -calculus for specifying dynamic and mobile software architectures. SIGSOFT Softw. Eng. Notes, 29(3), 1–14 (2004), doi:10.1145/986710.986728

[14] Pinto, M., Fuentes, L., Troya, J.M.: DAOP-ADL: An Architecture Description Language for Dynamic Component and Aspect-Based Development. In: Pfenning, F., Macko, M. (eds.) GPCE 2003. LNCS, vol. 2830, pp. 118–137. Springer, Heidelberg (2003)

[15] Rigo, S., Araujo, G., et al.: ArchC: a systemC-based architecture description language. Computer Architecture and High Performance Computing, SBAC-PAD 2004 (2004)

[16] Sandkuhl, K.: Capturing Product Development Knowledge with Task Patterns. Quarterly Journal of Control & Cybernetics (1) (2010)

[17] Sandkuhl, K.: Information Demand Patterns. In: Proc. PATTERNS 2011, The Third International Conferences on Pervasive Patterns and Applications, Rome, Italy, September 25-30, pp. 1–6 (2011) ISBN: 978-1-61208-158-8

[18] Sandkuhl, K.: Towards Intelligent Information Logistics Services: Case Study from Transportation. In: Ivanov, D., Kopfer, H., Haasis, H.D., Schönberger, J. (eds.) Dynamics and Sustainability in International Logistics and Supply Chain Management, pp. 317–328. Cuvillier Verlag, Göttingen (2011) ISBN 978-3-86955-703-8

[19] Sommerville, I.: Software Engineering, 8th edn. Pearson Education (2007)

[20] Sowa, J.F.: Knowledge Representation: Logical, Philosophical, and Computational Foundations. Brooks Cole Publishing Co., Pacific Grove (2000) ISBN 0-534-94965-7

Methods of the Assessment of Enterprise Architecture Practice Maturity in an Organization

Andrzej Sobczak

Department of Business Informatics, Warsaw School of Economics,
6/8 Madalińskiego St, Warsaw, Poland
Andrzej.Sobczak@sgh.waw.pl

Abstract. Both enterprises and public sector units take advantage of Enterprise Architecture concepts in an increasing manner. Therefore, a periodical assessment of its effectiveness (maturity) and suggesting certain improvements on the basis of obtained results is recommended (e.g. by TOGAF, a de facto Enterprise Architecture development standard). This article is an overview of existing approaches in this area, and identifies its weaknesses and strengths. Also, the author's approach to assessment of enterprise architecture practice is discussed and directions of further research work in this area are presented.

Keywords: Enterprise Architecture, architecture maturity assessment, architecture practice, CMM, TOGAF.

1   Introduction

Organizations which take advantage of Enterprise Architecture[1] concepts should provide periodical reviews of existing architecture practices and outcomes obtained by using them. In this article, the author defines architecture practice as follows: a coherent set of services, processes, roles and bodies (together with responsibilities assigned to them) which participate in the creation, maintenance and modification of architecture deliverables, and in the assistance in making certain decisions, putting them into effect and observing how these decisions are being realized.

If there exist areas where it is necessary to improve architecture practice, they should be identified and some actions in this field should be taken. Reviews should refer to a degree to which architecture practice is aligned to the organization's strategic goals, to how effectively measures which assess architecture practice are used (i.e. do they serve to perform architecture activities), and finally to whether the architectural undertaking delivers the planned outcomes (both at a business and IT level).

---

[1] Enterprise Architecture – a formal description of the enterprise, or a detailed plan of the enterprise at component level to guide its implementation. The structure of components, their inter-relationships, and the principles and guidelines governing their design and evolution over time [9].

A. Kobyliński and A. Sobczak (Eds.): BIR 2013, LNBIP 158, pp. 104–111, 2013.

These reviews must also include analysis of effectiveness of architecture processes and quality of architecture deliverables. Moreover, it is recommended that an organization assess human capability of developing architecture skills and knowledge. This is going to be a basis for the identification of competence gaps and reduction of them through training, recruitment and/or employment of external Enterprise Architecture experts.

This article aims to: analyze existing approaches to assess architecture practice maturity with the intention to identify its weaknesses and strengths and recommend the author's method for the assessment of architecture practice on the basis of obtained results. Because of these aims, this work should is constructed as follows: point 2 provides a review of approaches to the assessment of architecture practice; point 3 presents the author's method for the assessment of architecture practice; point 4 summarizes current discussions and indicated directions of further research work.

2   Analysis of Existing Approaches to the Assessment of Architecture Practice

Nowadays, there exist many methods for the assessment of architecture practice maturity. Three sources for models for the assessment of architecture practice maturity are available at the moment, namely:

- consultancies (such as Forrester, Gartner),
- public administration (mainly in USA),
- standardization organizations (e.g. The Open Group).

Most of these approaches are based on the maturity assessment model[2] CMMI for Development[3]. Starting from 1991, this model has been adapted to needs of various disciplines such as systems engineering, integrated product and process development. Also, a CMM-based approach for Enterprise Architecture has been adapted – there appeared Extended Enterprise Architecture Maturity Model developed by Institute for Enterprise Architecture Developments [4] and NASCIO Enterprise Architecture Maturity Model developed by National Association of State Chief Information Officers [8], among others. Also, a model used by the US Department of Commerce, i.e. A-CMM – Architecture Capability Maturity Model – [9], is frequently applied.

---

2   M. Kohlegger, R. Maier and S. Thalmann put forward the following definition of a maturity model: „a model which represents quantitatively or qualitatively stages of increasing capabilities of the model element of performing particular tasks in order to assess them regarding the defined areas". See [6].

3   Capability Maturity Model Integration – a model developed by Software Engineering Institute (SEI) which serves to assess the software development process. CMMI defines five levels of maturity: initial, repeatable, defined, managed and optimized. For each level, except the first, so-called key process areas and corresponding goals are defined. In this approach, an organization attains a certain level of maturity if it realizes all the goals belonging to all the areas assigned to each level and the lower ones. See [**Błąd! Nie można odnaleźć źródła odwołania.**].

Maturity models, including those adapted to Enterprise Architecture's specific features, have three functions:

- descriptive function which helps determine real organization's maturity level,
- prescriptive function which describes a desired target state and determines a gap between the current state and the desired state,
- function defining a transition scope, which tells how many and which actions should be taken in order to pass from the current state to the desired state.

A basic idea of an architecture practice maturity model is to give a possibility of assessing it in selected areas at one of five available subsequent maturity levels which are characterized in table 1.

Table 1. Maturity levels in Enterprise Architecture management

Level name	Level indicators
Initial level – no structured architecture practice elements	Enterprise Architecture activities in the organization are performed ad hoc. Many activities are performed chaotically. Few elements of activities are defined before the kick-off of works, and a final effect of many of them is dependent on an individual effort of particular organization's units. No historical knowledge on previous Enterprise Architecture initiatives.
Repeatable level – repeatable practice elements	Basic Enterprise Architecture activities in the organization are defined at a high level of abstraction; they have been mastered in management terms. Historical knowledge is a basis for the development of a plan for further Enterprise Architecture works.
Defined level – defined practice	A coherent set of Enterprise Architecture definitions and standards. Works intended for the identification of threats and inconsistencies regarding the course of performed activities are done before negative effects of these threats and inconsistencies influence another tasks. Smaller dependence of performed activities on single units.
Managed level – fully managed practice	Enterprise Architecture activities in the organization are of stable nature, but areas which require improvements can be still found. Detailed measurements and control of particular architecture activities.
Optimized level – continuously improved practice	All the Enterprise Architecture issues are well documented, structured and managed. Architecture activities' feedback loop is put into practice (the organization's learning process is present). More requirements for particular architecture activities. The organization can afford pilot projects which check new Enterprise Architecture initiatives in practice, both in financial and organizational terms. Only after such verification an initiative may become valid in the organization.

Source: the author's own study and [9].

In an analyzed unit, the model A-CMM included in TOGAF is used by an expert team in collaboration with the organization's representation team. They assess a maturity level in nine identified areas. Then a graphic analysis is prepared, e.g. in the form of a radar chart. It can be a basis for the assessment how a maturity level of selected Enterprise Architecture management aspects has changed over time.

By applying architecture maturity models, one can presume one of two ways of representing them: Staged or Continuous. In the representation Staged, the organization can be classified at one of five maturity levels, where the first level means the lowest maturity level. In this approach, it is possible to calculate the factor γ which describes an Enterprise Architecture management maturity level:

$$\gamma = \frac{\sum\limits_{k=1}^{n} P_k}{n},$$

where: n – a number of identified areas in which a maturity level of selected Enterprise Architecture management aspects is assessed; P_k – a maturity level of the area k of Enterprise Architecture management.

In the representation Continuous, each Enterprise Architecture area is assessed separately. In this way, it is possible to align the order of improvements to the organization's specific features and prioritize areas which are considered crucial or which involve the greatest risk.

Apart from the open architecture maturity assessment methods (like A-CMM), there exist other approaches, for example developed by consultancies. Unfortunately, in order to use them we should buy an appropriate license. We must also remember that they can be used only by customers of these consultancies. Table 2 summarizes properties of existing architecture practice assessment approaches.

Table 2. Comparison of properties of existing architecture practice assessment approaches

	Detailed description	Versatility	Support of IT tools	Licensing
Approaches developed for public administration units	Description is available free of charge, it gives much information about a given approach	Very little, intended for public units in a given country	Average or little	Free of charge for all interested parties
Approaches developed by consultancies	Few details available free of charge	Big or very big	Average or big	Necessity of paying license fees for use
Approaches developed by standardization organizations	Description if available free of charge, but gives relatively little information about a given approach	Big or very big	Average or little	Free of charge for all interested parties

Source: the author's own study.

3   Author's Concept of an Enterprise Architecture Practice Assessment Technique

The author's experiences with the deployment of Enterprise Architecture concepts over years have allowed him to develop his own architecture practice maturity assessment approach called TOPAZ. In TOPAZ, 15 control blocks regarding particular architecture practice aspects (see figure 1) are together assessed.

250 control question were defined in total. However, they are not related with a concrete architecture framework (thus, they can be used with regard to architecture practice based on the Gartner framework, for example), but they refer to TOGAF to a certain degree. Each question has a certain origin (e.g. TOGAF, but also the author's own experience).

An undoubted advantage of the approach is that we can use many variants of it, that is can use the architecture practice assessment technique for a full concept of Enterprise Architecture, and for Enterprise IT Architecture as well. The effect is that we have a various number of questions in particular control blocks (41 questions less in total for Enterprise IT Architecture than for Enterprise Architecture).

Information obtained in answers to control questions is a basis for the assessment of maturity level for a given control block. This technique provides an aggregated and normalized index which presents total maturity of the organization for 15 control blocks (the index takes values from the range 0-1) and a one-column matrix consisting of 15 elements for particular control blocks.

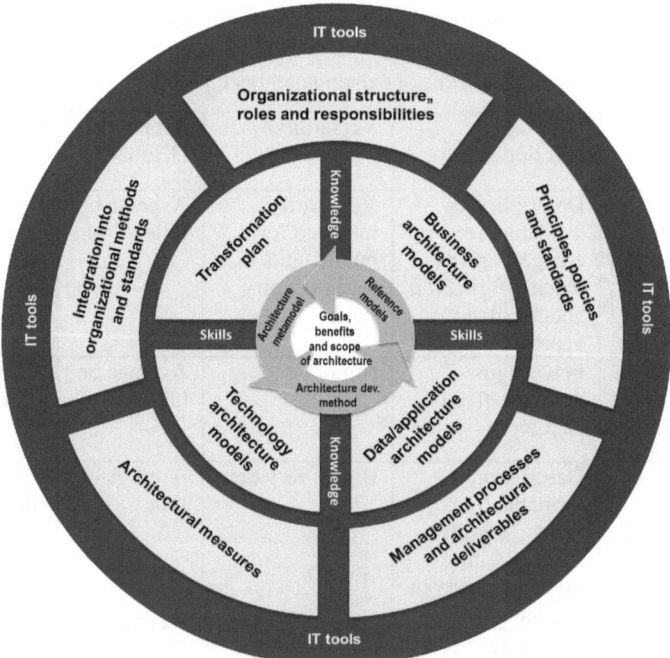

Fig. 1. Structure of control blocks in TOPAZ. Source: the author's own study.

Within the first control block the following aspects are assessed:
- Is a scope of the deployment of Enterprise Architecture defined, and how?
- Are goals of the deployment of Enterprise Architecture defined, and how?
- Are benefits of the deployment of Enterprise Architecture defined, and how?

Within the second control block the following aspects are assessed:
- Is an Enterprise Architecture development method defined, and how?

Within the third control block the following aspects are assessed:
- Is a content metamodel of architecture models defined, and how?

Within the fourth control block the following aspects are assessed:
- Is the use of reference models considered in the organization?
- How are reference models used during the creation of architecture models?
- Are architectural patterns used during the creation of architecture models, and how?

Within the fifth control block the following aspects are assessed:
- Are business architecture models defined (the architecture's as-is state, target state, transitional states, modeling scope), and how?

Within the sixth control block the following aspects are assessed:
- Are data and application architecture models defined (the architecture's as-is state, target state, transitional states, modeling scope), and how?

Within the seventh control block the following aspects are assessed:
- Are technical architecture models defined (the architecture's as-is state, target state, transitional states, modeling scope), and how?

Within the eighth control block the following aspects are assessed:
- Are transformation strategy and plan defined on the basis of architecture models, and how?

Within the ninth control block the following aspects are assessed:
- Are organizational structure, roles and responsibilities regarding architecture practice defined, and how?

Within the tenth control block the following aspects are assessed:
- Are architecture principles defined, and how?
- Are organizational policies defined, and how?
- Are architecture standards defined, and how?

Within the eleventh control block the following aspects are assessed:
- Are management processes defined, and how?
- How are management processes realized?
- Are management deliverables defined, and how?
- How are management deliverables used?

Within the twelfth control block the following aspects are assessed:
- Are architectural measures (KPI) defined, and how?
- Are the measures used systematically?

Within the thirteenth control block the following aspects are assessed:
- Is architecture practice integrated into organizational methods and standards – in particular areas (such as: strategic planning, software development, portfolio management, project management, security management) and how?

Within the fourteenth control block the following aspects are assessed:
- How is architectural knowledge communicated across the organization?
- How are architectural skills improved in the organization?

Within the fifteenth control block the following aspects are assessed:
- Are IT tools supporting the work of Enterprise Architects deployed in the organization (in particular modeling tools and architectural knowledge repository tools), and how?

This technique uses a simple tool (an MS Excel application) which allows to generate radar charts and to consult a dashboard (see figures 2 and 3, these figures present results of the deployment of a pilot method in a Polish company; because of signing an NDA, the author must not give more details apart from that the company employs almost 2000 people in Poland, the IT department personnel is about 60 people, and the organization has just started to deploy architectural approach).

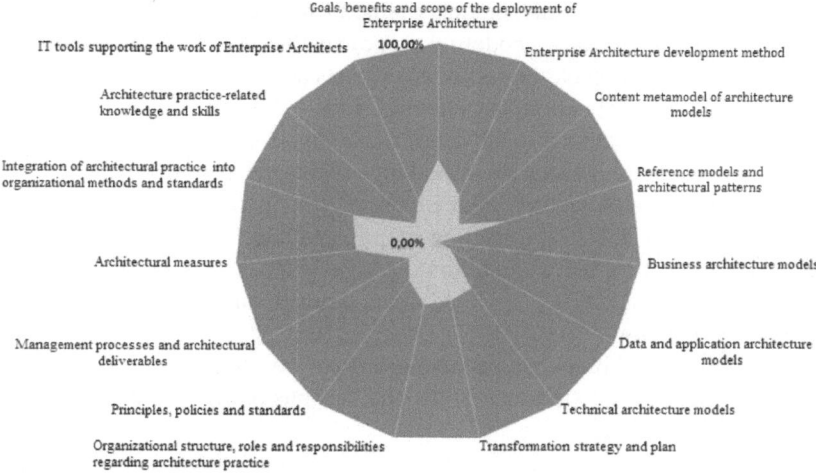

Fig. 2. Results of the use of TOPAZ in a Polish company. Source: the author's own study.

#	Area name		Index
1	Goals, benefits and scope of the deployment of Enterprise Architecture	●	42%
2	Enterprise Architecture development method	◐	26%
3	Content metamodel of architecture models	◐	14%
4	Reference models and architectural patterns	◯	36%
5	Business architecture models	●	0%
6	Data and application architecture models	◐	7%
7	Technical architecture models	◐	28%
8	Transformation strategy and plan	◐	30%
9	Organizational structure, roles and responsibilities regarding architecture practice	●	32%
10	Principles, policies and standards	◐	24%
11	Management processes and architectural deliverables	●	16%
12	Architectural measures	◯	41%
13	Integration of architectural approach into organizational methods and standards	●	44%
14	Architecture practice-related knowledge and skills	◐	15%
15	IT tools supporting the work of Enterprise Architects	◐	24%

Fig. 3. Dashboard for a Polish organization. Source: the author's own study.

As findings of the pilot deployment of TOPAZ show, graphic elements (such as a dashboard) used for the assessment of architecture practice allow to bring final results to decision-makers more easily. Hence, it is easier to convince them to take improvement actions.

4   Summary and Further Research

Raising architectural maturity in organizations involves certain costs. We must answer one question: is that rational from a business point of view? In 2011, SAP carried out research whose findings proved that organizations which represent a high level of architectural maturity invest more in innovative IT solutions and have definitely lower complexity of IT environments, what makes them more competitive on the market [5].

At the moment, there exist a number of architecture practice maturity assessment methods. In practice, it turns out that only general assumptions of the methods are available free of charge, they have no implementation details, or using them costs money (e.g. by paying license fees). The technique TOPAZ, the one proposed by the author, is distributed free of charge, with a detailed description (including a full list of control questions) and an IT tool supporting its use. Each organization may adapt it for its own needs in any scope. Initial verification of the method in a large Polish company proved its applicability. With the experience gained so far, the author is planning to extend the approach, he is planning to transform the existing architecture practice assessment technique into an architecture practice optimization technique (then assessment is only an initial stage of optimization).

References

1. van den Berg, M., van Steenbergen, M.: Building an Enterprise Architecture Practice. Springer, Netherlands (2006)
2. Commerce Maturity Model, Department of Commerce, Office of the Chief Information Officer (May 2003), http://ocio.os.doc.gov/ITPolicyandPrograms/ (last visit: April 04, 2013)
3. Enterprise Architecture Use across the Federal Government Can Be Improved, GAO, USA (February 2002)
4. Extended Enterprise Architecture Maturity Model, Institute for Enterprise Architecture Developments, ver. 2.0 (2004)
5. Gupta, S.: Building Effective Enterprise Architecture Developing a Business Case and Road Map for Mature, EA Practices to Maximize Value in IT Investments, SAP White Paper (2012)
6. CMMI Product Team, CMMI for Development, Version 1.3 (CMU/SEI-2010-TR-033). Software Engineering Insitute, Carnegie Mellon University, Pittsburgh, PA (2010)
7. Kohlegger, M., Maier, R., Thalmann, S.: Understanding Maturity Models Results of a Structured Content Analysis. In: Proceedings of I-KNOW 2009 and I-SEMANTICS 2009, Austria, September 2-4 (2009)
8. NASCIO Enterprise Architecture Maturity Model, National Association of State Chief Information Officers, ver. 1.3 (December 2003)
9. The Open Group Architecture Framework, The Open Group, version 9.1 (December 2011)

Development of an Enterprise Architecture Management Capability Catalog

Matthias Wißotzki[1], Hasan Koç[1], Tino Weichert[2], and Kurt Sandkuhl[1]

[1] University of Rostock, Institute for Business Informatics, Rostock, Germany
{matthias.wissotzki,hasan.koc,kurt.sandkuhl}@uni-rostock.de
[2] alfabet AG, Berlin, Germany
tino.weichert@alfabet.com

Abstract. Managing IT within the business context and not as a stand-alone function is becoming increasingly important for business success, the complex structures of enterprises have to be managed holistically. The integration of bordering processes, which address organizational changes, must be realized to guarantee an enterprise-wide management of the different architectures. This can be reached by implementing Enterprise Architecture Management (EAM). After introducing the challenges of EAM implementation that resulted from a number of investigations we performed, this paper introduces the state of our research proposing a general context for finding the capabilities in an enterprise - EAM capability catalog - and a preliminary draft of its structured development process, the EAM capability solution matrix, to overcome these challenges.

Keywords: Enterprise Architecture Management (EAM), Capability, Business-IT Alignment (BITA), Maturity Model.

1 Introduction

Enterprises are complex, highly integrated systems comprised of processes, organizational units, information and supporting technologies, with multifaceted interdependencies and interrelationships across their boundaries [1]. Organizations have to be more sensitive towards the interaction of business and IT-strategies as well as their consequences on processes, customers and application systems. Due to the complex relations between strategies, processes, applications, information infrastructures and roles, the enterprises are losing their focus in reacting to the rapid change demands as the decision makers no longer have a holistic perspective on the organization [2] and IT alone is not sufficient for business success without being managed in business context. The integration of bordering processes, which address organizational changes, must be realized to guarantee an enterprise-wide management of the different architectures [3]. Such an integrated view can be reached by implementing Enterprise Architecture Management (EAM).

Enterprises are competing in rapidly changing markets. To achieve their business objectives, organizations have to execute appropriate actions, which later on should be turned into so-called "enterprise initiatives" (see Figure 1). For the actions to be taken in

A. Kobyliński and A. Sobczak (Eds.): BIR 2013, LNBIP 158, pp. 112–126, 2013.

different perspectives, there is a need for an integrated management approach, which could be achieved by implementing EAM, since these initiatives cover various dimensions like strategy, projects, business, technology or their combinations. Nevertheless the successful adoption of EAM is accompanied by challenges that an enterprise has to face and to overcome. In order to be able to implement the operationalized initiatives efficiently and achieve a specific outcome the enterprises require specific combinations of know-how in terms of organizational knowledge, procedures and resources –the so-called "capabilities". This paper first introduces the EAM capability catalog, a blueprint to find such capabilities in an EAM context and to measure their potential to support the initiatives. Then it proposes a systematic capability design process, the EAM capability solution matrix that is based on a meta-model, the EAM capability constructor, and aims to overcome the challenges on EAM implementation.

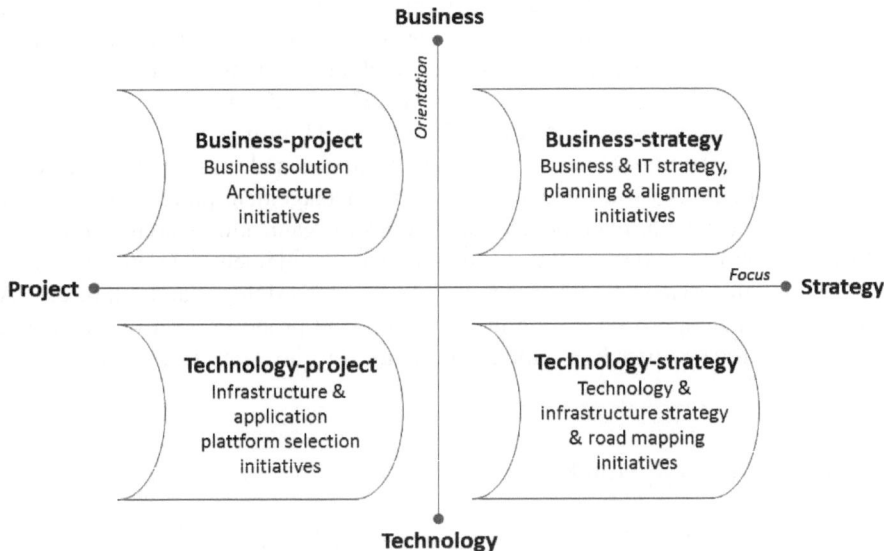

Fig. 1. Dimensions of Enterprise Initiatives based on [34]

After presenting the background on Enterprise Architecture (EA) and EAM, chapter 3 provides the research approach of this paper and lists the relevant studies, chapter 4 discusses the reasons for an EAM implementation and identifies the EAM challenges thereby. Chapter 5 introduces EAM capability catalog and the solution matrix, an approach that comprises of the architecture objects and management functions for EAM as well as the EAM capability constructor. Finally chapter 6 draws a conclusion of the work and gives an outlook.

2   Enterprise Architecture and Its Management

Architecture is defined as a fundamental organization of a system embodied in its components, their relationships to each other, and to the environment, and the principle guiding the organization's design and evolution [4]. Enterprise Architecture (EA) is the formal declaration of the basic structures of an organization, its components and relations, as well as the processes used for development [3]. Enterprise architecture means the comprehensive understanding and documenting of an organizational structure with all dependencies of artifacts and information objects necessary for business performance in an appropriate EA model.

The EA models are evolving from pure IT architecture models into control instruments that can be used by the management as a tool for their business decisions that allows an integrated view on enterprise [24]. In this context, EAM provides a powerful approach for a systematical development of the organization in accordance with its strategic vision [2], yet its value depends on the organizational capabilities to perform EAM effectively. EAM consists of three major functions such as transforming, monitoring and planning. Transforming is the alignment of an enterprise architecture towards the target state of the respective enterprise architecture domains. Monitoring is the controlling that needs to be applied to ensure the intended progress and planning is the analysis of the current-state enterprise architecture that provides on-going information for specific questions that facilitate decision-making.

The discussion and usage of EAM is focused on IT in practice, although there is knowledge about the importance of processes, strategies and organizational aspects as well [3]. EAM adopts various perspectives. As a management philosophy, it is a holistic way to understand, plan, develop and control organization´s architecture. EAM enables and improves existing strategic planning and implementation processes and in this way is an organizational function. As a methodology and culture, EAM represents an open approach among the managers and proposes a set of management practices in order to reach a global optimum for the firm free of egoism and opportunism [2].

3   Research Approach

Developing an EAM capability catalog has to be based on a solid grounding regarding existing scholarly work, established practices in industry and demands of the future target groups. In order to establish this grounding, we performed a number of investigations during the year summarized in Table 1. [24] conducts an empirical survey underlines the adaptability by researching the implementation of EAM in SME in practice. [23] executes a survey with TOGAF experienced users was performed to get a better understanding of the most important parts of the framework and the possibility of adapting TOGAF to the requirements of SME. [22] performs a systematic literature review of the papers presented at CAISE, EMMSAD, ICIS, and INCOM over the last seven years on the enterprise model reuse. [3] presents an overview of existing approaches of (EAM). [32] provides a systematic literature review in the field of IT Operation Management and distinguishes IT Operation Management approaches. [31] gives a comprehensive overview about relationship management, reveals limitations and analyzes new research phenomena like multi-sourcing. [28] proposes an approach to maturity model development that aims to eliminate the drawbacks of maturity models and fulfills the quality requirements in developing a maturity model. Finally, [18] introduces an approach to augment the EKD (Enterprise Knowledge Development) framework with additional features, like new visualization possibilities, and presents complexity reduction methods.

Table 1. List of Research Activities

#	Publication Name	Authors	Status	Research Scope	Mainly Conceptual	Empirical & Conceptual Quant.	Empirical & Conceptual Quali.	Mainly Empirical Quant.	Mainly Empirical Quali.
1	Adoption of Enterprise Architecture Management in Small and Medium Enterprises - A Comparison of Theory and Practice [24]	Wißotzki, Sonnenberger	submitted PoEM 2013	SLR on EAM (in SME Context) / Survey on EAM in SME		X			
2	TOGAF Adoption for Small and Medium Enterprises [23]	Alm, Wißotzki	accepted BITA@BIS 2013	Survey on TOGAF Implementation in SME				X	
3	EAM in the Utility Sector	Wißotzki, Starke	in progress paper	Survey on EAM (in the context of utility sector)				X	
4	EAM Performance Measurement in Practice	Wißotzki, Freiberg	in progress paper	Survey on EAM (in the context of performance measurement)				X	
5	State of research in reuse of enterprise models [22]	Wissotzki, Dunkel, Sandkuhl	published paper 2012	SLR on reuse of models	X				
6	Enterprise Architecture Management – State of Research Analysis and a Comparison of Selected Approaches [3]	Wißotzki, Sonnenberger	published paper 2012	SLR on EAM approaches	X				
7	State of Research in IT Operation Management - A Systematic Literature Review of ICIS, EDOC and BISE [32]	Wißotzki, Piontek, Hansen	submitted PoEM 2013	SLR on IT Operation Management	X				
8	Investigation of IT Sourcing, Relationship Management and Contractual Governance Approaches: State of the Art Literature Review [31]	Wißotzki, Timm, Wiebrig	submitted PoEM 2013	SLR on IT Sourcing, Supplier & Contract Management	X				
9	A Project Driven Approach for Enhanced Maturity Model Development for EAM Capability Evaluation [28]	Wißotzki, Koç	accepted EDOC 2013	Conceptual Framework for Maturity Model Development			X		
10	EA Visualization Technics for Complexity Reduction[18]	Wißotzki, Christiner	published book 2012	Complexity Reduction in Enterprise Modeling and in EA	X				

An elementary work in application of methods in Wirtschaftsinformatik[1] has been done by [6], [8] and [7]. Two main paradigms are identified in WI research, which cannot be thought of being dichotomous. The first paradigm is formed by behavioral-science research, which was created in psychology of science and thereby has its roots in natural sciences. In the context of WI, behavioristic research seeks to develop and justify theories (i.e., principles and laws) that explain or predict organizational and human phenomena surrounding the analysis, design, implementation, management, and use of information systems. Behavioral science starts with a hypothesis, then researches collect data, and either prove or disprove the hypothesis. Eventually a theory develops [9]. The second paradigm is design-science research, which is

---

[1] Wirtschaftsinformatik (WI) – the German term for (business) information systems - is a multi-pluralistic discipline between Economics and Computer Science, which emerged in the sixties of the last century in German speaking countries [5] and investigates subjects in information systems and foundational research methods [5, 7].

construction-oriented and in which a designer answers questions relevant to human problems via the creation of innovative artifacts, thereby contributing new knowledge to the body of scientific evidence. Unlike the natural sciences, the design science research is fundamentally a problem-solving paradigm whose end goal is to produce an artifact which must be built and then evaluated [10]. Simply put, behavioristic research resembles the truth and design-science research resembles utility. These research paradigms may be both conducted adopting quantitative and qualitative research methods.

A finer distinction in this paper has been be-tween empirical and conceptual research. Empirical research utilizes qualitative (expert interviews, case studies) and quantitative studies (surveys) whereas the conceptual research (design work, systematic literature analysis) is an artifact of the designer´s creative efforts that could however employ the empirical techniques to evaluate the quality and effectiveness of artifacts [9, 11]. The research for the EAM capability solution matrix development utilizes both paradigms to some extent and mostly uses the conceptual methods. As Table 1 shows, 5 of 10 publications regarding our research in the enterprise architectures topic carry out systematic literature reviews (SLR), which evaluates the collected data numerically and interprets the results in accordance with the research questions of the scope. In line with [11], we consider the systematic literature reviews as a conceptual research approach. Moreover, four out of the ten publications also conduct surveys as a method of data collection. Two publications adopt both empirical and conceptual research methods and one proposes a theoretical framework for the maturity model development. As the time of writing, two papers are accepted, three papers have already been submitted and alongside with a book, two papers have been published. In addition to that, two papers are in progress of writing and shall be submitted at the earliest time. Hence the research for the development of EAM capability catalog is a multi-methodological procedure [12].

4   Findings and Interpretations

In this chapter, the findings of our research activities are reflected and the reasons for implementing EAM as well as its challenges are identified and discussed. The organizations face an ever-increasing complexity accompanied by accelerated change due to the following reasons:

- Mergers & acquisitions require consolidation and elimination of redundancies to form a new appropriate enterprise architecture which supports the whole business with best performance at best cost [23, 24].
- Sourcing strategies like outsourcing, insourcing, offshoring or cloud computing create a distributed landscape with completely new requirements for the governance processes to manage this successfully [31].
- Internalization & Globalization requires a rapid replication of existing best practice blueprints who to execute certain parts of the business in a new organizational unit [23].
- Regulations and fast changing or new business models might require more agile EA to provide complete new capabilities, e.g. car manufacturers who become mobility providers or telecommunication infrastructure enterprises who become full service provides [29].

- Budget restrictions especially in the SME context limit the resources that can be used. [3, 24]
- External regulations like Dodd-Frank or SOX limit the flexibility while putting an extra workload [31, 33].
- High complexity in enterprise architectures might even restrict highly skilled and competent professionals [2, 33].

4.1 Reasons for EAM Implementation

The complexity of the interactions between processes and information systems caused by technological, economic, social and/ or industrial changes must be documented on all business levels [13]. The decision makers might take wrong decisions since they lose the overall view of such complex structures. Hence, there are a variety of reasons for implementing EAM, such as summarized by Weinberger [14]:

- EAM supports delivery of the business strategy by aligning IT transformation to business needs
- Effective management and exploitation of information is key to business success and competitive advantage
- EAM manages stakeholder concerns that need to be addressed by IT systems
- EAM manages complexity and changes to business and IT
- EAM enables the right balance between IT efficiency and business innovation
- EAM provides an enhanced transparency and makes it possible to manage risks better
- EAM optimizes the (fragmented) legacy processes (manual and automated) to an integrated environment

Still, the EAM implementation itself is perceived to be a complex and cost-intensive process which requires a continuous attention and know-how [3, 23, 24].

4.2 EAM Challenges

EAM challenges are the hurdles that an enterprise has to overcome to establish long-turn success when implementing enterprise initiatives or the change activities resulting from adjustments in business models, which affect the respective initiatives. On the basis of our research activities, we were able to identify a total of 8 EAM challenges that enterprises have to pay attention to, which are listed as follows:

Implement EAM as All Do Some Approach

EAM is not just a task for enterprise architects who only communicate with the development team without taking the general view of fundamental structures and their interplay into consideration due to lack of transparency and understanding, but also for the whole enterprise. Thus EAM has moved from being an ivory tower expert task to a cross-functional line activity that requires the participation of different departments. Enterprises need to be convinced that the relevant community is larger than assumed and convincing the employees can be difficult if the EA team is not prepared for more collaboration with different departments. The models have to be kept alive by introducing processes that update the models so one does not start modeling from scratch, but rather concentrates on the changes and benefits from the reuse of models [22]. Instead managing a certain domain, like the IT-focused architectures did in the past, the connection between different architecture layers has to be established in response to the dynamic environment, forcing to adapt and internal change of enterprises as well as understanding the complex structures and enterprise-wide processes [3, 24]. After the completion of two research papers, EAM in the Utility Sector and EAM Performance Measurement in Practice (nr. 3 and nr.4 papers in Table 1), it is expected to obtain actual information on this topic.

Organizations Are Not Prepared to Establish an All-Do-Some EAM

EA is the idea of modeling the elements, roles, responsibilities and systems, as part of the enterprise structure, and their relations. [15, 16]. In an enterprise this task is structured through corresponding roles and clearly defined roles are of vital importance when implementing EAM. In this context, the essential roles are only to some extent available in enterprises, e.g. Business Demand Manager, Domain Architect or Architecture Approval Board, which are required due to the increased change management activities and the above-described cross functional roles of EAM [3, 24].

In the SME context, there are other EAM challenges in terms of roles and responsibilities. Small enterprises have few employees with the necessary technological skills. The loss of expert knowledge is a high risk for smaller enterprises. Also expenses to introduce methods, tools, customizations and trainings might not be justifiable in SME [24]. After the completion of the research, EAM in the Utility Sector (nr. 3 in Table 1), we expect to find ongoing information on this topic.

EAM Awareness Insufficient

As having emerged from a technical perspective (Information Systems Engineering), EAM did not fully realize the importance of the social factors like human, organizational behavior and communication [2]. Moreover, there is always a behavioral resistance against a new methodology use, as the individuals might not share the goals of the organization in which they work [25].

alfabet[2] survey[3] shows that the delivery of a tangible EAM value proposition is one of the biggest challenges for companies. Hence, EAM value proposition needs to be communicated to the right stakeholders in the right way and its implementation has

---

[2]   University of Rostock and alfabet AG have launched a joint research project in May 2012. Within the framework of this project, a capability model is being developed and examined, which enables a simple performance assessment of EAM Capabilities that are necessary for an optimal alignment of business development with the enterprise architecture (EA) and suggests methods for their further development. According to Gartner and Forrester, the alfabet AG, known as one of the most innovative software houses, is leading internationally in the planning of Enterprise Architectures.

[3]   Customer satisfaction survey of alfabet AG (CSAT) 2012.

to be perceived to be beneficial. Success of any new process or topic comes in with the available benefits and the realization thereof.

Also in the SME perspective the value proposition and implementation has to be supported by a matching communication policy since there are doubts about cost - benefit ratio and the needed resources, which might produce resistance [3].

Lack of Ability to Express Information Demands

Without managing the overall context it is difficult for enterprises to satisfy their customers and to extend their market shares [3]. Organizations are often unable to express their information need, which makes it difficult if not impossible to design a fit-to-purpose solution.

For every enterprise a specific EAM has to be developed. The expense and complexity of introducing EAM as well as the first documentation is a central problem for a variety of reasons (e.g. selection, maintenance and quality of information) [24, 33]. As stated above and in [17], EAM "is such a complex topic that easy and general solutions are unlikely to appear". Still 9 out of 10 people responsible for an EAM rollout counter the questions when asking for the information needs of customers with "what is the best practice for this?". In most cases, the best practices help to some extent but company specific information is necessary to customize the best practices to the enterprise correctly. Additionally enterprises want to have fully developed solutions although they are not able to implement the required processes and use the provided tools. For example, an organization has requested the full-blown functionality of an EAM-Tool due to anxiety to miss a feature and the laziness not to analyze its information needs. Later it turned out that most of the occasional users were not able to run the process and use the tool because they were not adapted to the specific information needs.

Complex Tasks Require Complex Approaches

Even if you have the smartest approach, you need to get people to execute it in an organization and every time you work with people you have to deal with emotions, which can be quite unpredictable sometimes. Thus, people in the organization have to be motivated to learn new ways of working/ thinking and eventually break with their existing working habits.

Handling of complex tasks requires sometimes complex approaches which are difficult to teach and often difficult to depict graphically. Increasing complexity of enterprise models is a continuing trend, inevitably caused by the efforts to create ever better products. Visualizations of dependencies need to be produced from supporting tools like planningIT. Nevertheless, the results might be unusable if an incorrect visualization technique is used [18].

Common Language/ glossary Inside IT and between Business and IT

Since the roles and responsibilities in an organization have to be defined clearly, a consensus on a common terminology has to be achieved (for instance answering the questions like "what is an application?", "what is a service?" and "how does it relate to an application?") for an efficient EAM.

One would certainly discuss how rooms, windows or balconies should be constructed when contracting an architect to design the house [4]. Likewise a city planner would have to know the interplay between complex objects like streets, land use or waste disposal and communicate with the customer using the domain vocabulary [2]. Both examples prove the necessity of a framework to achieve a shared understanding.

A shared conceptualization as such can be achieved by deploying knowledge modeling methods, for example as developing a domain specific ontology [19] and ranking it under the upper ontologies. Benefits of such ontology would not only be the accomplishment of a common vocabulary in an organization but also the detection of inconsistencies due to the reasoning mechanism and assertion of new knowledge that can be shared in the enterprise.

Data Quality and Consolidation

Data quality issues seem to be one of the biggest obstacles on the way for EAM as the continuously changing business requirements caused by new technology, legal regulations or increased demands on security and compliance are not being integrated well to the existing infrastructures, thus leading to heterogeneity and complexity in the entire application structure which results in a technological diversity and a great number of interfaces [20]. Data quality in this context defines the degree of excellence presented by the data in relation to the portrayal of the actual scenario [21]. There are different dimensions to data quality like completeness, reliability, integrity and consistency. Due to the low data quality, the stakeholders and managers cannot be supplied with the right information at the right time. Moreover, enterprises are confronted with the challenges of data consolidation due to business transformations or technological changes [33].

Compliance Requirements

Increasing compliance requirements and new regulations are challenging especially for enterprises from banking, insurance, utilities and telecommunication sector. Facilitating the transparency in the organization is a prerequisite for an efficient compliance management. For an efficient and agile implementation of the compliance requirements the architectural dependencies have to be revealed. Furthermore, due to its focus on different layers and structural dependencies between information objects as well as its complexity, the architectural compliance check cannot be manually performed; thus tool support is an absolute necessity [27].

5   EAM Capability Solution Matrix and Constructor

The main objective of the research is development of a holistic approach that is utilized as a management function and overcomes the challenges described in the previous chapter. For this purpose an elementary approach is proposed that identifies the required EAM capabilities for an efficient operationalization of enterprise initiatives. These capabilities are derived systematically through structured process and then gathered in an enterprise specific repository. This chapter provides the general context of the EAM capability catalog and its integration to the overall process (see Figure 2), which is an ongoing research project with our project partner alfabet AG [28].

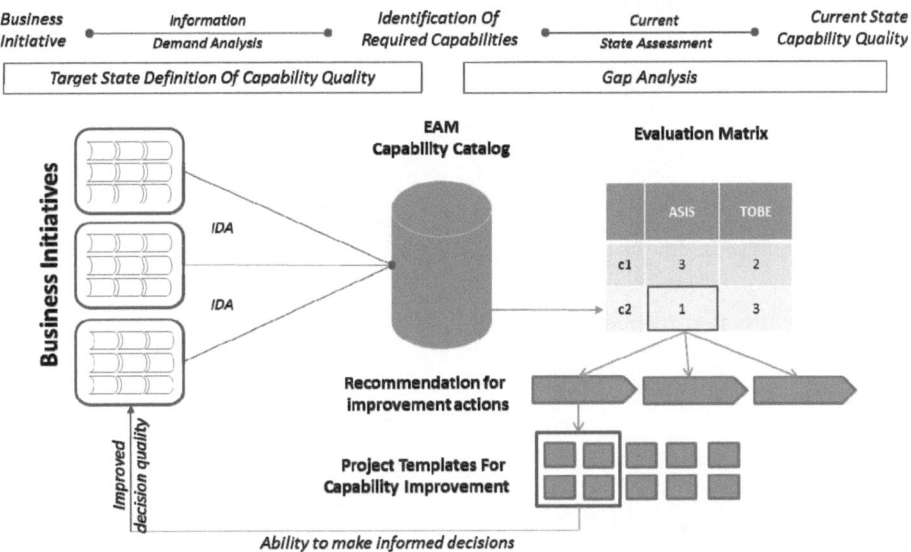

Fig. 2. Enterprise Initiatives and EAM Capability Catalog

A capability is defined as the organization's capacity to successfully perform a unique business activity to create a specific outcome [26] and the ability to continuously deliver a certain business value in dynamically changing business environments [36]. Capabilities are abstracted from the organizational model to capture business interests [35]. Enterprises are equipped with various capabilities that are specific to their organizations. An EAM capability in this context describes the specific combination of know-how in terms of organizational knowledge, procedures and resources able to externalize this knowledge in a specific process with appropriate resources to achieve a specific outcome for a defined enterprise initiative.

Initiatives are understood as initial impulses for actions to be taken about certain topics. Enterprise initiatives describe the operationalization of enterprise objectives in the EAM context and have various dimensions like project, strategy, business or technology. These can be derived from enterprise goals or business models and are implemented via EAM projects. To identify the relevant capabilities that help to implement an initiative, an adapted version of the information demand analysis method is executed [30]. The analysis supports the determination of the target state (to-be) maturity of the corresponding EAM capabilities. On this basis, the required capabilities are mapped into an EAM capability catalog which is a repository of present enterprise capabilities. The EAM capability catalog is enriched by the set of capabilities that are derived from the EAM capability solution matrix (see Figure 3) and EAM capability constructor (see Figure 4), which serves as a meta-model. Following this, if the required capability is already in the catalog, then a gap analysis is conducted in order to assess the current (as-is) state of the capability. If there is a gap between the target and current state, then the recommendations for improvement action are followed, which in turn improve the decision quality on the corresponding capabilities. The whole process is illustrated in Figure 2.

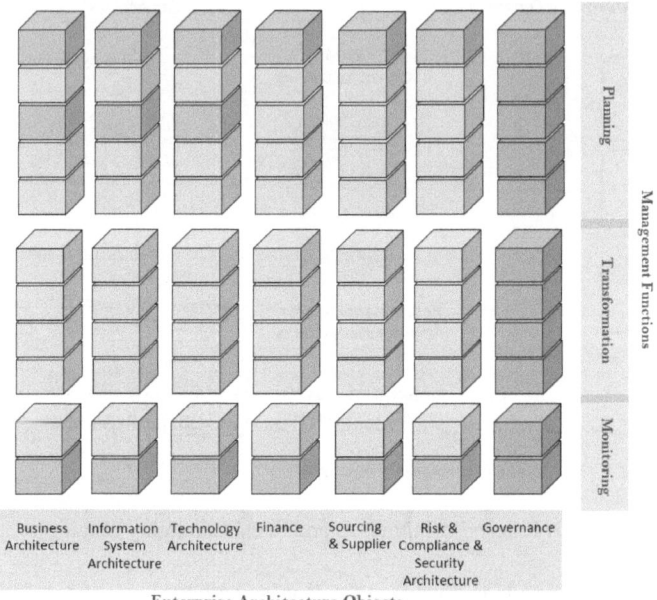

Fig. 3. EAM Capability Solution Matrix

The EAM capabilities that support enterprise initiatives are derived from the EAM capability solution matrix, which has two dimensions as illustrated in Figure 3. The management function dimension involves planning, transforming and monitoring functions, which are introduced in chapter 2. The enterprise architecture objects dimension comprises architecture objects from architecture layers like Business Architecture, Technology Architecture or Finance. By doing this, the solution matrix delivers a tool to have a complete understanding of capabilities, i.e. how they relate to different architecture objects, management functions and other capabilities.

But what if the enterprise does not have the required capability to perform the initiatives and the capability is not yet an element of the catalog? Considering the need to lower costs, to improve quality and to increase efficiency, reusability has been an important subject in information systems research and computer science [22] and competitive advantage can be achieved if the capabilities are re-used [2]. For an enhanced traceability and reusability, we propose the development of such solution matrix via a meta-model (Figure 4).

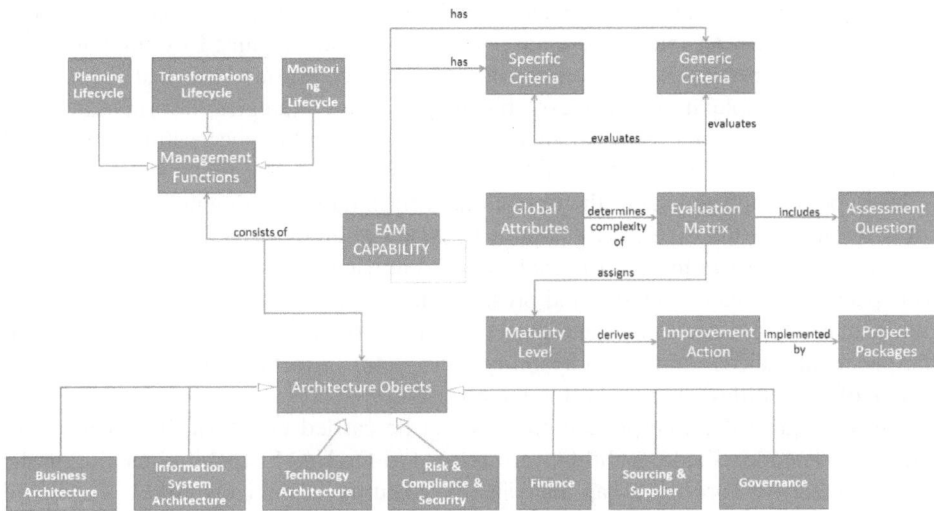

Fig. 4. EAM Capability Constructor

An EAM Capability is performed on management functions and/ or architecture objects. The capabilities can have i) information dependencies (information used to fulfill one capability that is produced by another), ii) support relationships (resources for use in other capabilities) and iii) close functional relationships (representing different aspects of the same area). EAM Capabilities have specific and generic criteria which are evaluated by a matrix including assessment questions. The complexity of an evaluation matrix is determined by the global attributes such as size of the enterprise, number of provided products/ services or processes. The results of the matrix help to assign a maturity level to the capability. The respective improvement actions derived from the maturity level are then implemented by project packages. As an example the capability "plan application landscape" delivers a value on the management function "planning lifecycle" and on the "information system architecture" object. The capability has specific criteria like used application versions or defined responsibilities and dependencies as well as generic criteria (available resources, skill level, etc.). Those criteria are subject to the evaluation matrix and their maturity level are to be determined. If an improvement is necessary, the actions should be executed in order to reach higher levels of maturity. These actions are to be implemented via project packages. If the capability has to be an element of the catalog, then, like all other capabilities, it is developed using the EAM capability constructor and then transferred to the solution matrix. Both the EAM capability solution matrix and the EAM capability constructor are still under development. These are depicted in Figure 3 and Figure 4 respectively.

6   Conclusion and Outlook

Enterprises reach their goals by applying their capabilities to various processes. In order to do so, organizations have to carry appropriate actions into execution, which later on should be turned into so-called "initiatives". For these actions to be taken there is a need for an integrated approach, which could be gained by implementing EAM. This is a prerequisite for an enhanced holistic enterprise view that reduces the management complexity of business objects, processes, strategies, information infrastructure and the relations between them. Nevertheless the successful adoption of EAM is accompanied by challenges that an enterprise has to face and to overcome. In order to be able to implement the operationalized initiatives efficiently and achieve a specific outcome the enterprises require EAM capabilities, which are the combinations of know-how in terms of organizational knowledge, procedures and resources. This paper proposes a blueprint and presents an overall context to find such capabilities in an enterprise and to measure their potential to support the initiatives. Moreover, the paper introduces the EAM capability constructor, a meta-model for a structured design of capabilities which is still in the progress.

On these grounds, enterprise initiatives can be carried out if via information demand analysis identified capabilities are present in the EAM capability catalog in the desired maturity. Through a gap analysis, the maturity of the capabilities is assessed and recommendations for improvement actions are proposed when necessary. If the required capabilities have not been introduced to the enterprise´s repertoire yet, then it can be developed via the EAM capability constructor.

Further purpose of the research is the elaboration of the EAM capability solution matrix and composition of the EAM capabilities via the meta-model to provide insights to the actual contents and to concretize, what the capabilities are capturing. Moreover the use of these approaches in practice or possible application scenarios should be evaluated. Following that, the capabilities have to be transferred into a flexible, feature-related measurement system, in a *maturity model*, which contains both the methodology for the determination and concepts for the further development of the relevant EAM capabilities of an enterprise [28] and is called Enterprise Architecture Management Capability Navigator.

References

1. Razavi, M., Shams Aliee, F., Badie, K.: An AHP-based approach toward enterprise architecture analysis based on enterprise architecture quality attributes. Knowl. Inf. Syst. 28(2), 449–472 (2011)
2. Ahlemann, F.: Strategic enterprise architecture management: challenges, best practices, and future developments. Springer, Berlin (2012)
3. Wißotzki, M., Sonnenberger, A.: Enterprise architecture management - state of research analysis & a comparison of selected approaches. In: Short Paper Proceedings of the 5th IFIP WG 8.1 Working Conference on the Practice of Enterprise Modeling, Rostock, Germany, November 7-8. CEUR-WS.org (2012)
4. Lankhorst, M.: Enterprise architecture at work: modelling, communication, and analysis, 2nd edn. Springer, Dordrecht (2009)
5. Frank, U.: Towards a pluralistic conception of research methods in information. Institut für Informatik und Wirtschaftsinformatik (ICB), Universität Duisburg-Essen, Essen (2006)

6. Wilde, T., Hess, T.: Forschungsmethoden der Wirtschaftsinformatik. Wirtschaftsinformatik 49(4), 280–287 (2007), http://dblp.uni-trier.de/db/journals/wi/wi49.html#WildeH07

7. Hess, T., Wilde, T.: Potenzial experimenteller Forschung in der Wirtschaftsinformatik: Ein Beitrag zur methodischen Fundierung. In: Quo vadis Wirtschaftsinformatik?, pp. 57–82. Gabler, Wiesbaden (2008)

8. Wilde, T., Hess, T.: Methodenspektrum der Wirtschaftsinformatik: Überblick und Portfoliobildung (2006), http://www.bibsonomy.org/api/users/taberski/posts/cb8294dc833d501e9a05b91fc6e3c47b

9. Hevner, A.R., March, S.T., Park, J., Ram, S.: Design science in information systems research. Management Information Systems Quarterly 28(1), 75–106 (2004), http://www.hec.unil.ch/yp/HCI/articles/hevner04.pdf

10. Hevner, A.R., Chatterjee, S.: Design research in information systems: theory and practice. Springer, New York (2010)

11. Niehaves, B., Pöppelbuß, J., Simons, A.: Maturity models in IS research

12. Becker, J., Knackstedt, R., Pöppelbuß, J.: Developing maturity models for IT management. Bus. Inf. Syst. Eng. 1(3), 213–222 (2009)

13. Dietzsch, A.: Architekturmanagement — Rahmen und Realisierung der Unternehmensarchitektur der Mobiliar. In: Schelp, J., Winter, R. (eds.) Business Engineering, Integrations-Management, pp. 231–266. Springer, Heidelberg (2006)

14. Weinberger, D.: ... und am Anfang steht die Geschäftsanforderung, oder?, http://www.sigsdatacom.de/fileadmin/user_upload/zeitschriften/os/2010/EAM/weinberger_OS_EAM_10.pdf

15. Aier, S., Riege, C., Winter, R.: Unternehmensarchitektur – Literaturüberblick und Stand der Praxis. Wirtschaftsinformatik 4(50), 292–304 (2008), http://www.alexandria.unisg.ch/publications/67528

16. Alaeddini, M., Salekfard, S.: Investigating the role of an enterprise architecture project in the business-IT alignment in Iran. Inf. Syst. Front. 15(1), 67–88 (2013)

17. Hagen, C., Schwinn, A.: Measured integration — Metriken für die Integrationsarchitektur. In: Schelp, J., Winter, R. (eds.) Business Engineering, Integrations-Management, pp. 267–292. Springer, Heidelberg (2006)

18. Wißotzki, M., Christiner, F.: Enterprise architecture visualization: techniques for complexity reduction, 1st edn. AV Akademikerverlag (2012)

19. Czarnecki, A., Orłowski, C.: IT business standards as an ontology domain. In: Jędrzejowicz, P., Nguyen, N.T., Hoang, K. (eds.) ICCCI 2011, Part I. LNCS, vol. 6922, pp. 582–591. Springer, Heidelberg (2011)

20. Hanschke, I.: Enterprise architecture management - einfach und effektiv: ein praktischer Leitfaden für die Einführung von EAM. Hanser, München (2012)

21. Roebuck, K.: Data quality: high-impact strategies - what you need to know: definitions, adoptions, impact, benefits, maturity, vendors. Emereo Pty Limited (2011)

22. Wißotzki, M., Sandkuhl, K., Dunkel, A.K., Christina, L.V.: State of research in reuse of enterprise models: Systematic literature analysis of CAISE, EMMSAD, ICIS and INCOM. In: Proc. IADIS International Conf. on Information Systems, pp. 82–90 (2012)

23. Alm, R., Wißotzki, M.: TOGAF adaption for small and medium enterprises (unpublished)

24. Wißotzki, M., Sonnenberger, A.: Adoption of enterprise architecture management in small and medium enterprises – a comparison of theory and practice (unpublished)

25. Mohan, K., Ahlemann, F.: What methodology attributes are critical for potential users? Understanding the effect of human needs. In: Advanced information systems engineering: Proceedings of the 23rd International Conference on Advanced Information Systems Engineering, pp. 314–328. Springer, Heidelberg (2011)
26. Scott, J., Cullen, A., An, M.: Business capabilities provide the rosetta stone for business-IT alignment: capability maps are a foundation for business architecture. Technical Report 2009 (2009)
27. Deiters, C., Dohrmann, P., Herold, S., Rausch, A.: Rule-based architectural compliance checks for enterprise architecture management. In: Proceedings of the 13th IEEE International Conference on Enterprise Distributed Object Computing: EDOC 2009, Auckland, New Zealand, September 1-4, pp. 158–167. IEEE Press, Piscataway (2009)
28. Wißotzki, M., Koç, H.: A project driven approach for enhanced maturity model development for EAM capability evaluation (unpublished)
29. Sandkuhl, K., Borchardt, U., Lantow, B., Stamer, D., Wißotzki, M.: Towards adaptive business models for intelligent information logistics in transportation. In: Satellite Workshops & Doctoral Consortium, pp. 43–59 (2012)
30. Lundqvist, M., Sandkuhl, K., Seigerroth, U.: Modelling information demand in an enterprise context. International Journal of Information System Modeling and Design 2(3), 75–95 (2011)
31. Wißotzki, M., Timm, F., Wiebring, J.: Investigation of IT sourcing, relationship management and contractual governance approaches: literature review (unpublished)
32. Wißotzki, M., Piontek, T., Hansen, M.: State of research in IT operation management - a systematic literature review of ICIS, EDOC and BISE (unpublished)
33. Berneaud, M., Buckl, S., Fuentes, A., Matthes, F., Monahov, I., Nowobilska, A., Roth, S., Schweda, C.M., Weber, U., Zeiner, M.: Trends for enterprise architecture management and tools. Technical Report 2012 (2012)
34. DeGennaro, T., Cullen, A., Peyret, H., Cahill, M.: The forrester wave™: EA management suites, Q2 2013: the 10 providers that matter most and how they stack up. Technical Report 2013 (2013)
35. Keller, W.: IT-Unternehmensarchitektur: von der Geschäftsstrategie zur optimalen IT-Unterstützung, 2nd edn. dpunkt.verlag, Heidelberg (2012)
36. Stirna, J., Grabis, J., Henkel, M., Zdravkovic, J.: Capability driven development – An approach to support evolving organizations. In: Sandkuhl, K., Seigerroth, U., Stirna, J. (eds.) PoEM 2012. LNBIP, vol. 134, pp. 117–131. Springer, Heidelberg (2012)

Developing Open Source ERP Systems for SMEs: Is That Still of Interest?

Björn Johansson

Department of Informatics, School of Economics and Management,
Lund University,
Ole Römers väg 6 SE-223 63 Lund, Sweden
bjorn.johansson@ics.lu.se

Abstract. There is an increasing interest in enterprise resource planning (ERPs) systems for small and medium sized enterprises (SMEs). This interest has created new delivery models of ERPs and one is the open source ERP. The question addressed in this paper is: What role has development of open source ERPs played in the diffusion of ERPs among SMEs? It can be stated that open source have gained momentum in organizations today, however, it is not that clear what role open source plays when it comes to specific business applications such as a ERPs. In order to explore this, a combination of literature reviews and an investigation of a distribution channel of open source projects were conducted. Based on this it is discussed if open source ERP systems still are of interest among SMEs. This is then compared with challenges, which a proprietary ERP vendor suggests exist in ERP development when they target the SME market. It can be concluded that open source ERP development has a great deal to offer, but the main conclusion is that the difference is mainly on the development side, which means that it can be suggested that for the actual diffusion of ERPs among SMEs, it does not matter whether the ERP is open source or proprietary, however for SMEs open source ERPs have probably made that new "business models" enhancing the possibility for SMEs to access ERPs have seen the light.

Keywords: Open source ERP, SourceForge, Diffusion, SMEs, ERP downloads.

1   Introduction

Diffusion of advanced integrated standardized software packages such as enterprise resource planning systems (ERPs) among small and medium-sized enterprises (SMEs) are of high interest. One reason for this could for example be found in the fact that the "original" market for ERP vendors – large enterprises – have reached saturation and they now aim at targeting SMEs. It is also a fact that increased globalization has as a consequence increased the need for ERPs among SMEs. However, at the same time as proprietary ERP vendor started to focus on SMEs, or even before that, new ERPs developed by "new vendors" building on open source started to show up, namely Open Source ERPs. This directs to the question addressed

A. Kobyliński and A. Sobczak (Eds.): BIR 2013, LNBIP 158, pp. 127–139, 2013.

in this research which is to discuss what role open source ERPs development has played in the diffusion of ERPs among SMEs. This is done by presenting research about open source ERP projects gained from the distribution channel SourceForge.

Earlier research have discussed what interest there are among SMEs for open source ERPs [1] as well as how challenges for proprietary ERP vendor potentially are dealt with in the open source ERP field [2], but also how the two counterparts proprietary ERPs and open source ERPs have become similar in many respects [3]. A question is then what the status is on open source ERP development, if the interest still exists or if it has increased or decreased? However, the main question discussed is: What role has development of open source ERPs played in the diffusion of ERPs among SMEs.

The rest of the paper is organized in the following way: Section 2 presents the research method, followed by Section 3 which describes ERP, open source and open source development. Section 4 then discusses open source ERPs and status of open source ERPs development from an investigation of downloads. Section 5 delivers a comparison of open source and proprietary ERPs characteristics in relation to ERP systems diffusion among SMEs. The final section of the paper offers some suggestions for future research related to diffusion of ERPs among SMEs and presents some conclusions on the question about development of open source ERPs role in the diffusion of ERPs among SMEs.

2   Research Method

This research builds mainly on a theoretical literature study focusing on articles on proprietary ERPs and open source ERPs development. In order to elaborate more on diffusion of open source ERPs, a study of the distribution channel of open source projects, SourceForge, was made. Based on a recommendation from a consultant in open source ERPs, and upon the ranking that SourceForge delivers (number of downloads) six different open source ERPs were selected. The study investigated downloads of and some other demographic data on these six open source ERPs (Table 1), during five years (2007 – 2012). The literature study and the study of downloads of open source ERPs were then compared to earlier presented research, which investigated challenges for a proprietary ERP software vendor. In that research interviews with 8 executives at different levels in the software vendor organization was made. From that research the challenges, reported in Johansson [4] and in Johansson [2], comes which means that challenges presented is a result from the analysis of a case study on a proprietary ERP vendor.

However, before presenting data about downloads from SourceForge and relating it to development of proprietary ERPs as well as open source ERPs and diffusion of ERPs among SMEs, the next section will provide a short introduction to ERP and open source software.

3   ERP and Open Source Software

Enterprise resource planning systems (ERPs) have received and still receive a lot of attention and there are many ERP research instances and quite a lot of literature reviews, e.g. Shehab, Sharp, Supramaniam, and Spedding [5], Esteves and Pastor [6] and Botta-Genoulaz, Millet and Grabot [7]. ERPs is often defined as standardized packaged software [8] designed with the aim of integrating the entire value chain in an organization [9, 10]. Wier et al. [11] argue that ERPs aim to integrate business processes and ICT into a synchronized suite of procedures, applications and metrics which goes over firms' boundaries. The evolution of ERPs [12] has increased the complexity both when it comes to usage as well as development of ERPs. The complexity comes from the fact that ERPs are systems that are supposed to integrate the organization, both inter-organizational as well as intra-organizational, and its business process in a one suite package [13].

When reviewing existing literature on ERPs, such as Shehab et al., [5], Esteves and Pastor [6] and Botta-Genoulaz et al. [7], it is found that a major problem presented is the misfit between ERP functionality and business requirements. Soh, Kien and Tay-Yap [14] describe this as a common problem when adopting software package. The problem of "misfit" means that there is a gap between functionality offered by the package and functionality required from the adopting organization. It can also be suggested that ERPs are complex business applications and the complexity has increased when the software has matured. It may be also suggested that the complexity, to a high extent, influences development, since the software aims at supporting the entire organization's business processes. This implies that ERPs need to have a high level of functionality adopted, which is supposed to support internal processes as well as external processes. It can also be said that development of ERPs is extremely difficult when it comes to fulfilment of requirements requested by the end-user organizations, since it tries to be a common software package and at the same time fulfil specific requirements from individual organizations. This have, to some extent, resulted in new delivery models for ERPs and ERPs related services, such as application service provision (ASP) or software as a service (SaaS). It could be said that these models, to a high extent, focus on SMEs as the target for existing ERPs. However, another delivery model, which has existed for some years, is the open source phenomenon. This delivery model could be described as a combination of delivery and development, and it could be asked if the attention that ASP and SaaS give, allows open source to become a more visible option for SMEs when they think about adoption of ERPs. Then, the question is if an organization adopts open source ERPs since decision-makers in the organization see open source ERPs as the way of developing a system that fits better and, thereby, by increasing alignment between business processes and supporting technology dealing with the misfit problem.

Bruce, Robson and Spaven [15] suggest that open source is mature and industry-strong in many areas, such as operating systems, application servers and security tools. Regarding applications, they state open source is not that mature, but some exceptions exist such as customer relationship management (CRM), enterprise resource planning (ERP), content management, and business intelligence. Open source in business applications is described by Bruce et al., [15] as the third wave of open source adoption. The first wave being the adoption of open source as operating systems, the second wave adoption of open source as infrastructure systems (middleware, browsers, and databases).

When investigating the interest behind open source development it is found that there are two different types of open source software - community open source and commercial open source [16]. Riehle describes these two types in the following way: Community open source is software developed by a community while commercial open source is software that are owned and developed by a for-profit entity. These types differ in who decides on the future direction of the software. In the community case, individual developers, often in the form of a broad community of volunteers, decide which contributions should be accepted in the source code base. The "community" also decides on where the software is heading. In the commercial case a company decides on what should be accepted into the software code base. In this case, the company also maintains the copyright and decides what to implement next. This means that, in the commercial open source, market-entry barriers exists. In the community open source situation no market-entry barriers exist, and therefore can, given the right license, anyone set up a company and start selling software according to Riehle [16]. He states that if someone starts a company delivering open source software they will not sell the software as such, instead they will sell its provision, maintenance, and support. Another way of describing open source can be found in Xu and Brinkkemper [8], they describe software as a product. They say that open source could either be seen as a product that is used to develop software or a product which is delivered as open source.

Riehle [16] as well as Hug, Shah and Mihailescu [17] describes costs as one reason why organizations adopt open source. However, Riehle states that the open source cost perspective is mainly a reason suggested by solution providers. The reason for this is that the customer pays for the software he or she uses from a market perspective. This means that customers pay the fee that the market demands. If then the solution provider can produce the software solution cheaper by using open source, they can increase their profit or decrease the cost for delivered services to each costumer. According to Riehle [16], this results in that solution providers gain the most from open source software because they increase profits through direct cost savings and the ability to reach more customers through improved pricing flexibility. Economides and Katsamakas [18] stipulate that open source, despite the fact that it can be used for free, has costs related to its usage, such as: costs of learning, costs for installing, and costs for maintaining. But there can also be higher support costs than for proprietary software, all this implies that the total cost of ownership (TCO) need to be considered. However, it also implies that open source is seen as a product used for development, and it can be suggested that open source ERPs should be understood as a product. So far the discussion on open source has been quite general. The next section looks more concretely into open source ERPs.

4   The Status of Open Source ERPs

There is no doubt that there is a great interest in open source. However, the question remains if this could be said also about open source ERPs. In order to get some kind of answer to this question, an investigation of the distribution channel SourceForge was made. Even if downloads not is a perfect approach to estimate diffusion of open source ERPs, downloads definitely gives an indication of interest and the status of open source ERPs. To get a grasp of the status over open source ERPs, a search was made in SourceForge (www.SourceForge.net) at the end of 2007; the same search was then repeated during five years. The search showed that there were 336 open source ERP projects registered on 13 September 2007. On January 23rd 2008, there were 392 open source ERP projects registered, an increase of 56 projects in eighteen weeks. At the end of 2012 there were 169 open source ERP projects registered.

Looking at the new projects in 2008 it was found that these to a high extent were connected to existing projects, developing ERPs for specific industries such as Compiere Garnment ERP but also on deployment of open source ERPs such as OpenTaps ERP Deployment. Doing the same search in the end of 2012, the results indicate that the number of projects has decreased a lot. Several reasons could probably explain this, first: it is a fact that some open source ERPs has started their own distribution channel. Second: it seems like the ongoing projects may have matured, indicating that forged projects are included in the "overall" project. A third reason could be abandonment of the project and transfer of developer to a competing project which is more complete. However, a fourth reason could be decreasing interest of open source ERPs among organizations. But, still it can be seen that a lot of downloads have been made and still are made. In Table 1, statistics about downloads from six open source ERPs projects is shown. The reason for showing just these six was a described above, based on a recommendation of an open source ERP consultant as well as on the ranking of downloads at SourceForge in 2007.

Table 1. Downloads of open source ERPs at SourceForge 2007 to 2012

Open source ERPs	Project start	Total number of downloads 31 December respectively year: In brackets is the number of downloads during one year for the specific year (+XXX)					
		2007	2008	2009	2010	2011	2012
Compiere	2001-06-09	1 310 796	1 449 410 (+138 614)	1 547 957 (+98 547)	1 620 303 (+72 346)	1 657 206 (+36 903)	1 689 334 (+32 128)
OpenBravo	2006-03-09	445 096	872 196 (+427 100)	1 181 978 (+309 782)	1 514 090 (+332 112)	1 750 827 (+236 737)	2 001 237 (+250 410)
OpenTaps	2005-08-10	321 245	419 297 (+98 052)	490 245 (+70 948)	562 912 (+72 667)	607 947 (+45 035)	646 754 (+38 807)
Facturalux	2006-09-01	237 543	253 312 (+15 769)	263 959 (+10 647)	287 270 (+23 311)	296 827 (+9 557)	299 279 (+2 452)
WebERP	2003-01-07	153 133	214 966 (+61 833)	284 787 (+69 821)	364 943 (+138 614)	426 267 (+80 156)	484 909 (+58 642)
TinyERP	2005-03-25	25 719	51 740 (+26 021)	59 658 (+7 918)	63 856 (+4 198)	67 162 (+3 306)	68 742 (+1 580)

In table 1 it is shown that open source ERPs have existed for several years, for instance, the Compiere project started already in 2001. It also shows that the interest seems to have been higher and lately started to decrease. In general there is a peak of interest for the different open source ERP in 2008. However, it differs to some extent between the different open source ERPs and for instance webERP had its peak of downloads in 2010. However, an interesting observation that could be made is that the software showing the highest amount of downloads is OpenBravo, which is the only system that clearly describes itself as having a focus on SMEs. This finding is of interest when comparing with the general interest on ERP for SMEs that have been expressed among both practitioners and academia's during the same time. So, one question is then who it is that downloads. When considering that the highest number of downloads is OpenBravo it could be easy to think that SMEs are the ones that downloads, since OpenBravo have a strong focus on SMEs. However, it is hard to find support for this and it can more or less only be speculations as support for that statement. Raymond [19] for instance state that SMEs are highly flexible and adaptable to change, which may be seen as one factor influencing them to download open source ERPs. However, another support could be that SMEs not have the necessary resources for adoption of critical applications such as ERPs [20] and it can be suggested that open source ERPs allow SMEs at least to use them as a source of supply, which according to Levenburg [21] is a crucial usage of Internet at least for micro firms.

But, looking at downloads it is as described above a decrease in the numbers. This decrease of interest (described as downloads) maybe is natural when it comes to any open source project. However, one reason for this could be as described above the usage of other ways of providing the software. For instance, the number of downloads of TinyERP is the lowest in the table, one reason for this is that TinyERP was replaced by openERP in October 2008, and at the same time started their own website from which downloads can be made. Also Compiere, OpenBravo and OpenTaps have their own websites supporting downloads. Despite that TinyERP was replaced by openERP there is still downloads of TinyERP that take place from SourceForge. WebERP shows first an increase in downloads and then a smaller drop, however, interesting to notice is that WebERP market itself as an entirely web-based system. Also webERP has an own website, however, the download part of that website redirects to SourceForge.

The data available at SourceForge does not provide any specific demographic data on who it is making downloads. However, it is possible to see geographic data on countries that makes most downloads. The top three countries for each of the six projects are shown in table 2. There is also data on which operating systems that the downloaded system runs on, if it is used.

Table 2. Information about top three countries and operating systems related to downloads

	Top three countries for downloads			Top three operating systems used		
Open source ERPs	1	2	3	1	2	3
Compiere	China (26%)	India	US	Windows (85%)	Linux	Unknown
OpenBravo	Mexico (12%)	Spain	China	Windows (70%)	Linux	Unknown
OpenTaps	China (25%)	US	India	Windows (82%)	Linux	Macintosh
Facturalux	Ecuador (32%)	Argentina	Spain	Linux (48%)	Windows	Unknown
WebERP	China (17%)	India	US	Windows (82%)	Linux	Unknown
TinyERP	India (25%)	Canada	China	Windows (72%)	Unknown	Linux

According to Serrano and Sarriegi [22], OpenBravo ERP has been successfully installed in SMEs. What they state is that the SMEs installed OpenBravo after evaluating proprietary ERPs, and the interesting fact is that the adopting SMEs were not interested in the open source license. Based on this, it can be suggested that it was not the fact that it was open source as such that made them install the specific ERP system. Looking at what operating system that downloaders used, it can be said that the major part does not used an open source inspired operating system when installing the open source ERP project. Another interesting finding is that China is a major downloader of open source ERPs. It had been interesting to get information about size of organization that downloads, however, that is not possible to get from just doing a study on downloads. What can be suggested anyway is that the systems showing the biggest interest among downloaders are OpenBravo and WebERP, and both these systems target SMEs.

5   Developing ERPs Aiming at Diffusion of ERPs among SMEs

Although many large corporations experience cost savings from implementing ERPs, an implementation may cost millions of USD [23]. According to Smets-Solanes and de Carvalho [24], the high cost has prevented ERP systems from spreading to SMEs. This is to some extent in conflict with what Eriksson and Hultman [25] found in their investigation of information and communication technology (ICT) adoption in SMEs. What they state is that scarce financial resources were rarely mentioned as a reason for non-adoption of ICT. Smets-Solanes and de Carvalho supports their opinion, that after ERP deployment, its "black box" nature prevents users from understanding and eventually improving the business processes the ERP implements, leaving some important business decisions to the software publisher rather than to the corporate manager.

Deciding on deployment of a specific system includes questions such as usability, compatibility, features, support costs and software quality and reliability [26]. Boulanger [26] argues that open source systems are a viable alternative to proprietary systems when taking software quality and reliability into consideration. However, Ven and Nuffel [27] claim that the main motives for non-adoption of open source ERPs are lack of functionality and lack of support. MacCormack, Rusnak and Baldwin [28] propose that open source and proprietary code show a difference in modularity, claiming that open source is more modular than proprietary software, since open source development demands a higher level of modularity. They also state that if this not had been the case, the huge number of developers in an open source project would have resulted in many problems with the software.

Boulanger [26] describes the feedback loop as one difference between development of proprietary software and open source software. A common approach in proprietary software development is the "waterfall model". This means that the development more or less follows a clear structure and uses the following set of five well-defined phases: The requirements phase, the system and software design phase, the implementation and unit-testing phase, the integration and system-testing phase, and the support and maintenance phase [26]. Boulanger [26] says that this structure, of course, is an iterative process. It is interesting to compare Boulanger's [26] description of proprietary software products with the description of open source projects that Bonaccorsi and Rossi [29] and Von Krogh and Spaeth [30] provide. Von Krogh and Spaeth [30] claim that there has been a huge interest in open source over the last decade, and they describe open source as having two distinct features. The first is that open source software is equipped with a license that provides rights to existing and future users to use, inspect, modify, and distribute modified and unmodified software to others. The second feature is the change in the development practice of open source. According to von Krogh and Spaeth [30], years of development have resulted in a new practice of innovation associated with open source software. The new practice displays a very distinct development process which means that open source projects often are initiated by a project leader or project entrepreneur. They state that volunteers then join this project depending on their knowledge. The result of it is that open source projects highlight a change in the nature of how software is developed. Von Krogh and Spaeth [30] argue that the pure top-down planned style of software development project has changed into an evolutionary manner involving many volunteers. But, it can be claimed by referring to Riehle [16], and his discussion about commercial open source, that the open source development have changed direction.

Regarding access to the source code, experience has shown that most adopters will not get involved in customization or even maintenance tasks. Still, open source ERPs could be a good choice, since it may reduce vendor dependency. Customer lock-in with the vendor was investigated e.g. by Chen and Ching [31]. Moreover, its code openness also makes adapting it to specific needs easier, thus reducing costs in customization and further evolution of the software. It can also be claimed that more and more open source development is carried out by developers that are paid by software vendors – the so-called Sponsored Open Source [32]. However, when thinking about customizing the ERP by itself, a critical question for an organization adopting ERPs is if they have the resources needed for implementing ERPs. In both proprietary ERP and open source ERP cases, it is as stated by Carvalho and Johansson [33] very unlikely that small companies have resources and the knowledge for making necessary modifications by themselves. This situation may support the shift to the SaaS business model, which indicates that in the future SaaS as delivery model could solve this problem for adoption of ERPs regardless if it is open source or proprietary ERP. As examples on the evolution of SaaS delivered ERPs there are for instance ERP5 Express on the open source ERP side and Fortnox on the proprietary ERP side. For the Medium Enterprise, which has more IT resources, it could be easier to adopt an open source ERP and take part on its customization, as occurred with some adopters. This is in line with what Ven and Nuffel [27] reports about adoption of open source ERP in Belgium.

In the case of open source ERPs, consulting certification is yet on the early stages, thus quality of service must be carefully addressed during contract negotiation [33]. On the other hand, although SMEs can change their business processes faster than bigger companies, cheaper but restrictive proprietary ERPs support contracts could result into that the software change slower than business processes in the organization does. Also on the economic side, following the common reasoning about free and open source software pricing, open source ERP vendors may have a potential advantage from other open source software because, according to Riehle [16], open source systems "increase profits through direct costs savings and the ability to reach more customers through improved pricing flexibility", allowing partners and free-lance vendors switch from more expensive proprietary software to less expensive open source software, since, as a general rule, open source ERPs relies on other open technologies [33]. For instance, while most proprietary ERPs export and import data to and from MS-Office, open source ERPs in general interacts with the also free Open Office. However, this statement contradicts the findings on use of operating systems as reported in Table 2 and the finding that Windows are the operating systems that are most commonly used. However, another economic factor is that proprietary ERP vendors, generally, impose high costs and a rigid set of rules for companies that desire to enter their partner network, raising the difficulties for smaller firms to become players in this market. In contrast, it can be assumed that this not is the case in the open source ERP market. With more partners entering the market, consulting costs can be reduced, help shifting the market perspective from vendor to adopter. On the other hand, the proprietary ERP partner networks rely on more mature consulting processes and experiences of global ERP players. In that sense, open source ERP must learn how to create certification and consulting processes that are, at the same time, high quality products, like the proprietary ERP ones, and cheaper than those, in order to survive on the market.

However, when analysing downloads open source ERPs seem to be of decreasing interest at the moment, but that is somewhat hard to justify. Another potential explanation is that the individual projects have reached a higher level of maturity. If this is the case it would be of interest to further explore the open source ERP development from the challenges reported by Johansson [2, 4] who suggested that a proprietary ERP vendor basically had the following problems related to ERP development: requirements gathering, ERP implementation, customization versus configuration, ERP architecture, ERP and support of business processes, and variations in ERP requirements. It can be argued that, to a great extent, these can be related to what, proponents of open source state are, the benefits when developing open source ERPs. If that is the case, software vendors of proprietary ERPs could probably earn a lot by looking closer into open source ERPs development. Another reason that could be assumed to have an impact on adoption of open source ERPs is that it is the same that makes organizations adopt open source, namely, that it engages individuals in open source projects. It would, definitely, be of interest to conduct more research about this, since it can be stated that decisions in organizations are made by individual decision-makers.

Open source development has changed in the recent years. When it started, it was more or less based on voluntary efforts. Now, most open source development is made by employees paid to do the development. This means that open source as such have moved in the direction of proprietary software development. It can be stated that at the beginning of open source development, the developer had a closer connection to end-user. A question is if this is still the case even when the open source development have changed into, what Riehle [16] describes as, commercial open source.

Summarizing the comparison of open source ERPs and proprietary ERPs characteristics in relation to SMEs it can be stated that the main difference lies in the cost for license fee. In the open source case the adopting organization does not have to pay any license fee, however, there are indications that the cost despite that is even higher for open source ERPs than for proprietary ERPs [34]. Another distinction when comparing proprietary ERPs and open source ERPs is if the adopting organization takes part in the development or not. As described by Riehle [16] there are two different types of open source software, community open source and commercial open source. For SMEs, this means that if they should take part of the development that has to be in what Riehle describe as community open source, and it can be stated that at least the open source ERPs that are described in Table 1 is not community open source ERPs.

6   Concluding Discussion and Future Research

From the comparison of the proprietary ERPs and the open source ERPs some conclusions can be drawn. The first is that lower costs in both open source ERPs and proprietary ERPs open new opportunities for SMEs to become ERP adopters. This is a fact since, both proprietary ERPs and open source ERPs have some basic modules that they offer for free, such as Microsoft's small ERP system Office Accounting (in US and UK), and the accounting module of ERP5 on its software as a service (SaaS) version. However, an interesting discussion related to this is what role the open source way of delivering software has played in the development of "new business model" for proprietary ERP vendors. Secondly, it can be said that lower costs can also mean that adopters have to deal with lower service levels, then stressing the necessity of carefully evaluating ERP options regarding service levels and pricing.

Another interesting question is then what the "new business models" of ERPs mean when it comes to differences between support in the open source ERP case and the proprietary ERP case. One possible outcome of this is that it will only be the solutions that have a high level of relevant services connected to the specific ERP solution delivered that will survive. It also means that open source ERPs and proprietary ERPs will become closer to each other and this movement maybe, to some extent, makes it harder for the adopting organization to decide on which kind of ERP to select. Following this reasoning, it can be stated that open source ERPs, when evaluated as products and not as services in a SaaS mode, can be harder to evaluate than proprietary ERPs. When evaluating open source ERPs the adopting organization is supposed to also carefully evaluate the maturity of the open source project, its survivability, and its partner network – having special attention on the risks associated with adopting a community founded ERP project.

Another interesting area for future investigation is post-implementation of open source ERP systems because according to Botta-Genoulaz et al., [7], only a very few authors focus on the ERP maintenance activities. The reason for why this is of especially importance in open source ERPs is the fact that it is unclear who assists the adopting organizations when they have problems with the software or want to have further development of the ERP system they use.

It can be said that the interest for open source ERPs is a result of maturity of open source, implying that open source ERPs more or less are ready for usage. Whether this is the case or not is unclear, when looking at the advertisement of open source ERPs at SourceForge; the impression is that the product seems to be rather mature. But, the interesting question is then how much adjustment is necessary for the SMEs when they download the product. Both Ven and Nuffel [27] as well as Carvalho and Johansson [33] indicate that open source ERPs is more suitable for medium-sized enterprises, because of the need for further development and that this size of enterprises more likely have access to necessary resources for doing the development.

It can be generalized that open source ERP developers are closer to end-users than proprietary ERP vendors, so gathering of requirements and their implementation into ERPs is faster in case of open source ERPs. There is also another factor contributing to superficially slower release of new versions (and/or service packs) of proprietary ERPs – intention of vendors to keep number of versions low because these vendors are expected to support virtually all the versions of their ERP systems.

To sum up, although the data gained from SourceForge suggest a decreasing interest in open source ERP, there are indications that the interest still is high among SMEs. One interesting conclusion is that the major part of downloads are made by downloaders using windows. From this it can be concluded that downloaders of open source ERPs are not organizations or people that usually are contributors to open source. It is also interesting to notice that the major part of downloads are made in countries that historically not are locked into the market of proprietary ERPs.

From this it can be concluded that the open source ERP development have most likely been an important driver for "new business model" , such as SaaS, for ERP provision, seeing the light which enhancing the possibility for SMEs to get access to advanced ERPs in the future.

References

1. Johansson, B., Sudzina, F.: ERP systems and open source: an initial review and some implications for SMEs. Journal of Enterprise Information Management 21(6), 649–658 (2008)
2. Johansson, B.: Exploring how open source ERP systems development impact ERP systems diffusion. Int. J. Business and Systems Research 6(4), 361–378 (2012)
3. Atem de Carvalho, R., Johansson, B.: Key aspects of free and open source enterprise resource planning systems. In: Atem de Carvalho, R., Johansson, B. (eds.) Free and Open Source Enterprise Resource Planning: Systems and Strategies. IGI Global (2012)
4. Johansson, B.: Pain Points Challenges for future Enterprise Resource Planning (ERP) systems. In: The First 3gERP workshop. 2007. Paper Presented at Copenhagen Business School at October 2007 in Conjunction with Microsoft Convergence 2007 EMEA in Copenhagen (2007)
5. Shehab, E.M., et al.: Enterprise resource planning: An integrative review. Business Process Management Journal 10(4), 359–386 (2004)
6. Esteves, J., Pastor, J.: Enterprise Resource Planning Systems Research: An Annotated Bibliography. Communications of AIS 7(8), 1–51 (2001)
7. Botta-Genoulaz, V., Millet, P.A., Grabot, B.: A survey on the recent research literature on ERP systems. Computers in Industry 56(6), 510–522 (2005)
8. Xu, L., Brinkkemper, S.: Concepts of product software. European Journal of Information Systems 16(5), 531–541 (2007)
9. Lengnick-Hall, C.A., Lengnick-Hall, M.L., Abdinnour-Helm, S.: The role of social and intellectual capital in achieving competitive advantage through enterprise resource planning (ERP) systems. Journal of Engineering and Technology Management 21(4), 307–330 (2004)
10. Rolland, C., Prakash, N.: Bridging the Gap Between Organisational Needs and ERP Functionality. Requirements Engineering 5(3), 180–193 (2000)
11. Wier, B., Hunton, J., HassabElnaby, H.R.: Enterprise resource planning systems and non-financial performance incentives: The joint impact on corporate performance. International Journal of Accounting Information Systems 8(3), 165–190 (2007)
12. Møller, C.: ERP II: a conceptual framework for next-generation enterprise systems? Journal of Enterprise Information Management 18(4), 483–497 (2005)
13. Koch, C.: ERP-systemer: erfaringer, ressourcer, forandringer, p. 224. Ingeniøren-bøger, København (2001)
14. Soh, C., Kien, S.S., Tay-Yap, J.: Cultural fits and misfits: Is ERP a universal solution? Communications of the ACM 43(4), 47–51 (2000)
15. Bruce, G., Robson, P., Spaven, R.: OSS opportunities in open source software — CRM and OSS standards. BT Technology Journal 24(1), 127–140 (2006)
16. Riehle, D.: The Economic Motivation of Open Source: Stakeholders Perspectives. Computer, 25–32 (2007)
17. Hug, N., Shah, S.M.A., Mihailescu, D.: Why select an open source ERP over proprietary ERP? A focus on SMEs and supplier's perspective, In: Atem de Carvalho, R., Johansson, B. (eds.) Free and Open Source Enterprise Resource Planning: Systems and Strategies, pp. 33–55. IGI Global (2012)

18. Economides, N., Katsamakas, E.: Two-Sided Competition of Proprietary vs. open Source Technology Platforms and the Implications for the Software Industry. Management Science 52(7), 1057–1071 (2006)

19. Raymond, L.: Operations management and advanced manufacturing technologies in SMEs: A contingency approach. Journal of Manufacturing Technology Management, 16(8), 936–955 (2005)

20. Brown, D.H., Lockett, N.: Potential of critical e-applications for engaging SMEs in e-business: a provider perspective. European Journal of Information Systems 13(1), 21–34 (2004)

21. Levenburg, N.M.: Does Size Matter? Small Firms' Use of E-Business Tools in the Supply Chain. Electronic Markets 15(2), 94–105 (2005)

22. Serrano, N.S., Sarriegi, J.M.: Open Source Software ERPs: A New Alternative for an Old Need. IEEE Software 23(3), 94–97 (2006)

23. Jutras, C.: The Total Cost of ERP Ownership in Large Companies (2007), http://www.aberdeen.com/summary/report/sector_insights/4363-SI-erp-cost-large.asp

24. Smets-Solanes, J.-P., de Carvalho, R.A.: ERP5: A Next-Generation, Open-Source ERP Architecture. IT Professional 5(4), 38–44 (2003)

25. Eriksson, L.T., Hultman, J.: One digital leap or a step-by-step approach? - An empirical study of e-commerce development among Swedish SMEs. International Journal of Electronic Business 3(5), 447–460 (2005)

26. Boulanger, A.: Open-source versus proprietary software: Is one more reliable and secure than the other? IBM Systems Journal 44(2), 239–248 (2005)

27. Ven, K., Van Nuffel, D.: An exploratory investigation of the barriers to the adoption of open source ERP by Belgian SMEs. In: Atem de Carvalho, R., Johansson, B. (eds.) Free and Open Source Enterprise Resource Planning: Systems and Strategies, pp. 145–164. IGI Global (2012)

28. MacCormack, A., Rusnak, J., Baldwin, C.Y.: Exploring the Structure of Complex Software Designs: An Empirical Study of Open Source and Proprietary Code. Management Science 52(7), 1015–1030 (2006)

29. Bonaccorsi, A., Rossi, C.: Why Open Source software can succeed. Research Policy 32(7), 1243–1258 (2003)

30. von Krogh, G., Spaeth, S.: The open source software phenomenon: Characteristics that promote research. The Journal of Strategic Information Systems 16(3), 236–253 (2007)

31. Chen, J.-S., Ching, R.K.H.: The effects of Information and Communication Technology on Customer Relationship Management and customer lock-in. International Journal of Electronic Business 5(5), 478–498 (2007)

32. West, J. and S. O'Mahony. Contrasting Community Building in Sponsored and Community Founded Open Source Projects. in 38th Annual Hawaii International Conference on System Sciences. 2005. Hawaii.

33. Atem de Carvalho, R., Johansson, B.: ERP Licensing Perspectives on Adoption of ERPs in Small and Medium-sized Enterprises. In: Chaudbry, S. (ed.) The IV IFIP International Conference on Research and Pratical Issues of Enterprise Systems (CONFENIS), Barcellos de Andrade, Inez, Rio Grande do Norte (2010)

34. Danielsson, L.: Oppen källkod dubblar lönen (Open Source code doubles the salary) (2007), http://www.idg.se/2.1085/1.135393 (accessed December 10, 2007)

Relationships among Open Innovation Processes, Entrepreneurial Orientation, and Organizational Performance of SMEs: The Moderating Role of Technological Turbulence

Pei-Hung Ju[1], Deng-Neng Chen[2], Yu-Chun Yu[3], and Hsiao-Lan Wei[4]

[1] National Kaohsuing University of Applied Sciences
Chien Kung Campus 415 Chien Kung Road Kaohsiung 807, Taiwan
peihung.chu@cc.kuas.edu.tw
[2] National Pingtung University of Science and Technology
1 Shuefu Road, Neipu, Pingtung 912, Taiwan
dnchen@mail.npust.edu.tw
[3] National Kaohsuing University of Applied Sciences
Chien Kung Campus 415 Chien Kung Road Kaohsiung 807, Taiwan
jimmy.yc.yu@gmail.com
[4] National Taiwan University of Science and Technology
43, Section 4, Jīlóng Rd, Da'an District, Taipei City 106, Taiwan
hlwei@cs.ntust.edu.tw

Abstract. Open innovation processes have become important mechanisms that are integrated into organization's innovation strategies to improve performance among small and medium-sized enterprises (SMEs) under dynamic technological settings. This study explored the relationships among open innovation processes (outside-in, inside-out, and coupled), entrepreneurial orientation (EO), and organizational performances (innovation and financial) of SMEs and analyzed the moderating role of technological turbulence on these relationships. Drawing on the technology-based view, we proposed a conceptual framework that depicts how SMEs' EO facilitates open innovation processes, which consequently affect performance. The empirical results from a sample of 161 Taiwan-based SMEs reveal that EO serves as a precursor for open innovation processes, and practicing specific open innovation processes improve specific performance outcomes. Outside-in process is positively related to both performance outcomes. Inside-out process is linked to financial performance, and the coupled process is linked to innovation performance. Under high degree of technological turbulence, the positive relationship between EO to outside-in and inside-out processes and the relationship between outside-in process to both innovation and financial performance are strengthened. However, high technological turbulence does not facilitate the relationship between EO to the coupled process or the coupled process to both performance outcomes.

Keywords: open innovation, entrepreneurial orientation, organizational performance, technological turbulence, small and medium-sized enterprises.

A. Kobyliński and A. Sobczak (Eds.): BIR 2013, LNBIP 158, pp. 140–160, 2013.
© Springer-Verlag Berlin Heidelberg 2013

1   Introduction

Nowadays organizations are challenged by rapid technological changes, shortened innovation cycles, and escalation of research and development (R&D) costs. These have caused organizations, including small and medium-sized enterprises (SMEs), to gradually move toward the "open innovation" model by actively seeking linkages with external environment [1], [2], [3], [4]. This global trend of open innovation encourages that an organization should access both internal and external sources of R&D to improve their innovation competencies. Furthermore, an organization should also use internal and external commercialization paths to advance their technologies [1], [2].

Among others, Gassmann & Enkel [5] from a process perspective developed an open innovation theory. The theory asserts that there are three core processes of open innovation: outside-in, inside-out, and coupled process [3], [5]. The outside-in process is the search for and adoption of knowledge and technologies from outside an organization's boundaries. Inside-out process is the various ways in which internally developed innovations can be commercialized and entered into new markets. The coupled process links the integration and commercialization of knowledge and technologies through collaborating with other organizations in innovation networks, such as strategic alliances and joint ventures [3], [5].

Since then, studies on the relationship between open innovation processes and organizational performance have increased [6], [7], [8], [9]. Despite the growing interest, the majority of these studies had only separately investigated the effects of each open innovation process on performance. Likewise, there is a lack of empirical studies simultaneously examining all three processes in a single integrated research model [9], [10], [11]. This research gap is unfortunate because in practice, organizations usually utilize all or a mix of the three processes of open innovation to improve their innovation efforts and economic returns. Hence, a motive for this study is to fill this gap by simultaneously investigating the impact of all three processes on organizational performance.

Scholars have also asserted that practicing open innovation not only can be beneficial for large enterprises, but it's crucial for the success of SMEs as well [1], [2], [12], [13], [14], [15], [16]. SMEs are clearly different from their larger counterparts with the respect to how they can utilize open innovation. On one hand, innovative developments is often challenging for SMEs because SMEs usually suffer from the "liability of smallness" due to limited resources for R&D, undeveloped competencies, and unstructured innovation processes [13], [17]. Yet, on the other hand, SMEs often benefit from their entrepreneurship. *Entrepreneurial traits* such as the willingness to take risks, the stress on being innovative, the eagerness for learning, and the ability to adapt easily and rapidly to environmental changes are the key strengths of many SMEs [13], [18]. Collectively these entrepreneurial characteristics enable SMEs to become proficient in applying open innovation while concurrently compensate for their liability of smallness [13], [15].

In accordance, a growing number of SMEs have practiced open innovation processes during this past decade [13], [14], [16], [19], [20], [21]. This movement is crucial not only to the sustainability of individual organizations, but also to the economy of many countries, such as China [22], Brazil [23], Australia [19], Sweden [13], and Taiwan [18], [24], where SMEs are the powerhouse for driving economic growth. For example, Taiwan relies heavily on SMEs' innovation performance and entrepreneurship. In terms of innovation records, Taiwan ranked 6th in the Economist Intelligence Unit's Global Innovation Index of 2009-2013 and ranked 3rd in the world's most entrepreneurial country [25]. SMEs not only account for more than 97.63% of Taiwan's total enterprises, but also SMEs' total R&D expenditure in Taiwan has risen with a growth rate of 17.17% in 2008, 2.05% in 2009 and to 4.46% in 2010 [26]. Therefore, an integrated examination on how open innovation processes improve Taiwan-based SMEs' performance is not only important to Taiwan, but also can be beneficial to other countries where SMEs and innovation play a crucial role in facilitating economic growth.

In addition, open innovation studies have focused on several aspects of an organization that may influence its open innovation strategies and organizational performance [6], [10], [11], [18], [19], [27], [28]. For instance, the absorptive capacity of organizations has been frequently highlighted as a crucial characteristic that helps to achieve a sustainable competitive advantage [19], [28], [29]. However, the direct impact of entrepreneurial orientation on open innovation practice to organizational performance is less explored. In summary, the objective of this study is to have a closer look at Taiwan-based SMEs' entrepreneurial orientation and their impact on their open innovation practices and organizational performance.

Based on the research background and motives listed above, the contribution of this study is threefold: (1) it investigated the potential antecedent role of EO of SMEs in driving their implementation of open innovation processes; (2) it simultaneously examined the effect of each open innovation process on both innovation performance and financial performance; (3) it investigated the potential moderating role of technological turbulence on the previous two relationships.

2   Conceptual Background and Hypothesis Development

Reflecting on the contributions listed in the previous section, Figure 1 presents the conceptual framework and respective hypotheses. The framework indicates that SMEs' EO acts as a precursor towards the three core processes of open innovation, and practicing open innovation process improves a specific performance outcome. In addition, technological turbulence is included in the model to serve as a moderator to the previous two relationships. In summary, this framework guides the proposition of the hypotheses, which are presented below.

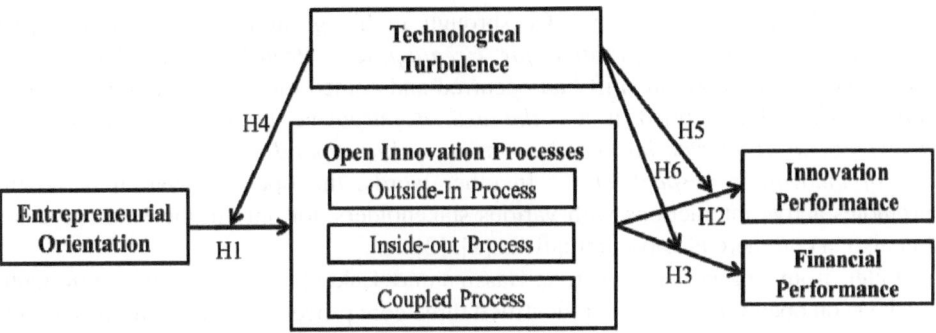

Fig. 1. Conceptual Framework

2.1   Technology-Based View

With the growing importance of technological knowledge, intellectual property and the integration of internal and external sources as a resource in economic and technological development, understanding the key perspectives on collaborative innovation and knowledge sharing are essential [10], [11], [30]. A significant theory in strategic management that has served as a theoretical foundation for studying collaborative efforts is the resource-based view (RBV) [31]. The key concept of the RBV is that organizations possess a set of resources or capabilities that differ among organizations, and these unique resources and capabilities can lead them to a sustainable competitive advantage [31]. Various perspectives related to RBV have arisen, and the most notable one is the technology-based view.

Technology-based view focuses on the technological competencies as a central part of an organization's resource base. Simply put, technology-based view considers an organization's technologies and resources as being a special kind of knowledge that assist in dealing with technological uncertainties [32], [33]. Thus, technology-based view is suggesting that collaboration innovation is a strategy for organizations to develop appropriate acquisition and exploitation strategies to externalize their technological competencies to deal with technological uncertainties. This perspective can be used to explain the impacts of EO to open innovation processes and open innovation processes on organizational performance which will be presented below.

2.2   Open Innovation and Its Core Processes

Traditionally, organizations had operated under a fundamentally *closed* innovation paradigm. All innovation processes must be tightly controlled within the organizations and not exposed externally, even if the R&D projects had already been discarded or put on hold [1], [34]. However, in an era where technological knowledge is diffused across organizations combined with the increasing importance of porous boundaries, organizations can no longer depend on their own R&D to innovate. In accordance, Henry Chesbrough in his ground-breaking book, *Open Innovation: The New Imperative for Creating and Profiting from Technology*; suggested that a paradigm shift had occurred and coined the new paradigm as *"open innovation."* He defined it as *"the use of purposive inflows and outflows of knowledge to accelerate internal innovation and to expand the markets for external use of innovation, respectively."* In other words, the open innovation paradigm promotes active interactions with various stakeholders not only in the R&D process, but also in commercialization initiatives [1], [2].

Later, from a process perspective, Gassmann & Enkel [5] had provided an in-depth analysis on open innovation and identified three core processes: outside-in, inside-out, and coupled process. The *outside-in process* involves the usage of external sources of knowledge to enrich the knowledge base within an organization. It opens the innovation process to external knowledge exploration through the integration of suppliers and customers' knowledge and competencies [3], [4], [5]. In addition, organization can also integrate non-profit organizations like universities, government agencies, and other research institutions to integrate their different competencies to enrich its own innovation competencies. For instance, many large pharmaceutical firms, such as Eli Lilly, actively acquire a significant amount of their technologies from external partners to enhance their internal capabilities [8], [12].

The *inside-out process* involves externally commercializing and/or transferring of internally developed technologies in order to gain monetary and strategic benefits [3], [5], [35]. This process results in faster time-to-market for products and technologies, and it also makes them more valuable than when they are initially developed [1], [2]. For example, IBM not only benefitted from their internal innovations, but IBM also generated millions of dollars in licensed technologies annually [1], [2], [8], [36].

Organizations may also integrate both outside-in and inside-out processes to yield the *coupled process* by closely collaborating with other organizations through strategic alliances or joint collaborations [3], [5], [30]. In order to collaborate and cooperate successfully, a right balance of give and take is crucial. Cooperation is usually characterized by a profound form of interaction between organizations over a long period of time. This interaction tends to result in intensive exchanges of knowledge and initiates a process of mutual learning [5]. Furthermore, the coupled process allows the transfer of tacit knowledge among organizations which normally cannot be easily blueprinted or packaged through licensing or market transactions [5].

Although the idea of practicing the three core processes of open innovation is rather intriguing, nevertheless, through a comprehensive review of prior studies, we have identified that the majority of the studies had only explored the impacts of outside-in, inside-out, and coupled process individually. In addition, to date, the majority of prior research has focused on large enterprises and less on SMEs [13], [14], [15], [16] as shown in Table 1. As a result, we find that it is practical and theoretically relevant to focus on the topic of SMEs and simultaneously investigate how all three processes can influence performance in a single research model.

Table 1. Prior Studies on Open Innovation and Organizational Performance Based on Organization Size

Focus	Outside-In	Inside-out	Coupled
Large Enterprises	Chiang & Hung [24] Ebersberger et al. [37] Hung & Chiang [18] Inauen & Schenker-Wicki [10] Laursen & Salter [38] Lee et al. [17] Lin & Wu [39] Mazzola et al. [9] Spithoven et al. [28], [40] Tsai et al. [41] Un et al. [42]	Belderbos et al. [43] Inauen & Schenker-Wicki [11] Kutvonen [44] Lichtenthaler [45], [46], [47] Lichtenthaler & Ernst [35], [48] Mazzola et al. [9]	Belderbos et al. [43] Bogers [30] Faems et al. [49] Mazzola et al. [9] Lin et al. [50] Nieto & Santamaria, [51]
SMEs	Huang & Rice [19], [52] Kim & Park [20] Lasagni [21] Neyens et al. [53] Parida et al. [13] Suh & Kim [54] Zeng et al. [22]	Bianchi et al. [14]	Lee et al. [17] Neyens et al. [53] Suh & Kim [54]

2.3   Entrepreneurial Orientation (EO) and Open Innovation

Entrepreneurial orientation (EO) has been recognized as the key for innovative activities for many organizations especially SMEs [13], [18], [22], [54]. EO refers to an organization's strategic orientation that reflects specific aspects of an organization[55], [56]. These aspects of EO are demonstrated by the extent to which the top managers or chief executive officers (CEO) are inclined to take business-related risks (inclination to risk-taking), to favor change and novelty in order to obtain a competitive advantage (innovativeness), and to compete aggressively with other organizations (pro-activeness) [56], [57], [58].

More specifically, risk-taking is the willingness of an organization to take bold actions such as exploiting significant resources or utilizing business strategies where the outcome is highly uncertain. Innovativeness refers to the organization's willingness to engage in creative processes, to try new technological processes, and to improve existing or to create new products and/or experiment with new ideas and technologies. Pro-activeness refers to actively seeking new opportunities, such as taking advantage of first mover strategies in a competitive environment [56], [57], [59], [60]. Altogether, these three dimensions of EO facilitate organizations to be flexible to environmental changes and be responsive to external opportunities; hence, they may assist organizations in adopting open innovation [3], [4], [14].

Based on this logic, we argue that high EO can assist an organization in implementing open innovation processes. First, organizations with high EO will actively scan its task environment to look for adequate sources of knowledge, in turn allowing them to deepen the pool of technological opportunities available to them. Prior studies on open innovation have asserted that searching for external sources of knowledge can increase the chance for organizations to improve its internal knowledge base [10], [24], [37], [38]. Second, an organization with high EO is more willing to take risks by adopting innovative strategies such as divesting and/or transferring of a given technology into new markets. Such processes accelerate commercialization of innovations which provide both monetary and strategic benefits [44], [45], [46]. Third, organizations with high EO are more inclined to initiate collaboration projects, where one organization provides the specialized knowledge and the other organization provides the needed infrastructure and resources for producing, marketing, and commercializing an innovative product or service [13], [18]. Overall, organizations possessing a high EO are more equipped to adopt open innovation processes to improve their innovation efforts than their counterparts with low EO. Prior studies have found a positive relationship between EO and innovative strategies [15], [18], [55], [58].

H1a: EO is positively related to the outside-in process of open innovation.
H1b: EO is positively related to the inside-out process of open innovation.
H1c: EO is positively related to the coupled process of open innovation.

2.4   Open Innovation and Innovation Outputs

The technology-based view has emphasized that with the growing importance of technological knowledge and intellectual capital, organizations should actively engage in collaborative innovation with the external environment [4], [30]. Scholars have also indicated that the reason organizations have adopted open innovation is because organizations believe that utilizing the paradigm is critical to growth in profits and improvement in their innovation efforts [1], [2], [3], [6], [7], [8], [61]. In other words, with the three open innovation processes (outside-in, inside-out, and coupled process), organizations can greatly improve their performance outcomes.

First of all, outside-in process refers to the integration of external knowledge, competencies, and resources gained from stakeholders outside the boundaries of an organization [3], [5]. Practicing the outside-in process can enrich an organization's internal knowledge base and in turn increase its overall innovativeness. The concept of absorptive capacity illustrates that new knowledge that is complementary to prior knowledge can enhance an organization's innovation capabilities [29], [62]. Through absorptive capacity, organizations can expand their knowledge base, improve their ability to assimilate, utilize new information, and enhance their innovation outputs [19], [28]. Previous studies have asserted that by accepting and utilizing external sources of R&D, organizations can improve their innovation efforts such as innovations' flexibility and value added to customers [10], [20], [28], [38], [52]. Moreover, Parida et al [13] suggested that by utilizing outside-in strategies, such as technology scouting of new technological developments and technology sourcing of complementary knowledge, organizations can keep up with new developments and innovations to improve their innovation performance [21], [27].

Besides impacting the innovation performance, the outside-in process affects an organization's financial performance as well. Many prior empirical studies have indicated that the integration of external parties' knowledge and expertise tend to be beneficial for organizations in terms of revenue, net-profit, and sales [9], [10], [18],

[43].   In summary, relying on external developed technologies or knowledge enables an organization to improve both its innovation and financial performance. For this reason, we suggest the following hypotheses:

H2a: The outside-in process of open innovation is positively related to innovation performance.
H3a: The outside-in process of open innovation is positively related to financial performance.

The inside-out process is increasingly considered as a strategic practice, in which an organization can profit from its own technological developments through various contracts such as out-licensing, spin-offs, and/or technology commercialization. Gassmann & Enkel [5] suggested that for organizations to successfully transfer its knowledge to the external environment, a *multiplicative capability* is required. The concept of multiplicative capability illustrates that for an organization to transfers their knowledge, a strategic selection of partners that are willing to multiply the application of the technology is essential. Basically, when an in-house technology does not match with the organization's business model, the organization should look for others with business models that are better suited [1], [2], [35].   By commercializing or transferring internal unused technological knowledge to the market, organizations are able to gain strategic opportunities, which result in a positive impact on both innovation and financial performance [11], [44], [46].

Although prior empirical studies on the inside-out process mostly focused on the results on financial performance, non-monetary benefits can be gained as well [35], [43], [47]. The most commonly acknowledge non-monetary benefit for inside-out process is accelerating the commercialization of an innovation and identifying the potential various applications of a given technology [1], [2], [35]. Based on this logic, we suggest the following:

H2b: The inside out process of open innovation is positively related to innovation performance.
H3b: The inside-out process of open innovation is positively related to financial performance.

Lastly, coupled process refers to co-creation with complementary organizations through strategic alliances and/or joint ventures. Organizations that practice the coupled process are heavily involved in inter-organizational relationships, where the critical factor for success is a cooperatively pattern of giving and taking of complementary resources [3], [4], [5]. According to Dyer & Singh [63], the concept of relational capacity illustrates that an organization can be differentiated from their competitors by the networks in which it is connected to.   In other words, an organization's competitive advantage is its capability to build and maintain a strong innovative network with partners [63].   Working in R&D collaboration with complementary partners facilitates organizations to scan the external environment for potential new innovation opportunities and complementary technologies [12], [50].

Overall, practicing the coupled process enables organizations to jointly produce efficient performance outcomes measured by the variety of offered products and services, sales and revenue growth, and overall customer satisfaction [37]. Prior studies on inter-organizational collaboration asserted that forming both R&D and manufacturing alliances are of crucial importance in achieving higher degree of novelty and quality in product innovation [50], [51]. In summary, by co-developing new products and services together, organizations can improve both performance outcomes since both parties can reduce costs and production time. Therefore, we hypothesize:

H2c: The coupled process of open innovation is positively related to innovation performance.

H3c: The coupled process of open innovation is positively related to financial performance.

2.5   Technological Turbulence's Moderating Effects

Contingency theory asserts that an organization's strategic orientation and innovation strategies will not be equally effective under unconventional environmental conditions [59], [60]. Accordingly, the external environment of an organization is a key intervening variable that affects how EO functions in terms of driving an organization's innovation practices. A particular environmental condition that is believed to pressure SMEs into practicing open innovation is technological turbulence [16], [64]. Technological turbulence refers to the extent which the industry that an organization is embedded in is impacted by rapid changes in technological conditions [65].

Within a setting of high technological turbulence, competitions among organizations can be characterized by extreme short innovation cycles [1], [2], [46]. New products and services can emerge very unpredictably and quickly. The constant change of technologies also yields greater risks such as technical obsolescence and high R&D cost [14]. To cope with these increased risks, organizations with a high EO tend to intensify their risk-reduction initiatives [18], [30], [56], [59]. For instance, by adopting outside-in process, organizations can shorten product development cycles through leveraging external sources of technologies and knowledge [19], [38], [52]. By adopting inside-out process, organizations can avoid the risk of technical obsolescence [35], [46]. In addition, by adopting coupled process such as long-term collaborative arrangements, organizations can constitute an effective risk-sharing mechanism [30]. Studies on open innovation have argued that under high levels of technological uncertainty, an organization's strategic orientation will facilitate the gathering and transferring of knowledge and technologies for superior responsiveness [46], [66], [67]. Based on the argument above, we propose the following:

H4a: Technology turbulence positively moderates the relation between EO and outside-in process of open innovation.

H4b: Technology turbulence positively moderates the relation between EO and inside-out process of open innovation.

H4c: Technology turbulence positively moderates the relation between EO and coupled process of open innovation.

Existing studies on open innovation have stressed that technological turbulence can moderate the effectiveness of open innovation processes on both innovation and monetary outcomes [16], [46], [68]. Technology-based view also suggested that with the emergence of a technological and knowledge-abundant economy, an organization needs to ensure that it captures value from its technological and knowledge resources as a mean to improve performance and sustain competitive advantage [30], [32], [33]. In high technological turbulent environments, there are higher technical obsolescence and shorter innovation cycles, in which the benefits from practicing innovations may be undermined [10], [11], [46]. For example, the possibilities of achieving more profits from R&D investments are limited when technologies are constantly changing. Hence, technology-based view suggested that organizations need to concentrate on the exploitation of their technological resources to capture value from innovations if technologies are developing rapidly [30], [32], [33]. In other words, high technological turbulence facilitates the relationship between open innovation processes and both innovation outputs and economical returns. Lichtenthaler [46], [47] suggested that in environments characterized as high technological turbulence, it motivates organizations to utilize the inside-out process to create opportunities for superior financial returns by actively commercializing or licensing out unused technologies. In addition, high technological turbulence demands active acquisitions of external sources of R&D resources because organizations are not able to cover all technological developments independently [11], [44], [46], [68] . Base on the arguments above, we propose the following:

H5a: Technology turbulence positively moderates the relation between outside-in and innovation performance.

H5b: Technology turbulence positively moderates the relation between inside-out and innovation performance.

H5c: Technology turbulence positively moderates the relation between coupled and innovation performance.

H6a: Technology turbulence positively moderates the relation between outside-in and financial performance.

H6b: Technology turbulence positively moderates the relation between inside-out and financial performance.

H6c: Technology turbulence positively moderates the relation between coupled and financial performance.

3   Research Methodology

3.1   Data and Sample

The sampling frame for this study is SMEs in Taiwan. It is difficult to define SMEs since the definition not only varies across countries to countries, but also the definition changes over time [13], [22]. According to small and medium enterprises administration (SMEA), SMEs in Taiwan are mainly composed of two sectors, manufacturing and services [26]. The average number of employees is 200 or less, with a paid capital of New Taiwanese dollars (NT$) 80-100 million or less. The definition of SMEs in Taiwan is obviously different from other countries; therefore, we followed the U.S. Small Business Administration's definition and labeled the size of our sampled Taiwan-based SMEs as enterprises with fewer than 500 employees [69].

For data collection, we used a questionnaire survey on Executive Master of Business Administration (EMBA) students from several well-known universities across Taiwan. EMBA students represent an appropriate sample as SMEs for various reasons. First of all, many of these EMBA students are CEOs or top executives of SMEs. In addition, they are people engaged in further enrichment of their knowledge and relational networks, and this fulfills the requirements for wanting to operate in an open environment where knowledge is abundant. These features make EMBA students suitable targets for studying the relationship between open innovation processes and organizational performance in SMEs. A total of 161 useable questionnaires were obtained. Out of the 161 respondents: 112 (69.5%) are from the manufacturing sector and 49 (30.4%) are from the services sector.

3.2   Variables and Measures

This study adopted survey measurement items from past studies based on relevant literature. Modifications were made to fit the context of the study. All scales were measured using a five-point Likert scale ranging from 1 (strongly disagree/low) to 5 (strongly agree/high) (see Appendix).

Open innovation is a broad concept that includes different dimensions; thus, based on Gassmann & Enkel [5]'s theory and Inauen & Schenker-Wicki [10], [11]'s descriptions, we operationalized open innovation as consisting of three dimensions (outside-in, inside-out, and coupled) and developed measurement scales for each process. *Outside-in process* measures the practices to which an organization integrates external initiatives into their innovation process. *Inside-out process* measures the practices to which an organization externally transfers or commercializes its internally developed resources. *Coupled process* captures an organization's interaction characteristics with their innovation partners.

To ensure adequate reliability and validity of our composed measurement scales, we conducted a pilot test with a convenience sample of 67 EMBA students. The data of the pilot test were then subjected to evaluation using Cronbach's alpha and factor analysis [70]. Cronbach's alpha assesses the reliability of the scales. Items that did not significantly contribute to the reliability were eliminated [70]; as a result, one item was removed from each process (see Appendix). The overall reliability coefficients for the dimensions were 0.873, 0.873, and 0.808 respectively. All coefficient scores were over the cutoff of 0.70 [70], [71]. To examine whether the scales of each open innovation processes could load on to three components respectively, we subjected the data to exploratory factor analysis (EFA) [70]. EFA found all items loaded onto their respective factors, which concurred with Gassmann & Enkel [5] and Inauen & Schenker-Wicki [10], [11]'s descriptions. These findings provided preliminary support for the adequacy of our scales for open innovation processes.

Following Covin & Slevin [56], we measured *entrepreneurial orientation* as a uni-dimensional construct and adapted items to measure an organization's tendency to risk-taking, innovativeness, and pro-activeness (Alpha=0.939).

Innovation performance was assessed as product innovation adapted from Prajogo and Ahmed [56]'s indicators representing the generation and creation of new ideas that were reflected in the end product or service (Alpha= 0.775).

For *financial performance*, we adapted Wiklund & Shepherd [58]'s scale to measure the sales, net profit, and revenue growth of the respondent's organizations in comparison to their competitors in the past three years (Alpha=0.813).

Technological turbulence was adapted using scales derived from Jaworski and Kohli [65]. Respondents were ask to rank the intensity of each based on the changes in their industry. The construct's reliability coefficient is 0.854.

4   Results

The descriptive statistics and correlations of variables are presented in Table 2. The mean and standard deviations showed enough variance in all variables, while correlation coefficients suggested functional inter-relationship between variables. In order to test our hypotheses, a two-step moderated hierarchical regression analysis was carried out using the approach described by Cohen et al. [72]. In the first step of the hierarchical regression, the dependent variables were being regressed on the independent variables to assess the main effects. In step two, we added the moderating variables and the interaction terms of moderator * independent variables respectively. In order to prevent multi-collinearity on the interaction terms, we took a mean-centered approach for all the independent variables before conducting regression analysis. In addition, we followed the suggestions in the literature and only considered one interaction term per model [72]. Regression analysis results are provided in Table 3-5.

Table 2. Descriptive Statistics and Correlation Matrix

Measures	1	2	3	4	5	6	7
1. Outside-in	1						
2. Inside-out	0.516^{**}	1					
3. Coupled	0.248^{**}	0.172^{*}	1				
4. EO	0.678^{**}	0.405^{**}	0.281^{**}	1			
5. Product Innovation	0.626^{**}	0.306^{**}	0.194^{*}	0.671^{**}	1		
6. Financial Performance	0.464^{**}	0.516^{**}	0.147	0.505^{**}	0.451^{**}	1	
7. TT	0.407^{**}	0.411^{**}	0.0.17	0.481^{**}	0.470^{**}	0.247^{**}	1
Mean	3.94	3.39	3.77	3.96	4.01	3.59	3.68
S.D.	0.55	0.60	0.38	0.60	0.55	0.48	0.67
Cronbach's α	0.873	0.873	0.808	0.939	0.775	0.813	0.854
Factor loading	0.78-0.86	0.74-0.88	0.75-0.86	0.72-0.90	0.66-0.86	0.81-0.86	0.79-0.92

EO: Entrepreneurial Orientation; TT: Technological Turbulence
N = 161; ***$p<0.001$, **$p<0.01$, *$p<0.05$

Table 3. Regression Analysis for H1 and H4

Variable	Outside-in Process		Inside-out Process		Coupled Process	
	Model 1	Model 2	Model 3	Model 4	Model 5	Model 6
EO	*0.678****	0.557***	*0.455****	0.280***	*0.281****	0.317***
TT		0.208**		0.330***		-0.148
Moderators						
EO * TT		*0.247****		*0.193***		0.094
R^2	0.459	0.520	0.207	0.287	0.079	0.099
Adjusted R^2	0.456	0.511	0.205	0.273	0.073	0.081
F	135.050	56.735	41.552	21.061	13.629	5.719

EO: Entrepreneurial Orientation; TT: Technological Turbulence
N=161; ***$p<0.001$, **$p<0.01$, *$p<0.05$, +$p<0.1$

Table 4. Regression Analysis for H2 and H5

Variables	Innovation Performance			
	Model 7	Model 8	Model 9	Model 10
Outside-in Process	0.623***	0.465***		
Inside-out Process	-0.046		0.127+	
Coupled Process	0.112+			0.172*
Technology Turbulence (TT)		0.302***	0.416***	0.467***
Moderators				
Outside-in * TT		0.165**		
Inside-out * TT			0.150**	
Coupled * TT				0.071
R^2	0.413	0.472	0.258	0.257
Adjusted R^2	0.402	0.462	0.244	0.243
F	36.838	46.727	18.237	18.134
		N=161; ***p<0.001, **p<0.01, *p<0.05, +p<0.1		

Table 5. Regression Analysis for H3 and H6

Variables	Financial Performance			
	Model 11	Model 12	Model 13	Model 14
Outside-in Process	0.265***	0.400***		
Inside-out Process	0.377***		0.502***	
Coupled Process	0.017			0.155*
Technology Turbulence (TT)		0.098	0.041	0.252***
Moderators				
Outside-in * TT		0.176*		
Inside-out * TT			-0.102	
Coupled * TT				-0.020
R^2	0.320	0.229	0.70	0.085
Adjusted R^2	0.307	0.214	0.256	0.067
F	24.632	15.543	19.323	4.857
		N=161; ***p<0.001, **p<0.01, *p<0.05, +p<0.1		

Within all the basic models before inclusion of the interaction terms, we found significant direct effects of EO on all three processes of open innovation (as shown in model 1, 3 and 5). These findings provide support for hypothesis 1: EO is positively related the core processes of open innovation. With regard to the relationships between each open innovation process to organizational performance, only outside-in process is positively and significantly related to both performance variables. Inside-out process is positively related to financial performance, and coupled process is positively linked to innovation performance (see models 7 and 11). These findings provide partial support for both hypothesis 2 and 3.

As for the moderating effects, hypothesis 4 proposes that technological turbulence has a positive moderating effect on the relationships between the open innovation process and EO. Model 2 and 4 indicate that technological turbulence only moderates the relationship between outside-in process (Beta = 0.247, p<0.001) and inside-out process (Beta = 0.193, p<0.01) to EO and thus providing partial support for hypothesis 4. Model 8 and 9 demonstrate that technological turbulence strengthens the relationship between outside-in process (Beta = 0.165, p<0.01) and inside-out process (Beta = 0.150, p<0.01) on innovation performance, while no such interaction effect can be observed for the coupled process; therefore, the data only partially support hypothesis 5. In support of hypothesis 6, the interaction term for outside-in process (0.176, p<0.05) is positive and significant, while the interaction terms for inside-out process and coupled process are not significant as shown in Models 12-14.

5   Discussion and Conclusions

Despite the recent emergence of research on open innovation [2], [3], [4], [7], [8], [61], analyses in the context of SMEs are still lacking. In addition, studies relating to the impact of an organization's entrepreneurial orientation (EO) to their open innovation practices have not yet been explored as well [55]. Furthermore, to the best of our knowledge, studies that simultaneously explore the impact of outside-in, inside-out, and coupled processes of open innovation on organizational performance in a single framework are also lacking. Therefore, this study acts as a pioneering effort to further the understanding regarding these issues by investigating the potential impact of SMEs' EO on outside-in, inside-out, and coupled process, and how these impacts in turn influence their organizational performance. We also examined the potential moderating role of technological turbulence in this context. Using data collected from 161 EMBA students from well-known universities across Taiwan, our empirical results have provided strong support for the importance of open innovation for SMEs in Taiwan.

Table 6 illustrates a summary of the empirical findings to the proposed hypotheses based on our conceptual framework (see Figure 1). There are a number of interesting findings from our empirical results. First, as seen in the descriptive statistics of the variables (Table 2), the mean score of outside-in process (3.94) exceeds both inside-out process (3.39) and coupled process (3.77), which suggests that Taiwan-based SMEs tend to engage more in outside-in process of open innovation. Additionally, our regression results indicated that under technological turbulent settings, SMEs focus more on outside-in process to improve both their innovation and financial performance than the other two processes. Second, previous studies have asserted that an organization's strategic orientation may serve as a precursor on the relationship between open innovation and organizational performance. Our empirical findings further contribute by confirming that EO may serve as a precursor for open innovation processes [18], [55].

Perhaps a more interesting finding is that under technological turbulent settings, possessing a high EO does not support SMEs in adopting the coupled processes. Despite the importance of collaborative innovation under technological turbulent conditions claimed by prior studies [30], [46], [68], strong EO does not intuitively facilitate the coupled process and in turn improve organizational performance. According to SMEA, when SMEs in Taiwan are faced with uncertainty in technological development, they prefer to tackle it alone and are reluctant to collaborate with others [26]. Thus, Taiwan-based SMEs only practice the coupled practice if the imperfections in technological turbulence are reduced.

In summary, the findings of this study confirm the insights of previous studies that the trend towards open innovation may be a global phenomenon since the implementation of open innovation is found not only in developed countries such as USA and Europe [2], [8], but also in developing countries such as Taiwan, China, and Brazil [13], [18], [19], [20], [21], [22], [54].

Table 6. Results of Hypotheses Testing

Hypotheses	Supported
H1a: EO is positively related to the outside-in process of open innovation.	Yes
H2b: EO is positively related to the inside-out process of open innovation.	Yes
H3c: EO is positively related to the coupled process of open innovation.	Yes
H2a: The outside-in process is positively related to innovation performance.	Yes
H2b: The inside-out process is positively related to innovation performance.	No
H2c: The coupled process is positively related to innovation performance.	Yes
H3a: The outside-in process is positively related to financial performance.	Yes
H3b: The inside-out process is positively related to financial performance.	No
H3c: The coupled process is positively related to financial performance.	No
H4a: TT positively moderates the relation between EO and outside-in process.	Yes
H4b: TT positively moderates the relation between EO and inside-out process.	Yes
H4c: TT positively moderates the relation between EO and coupled process.	No
H5a: TT positively moderates the relation between outside-in and innovation performance.	Yes
H5b: TT positively moderates the relation between inside-out and innovation performance.	Yes
H5c: TT positively moderates the relation between coupled and innovation performance.	No
H6a: TT positively moderates the relation between outside-in and financial performance.	Yes
H6b: TT positively moderates the relation between inside-out and financial performance.	No
H6c: TT positively moderates the relation between coupled and financial performance.	No

5.1   Theoretical and Managerial Implications

The contributions and implications of this study are relevant to the growing interest of both scholars and practitioners of open innovation and SMEs. First, our study contributes to existing open innovation literature by providing further insights on how each open innovation processes could improve both innovation performance and financial performance [2], [3], [4], [7], [8], [9]. It also contributes to SMEs' literature by augmenting to the body of knowledge on how SMEs' EO drives the adoption and implementation of open innovation processes [12], [13], [16], [18]. Our study also developed and validated new metrics for Gassmann & Enkel [5]'s theory of open innovation. These measurement scales may be useful to future researchers in gauging the extent of organizations' engagement in open innovation processes.

From the managerial perspective, our findings provide understandings for managers of SMEs in selecting the appropriate open innovation process to improve performance outcomes under a specific environmental setting. More specifically, in high technological turbulent settings, SMEs should actively practice the outside-in process to overcome their liability of smallness.

5.2   Limitations and Future Research Directions

Despite the contributions and implications that are previously mentioned, this study has several limitations that may be considered and possibly addressed in future research. First of all, we have focused on a sample of SMEs from a single country, which limits the generalization of results. Moreover, the data we had used to empirically test our research model is a convenience sample of EMBA students. Considering the number of variables in the study, the sample size is not that large. A larger scale of survey with random sampling is suggested for future research. In addition, since innovation is a long process and sometimes outcomes are not seen instantaneously, future studies may adopt a longitudinal research design with larger data set from different industries and countries to examine the complex relationships among open innovation process, entrepreneurial orientation, technological turbulence, and organizational performance. Secondly, we have only considered the precursory role of EO and the moderating influence of technological turbulence. It is possible that others variables may moderate and even mediate the relationships between open innovation process and organizational performance. Therefore, incorporating other potential variables into our conceptual framework is also a very promising research field in the future. Thirdly, we have only further contributed to extant open innovation literature by simultaneously examining the impact of outside-in, inside-out, and coupled process of open innovation on both innovation and financial performance. Future research may want to discuss the combined or interacting effects of three processes of open innovation on organizational performance. In conclusion, addressing these limitations can further advance our understanding on the complex relationship between open innovation and organizational performance.

References

1. Chesbrough, H.: Open innovation: The new imperative for creating and profiting from technology. Harvard Business School Publishing Corporation, Boston (2003)
2. Chesbrough, H., Vanhaverbeke, W., West, J.: Open innovation: Researching a new paradigm. Oxford University Press, New York (2006)
3. Enkel, E., Gassmann, O., Chesbrough, H.: Open R&D and open innovation: exploring the phenomenon. R&D Management 39(4), 311–316 (2009)
4. Gassmann, O., Enkel, E., Chesbrough, H.: The future of open innovation. R&D Management 40(3), 213–221 (2010)
5. Gassmann, O., Enkel, E.: Towards a theory of open innovation: three core process archetypes. In: R&D Management Conference, Lisbon, Portugal (2004)
6. Dahlander, L., Gann, D.M.: How open is innovation? Research Policy 36(9), 699–709 (2010)
7. Huizingh, E.K.: Open innovation: state of the art and future perspectives. Technovation 31(1), 2–9 (2011)

8. Lichtenthaler, U.: Open innovation: Past research, current debates, and future directions. Academy of Management Perspectives 25(1), 75–93 (2011)
9. Mazzola, E., Bruccoleri, M., Perrone, G.: The Effect of Inbound, Outbound and Coupled Innovation on Performance. International Journal of Innovation Management 16(6) (2012)
10. Inauen, M., Schenker-Wicki, A.: The impact of outside-in open innovation on innovation performance. European Journal of Innovation Management 14, 496–520 (2011)
11. Inauen, M., Schenker-Wicki, A.: Fostering radical innovations with open innovation. European Journal of Innovation Management 15, 212–231 (2012)
12. Chesbrough, H., Crowther, A.K.: Beyond high tech: Early adopters of open innovation in other industries. R&D Management 36(3), 229–236 (2006)
13. Parida, V., Westerberg, M., Frishammar, J.: Inbound open innovation activities in high-tech SMEs: The impact on innovation performance. Journal of Small Business Management 50(2), 283–309 (2012)
14. Bianchi, M., Campodall'Orto, S., Frattini, F., Vercesi, P.: Enabling open innovation in small and medium-sized enterprises: how to find alternative applications for your technologies. R&D Management 40(4), 414–431 (2010)
15. Christensen, J.F., Olesen, M.H., Kjær, J.S.: The industrial dynamics of open innovation: Evidence from the transformation of consumer electronics. Research Policy 34(10), 1533–1549 (2005)
16. Van De Vrande, V., De Jong, J.P.J., Vanhaverbeke, W., De Rochemont, M.: Open innovation in SMEs: Trends, motives, and management challenges. Technovation 29(7), 423–437 (2009)
17. Lee, S., Park, G., Yoon, B., Park, J.: Open innovation in SMEs - An intermediated network model. Research Policy 39(2), 290–300 (2010)
18. Hung, K.P., Chiang, Y.H.: Open innovation proclivity, entrepreneurial orientation, and perceived firm performance. International Journal of Technology Management 52, 257–274 (2010)
19. Huang, F., Rice, J.: The role of absorptive capacity in facilitating "Open innovation" outcomes: A study of Australian SMEs in the manufacturing sector. International Journal of Innovation Management 13(2), 201–220 (2009)
20. Kim, H., Park, Y.: The effects of open innovation activity on performance of SMEs: The case of Korea. International Journal of Technology Management 52(3), 236–256 (2010)
21. Lasagni, A.: How can external relationships enhance innovation in SMEs? New evidence for Europe. Journal of Small Business Management 50(2), 310–339 (2012)
22. Zeng, S.X., Xie, X.M., Tam, C.M.: Relationship between cooperation networks and innovation performance of SMEs. Technovation 30(3), 181–194 (2010)
23. Kaminski, P.C., De Oliveira, A.C., Lopes, T.M.: Knowledge transfer in product development processes: A case study in small and medium enterprises (SMEs) of the metal-mechanic sector from Sao Paulo, Brazil. Technovation 28, 29–36 (2008)
24. Chiang, Y.H., Hung, K.P.: Exploring open search strategies and perceived innovation performance from the perspective of inter-organizational knowledge flow. R&D Management 40(3), 292–299 (2010)
25. Economist Intelligence Unit. A new ranking of the world's most innovative countries. An Economist Intelligence Unit Report Sponsored Cisco (2009)
26. Small and Medium Enterprise Administration Ministry of Economic Affairs. White paper on small and medium enterprises in Taiwan. White Paper (2012)
27. Keupp, M.M., Gassmann, O.: Determinants and archetype users of open innovation. R&D Management 39(4), 331–341 (2009)

28. Spithoven, A., Clarysse, B., Knockaert, M.: Building absorptive capacity to organise inbound open innovation in traditional industries. Technovation 31, 10–21 (2011)
29. Cohen, W.M., Levinthal, D.A.: Absorptive capacity: A new perspective on learning and innovation. Administrative Science Quarterly 35(1), 128–152 (1990)
30. Bogers, M.: The open innovation paradox: knowledge sharing and protection in R&D collaborations. European Journal of Innovation Management 14(1), 496–520 (2011)
31. Barney, J.: Firm resources and sustained competitive advantage. Journal of Management 17(1), 99–120 (1991)
32. Granstrand, O.: The economics and management of intellectual property: towards intellectual capitalism. Edward Elgar Publishing, Cheltenham (2000)
33. Granstrand, O.: Multi-technology management. In: Cantwell, J., Gambardella, A., Granstrand, O. (eds.) The Economics and Management of Technological Diversification, pp. 296–332. Routledge, London (2004)
34. March, J.G.: Exploration and exploitation organizational learning. Organization Science 2(1), 71–87 (1991)
35. Lichtenthaler, U., Ernst, H.: External technology commercialization in large firms: Results of a quantitative benchmarking study. R&D Management 37(5), 383–397 (2007)
36. Chesbrough, H., Schwartz, K.: Innovating business models with co-development partnerships. Research-Technology Management 50(1), 55–59 (2007)
37. Ebersberger, B., Bloch, C., Herstad, S.J., Van De Velde, E.: Open innovation practices and their effect on innovation performance. International Journal of Innovation and Technology Management (2010)
38. Laursen, K., Salter, A.: Open for innovation: The role of openness in explaining innovation performance among U.K. manufacturing firms. Strategic Management Journal 27(2), 131–150 (2006)
39. Lin, B.W., Wu, C.H.: How does knowledge depth moderate the performance of internal and external knowledge sourcing strategies? Technovation 30(11), 582–589 (2010)
40. Spithoven, A., Frantzen, D., Clarysse, B.: Heterogeneous Firm-Level Effects of Knowledge Exchanges on Product Innovation: Differences between Dynamic and Lagging Product Innovators. Journal of Product Innovation Management 27, 362–381 (2010)
41. Tsai, K.H., Hsieh, M.H., Hultink, E.J.: External technology acquisition and product innovativeness: The moderating roles of R&D investment and configurational context. Journal of Engineering and Technology Management 28, 184–200 (2011)
42. Un, C.A., Cuervo-Cazurra, A., Asakawa, K.: R&D Collaborations and Product Innovation. Journal of Product Innovation Management 27, 673–689 (2010)
43. Belderbos, R., Faems, D., Leten, B., Van Looy, B.: Technological Activities and Their Impact on the Financial Performance of the Firm: Exploitation and Exploration within and between Firms. Journal of Product Innovation Management 27(6), 869–882 (2010)
44. Kutvonen, A.: Strategic application of outbound open innovation. European Journal of Innovation Management 14(4), 460–474 (2011)
45. Lichtenthaler, U.: External commercialization of knowledge: Review and research agenda. International Journal of Management Reviews 7(4), 231–255 (2006)
46. Lichtenthaler, U.: Outbound open innovation and its effect on firm performance: Examining environmental influences. R&D Management 39(4), 317–330 (2009)
47. Lichtenthaler, U.: Technology exploitation in the context of open innovation: Finding the right "job" for your technology. Technovation 30(7), 429–435 (2010)
48. Lichtenthaler, U., Ernst, H.: Opening up the innovation process: The role of technology aggressiveness. R&D Management 39(1), 38–54 (2009)

49. Faems, D., De Visser, M., Andries, P., Van Looy, B.: Technology Alliance Portfolios and Financial Performance: Value-Enhancing and Cost-Increasing Effects of Open Innovation. Journal of Product Innovation Management 27, 785–796 (2010)
50. Lin, C., Wu, Y.J., Chang, C., Wang, W., Lee, C.Y.: The alliance innovation performance of R&D alliances-the absorptive capacity perspective. Technovation 32(5), 282–292 (2012)
51. Nieto, M.J., Santamaria, L.: The importance of diverse collaborative networks for the novelty of product innovation. Technovation 26(6), 367–377 (2007)
52. Huang, F., Rice, J.: Openness in Product and Process Innovation. International Journal of Innovation Management 16(4) (2012)
53. Neyens, I., Faems, D., Sels, L.: The impact of continuous and discontinuous alliance trategies on startup innovation performance. International Journal of Technology Management 52(3/4), 392–410 (2010)
54. Suh, Y., Kim, M.S.: Effects of SME collaboration on R&D in the service sector in open innovation. Innovation: Management, Policy & Practice 14(3), 349–362 (2012)
55. Chaston, I., Scott, G.J.: Entrepreneurship and open innovation in an emerging economy. Management Decision 50(7), 1161–1177 (2012)
56. Covin, J.G., Slevin, D.P.: Strategic management of small firms in hostile and benign environments. Strategic Management Journal 10(1), 75–87 (1989)
57. Miller, D.: The correlates of entrepreneurship in three types of firms. Management Science 29(7), 770–791 (1983)
58. Wiklund, J., Shepherd, D.: Knowledge-based resources, entrepreneurial orientation, and the performance of small and medium-sized businesses. Strategic Management Journal 24(13), 1307–1314 (2003)
59. Lumpkin, G.T., Dess, G.G.: Clarifying the entrepreneurial orientation construct and linking it to performance. Academy of Management Review 21(1), 135–172 (1996)
60. Lumpkin, G.T., Dess, G.G.: Linking two dimensions of entrepreneurial orientation to firm performance: The moderating role of environment and industry life cycle. Journal of Business Venturing 16(5), 429–451 (2001)
61. Van De Vrande, V., Vanhaverbeke, W., Gassmann, O.: Broadening the scope of open innovation: past research, current state and future directions. International Journal of Technology Management 52(3/4), 221–235 (2010)
62. Zahra, S.A., George, G.: Absorptive capacity: A review, reconceptualization, and extension. Academy of Management Review 27(2), 185–203 (2002)
63. Dyer, J.H., Singh, H.: The relational view: Cooperative strategy and sources of inter-organizational competitive advantage. Academy of Management Review 23(4), 660–679 (1998)
64. Terziovski, M.: Innovation practice and its performance implications in small and medium enterprises (SMEs) in the manufacturing sector: A resource-based view. Strategic Management Journal 31(8), 892–902 (2010)
65. Jaworski, B.J., Kohli, A.K.: Market orientation: Antecedents and consequences. Journal of Marketing 57(3), 53–70 (1993)
66. Chiaroni, D., Chiesa, V., Frattini, F.: The Open Innovation Journey: how firms dynamically implement the emerging innovation management paradigm. Technovation (2009)
67. Chiaroni, D., Chiesa, V., Frattini, F.: Unravelling the process from Closed to Open Innovation: evidence from mature, asset-intensive industries. R&D Management 40(3), 222–245 (2010)

68. Schweitzer, F.M., Gassmann, O., Gaubinger, K.: Open innovation and its effectiveness to embrace turbulent environments. International Journal of Innovation Management 15(6), 1191–1207 (2011)
69. The U.S. Small Business Administration (2013), http://www.sba.gov
70. Hair, J.F., Black, W.C., Babin, B.J., Anderson, R.E., Tatham, R.L.: Multivariate data analysis: A global perspective, 7th edn. Prentice Hall, Upper Saddle River (2010)
71. Nunnally, J.C.: Psychometric theory, 3rd edn. Tata McGraw-Hill Education, New York (2010)
72. Cohen, J., Cohen, P., West, S.G., Aiken, L.S.: Applied Multiple Regression/Correlation Analysis for the Behavioral Science, 2nd edn. Lawrence Erlbaum, New Jersey (2003)

Appendix

Notes: (X), Items were removed from final analyses due to low item-to-total correlation

Outside-in Process	
OIOI-1	Your company sources external R&D initiatives from other organizations (e.g. ideas, knowledge, personnel, and technologies). (X)
OIOI-2	Your company integrates customers' R&D initiatives (e.g. ideas and knowledge).
OIOI-3	Your company integrates suppliers' R&D initiatives (e.g. ideas, knowledge, personnel, and technologies).
OIOI-4	Your company integrates non-profit organizations' R&D initiatives (universities, government agencies, and other institutions).
OIOI-5	Your company licenses-in external sources of R&D initiatives (e.g. patents, intellectual property, and technologies).
Inside-out Process	
IOOI-1	Your company commercializes internally developed R&D initiatives (e.g. knowledge and technologies). (X)
IOOI-2	Your company transfers internally developed R&D initiatives (e.g. knowledge, personnel, and technologies).
IOOI-3	Your company licenses-out internally developed R&D initiatives (e.g. patents, IP, and technologies).
IOOI-4	Your company sells internally developed R&D initiatives (e.g. patents, IP, and technologies).
IOOI-5	Your company starts up new ventures drawing on internally developed R&D initiatives.
Coupled Process:	
COI-1	Your company and R&D partners have a high degree of trust.
COI-2	Your company and R&D partners interact with each other on a regular basis.
COI-3	Your company exchange knowledge with R&D partners intensively.
COI-4	Your company and R&D partners have a process of mutual learning. (X)
COI-5	There is a right balance of give and take between your company and R&D partners.

Entrepreneurial Orientation:

EO-1   Your company has a strong proclivity for high-risk projects with chances of very high return.

EO-2   Your company believes bold, wide-ranging acts are necessary to achieve the business objectives.

EO-3   When confronted with uncertainty, your company adopts an aggressive posture in order to exploit potential opportunities.

EO-4   In dealing with competitors, your company initiates actions which competitors then respond to.

EO-5   Your company is often the first to introduce new products/services, administrative techniques, or operating technologies, etc. (X)

EO-6   Your company typically adopts a very competitive "undo-the-competitors" posture.

EO-7   Your company has a strong emphasis on R&D, technological leadership, and innovations. (X)

EO-8   Your company has marketed many new products or services in the past three years.

EO-9   Changes in the product or service line in your company has been dramatic.

Product Innovation

ProdI-1   Level of newness (novelty) of your new/improved products for the past three years.

ProdI-2   Development speed of your new/improved products for the past three years.

ProdI-3   Number of new/improved products introduced to the market for the past three years.

Financial Performance

FinP-1   Compared the performance of your company with that of your competitors for the past three years in terms of growth in sales.

FinP-2   Compared the performance of your company with that of your competitors for the past three years in terms of growth in revenue.

FinP-3   Compared the performance of your company with that of your competitors for the past three years in terms of growth in net profits.

Technological Turbulence

TT-1   Technology in our industry is changing rapidly.

TT-2   Technological changes in our industry are unpredictable.

TT-3   Technological breakthrough results in many new product ideas in our industry.

The Relationships between Software Development Processes and Software Product Quality

Andrzej Kobyliński

Warsaw School of Economics, Al. Niepodległości 162,
02-554 Warsaw, Poland
Andrzej.Kobylinski@sgh.waw.pl

Abstract. The main motivation for software process assessment and improvement (i.e. performed in accordance with standard ISO/IEC 15504) is that the software product, developed according to improved processes, will be of higher quality (determined by ISO/IEC 25010). ISO/IEC 15504 refer to the ISO/IEC 12207 which describes processes performed in software acquiring or developing organizations. The relations between software processes and quality characteristics seem intuitive but there is little empirical evidence to prove its validity. The paper describes the first stage of research where practitioners try to find and explain relationships between software quality characteristics (ISO/IEC 25010) and software life cycle processes (ISO/IEC 12207). The motivation for the research lies in the assumption that if the acquirer is particularly interested in a certain quality characteristic of the product, the supplier may put special emphasis on these software processes that have a significant impact on this attribute.

Keywords: software quality, ISO/IEC 25010, software life cycle processes, ISO/IEC 12207, software process assessment, ISO/IEC 15504.

1 Introduction

Software product quality is different from software production quality. A mature process ensures good production quality (functional correctness, predictable cost and schedule, low defect rate). But product quality addresses the question "Is it the right product?" which means if the product fulfills customer expectations and if it has been built right from the perspective of the customer's organization in terms of reliability, usability, security etc. The main assumption for software process improvement is that improvement in software process performance results in higher software product quality.

1.1 The Quality Concept

The term "product quality" is a very general concept. There are a lot of different views on quality, each of which is valid when used in a certain context. It can be assumed as "degree of excellence" [1], "conformity to requirements" (Crosby) [2], "freedom from

A. Kobyliński and A. Sobczak (Eds.): BIR 2013, LNBIP 158, pp. 161–169, 2013.

deficiencies or defects" (Juran) [3], "fitness for use" (Juran) [4], "fitness for purpose" [5], "sustained satisfaction" (Deming) [6] etc. The newest terminological standard ISO 9000:2005 [7] defines quality as "the degree to which a set of inherent characteristics fulfills requirements", which sounds rather outdated but combining the definition of "quality" and "requirements", quality can be expressed as "the degree to which a set of inherent characteristics fulfills a need or an expectation that is stated, generally implied or obligatory". The term "software quality" has different meaning for different people in the same time, and their views are often competing, which can lead to confusion [8]. What's more, throughout the life cycle of a product the view on the quality of the people involved in the development often change a few times [9].

1.2   Software Quality Attributes

A direct attempt to assess the overall quality is doomed to failure. Therefore, commonly used procedure consists of the fact that the intangible concept of software quality is decomposed into a number of *attributes* (characteristics). Attributes (such as usability, functionality, maintainability etc.) are too general to be measured directly. Therefore quality attributes are usually decomposed into few more detailed characteristics, called *criteria* (or sub-characteristics). Criteria, in turn, can be assessed according to a number of *metrics*.

Over the past decades many models based on such a framework were established. The first was model designed in 1977 by McCall et al. [10], containing 11 characteristics. The second was Boehm's model [11], consisting of seven characteristics. In the subsequent years, a few other software quality models were prepared [9]. Emergence of so many models created confusing situation. Although the nature of the models is similar:

1. different definitions are assigned to identical terms (terminological inconsistency),
2. identical definitions may be referred by various terms (synonyms),
3. what in some models was considered as attribute, in other models was recognized as criteria.

The situation called for normalization. And so, in 1991, the International Organization for Standardization (ISO) developed the ISO/IEC 9126 [12], which led to the agreement what are the attributes of software quality. ISO/IEC 9126 software quality model was containing 6 characteristics. A revision was issued in 2001 in four parts (ISO/IEC 9126-1 to 9126-4) [13]. Characteristics of the model were supplemented with 27 sub-characteristics and dozens of metrics. ISO (with cooperation with IEC) then started work on more extensive series of standards to replace ISO/IEC 9126. Initiative SQuaRE (Software product Quality Requirements and Evaluation) resulted in a series of standards numbered ISO/IEC 250xy. The first standard of this series was published in 2005 (ISO/IEC 25000 [14]), and in 2011 was issued ISO/IEC 25010 [15], which supersedes ISO/IEC 9126-1. While ISO/IEC 9126-1 had six product quality characteristics, ISO/IEC 25010 has eight. They have been listed below, including the definitions and comprising a set of sub-characteristics.

Functional Suitability: degree to which a product or system provides functions that meet stated and implied needs when used under specified conditions (sub-characteristics: functional completeness, functional correctness, functional appropriateness).

Performance Efficiency: performance related to the amount of resources used under stated conditions (sub-characteristics: time behaviour, resource utilization, capacity).

Compatibility: degree to which a product, system or component can exchange information with other products, systems, or components and/or perform its required functions, while sharing the same hardware or software environment (sub-characteristics: co-existence, interoperability).

Usability: degree to which a product or system can be used by specified users to achieve specified goals with effectiveness, efficiency and satisfaction in a specified context of use (sub-characteristics: appropriateness, recognisability, learnability, operability, user error protection, user interface aesthetics, accessibility).

Reliability: degree to which a system, product or component performs specified functions under specified conditions for a specified period of time (sub-characteristics: maturity, availability, fault tolerance, recoverability).

Security: degree to which a product or system protects information and data so that persons or other products or systems have the degree of data access appropriate to their types and levels of authorization (sub-characteristics: confidentiality, integrity, non-repudiation, accountability, authenticity).

Maintainability: degree of effectiveness and efficiency with which a product or a system can be modified by the intended maintainers (sub-characteristics: modularity, reusability, analysability, modifiability, testability).

Portability: degree of effectiveness and efficiency with which a system, product or component can be transferred from one hardware, software or other operational or usage environment to another (sub-characteristics: adaptability, installability, replaceability).

1.3 Software Processes Maturity

The quality of the software product is mostly driven by the maturity (quality) of the development process. This is the main assumption lying in the bases of all software process improvement initiatives. In recent years, many such initiatives emerged. The best known is Capability Maturity Model (CMM-SW) [16], and its successor Capability Maturity Model Integration (CMMI) [17], but also several other models gained some popularity, for example: Trillium [18] and Bootstrap [19].

Model ISO/IEC 15504. Simultaneously in Europe a project called Software Process Improvement and Capability dEtermination (SPICE) has been initiated. The result of its work was Technical Report, which took the form of standard ISO/IEC TR 15504 in 1998 [20]. The standard in its Part 2 contained a two dimensional *reference model*. The reference model defined *process dimension* and *capability dimension*.

Process dimension defined processes that are typical not only for software developing organizations, but for all software business organizations, that acquire, supply, develop, operate and maintain software products. The processes have been defined in alignment with standard ISO/IEC 12207:1995, Information technology - Software life cycle processes [21], but there were included a number of additional processes (compare ISO/IEC 12207:1995 Fig. 1 and ISO/IEC TR 15504:1998 Fig. 1). Finally, all processes (both from ISO/IEC 12207 and additional) were divided into five process categories:

- customer / supplier,
- engineering,
- supporting,
- management,
- organization.

The second dimension of the reference model is the process *capability dimension* which characterizes the level of capability that an organization unit has attained for a particular process. It is characterized by a series of nine process attributes, applicable to any process, and represents measurable features necessary to manage process and improve its capabilities to perform. ISO/IEC TR 15504 specified six capabilities levels on the following scale:

Level 5. Optimizing process.
Level 4. Predictable process.
Level 3. Established process.
Level 2. Managed process.
Level 1. Performed process.
Level 0. Incomplete process.

Standard ISO/IEC 12207:1995 was revised by two Amendments from 2002 and 2004 respectively. This contributed to the need for a major revision of the standard: in 2003/2004 subsequent parts of the standard were updated as ISO/IEC 15504:2004 Information technology -- Process assessment [22]. The biggest difference compared with 1998 edition was the removal of the process reference model. Now, the user of the standard can use different process reference models but it's suggested, that in the field of software engineering, the process models in ISO/IEC 12207 apply ([22] Part 1, p. 13; [22] Part 2, p. 5). Process assessment model described in Part 5 of ISO/IEC 15504-5:2006 is fully based on the process reference model for software ISO/IEC 12207:1995+2 Amendments. In 2008 standard ISO/IEC 12207 [23] has been significantly changed. The old one enumerated 17 software processes grouped in 3 areas (primary, supporting, organizational), while the new one: 43 system and software processes (and more than 100 activities, a few hundred tasks and outcomes) classified in 7 main groups. As a consequence in 2012 Part 5 of ISO/IEC 15504-5 [24] has been changed.

2   Product Attributes versus Development Processes

2.1   Literature Review

The impact of different processes (described for example in ISO/IEC 12207) on the quality characteristics of the software product hasn't been extensively examined yet. Moreover, in the literature on a software quality there is little theoretical discussion on the topic. In 1994 Woodman in [25] presented the results of his reflection on this subject. Ashrafi in 2003 [26] investigated the impact of SPI methodologies on software quality. In 2008 van Solingen and Berghout published [27], where they described the impact of different software engineering techniques on quality attributes. They also supported author's impression on scarcity of research on the subject ([27], p. 3).

A clear and complete example how to apply a process point of view on usability attribute is described in Annex E of ([23], pp. 108-109). Unfortunately, there are no similar examples on software development processes impact on other quality attributes of software products. Fragmentary work on the subject was done during ESSI-SCOPE project [28]. Some discussion on the impact of the software development phases on the quality characteristics is contained in ([29], chap. 2).

An exhaustive review of the literature (148 papers) of the impact of various SPI practices at quality, cost, schedule is presented in [30].

2.2 Purpose of the Research

The goal of the research is to establish the impact of different processes, activities and tasks specified in ISO/IEC 12207:2008 on quality characteristics enumerated in ISO/IEC 25010:2011. As there are so many activities and tasks – hundreds, in the first stage of the research only seven groups of processes (management, organizational, engineering etc.) were taken into account. A more detailed analysis, taking into account all 47 processes will be conducted in the second phase of the research. If the client is particularly interested in a certain quality characteristic of the product, the supplier may put special emphasis on these software processes that have a significant impact on this attribute. Conducting the analysis the author relied on his own experience, interviews with practitioners, and a review of the literature.

2.3 Relationships

The table is the most convenient way to describe the relationships between process and product attributes. The cells located at the intersection of the appropriate rows (describing processes) and columns (product characteristics) contain information about the impact of the particular process on the certain product attribute. An example of such an array is given in Table 1.

Agreement Processes Group (AGR). This group of two processes (Acquisition Process and Supply Process) defines functions necessary to set up an agreement between two organizations: acquirer and supplier. When the process is successfully implemented, the contract that clearly expresses the client's expectations, responsibilities, liabilities of both the supplier and the customer should be developed. The acquisition is managed in a way that particular constrains (i.e. cost, schedule, quality) are met. Supply Process should ensure that a product or service that meet the agreed requirements are provided.

Table 1. Relationships between groups of processes versus product characteristics

Processes	Functional suitability	Performance efficiency	Compatibility	Usability	Reliability	Security	Maintainability	Portability
Agreement Processes (AGR)	++	+	+	+	+	+	+	+
Organizational Project-Enabling Processes (ORG)	+	+	+	+	+	+	+	+
Project Processes (PRO)	0	0	0	0	0	0	0	0
Technical Processes (ENG)	+++	+++	+++	+++	+++	+++	+++	+++
Software Implementation Processes (DEV)	+++	+++	+++	+++	+++	+++	+++	+++
Software Support Processes (SUP)	+	+	+	++	+	+	++	+
Software Reuse Processes (REU)	0	+	+	0	++	+	++	++

„0" – no direct relationship between the process and the quality attribute,
„+" – positive impact of process capabilities on the product quality characteristic (the number of signs + indicates the strength of the relationship).

The impact of Agreement Processes on quality characteristics is large, especially on the functionality, but also on other qualities of the system. The task of gathering requirements from the customer and the change management in the software development process is particularly important. That group of processes is rather general, the detail development processes are included in other groups (ENG and DEV), that's why it was decided to put only one sign + (except functionality) in the corresponding row.

Organizational Project-Enabling Processes (ORG). This group consists of five processes that establish organization's skills to acquire and supply products (or services) through the initiation, support and control of projects. Organizational processes (Life Cycle Model Management, Infrastructure Management, Project Portfolio Management, Human Resource Management, Quality Management) build organizational infrastructure, where individual projects can proceed. These processes seem to be of a different nature to the other process groups, as the whole group is at a much higher level.

While four of the mentioned processes has only an indirect effect on the quality of the software products, the Quality Management Process' significance can't be overestimated. Roughly speaking it can be concluded that all activities described in standard ISO 9001:2008 [31] can be assigned to Quality Management Process.

Project Processes (PRO). All 7 Project Processes can be divided into two internal groups: Project Management Processes (2 processes) and Project Support Processes (5 processes). Project Management Processes (Project Planning, Project Assessment and Control) are used to establish project plans, assess the progress against the plans and control execution of the project. The Project Support Processes (Decision Management, Risk Management, Configuration Management, Information Management, Measurement) are of a generic nature and may be used by anyone who manages any sort of project or process within a system lifecycle. Of course they are very supportive to perform other processes, but it's difficult to find clear relations between mentioned processes and product quality attributes.

Technical Processes (ENG). All 11 processes included in the technical (engineering) group are used to analyze, specify, design, implement, integrate, test, install, operate maintenance and removal a system. There are the following processes in this group: Stakeholder Requirements Definition, System Requirements Analysis, System Architectural Design, Software Implementation, System Integration, System Qualification Testing, Software Installation, Software Acceptance Support, Software Operation, Software Maintenance, Software Disposal.

This group of processes is essential for obtaining all analyzed quality characteristics by the product. Properly conducted system requirements analysis, well thought design, professional implementation, careful integration, honest testing of the product - make that the final product is formed and quality characteristics begin to manifest. Well performed processes result in obtaining a product of better or worse quality characteristics.

Software Implementation Processes (DEV). This group of process is very similar to the previous one. The former one was more general, the processes were used to create, operate, maintain, dispose a system, which consist of hardware and software items. Processes in DEV group (Software Requirements Analysis, Software Architectural Design, Software Detailed Design, Software Construction, Software Integration, Software Qualification Testing) are used to produce a software part of the system. Its impact on product quality characteristics is comparable to that in the preceding paragraph.

Software Support Processes (SUP). The Software Support Processes group consists of processes: Software Documentation Management, Software Configuration Management, Software Quality Assurance, Software Verification, Software Validation, Software Review, Software Audit, Software Problem Resolution that may be used by any other process at various stages of the software lifecycle. They are supporting processes enumerated in DEV group, contributing to the success of the software project.

It's obvious that five of the above processes: quality assurance, verification, validation, review, audit, carried out at various stages of the development process, contribute directly to obtain software that will be tailored to customer requirements gathered during the Software Requirements Analysis Process – these processes impose proper control of the development. But also Software Documentation Management Process has a strong impact on the two attributes of the software product: usability and maintainability. The quality of documentation has a direct impact on the software ease-of-use – both from the user's (usability) and maintainer's (maintainability) point of view.

Software Reuse Processes (REU). The three processes included in this group: Domain Engineering, Reuse Asset Management and Reuse Program Management, support organization's ability to reuse different software items: domain models, domain architectures, assets for the domain; manage the life of reusable assets; plan, establish, manage, control, monitor organization's reuse program and exploit reuse opportunities.

The use of reusable elements at all levels of abstraction is recommended due to the common belief that reusability reduce development time and increase the likelihood that prior testing and use eliminated defects. Reusable elements are generally considered to be more reliable, correct, flexible, adaptable, fast etc. than the elements developed from scratch. In Table 1 this is illustrated by the large number of signs + in the corresponding row. Reusability has a particularly big impact on reliability, maintainability and portability of the software product.

3   Conclusion

There is a direct correlation between the quality of the processes and the quality of software products. The influence of individual process on the quality of the software product is differentiated. None of the considered process groups has negative impact on the quality of the product, and most have a positive effect. The most important are Technical Processes (ENG) and Software Implementation Processes (DEV) groups, which directly affect the attributes of the newly developed product. Other processes are rather auxiliary. The exceptions are the processes included in the group Software Support Processes (SUP), as they influence the usability and maintainability, and Software Reuse Processes (REU), which are important for reliability, maintainability and portability.

There is insufficient empirical research on detailed relationships between software product quality characteristics and sub-characteristics and individual processes. There is a lack of experiments, which findings allow us to conclude what is the impact of new methodologies, techniques and tools on software products quality. Many publications about new methods, techniques and tools reported obtained "better quality", but this term is rarely explained, and certainly never in relation to the international standard ISO / IEC 25010.

The conclusion from the above discussion is quite obvious – most of the processes have a positive influence on software quality attributes. But the results of the initial works done in the next stage of the research (not included in this paper yet) is much more impressive – the analysis clearly shows which individual processes affect different software product's attributes.

References

1. New Webster's Expanded Dictionary (2005)
2. Crosby, P.B.: Quality is Free. McGraw-Hill Inc. (1979)
3. Juran, J.M.: Juran on Quality by Design. The Free Press, Division of Macmillan Inc. (1992)
4. Juran, J.M.: Quality Control Handbook, 3rd edn. McGraw-Hill Inc. (1974)
5. UK Sales and Supply of Goods Act (1994)

6. Deming, W.E.: The New Economics. MIT Press (2000)
7. ISO 9000:2005 Quality management systems – Fundamentals and vocabulary
8. Garvin, D.A.: What Does "Product Quality" Really Mean? Sloan Management Review, 25–43 (Fall 1984)
9. Kobyliński, A.: Modele jakości produktów i procesów programowych, OW SGH, Warszawa (2005)
10. McCall, J.A., Richards, P.K., Walters, G.F.: Factors in Software Quality, 1-3, RADC-TR-77-369, Rome Air Development Center, Griffiss Air Force Base, NY 13441-5700 (November 1977)
11. Boehm, B.W., Brown, J.R., Kaspar, H., Lipow, M., MacLeod, G.J., Merritt, M.J.: Characteristics of Software Quality, Amsterdam (1978)
12. ISO/IEC 9126:1991 Software engineering – Product quality
13. ISO/IEC 9126-1:2001 Software engineering – Product quality – Part 1: Quality model; ISO/IEC TR 9126-2:2003 Software engineering – Product quality – Part 2: External metrics; ISO/IEC TR 9126-3:2003 Software engineering – Product quality – Part 3: Internal metrics; ISO/IEC TR 9126-4:2004 Software engineering – Product quality – Part 4: Quality in use metrics
14. ISO/IEC 25000:2005 Software Engineering – Software product Quality Requirements and Evaluation (SQuaRE) – Guide to SQuaRE
15. ISO/IEC 25010:2011 Systems and software engineering – Systems and software Quality Requirements and Evaluation (SQuaRE) – System and software quality models
16. Paulk, M.C., Weber, C.V., Curtis, B., Chrissis, M.B.: The Capability Maturity Model: Guidelines for Improving the Software Process. Addison-Wesley Publishing Company (1995)
17. Chrissis, M.B., Konrad, M., Shrum, S.: CMMI for Development: Guidelines for Process Integration and Product Improvement, 3rd edn. Addison-Wesley Professional (2011)
18. Bell Canada, The Trillium Model (1994), http://www.sqi.griffith.edu.au/trillium/ (access: May 1, 2013)
19. Bicego, A., Khurana, M., Kuvaja, P.: Bootstrap 3.0 – Software Process Assessment Methodology. In: Hawkins, C., Ross, M., Staples, G. (eds.) Software Quality Management VI. Springer (1998)
20. ISO/IEC TR 15504:1998 Information technology - Software process assessment - Part 1–9
21. ISO/IEC 12207:1995 Information technology – Software life cycle processes
22. ISO/IEC 15504:2004 Information technology – Process assessment – Part 1–9 (part 2 was issued earlier; parts 5-9 were issued later)
23. ISO/IEC 12207:2008 Systems and software engineering – Software life cycle processes
24. ISO/IEC 15504-5:2012 Information technology – Process assessment – Part 5: An exemplar software life cycle process assessment model
25. Woodman, I.H.G.: Relationship Between the Activities of Software Process and the Quality of the Software Product. University Of Strathclyde, Department of Computer Science, Research Report/94/171
26. Ashrafi, N.: The Impact of Software Process Improvement on Quality: in Theory and Practice. Information and Management 40(7), 677–690 (2003)
27. van Solingen, R., Berghout, E.: Causal Relationships between Improvements in Software Development Processes and Final Software Product Quality. The Electronic Journal Information Systems Evaluation 11(1), 1–10 (2008)
28. ESSI-SCOPE, http://www.cse.dcu.ie/essiscope/sm5/relation.html (access May 1, 2013)
29. Chemuturi, M.: Mastering Software Quality Assurance: Best Practices, Tools and Techniques for Software Developers. J. Ross Publishing, Inc. (2011)
30. Islam, A.K.M.M., Gorschek, T., Unterkalmsteiner, M., Feldt, R., Permadi, R.B., Cheng, C.K.: Evaluation and Measurement of Software Process Improvement—A Systematic Literature Review. IEEE Transactions on Software Engineering 38(2), 398–424 (2012)
31. ISO 9001:2008 Quality management systems – Requirements

Ontological Foundations of Multi-agent Framework for Organizational Diagnosis

Tatiana Poletaeva[1], Habib Abdulrab[2], and Eduard Babkin[1]

[1] National Research University Higher School of Economics, Nizhny Novgorod, Russia
ta.poletaeva@gmail.com, eababkin@hse.ru
[2] INSA de Rouen, LITIS lab., Rouen, France
abdulrab@insa-rouen.fr

Abstract. In order to support management functions in dynamically changing corporate enterprises, adequate information systems need to be built, automating desirable adaptation of inter- and intra- organizational business processes. This paper therefore introduces a new approach to the design of multi-agent information systems meant for planning, discovering, monitoring deviations, and optimizing business processes. Expected qualitative breakthrough in the system's capacity is based on the matching of its constructional and behavioral perspective with the ontological model of supported enterprise. Besides, conformity between organizational and information systems is supplemented by their conceptual alignment in the description of states and processes. The method of multi-agent framework construction and its application for traceability in supply chains are presented in this paper.

Keywords: Organizational Diagnosis, Business Process Model, Object-Paradigm, Multi-agent, Meta-model.

1 Introduction

The research that is reported in this paper concerns the use of business information systems [1] for the purpose of organizational diagnosis that is to establish the widely shared understanding of a system and, based on that understanding, to determine whether change is desirable [2].

Globalization leads to the formation of dynamically changing, large-scale enterprises comprised of interacting business parties. The considerable growth of dependencies within corporate enterprises inevitably results in the complication of management activities related to organizational diagnosis. Provided that all the nodes of the ideal multi-organizational network agreed on their functions, standardized description of data and processes, and established flawless software interaction, even so the consolidated efforts of involved companies still would not guarantee their ability to react operatively to all the changes in the business world.

Furthermore, although the newest information systems are capable of fulfilling many human analytical and social functions, they still lack the ability to perform real-time analysis of deviations in the dynamic flow of business activities and automate

A. Kobyliński and A. Sobczak (Eds.): BIR 2013, LNBIP 158, pp. 170–184, 2013.

adaptation of inter- and intra- organizational business processes to erratic business conditions. The considerable degradation of existent business information systems in functional support of corporate enterprises arises due to reasons that are stated below.

At first, a theoretical basis for intellectual information systems for social organizations [3-5] is developed without taking into consideration the knowledge of enterprise engineering [6]. Implemented programming objects often have no links with the objects in the business world that they are meant to refer to. The fallacy in this approach is that resulted socio-technical systems [5] contain dissimilarities between models of information systems and business models of supported organizations. Consequently, the relationships between functions of developed software and constructions of social organizations are broken. Therefore, existing solutions do not meet contemporary business requirements.

Secondly, for the majority of information systems, embedded information patterns do not properly correspond to the concepts used in the real world to talk and think about business objects [7]. Representation of our world through inconsistent set of concepts creates unnecessary constraints and impedes data integration. Besides, progressive perdurantist approaches addressing temporality in data modeling still have not yielded complete, application-independent, and practically proved frameworks [8] for the modeling of business objects and processes. As a result, socio-technical systems are suffering from the isolation of data analysis from actual business activities.

Our research introduces a new approach to the design of information systems meant for planning, discovering, monitoring deviations, and optimizing business processes. Expected qualitative breakthrough in the system's capacity is based on the matching of its constructional and behavioral perspectives with the ontological model of supported enterprise. Besides, conformity between organizational and information systems is supplemented by their consistent abstractions for the description of states and processes of federated enterprises. Unified abstractions also help to improve the integration of business information systems of separated nodes into networks of organizations.

As will be presented and elaborated in this paper, integrated conceptualization of enterprise ontology [9], data models, and software architecture have a strong theoretical basis. Thus, to derive needed abstractions and a meta-description of business processes our approach uses the Design and Methodology for Organizations (DEMO) [6], which focuses on the communicative acts that take place between human actors in the organizations. One of perdurantist approaches, the Object Paradigm [7], accompanied with conceptual modeling technique BORO [7], facilitate tight integration among systems and data through semantic interoperability. ISO 15926 standard [10] is used for the representation of business-valuable data in a universal format. The WOSL (World Ontology Specification Language) language advantageously used in DEMO methodology for the specification of world ontologies is conceptually aligned with three-level metadata model ISO 15926. This creates necessary pre-conditions to both integrate concepts and predicates of these ontological models and build a generic process-data model.

On the other hand, we may see federated enterprises as social entities with collaborative human actors. From such a viewpoint, a supportive information system for organizational diagnosis naturally becomes a part of a 'collaboration' design domain intended for information sharing, learning and decision support [9]. The distributed manner of such systems and the large amount of autonomy among their components tempt us to use multi-agent approach [4] to design the needed abstractions of software architecture. A multi-agent solution adjusted with an ontological view on data model and business processes of organizations meets the requirement of some flexible reaction to changes in the dynamically changing enterprises.

The proposed approach to designing business information systems can be applied for the creation of a new class of traceability applications [11]. These applications are aimed at tracing the state of objects, discovering information regarding its past states, correctly predicting future states and estimating different kinds of risks. Particularly, traceability applications in transportation are essential for participants of supply chain activities, who want to carry out, plan and coordinate their business processes in accordance with the state and location of transportable objects. Logically and technically correspondent cornerstones of proposed multi-agent systems create the necessary conditions for the building of a cohesive transportation traceability system, which can be modified and extended continuously in order to support changes in the supply network. The method for multi-agent framework construction and its application for traceability in supply chains are presented upon in this paper.

The outline of the paper is as follows. First, the state of existing solutions is described in section 2. The theoretical background of our work is summarized in section 3. The research methodology is outlined in section 4. Then the application of proposed method of multi-agent framework construction is described in section 5. Finally, section 6 provides conclusions and directions for further research.

2   Existing Solutions for Organizational Diagnosis

In spite of rapid technological progress, there is a lack of information systems for organizational diagnosis in networking organizations [3], [5]. This new form of organizations is comprised by autonomous parties, which are free to join and leave the network. Traditional business information systems from SAP, BAAN, Navision et al. were found inefficient in supporting dynamically changing business processes within networking organizations [3]. That is why increasing number of the organizations with open, distributed and variable structure led to developing a theoretical basis for deployment of information technologies in social organizations [3-5]. In the early stages researches matured from abstracting of computing environment to model-oriented development in compliance with the application domain. At that time, the paradigm of model-oriented development was formulated by the international consortium OMG as Model Driven Architecture (MDA) [12]. At once multi-agent technologies were recognized as promising approach for operational data processing in the realm of organizational diagnosis [4]. However, the design principles of multi-agent systems for monitoring and optimization of business processes in accordance with the business models of the application domain have not been formulated until now.

One may think that thorough processing of the log files of business activities in networking organizations could satisfy the same goals as our approach. Thus we could advantageously avoid the necessity of correspondence between the conceptual model of an enterprise and the architecture of a multi-agent system, as well as eliminate the requirements for semantic interoperability between business level and supportive business information system. However, it is admitted that the most of the currently available process mining tools are still rather immature in operational support [13]. On the other hand, some stages of a common process mining project are covered in our framework, to wit: understanding of the domain; definition of the event data format and artifacts, process and organizational models. Furthermore, we will use process mining techniques at the implementation stage of multi-agent system.

3   Theoretical Background

3.1   DEMO Methodology for Enterprise Engineering

In our research we apply DEMO methodology [6] for the description of business processes of organizations at the conceptual level. DEMO, as the complete theory and the methodology of enterprise ontology, was published by J. Dietz in 2006. Nowadays the Enterprise Engineering Institute [14] advances and disseminates this methodology.

DEMO is a methodology for the design, engineering, and implementation of organizations and networks of organizations. Based on the strong theoretical basis, this methodology describes the function and construction of social organizations by their ontological models that are essential and complete at the conceptual level, logical and free from contradictions, compact and succinct, independent of its realization and implementation issues [6]. Besides, the interpretive perspective of the methodology comes from considering an enterprise as a social entity, the focus on social individuals, Habermas' theory of communicative action, the autonomy that is basically allowed to actor roles [6].

DEMO methodology builds a comprehensive view on the interaction and management processes of an enterprise from four Aspect Models [6]. On the other hand, these models are concise (i.e. contain a small set of concepts), therefore they can be considered as the core for unified description of business processes in networking organizations. In addition the Aspect Models represent business processes in the format suitable for automatic [15], [16] processing, and thereby provide the design-oriented foundation for IT alignment [9]. Moreover, since the Aspect Models are expressible in natural language sentences, they are free from Entity Paradigm's defects of seeing things [7], such as foundation on an inconsistent set of concepts as well as poor semantics for the description of relationships, identity and changes of objects over time.

3.2   Object Paradigm for Data Modeling

Supportive information systems perceive the reality through the data flow. Conceptualization plays a crucial role for data modeling because of the following reasons. At first, it expresses the ontological description of an application domain. Then, secure precise meaning and equal understanding of the exchanged data in a federated enterprise provides semantic interoperability between all its' parties. Finally, operation with the same data concepts in the description of an enterprise and related business information system helps to avoid information loss, simplifies and speeds up data analysis.

For the engineering of conceptual data modeling patterns, we strictly adhere to the Object Paradigm [7]. As other perdurantist approaches, the Object Paradigm assumes that all objects have four dimensions (spatial and temporal). The consideration of temporality unambiguously explains objects' identity through changes, their relationships and classification principles.

The idea about data standardization in networking organizations on both conceptual and domain-specific levels was substantiated in 2007 by a group of large-scale energy companies [17]. They encouraged the development of a unified ontology for data aggregation and support of manufacturing lifecycle management. As a result, ISO 15926 "Integration of lifecycle data for process plants including oil and gas production facilities" standard [10] was issued. The core data model of the standard is based on the Object Paradigm. Consequently, it includes interconnected concepts for the presentation of information about changes (processes) in federated enterprises.

Though initial reference data defined by the ISO 15926 relates to oil and gas industry, it can be easily extended for the application in other domains. Reference data is currently maintained and enhanced by Special Interest Groups within POSC Caesar Association (PCA) [18].

4   Steps of Solution Implementation

Hereafter we outline four main steps to be performed in order to design the multi-agent framework (MAS) for organizational diagnosis.

The ontological foundations of proposed multi-agent framework are formed by conceptual alignment between the meta-models of enterprise ontology [9], data, and multi-agent system. Therefore, at the first step, we will develop the meta-model of multi-agent framework.

It makes sense to consider functioning of MAS framework at two levels: business and information. Business level of the framework is formed by analytical and communicative abilities of intellectual agents implemented by the algorithms for data and events processing. Provided that meta-model of the framework matches with the DEMO meta-model, the rules for agents' interactions and their perception of the world can be specified by DEMO Aspect Models of supported enterprise for a particular case.

In the proposed solution information level of the multi-agent system is based on the cohesive theoretical foundations of DEMO and BORO methodologies. Every individual concept (predicate) of the WOSL language [6] represents an individual fact in the world. Thus, we will extract the concepts and their descriptions by the means of BORO methodology [7] from the DEMO meta-model and from DEMO aspect models of standardized business processes of networking organizations. In view of the fact that all individual facts and relations between them can be unambiguously classified based on the reference data of ISO 15926, we will integrate extracted concepts with ISO 15926 reference data. The resulted conceptual schema will specify the information structure of multi-agent system. Provided that intellectual agents implement the created data model, they will be able to follow and support business processes of prototypal organization.

At the next stage of our research, we will specify the co-influence of business strategy, business model, business capabilities and processes with the functions of multi-agent framework. As a result, multi-agent framework will be enhanced by the ability to support organizational interoperability.

Then we will implement the algorithms for run-time monitoring and control of processes enactment by intellectual agents. This stage includes implementation of Process Mining techniques [13] in the multi-agent system; implementation of reasoning abilities of intellectual agents; development of a runtime mechanism for adaptive change of business processes based on self-organization principles of intellectual agents.

Finally, the functions of created multi-agent framework should be validated and adjusted iteratively to support operation of artificial networking organization.

5 Multi-agent Framework for Organizational Diagnosis in Supply Network

In this section we present the first results of our research. The first step of proposed methodology (section 4) was applied to build the conceptual basis of multi-agent framework for organizational diagnosis in supply network. Supply networks can be considered as one of the forms of networking organizations, where volatility of supply processes is reflected in tracing data. The applications for tracing data processing (traceability applications) exemplify the means of organizational diagnosis. As confirmed by multiple researches [11], [20-24], nowadays the results of traceability data processing and analysis do not satisfy the needs of supply parties.

5.1 Traceability Artifacts in Supply Chain Management

Expected responsiveness of proposed multi-agent system for tracing data processing is based on the implementation of tracing data in a computer system (i.e. in the shape of concepts) as closer as possible to the business understanding of tracing information. That is why the first step in developing of abstraction framework for traceability applications is the accurate specification of the artifacts to work with. Based on the definition of traceability given in the Introduction, we deem that all processes, activities, information inputs and outputs, metrics, and assigned people roles related to tracing objects constitute the full set of traceability artifacts. Where relevant subset of the artifacts can be found in the specifications and practices of supply activities.

Consequently, generalization of supply chain practices can be considered as the most reliable method of specification of traceability artifacts.

In our work the description of common patterns for supply chain activities and metrics is founded on the Supply-Chain Operations Reference-model (SCOR-model) [25]. This model summarizes the best practices and technologies and put them into a unified structure in order to improve supply chain management [25]. Basic supply chain of the SCOR-model is a "chain" of Source, Make, and Deliver execution processes aimed to transform or transport materials and/or products. Each process in the chain is a customer of the previous process and a supplier to the next. Within this paper we exemplify our approach by using the second decomposition level of the Source Stocked Product (S1) process [25], which provides the reference model for procurement of inventory driven or standard goods and services.

According to the SCOR-model, chosen process S1 consists of the following stages: (S1.1) Schedule Product Deliveries, (S1.2) Receive Product, (S1.3) Verify Product, (S1.4) Transfer Product, (S1.5) Authorize Supplier Payment. The simplest S1 process is self-activated and encloses one transaction (the set of coordination and production acts) with some actor of the Delivery process at the Receive Product (S1.2) stage.

Though the SCOR-model provides a good vocabulary to speak about traceability in ordinary language, its semantics is still inconsistent and incomplete to be used as the ontological basis [26] for definition of the full set of traceability artifacts. This model entails resources exchanged between process elements and actors, but lacks semantic precision [26]. In the next section we enhance the semantics of the SCOR-model by new concepts extracted from the ontological description of social organization then link this world ontology with the reference concepts of ISO 15926.

5.2   Meta-description of Business Processes

Conceptual model expressed by PSI (Ψ) theory (Performance in Social Interaction) along with CRISP meta-model of organizations [6], provided by DEMO methodology, define universal fundamental concepts for description of business processes in and between organizations. Applying methods of BORO methodology to DEMO models, we built the set of business objects and their signs [7] in order to construct a core of our data model. The description of some extracted concepts is presented hereafter.

The Operation Axiom of PSI theory [6] states that people in an organization are *actors* (concept: "actor") which can play different *actor roles* (concept: "actor role") and perform two kinds of *acts* (concept: "act"): production acts and coordination acts. By performing *production acts* (concept: "production act") actors contribute to bringing about the goods and/or services delivered to the environment of the enterprise. By performing *coordination acts* (concept: "coordination act") actors express their *intensions* (concept: "intension") and comply with commitments towards each other regarding the performance of production acts [6]. The Transaction Axiom [6] states that production and coordination acts are performed as the steps of universal patterns, called *transactions* (concept: "transaction").

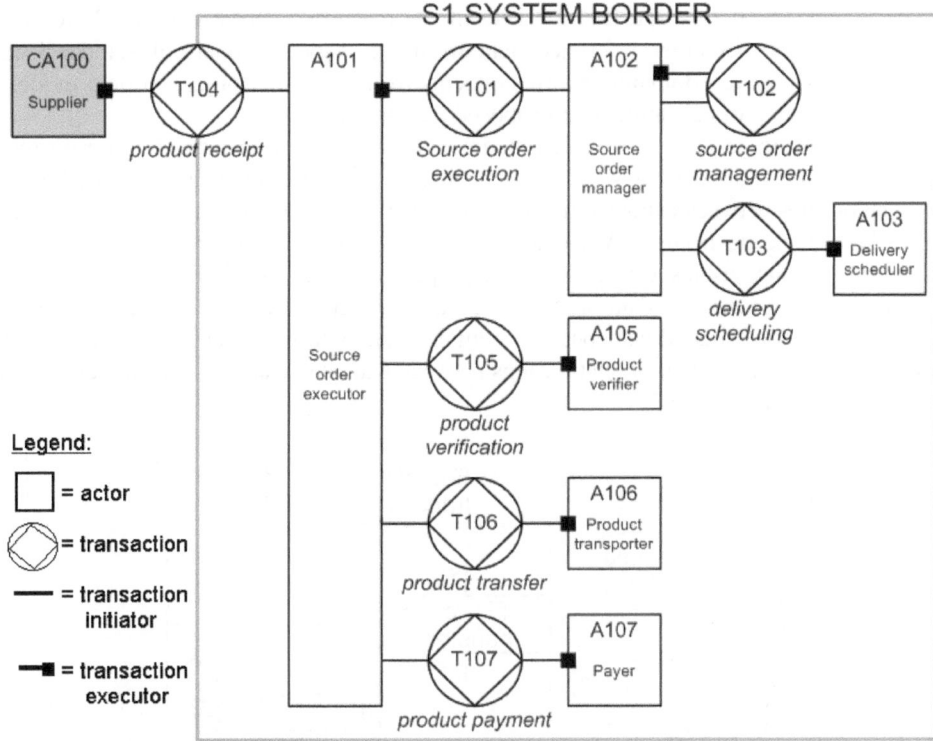

Fig. 1. Interaction Model of the Source Stocked Product process (S1) expressed in the Actor Transaction Diagram

Less general concepts can be extracted from DEMO Aspect models [6] of specified business processes. For example, the following classes of traceability artifacts were referenced to product transfer activity (S1.5) using the Interaction Model (fig. 1) of the Source Stocked Product process from section 5.1: "product transfer" and "Product transporter". Analysis of another Aspect model – the State Model – of the same process (S1) let us reveal target traced object of the process: "Product On Order". During S1 this object is received from supplier, verified, transported, and paid-up.

As founded on ontological approach authors believe that the core elements of the Aspect Models, which describe the same kind of organizations in supply chain, are the same. Consequently, complete number of universal concepts and their classes can be extracted from organization models of standardized supply chain processes and used as basic nodes of unified data meta-model (section 5.3).

5.3   Meta-description of Data

In compliance with the request of conceptual alignment between meta-description of business processes and meta-description of data, reference data ontology of the supply chain domain must include aforementioned concepts derived from CRISP meta-model, PSI theory and DEMO meta-model (section 5.2). In section 5.2 we also proposed to extract other reference data from the Aspect Models of standardized processes. Moreover, domain-specific concepts from particular organizational models of supply chain parties supplement proposed data model.

The following general steps of data-model construction were specified in our research. Step 1: extraction of business-valuable data concepts from DEMO meta-model; definition of relationships between extracted metadata and ISO 15926 reference data. Step 2: extraction of data concepts from the Aspect Models [13] of standardized supply chain processes; definition of relationships, cardinalities, and properties [11] of extracted metadata in compliance with the reference data of ISO 15926 and new reference data defined on step 1. Step 3: extraction of additional concepts from national, industry, and branch standards for traceability data; definition of relationships between extracted data and new reference data defined on step 1 and step 2.

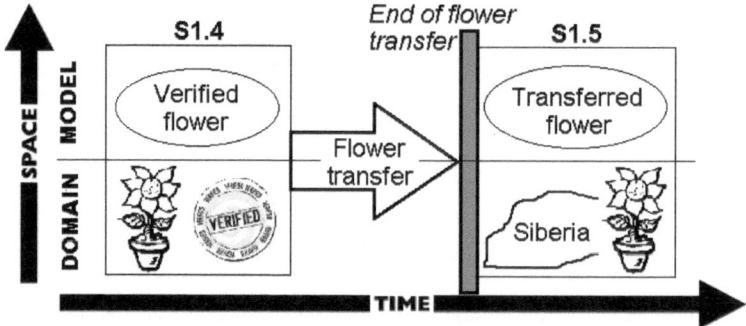

Fig. 2. Two stages (S1.4 and S1.5) of instantiated Source Stocked Product process (S1) on the time-space diagram

Some data concepts of proposed two first steps of data modeling process were described in section 5.2. In order to exemplify reference data of step 3, Source Stocked Product process (S1) was instantiated as follows: one florist is responsible for regular supply of a flower to Siberia. Normally he follows the best practices of supply chain management and acts according to S1 specifications. A flower is usually accompanied with RFID tag and is tracked during its lifecycle. Two stages of the flower are depicted in fig. 2. This picture contains domain-specific description of the process as well as corresponding data model concepts derived from Interaction Model of flower supply. Interaction Model components are similar to ones depicted in fig. 1. Thus, "Source order executor" is instantiated by a florist, and product is a flower. Space-time diagram of figure 2 emphasizes our goal to describe whole product lifecycle within the data model in terms corresponded with organizational models of related supply parties.

Following BORO methodology we defined data concepts and their interrelations to track a flower from the end of stage S1.4 till the end of stage S1.5: time-space dimensional object (product on order) - "Flower on order", activity -"Flower Transfer", result of activity (new stage of a flower) - "Transferred flower", event – "End of flower transfer", and location – "Siberia". According to our approach to data modeling, these concepts are classes, which for concepts related to particular flowers are members.

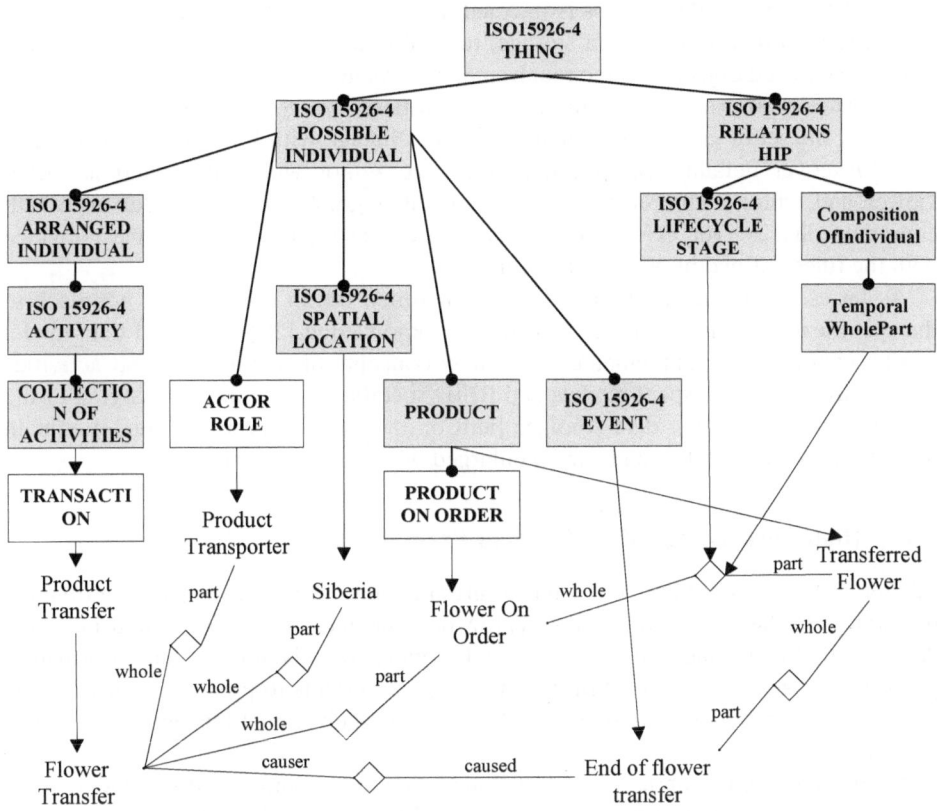

Fig. 3. Our extension of ISO 15926 data model

All aforementioned concepts were embedded into standardized data model of ISO 15926. In figure 3 all reference elements of ISO 15926 are highlighted in grey, whereas new elements of the data model are represented by white rectangles with their names inside. All data elements in rectangles are not linked to any special domain. Specification of the model is depicted by data elements without rectangles.

ISO 15926 standard defines not only the full set of core reference data elements, but it also specifies and classifies strong relationships between them. Thus, there are three types of links between elements are depicted in fig. 3: arrows for classification relationships, lines with bold dot at the end for specification relationships, and lines with diamond in the middle for other types of relationships. Due to lack of space and limitations of graphical representation of ISO 15926 meta-model, not all possible relationships between elements are shown in fig. 3.

Comparing proposed data meta-model with the ontology developed by Zdravkovic et al. [26], which is also aimed to support supply chain operations based on SCOR concepts, our extension of ISO 15926 meta-model is not only perfectly connected with the concepts of organizational structure and functions, but establishes tight links between tracing information and related processes. Thus, as soon as the information about other stages of the process is injected into the model, and real-time data is consequently recorded into the data storage, the information system can easily correlate state of the traced object with the requirements of related business process model.

Freeware platform .15926 Editor [27] facilitates extension of the standard data model by the set of graphical elements and their linkage with ISO 15926 upper ontology. Moreover default configuration of .15926 Editor with fully functional RDF viewer and editor at the core, transforms created graphical meta-model into RDF compliant data set (or OWL with many restrictions for conversion) in accordance with the rules defined by W3C consortium.

As far as ontologies are known to be well suited for an evolutionary approach to the specification of requirements and domain knowledge [28], proposed data-model can be continuously supplemented with new concepts of tracing data and activities derived from DEMO aspect models and RFID specifications without damaging of the model. It means that the data storages built on the basis of proposed model contain universally organized data and can be enlarged when it is necessary.

5.4   High-Level Design of Multi-agent Framework

Inherently business models of organizations are static because they map the time dimension onto the spatial dimensions [7]. Moreover, the information stored in accordance with the business model of social organization is not yet an information processing system. Only the ability of multi-agent systems to process business information and implement two-dimensional view of organizational business model does make processing.

Intellectual agents can partially fulfill analytical and communicative functions assigned to people (or "actors" in terms of DEMO) involved in business processes. Therefore real-time supply network can be imitated by multi-agent framework where agents get tracing data from data stores, analyze the information, overcome discovered problems and mistakes in supply processes, and provide actors with the graphical interface for manual control and representation of the results of their activities. In order to facilitate decision making of supply chain parties, the framework must be implemented as to detect automatically any deviations of process chains from projected traffic activities by comparing tracing real-time and historical data with the data quantifications and customer requirements come from business process guidelines and procedures.

As soon as a new request to analyze tracing data comes to the framework from agents' GUI or another application, related data is extracted from the supported traceability network and stored into agents' data structures. Afterwards agents compare incoming information with predefined knowledge about business objects and processes under their responsibilities. Agents' responsibilities for intelligent analysis of tracing data reflect proactive human roles in transactions and their abilities to over-come inconsistencies between real information about business objects and projected data by changing supply network topology.

Business processes in terms of MAS framework are built from the activities to be executed by agents and carried out by transactions between them. Expected outcome of tracing data analysis and agents' interactions correspond to the new facts [6]. These new facts correspond to completed coordination or production actions [6] of people involved in business activities. Proposed data meta-model establishes unequivocal connections between the types of all possible new facts and transactions described by DEMO Aspect Models. Therefore, real facts extracted from tracing data by intellec-tual agents lead to changes of multi-agent system together with supply network variation in time, and allow detection of failures in business operations by force of unidentified new facts. Since DEMO models of organizations in supply network pro-vide ontological description of business objects and related business processes, proposed data-process model of multi-agent framework can be considered as a basis for creation of flexible and scalable application for traceability data processing.

Ontological approach to definition of the main elements of the framework provides essential description of business objects and processes and makes it possible to apply the same multi-agent solution for data processing in the intermodal logistics systems, which consist of variety of supply chain parties and different types of business processes. Because of their nature, components of multi-agent system can be re-used on the new nodes of supply network and easily adapted to their special features in order to unite fragmented traceability applications to complex logistics system.

Proposed Model of Intellectual Agents. Design of programming agents described below is based on the ontological system model SMART [19] which is perfectly cor-respondent with CRISP meta-model [6] of organizations and proposed model of mul-ti-agent framework. In addition JADE framework [29] is used to develop multi-agent system that leads to some additional limitations on agents' construction.

In accordance to J. Dietz [19], agent model, as an atomic unit of traceability sys-tem, can be built from the following concepts:

— *Role* of agent correspond to actor role in DEMO methodology; *RoleID* is the *Role* identificator. Because of JADE limitations, one agent can fulfill only one actor role.
— *State* is the number of facts, which describe the state of agent at the current mo-ment.
— *State base* is the set of all permissible States of the agent.
— *Action* is the task assigned to the agent according to its Role.
— *Action base* consists of all possible Actions that can be performed by the agent. Ability of the agent to perform the Action is defined by the set of *behaviors* in terms of JADE framework.
— *Command* is a tuple in the form <Action, Time>, where Time is the moment when the Action is required to be performed. Each agent is able to accept, execute and generate commands, presented in the form of ACL messages.

— *Mutation* is the set of productions facts [13] that appear after Command execution. Notifications about occurred Mutations are sent to all subscribed agents in the form of ACL messages.
— *Mutation base* is the set of all permissible Mutations of the agent.
— *Reaction* is the set of Commands generated after Action execution.
— *Reaction Base* is the set of actions included into all permissible Reactions of the agent.
— *Transition Rule* is a tuple in the form <Action, State, Reaction, Mutation>, which defines all permissible changes of the agent at the current moment.
— *Transition base* is the set of all existent Transition Rules.

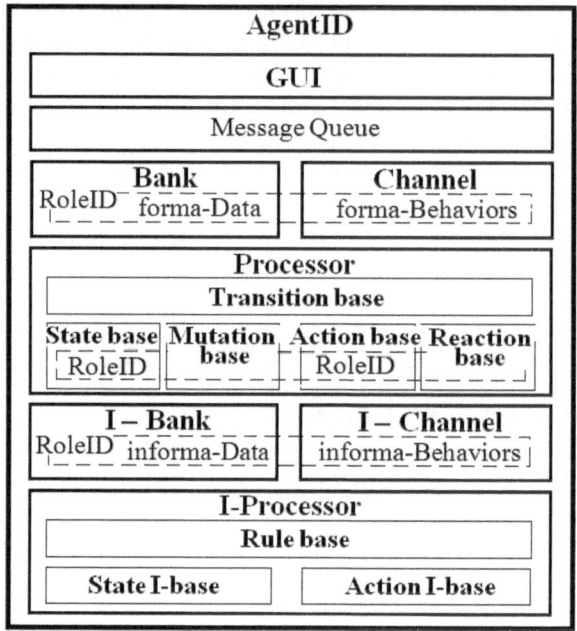

Fig. 4. Design of programming agent

Main components of the agent model are depicted in fig.4. Where GUI is a Graphical User Interface of the agent, which allows users of traceability system (i.e. actors of related organizations) manage the agent. Message Queue is used to exchange messages with other agents. It is assumed that information links between actor roles in the Interstriction Model of DEMO methodology are embodied into information links between agents.

Bank contains descriptors of current State in the form of data structures consistent with defined meta-data model (section 5.3). Channel contains the list of behaviors which have been activated by commands and have to be executed. Processor is responsible for agent's behavior and content of Bank and Channel. Since agents are able to act on information and business levels, these three components (Bank, Channel and Processor) are double inside of the agent. The only difference is between structure of Processor and I-Processor. State I-base and Action I-base components of I-Processor define the rules used by the agent to assess incoming information and form new information messages.

6   Conclusions

Our research presents a scientific approach to architectural design of business information systems for planning, discovering, monitoring deviations, and optimizing business processes. Semantically consistent abstractions in description of business-processes, data, and information system help to improve integration of information and processes. Logical and technical correspondence of proposed abstractions creates conditions for building of a cohesive information system for organizational diagnosis. Multi-agent solution adjusted with an ontological view on data model and business processes of organizations implements the ability to flexibly react on any deviations of business activities within networking organizations.

At the present stage of our research, the method of data modeling consistent with the business view on supply chain activities is introduced and exemplified. High-level design of multi-agent framework is presented. In the nearest future original architecture of multi-agent framework will be designed in details and implemented.

The proposed multi-agent framework accompanied with the methodology for its implementation in a particular application domain will structure and simplify creation of business information systems, will allow software designers to concentrate on the analysis of business-models and domain ontologies instead of designing the applications for organizational diagnosis from scratch.

References

1. Dietz, J.L.G.: Designing technical systems as social systems. In: Weigand, H., Goldkuhl, G., de Moor, A. (eds.) Proceedings of the 8th International Working Conference on the Language-Action Perspective on Communication Modeling (LAP 2003), pp. 187–207 (2003), http://infolab.uvt.nl/research/lap2003
2. Alderfer, C.P.: The Methodology of Organizational Diagnosis. Professional Psychology 11(3), 459–468 (1980)
3. Skobelev, P.O.: Open multi-agent systems for operational information processing in decision theory: PhD theses. RGB, Moscow (2003) (in Russian)
4. Tarasov, V.B.: From multi-agent systems towards intellectual organizations. URSS, Moscow (2002) (in Russian)
5. Vittih, V.A.: Introduction into inter-subjective control theory. Samara (2013) (in Russian)
6. Dietz, J.: Enterprise Ontology – Theory and Methodology. Springer, Heidelberg (2006)
7. Partridge, C.: Business Objects: Re-Engineering for Re-Use, 2nd edn. The BORO Center, London (2005)
8. Asswad, M.M.A., Al-Debei, M.M., Cesare, S.D., Lycett, M.: Conceptual modeling and the quality of ontologies: A comparison between object-role modeling and the object paradigm. In: ECIS (2010)

9. Hoogervorst, J.A.P.: Eterprise Governance and Enterprise Engineering. Springer, Heidelberg (2009)
10. ISO (International Organization for Standardization), http://www.iso.org/iso/home.html
11. Ilie-Zudor, E., Kemeny, Z., Blommestein, F., Monostori, L., Meulen, A.: A survey of applications and requirements of unique identification systems and RFID techniques. Computers in Industry 62, 227–252 (2011)
12. OMG Model Driven Architecture. Object Management Group Inc., http://www.omg.org/mda
13. Wil van der Aalst, M.P.: Process Mining. Discovery, Conformance and Enhancement of Business Processes. Springer, Heidelberg (2011)
14. Enterprise Engineering Institute, http://www.demo.nl
15. Wang, Y., Albani, A., Barjis, J.: Transformation of DEMO Metamodel into XML Schema. In: Albani, A., Dietz, J.L.G., Verelst, J. (eds.) EEWC 2011. LNBIP, vol. 79, pp. 46–60. Springer, Heidelberg (2011)
16. Barjis, J.: Developing executable models of business systems. In: ICEIS 2007 - 9th International Conference on Enterprise Information Systems, Proceedings ISAS, pp. 5–13 (2007)
17. Sampson, J.: Technical report. RFID and ISO 15926. Posccaesar Co. (2010), http://www.posccaesar.org
18. POSC Caesar Association, http://www.posccaesar.org
19. Dietz, J.L.G.: System Ontology and its role in Software Development. In: Missikoff, M., Nicola, A. (eds.) EMOI-INTEROP 2005, Co-located with CAiSE 2005 Conference. CEUR Workshop Proceedings, vol. 160 (2005), http://ceur-ws.org
20. OLF Co.: Guideline No.112. Deployment of Radio Frequency Identification (RFID) in the Oil and Gas Industry. Part 2: Architecture and Integration. OLF Oljeindustriens Landsforening, Sandnes (2010), http://www.olf.no/retningslinjer
21. Motamedi, A., Saini, R., Hammad, A., Zhu, B.: Role-based access to facilities lifecycle information on RFID tags. Advanced Engineering Informatics 25, 559–568 (2011)
22. Lee, C.K.M., Ho, W., Ho, G.T.S., Lau, H.C.W.: Design and development of logistics workflow systems for demand management with RFID. Expert Systems with Applications 38, 5428–5437 (2011)
23. Jakkhupan, W., Arch-int, S., Li, Y.: Business process analysis and simulation for the RFID and EPCglobal Network enabled supply chain: A proof-of-concept approach. J. of Network and Computer Applications 34, 949–957 (2011)
24. Chen, R.-S., Tu, M.: Development of an agent-based system for manufacturing control and coordination with ontology and RFID technology. Expert System with Applications 36, 7581–7593 (2011)
25. SCOR Frameworks, http://supply-chain.org/resources/scor
26. Zdravkovic, M., Panetto, H., Trajanovic, M., Aubry, A.: An approach for formalizing the supply chain operations. J. of Enterprise Information Systems 5, 401–421 (2011)
27. TechInvestLab.ru, http://techinvestlab.ru/dot15926Editor
28. Babkin, E., Potapova, E.: Towards Ontology-Based Methodology for Requirements Formalization. In: Forbrig, P., Günther, H. (eds.) BIR 2010. LNBIP, vol. 64, pp. 73–85. Springer, Heidelberg (2010)
29. Java Agent DEvelopment Framework (JADE), http://jade.tilab.com

Verification of Models in Agent Based Computational Economics — Lessons from Software Engineering

Bogumił Kamiński and Przemysław Szufel

Warsaw School of Economics, Decision Support and Analysis Division, Poland
{bkamins,pszufe}@sgh.waw.pl

Abstract. Agent based models are highly complex and usually are being implemented using programming languages. This situation calls for adequate methods allowing for their verification that are not used in standard economic research. In order to organize this process we propose to logically decompose agent based model into three layers: conceptual model, computerized model and metamodel. The main possible problems identified using this decomposition are: (a) incomplete specification of conceptual model, (b) unexpected behavior of computerized model and (c) problems with reproduction simulation results. In order to address these issues based on literature review we draw recommendations concerning model documentation, testing and simulation reproduction that are crucial to improve their quality and precision of communication.

Keywords: agent based modeling, computational economics, model verification, software engineering.

1 Introduction

In order to accurately capture the complexities of markets economic models are becoming increasingly complex. This tendency often leads to difficulties in application of analytical methods to their analysis. In such cases application of computational methods using agent based approach is a methodology gaining a progressing acceptance among economists [13].

Agent based computational economics is considered a promising approach allowing to solve problems that are not traceable using standard modeling techniques [12,24,27]. However, Richiardi et al. [37] notice that the research methodology needed to properly apply this paradigm is very different from traditional mathematical economics. In particular new challenges related with (a) methods of verification of model specification, (b) model calibration and (c) methods of computer experiments design and analysis have to be addressed by the researchers [20].

In this paper we focus on problems with verification of model specification. Our goal is to develop a unified agent based model development process. We base our recommendations on an extensive literature review on how software engineering methodologies based on object oriented approach and UML modeling

A. Kobyliński and A. Sobczak (Eds.): BIR 2013, LNBIP 158, pp. 185–199, 2013.

can be used to assist development and communication of computational models of complex economic systems.

The paper is organized in three sections. Section 2 presents a short introduction to agent based modeling methodology and concepts. Next, in Section 3 we review common problems related with verification of such models during their development and communication on practical examples. Finally, in Section 4 we present recommendations how software engineering tools can assist researchers in improving the quality of agent based models. The research methodology we apply in this paper is based on detailed review of current literature on the subject that allows us to derive model development guidelines.

2   Agent Based Computational Economics

Simulation techniques as a research area of operations research have appeared around the year 1950. However, first tools for agent based modeling have been developed after the year 1990 with the first comprehensive description of the approach given in 2006 by Tesfatsion and Judd [45]. Tesfatsion [44] observes that a rapid increase in development of simulations in complex system modeling is driven by falling price and increasing accessibility of computing power.

The agent based approach to economic modeling is grounded on an observation that the behavior of an economic system on a macro scale is a result of interacting behaviors on micro scale [18,31,41]. Hence, it is possible to model an economy in a micro level (e.g. agents, their behavior, social networks) and next observe the dynamics of aggregated indicators in macro scale. Additionally, Holland [19] points out that classical economic models assume full rationality of economic agents while in reality full rationality is not possible and he recommends agent based approach as a way to model complex economic systems.

Agent based simulation is a technique to analyze dynamics of a complex systems. The main characteristics of agent based approach is to divide the system into independent elements — agents. The most important part of such a definition is a detailed description of agents' attributes and their behavior. Hence let us now present the definition of an agent we use in this paper.

The meaning of an agent is often ambiguous. The review of literature done by Macal and North [25] concludes that an agent is an independent component capable of making decisions — this definition is close to one given by Bonabeau [3]. Independence means that an agent is identifiable and self contained — it has a clear boundary from the system which his an element of. Macal and North [25] further point out that in many scenarios an important feature of an agent is to adaptively adjust to its environment as explained by Casti [6]. Casti proposes that an adaptive agents should have two groups of rules: rules of behavior and rules for adapting rules of behavior to a changing environment. Another definition was given by Gilbert [15] when an agent is represented as a computer program or part of a computer program that can be considered as being independent and that represents an individual or an organization or a government or another social actor. In this paper, following Kamiński [20], we take a wide definition of an agent and assume that it is a distinct entity in the model that intends to represent some actor in the system that is modeled.

Notable classic agent based models include The Santa Fe Institute artificial stock market [32] and Electricity Market Complex Adaptive System [7]. They both present the main characteristics of agent based models. Agents have relatively simple behavior rules that lead to complex dynamics of the model as a whole. Such intricate models can exhibit unexpected characteristics due to problems with their specification, implementation or analysis. They are outlined in the Section 3.

3 Pitfalls of Agent Based Models Verification

The agent based modeling is an attractive methodology when standard tools form mathematical economics are insufficient. However, as is noted by Leombruni [23], its acceptance process among economics is slow. One of the reasons for such a situation given in the literature is their complex nature [36]. Additionally agent based models have dual specification: *conceptual* and *computerized* [20]. Conceptual specification is descriptive. It uses verbal explanation of model elements and their relationships and possibly mathematical formulas specifying them. Computerized specification is an implementation of the model using a selected programming language and framework. Finally, computerized model is executed during simulation process. Simulation results are stored and analyzed. Results of this analysis usually leads to creation of simplified model, called *metamodel*, that captures the most important characteristics of original agent based model [40]. Usually metamodels are built using econometrics or data mining tools. This process is presented on Fig. 1.

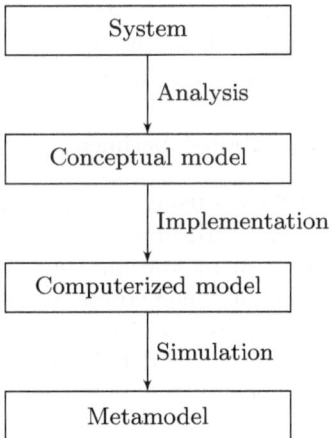

Fig. 1. Process of creation and analysis of an agent based model

An important distinction that has to be made is between conceptual model of a simulation (CMoS) and conceptual model of an information system (CMoIS) used to execute that simulation. The CMoS is a simplification of a real system that is created — Law in his classic book [22] defines CMoS as an assumption document that is «*not an "exact" description how the system works, but rather a description how it works relative to the particular issues that the model is to address*». On the other hand the computer science literature (for a review see [39]) defines conceptual modeling as «*the activity of formally describing some aspects of the physical and social world around us for purposes of understanding and communication*».

In the paper we assume that CMoS and CMoIS are two separate stages of building and executing simulation models. There are several reasons for that. Firstly, the addressee of a CMoS are domain specialists rather than programmers [22]. Secondly, a central part of a CMoS is a description of agents' rationality and their decision rules. Thirdly, CMoIS includes information on data processing (i.e. logging, object serialization, managing simulation runs, multi-threading) while in CMoS all that information is irrelevant. Moreover, CMoS describes only those parts of system (classes, flow diagrams) that explain simulation model behavior skipping the rest. Finally CMoS in general should assume that it could be implemented and executed without an information system. For example a classic simulation model proposed by Schelling [41] was actually first implemented by Schelling on the chessboard. Similarly Philips [33] created a physical, hydraulic simulation model of an economic system.

Further in the paper we focus on modeling only the conceptual modeling of simulation (CMoS) rather than conceptual modeling of information system (CMoIS) required to execute a particular simulation.

Existence of three stages in the process of creation and analysis of agent based model can lead to several important problems:

1. conceptual specification can be incomplete;
2. computerized specification might be unpublished;
3. computerized specification can contain implementation errors or design induced unexpected behavior;
4. design and analysis of simulation experiment might be flawed.

Next we will present these problems using examples from the literature.

First let us focus on problems with understanding model specification. Very often it omits details of model implementation which are crucial for the obtained results. This is especially important when computerized specification is not published by the authors. Take the paper by Dosi et al. [10] as an example. They propose an important and recognized model of endogenous growth and business cycles (with 57 citations reported by Google Scholar in May 2013). One of the authors of this paper was a member of the research team trying to replicate this model. Unfortunately the source code of the model is unpublished and it was not possible to obtain it from the authors. In such a situation an attempt to replicate it using conceptual model presented in the paper was tried. However, it also failed. Almost 100 details of the model were found not to be precisely defined in the description, including in particular: missing information of starting parameterization of the simulation, undefined detailed functional relationships between variables in the model or imprecise descriptions of all processes taking place in agent based simulation.

Next example of problems with verification of agent based models is presented by Edmonds and Hales [11] and stresses issues related to implementation errors and unexpected behavior of the model due to small specification changes. They are analyzing another well recognized paper by Riolo et al. [38] (with 443 citations reported by Google Scholar in May 2013). Edmonds and Hales created independently two computerized models using conceptual model given by Riolo et al. It was found that both replicated models gave consistent results that did not match those reported by Riolo et al [38]. Edmonds and Hales [11] identified the reason for this situation to be a seemingly insignificant design feature related to randomization of the simulation. Another issue found was that a small change in implementation of agents' decision making rule (changing from not strict inequality $\leq$ to a strict one $<$) significantly changed the results of the simulation.

Finally, Kamiński [20] presents problems with design of simulation experiments. The analysis focuses on the model of Cont [8]. It presents a simple agent based model showing that volatility clustering and leptokurtosis of financial asset prices can be observed even if the population of investors uses only one type of decision making rules. Cont presents the conceptual model very clearly and there is no problem with its computerized replication. Unfortunately, the argument about volatility clustering and leptokurtosis is given only by showing graphs of several runs of the simulation. Kamiński tests the leptokurtosis hypothesis for the range of parameters given by Cont using a formal procedure and finds that it is true only in $\approx 56\%$ of all simulations.

In summary it can be concluded that agent based models can suffer from the problem of improper specification. The flaws can be found on the conceptual model, computerized model or metamodel levels. The core problem that needs to be addressed is that agent based models have usually a very complex structure. In such situations standard methods of verbal model description used by economists is insufficient. Moreover, improvements are needed not only in the way models are created but also how they are tested. In the next section we review the literature focusing on the problem of development process of agent based models and draw recommendations that can help researchers to avoid pitfalls described in this section.

4   Best Practices for Agent Based Model Development

In order to overcome the issues highlighted in Section 3 we propose good practices of agent based model development in the following areas: (a) specifying conceptual model of simulation, (b) describing and publishing computerized model, (c) debugging and controlling the model in order to remove implementation errors and (d) describing scenarios for simulation experiments. There are several alternative approaches to describe simulation model. Partial approaches to those issues have been presented, e.g. see [16]. However, there is no unified methodology accepted in the literature addressing all the issues we identified.

In the description of simulation modeling and model building techniques we use the system approach (as defined by Ackoff [1]) because this is a standard approach in simulation analysis [14,22].

The section is organized as follows. Firstly, we propose an iterative model of a simulation process. It includes modeling, implementation, testing and experimenting. Secondly, for each modeling process phases we describe state-of-the-art approaches to agent based simulation development. We stress the importance of both conceptual description of a simulation model in modeling phase and of a computerized description in implementation phase. For the model experimenting phase we discuss issues related to management of parameter sweep and metamodeling in agent based computational models.

4.1   Process of Building Simulation Models

Simulation process is extensively described in the literature. Bennett [2] proposes to divide it into three stages: constructing model, testing and numerical calculations. Model construction includes defining the research problem and formulating hypothesis and designing model assumptions. After a model is constructed it can implemented. Bennett proposes two phases of model testing: validation and verification which is a standard in modeling literature, e.g. see [14,22,42]. The verification phase is about testing whether a computerized model is acting consistently with its conceptual specification while the validation phase is about checking similarity of model and a real system. After a simulation model is verified and validated it can be used to perform simulation experiments.

Gilbert and Troitzsch [14] propose a similar approach to simulation process modeling. They note that the process includes the following steps: (1) analyzing a real system and finding problem boundary, (2) observing a real system in order to find starting parameters, (3) making assumptions and constructing a model, (4) verification whether there are no programming errors in the source code, (5) model validation through analysis of similarities of a model and a real system, (6) sensitivity analysis in order to check how various initial parameters influence the final output of a simulation model.

Our experience with creation of agent based simulation model is that the model creation is an interactive process what requires to move between subsequent steps. Hence, we propose to see the simulation model building process as an *iterative and incremental development* as defined by Larman [21].

Provision of good quality simulation models requires from model creators awareness of moving between steps of model building process. We integrate postulates formulated in [14,22,42] with the need of maintaining the quality of model building process which requires to consider all small steps in the iterative and incremental development process. Based on this consideration we propose a reference agent based model development procedure presented in Fig. 2.

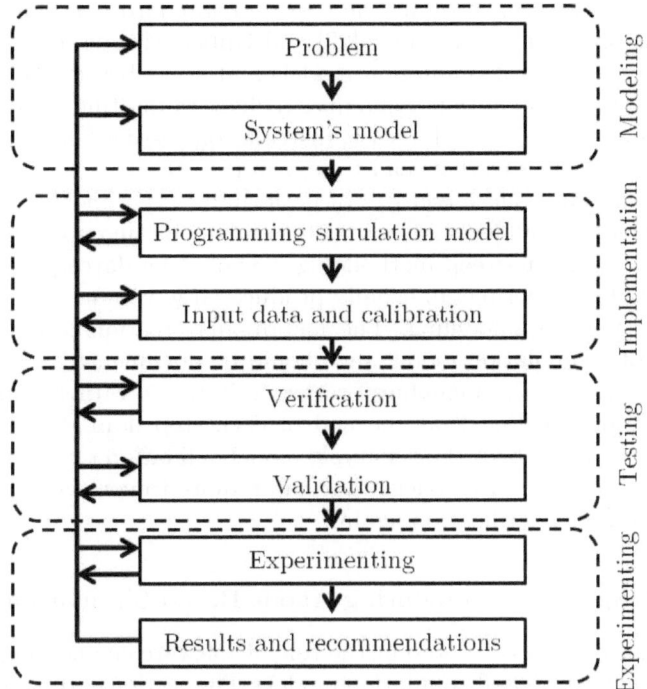

Fig. 2. Proposed stages of a simulation model building and programming process in an iterative and incremental development

In our approach we proposed to divide the modeling process into four main steps: Modeling, Implementation, Testing and Experimenting.

The *Modeling* phase includes problem formulation and a building a theoretical model of a real system. The theoretical system model also includes UML diagrams that are presented in Section 4.2. After the modeling process is completed the model implementation can be started.

The *Implementation* consist of two parts: programming and input data calibration. The *programming* is understood as designing the source code in a selected language and documenting it with detailed UML class diagrams. The *calibration* of the input data is required to get the model up and running. After a model is programmed and calibrated the testing phase can be started. A well documented implementation is crucial for reproducibility of simulation results. This issue is further discussed in the Section 4.2.

The *Testing* phase can be divided into two parts: verification and validation. The *verification* is about checking whether a simulation model is properly implemented (i.e. the source code has no bugs). The verification process can be supported by software engineering techniques such as the unit testing and tools. The unit testing for agent based models has been described by Poutakidis et al. [34]. The tools include for example debuggers in Integraded Development Environments. The goal of the *validation* process is to compare how much similar a given simulation model is to a real world system. The validation process is more complex than verification as there are no standards for this process and each time it is problem specific. Law [22] and Gilbert [14] discuss model validation techniques in general simulation models and agent based economic models respectively. Some of validation techniques include calibrating a model with historical data and observing its forecast, distribution testing for output variables and testing marginal cases that lead to known results.

The *Experimenting* phase consists of performing experiments and preparing recommendations. Simulation experiments need to be unambiguously defined. That is why parameter sweep methodologies should be developed as discussed in Section 4.3. The experiments usually produce large volumes of data that can be explored using metamodeling. The metamodel creation procedures are an integral part of a simulation model and should be documented.

Finally, we assume the modeling process is iterative rather than linear. As it is presented on the Fig. 2 at the end of each step it may turn out that a modeler needs to move back. For example model validation results may allow to discover implementation drawbacks that will require to correct implementation and perform a model verification again.

4.2   Designing and Documenting Agent-Based Simulation Models

The goal of this section is to present the role of software engineering approaches in documenting agent based simulation models. The section corresponds to problem formulation and implementation phases of simulation modeling presented in Section 4.1.

Object Oriented Approach in System Simulation and UML Modeling.
Software engineering handbooks, e.g. [5], postulate to use UML diagrams to describe object oriented software architecture. Oechslein et al. [30] point out that agent oriented simulation models also should be presented with UML diagrams.

The Object Management Group [29] defines 14 types of UML diagrams divided into two classes: structure diagrams and action diagrams. Diagrams of both theses classes should be included in documenting agent based simulation models.

A *structure* diagram represents a static state of objects in an analyzed system. Common structure diagram classes include: class diagram, component diagram, collaboration diagram and deployment diagram. The class diagram can be very useful in presenting a structure of an agent based model. However, we do not recommend to use the other three types of structure diagrams. Components diagrams present too high level of modeling as they focus on components rather the agents (that are represented as objects). Collaboration diagrams are unsuitable because interactions between agents are being defined from model perspective. Finally, deployment diagrams present a physical structure of deployment which is not a part of an agent based model.

A *behavior* diagram represents a dynamic behavior of of objects in a modeled system. Common behavior diagram types include activity diagram, interaction diagram, state diagram and use case diagram. We recommend to use activity and state diagrams to represent dynamics of an agent based simulation model. We do not recommend use case and interaction diagrams as there are usually no users of an agent based model who should be modeled within the model.

Hence, only three UML diagram types can be recommended for documentation of a typical agent based model:

1. class diagrams for high level model structure, capturing all agent types with their actions and attributes, see Fig. 3;
2. activity diagrams for overall model dynamics, see Fig. 4;
3. state diagrams to explain detailed dynamics of attributes for particular agent classes, see Fig. 5.

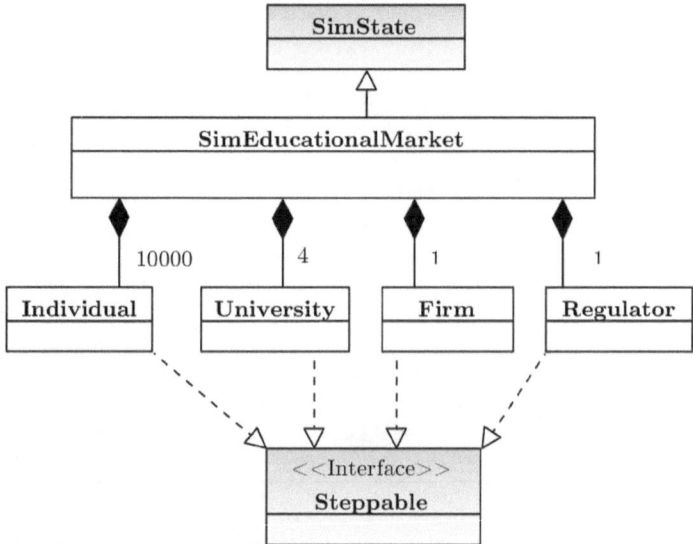

Fig. 3. This is a simplified class diagram from [43]. Agent classes are presented together with their references to multiagent framework. Detailed lists of actions and attributes are omitted.

Pseudocode in Documenting Agent Based Models. UML diagrams give a very good overview of model structure and dynamics. However they are insufficient to fully and unambiguously describe an agent based model and ensure reproducibility of simulation results. This is caused by several reasons. Firstly, the class diagram gives a good overview of classes and their dependencies. However, without the implementation content it is only known what methods are possessed by classes but their functionality is unknown. Secondly, activity diagram can explain behavior of particular agents in a simulation model. However, usually in simulation implementation there are important implementation details that have strong influence on model behavior.

Such considerations lead to the conclusion that application of UML diagrams should be used only as a tool that simplifies communication of the model on

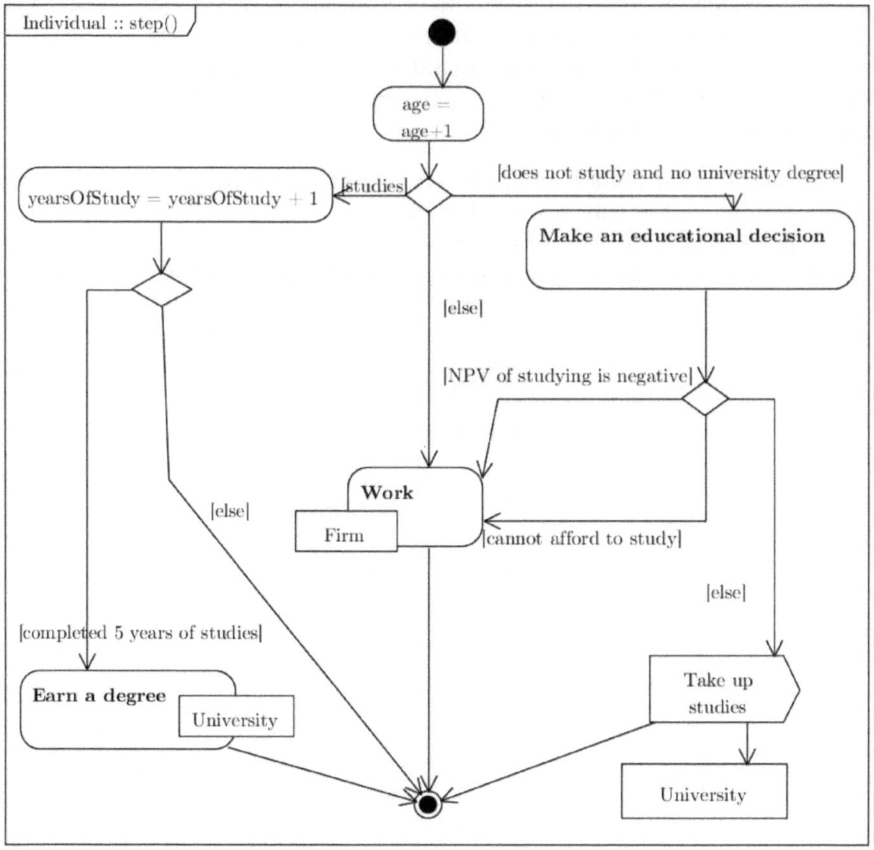

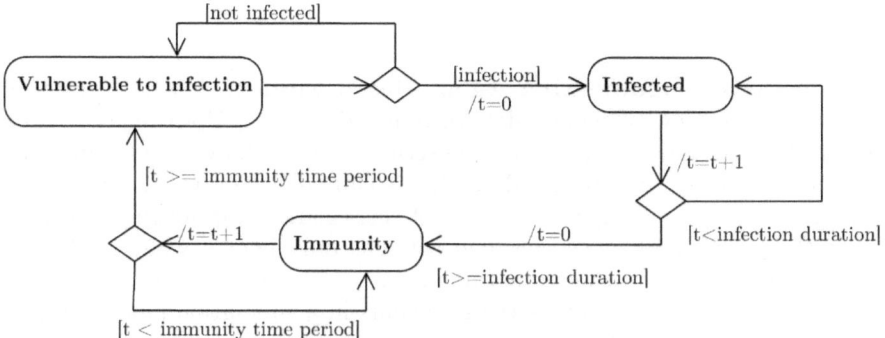

Fig. 4. Sample activity diagram for a agent based education market model presented in [43]. Diagram represents actions taken by each individual in each simulation step.

Fig. 5. Sample state diagram for individual in an agent based model of disease spread. Diagram taken from [20].

general level, but is not sufficient to fully document an agent based model. Hence, pseudocode should be also used to document agent based models.

Grimm [17] notes that the pseudocode plays an important role in ensuring reproducibility of a simulation model results.

Listing 1.1. A sample pseudocode for a simulation simulation process of an economic model

```
INITIALIZE agent_population
t = 0
REPEAT
  t = t + 1
  IF t == time_of_model_shock
    PERFORM_POLICY_CHANGE
    CALCULATE_GLOBAL_VARIABLES
    FOR EACH agent IN agent_population
      ADAPT_RULESET_TO_CURRENT_ECONOMIC_POLICY
    END FOR EACH
  END IF
  RANDOMLY_SHUFFLE agent_population
  FOR EACH agent IN agent_population
    PERFORM_ACTIONS_ACCORDING_TO_RULESET
  END FOR EACH
UNTIL t <= max_simulation_time
```

The pseudocode represented in Listing 1.1 represents an overview of a dynamic agent based model where an impact of a policy change on an economic system is analyzed. The psuedocode gives large amount of information on the dynamics of an agent based model. However, from our experience we know that pseudocode is not always sufficient in documenting an agent based model and some more complicated parts of pseudocode should still be explained with an actual source code.

A pseudocode is particularly appropriate in documenting overall model execution and implementation of particular methods and decision rules within agents. Interactions between model objects should be rather documented with UML.

However, as we have pointed earlier a pseudocode is not sufficient to ensure agent based model replication. Hence, more complicated or library dependent implementation details should be illustrated by an actual source code.

Sharing Source Code. Conceptual model augmented with UML diagrams and pseudocode should be an adequate basis for precise understanding of agent based model. However, because of high complexity of such models in practice this is not enough to fully understand them. Hence, in the literature a strong emphasis is put on important role of sharing model source code [26]. In particular in order to understand the mechanisms of the model it is often crucial to be able to run it independently and reproduce the simulation results obtained by authors of the model [20]. Good examples showing such an approach are: a classic book on simulation modeling by Law [22] where all model are being illustrated by C++ code examples and Gilbert [15] where NetLogo code is available.

It is also worth noting that because reader might want to replicate simulation results in fact agent based simulations are usually composed of three types of source code: a) model code, b) testing code and c) simulation experiment and data analysis code. The *model code* includes the core code required to run the calculations. The *testing code* includes the code that was used to verify and validate the model. Testing code can include unit tests for particular classes or code used run the model in marginal scenarios. Finally, the *code for simulation experiments* includes the code used to define the parameter sweep and code for metamodel creation.

Standard recommendations focus on sharing of core model source code. However, we strongly advise that all three types of source code should be shared and documented by the authors. By documentation of source code we understand required setup of execution environment required to run the model. This is particularly important when source code depends on third party libraries, where from our experience it is crucial to know exact versions of the libraries required to execute it.

4.3   Managing Parameter Sweep of Agent Based Models

Simulation experiment code requires input of model parametrization in order to assure possibility of its reproduction. At present there is no unified approach in the literature that allows for description of parameter space of a simulation model. Different authors use various approaches to model space exploration.

The simplest approach is introduction of several nested for-type loops within source code that executes the simulation model for various parameter sets. However, we do not recommend such an approach as it does not feature the separation of the model source code from the run time environment and is difficult to manage when a parameter set dynamically changes during a simulation process. Moreover changes in the parameter sets are not possible without an in depth knowledge of the source code. The problem of separating configuration from he model is acknowledged in the literature and various approaches including graphical configuration and use of external configuration files have been proposed [9,35]. Also several tools supporting simulation model configuration have been implemented including NetLogo BehaviourSpace [28], Repast Batch Parameters [4] and RNetLogo [46]. Independently of which method for implementation of parameter sweep is used by model authors it is crucial that unambiguous parameter sweep description is provided in order to allow for replication of simulation and metamodeling results.

In particular it is worth stressing that ensuring simulation reproducibility also requires standard methods to represent random number generators that are being used within a model as well as storing random seed numbers that were used to carry out simulation experiments.

5   Concluding Remarks

Agent based models are becoming increasingly popular among economists. However, because of their high complexity they introduce new challenges for model design and analysis. In order to analyze this problem we propose to approach these problems by logically decomposing agent based models into three layers: conceptual model, computerized model and metamodel. As we have presented in every layer and between them there are potential problems that are outside of standard mathematical economics model development framework. The main issues we identify are: (a) incomplete and hard to understand specification of conceptual model, (b) implementation errors or unreported behavior of computerized model and (c) problems with reproduction of model simulation results.

Based on an review of the literature we have proposed four stages of simulation model development and analysis (Fig. 2). For each of the stages we recommend various tools and approaches from software engineering including UML, pseudocode and unit testing that can help model authors to improve their quality. Within the proposed framework the use of UML helps reader to understand high level working of the model while a pseudocode enables to document its most important elements. Additionally because replication of simulation results is a crucial step allowing reader to understand the working of agent based model and gain confidence in it it is crucial that not only model but also simulation experiment source code and parameter sweep definition is shared with model reader.

Further developments of the proposed agent based simulation modeling framework include creating extensions of UML diagrams that address specific requirements or agent based models, proposing agent oriented pseudocode standards and creation of tools and methodologies that will enable parameter sweep process standardization.

References

1. Ackoff, R.L.: Towards a system of system concepts. Management Science 17(11), 661–671 (1971)
2. Bennett, B.S.: Simulation Fundamentals. Prentice Hall, London (1995)
3. Bonabeau, E.: Agent-based modeling: methods and techniques for simulating human systems, in: Proceedings of National Academy of Sciences 99(3): 7280–7287, (2001)
4. Bragen, M., Altaweel, M.: Repast Parameters Sweeps Getting started, (2013), http://repast.sourceforge.net/docs/RepastParameterSweepsGettingStarted.pdf (accessed on May 10, 2013)
5. Bruegge, B., Dutoit, A.H.: Object-Oriented Software Engineering: Using UML, Patterns and Java. Prentice Hall, Upper Saddle River (2009)
6. Casti, J.: Would-be worlds: how simulation is changing the world of science. Wiley, New York (1997)

7. Cirillo, R., Thimmapuram, P., Veselka, T., Koritarov, V., Conzelmann, G., Macal, C., Boyd, G., North, M., Overbye, T., Cheng, X.: Evaluating the Potential Impact of Transmission Constraints on the Operation of a Competitive Electricity Market in Illinois, Argonne National Laboratory, Argonne, IL, ANL-06/16 (report prepared for the Illinois Commerce Commission) (2006)
8. Cont, R.: Volatility Clustering in Financial Markets: Empirical Facts and Agent-Based Models. In: Teyssière, G., Kirman, A. (eds.) Long Memory in Economics. Springer (2007)
9. Daum, T., Sargent, R.G.: Experimental frames in a modern modeling and simulation system. IIE Transactions 33, 181–192 (2001)
10. Dosi, G., Fagiolo, G., Roventini, A.: Schumpeter meeting Keynes: A policy-friendly model of endogenous growth and business cycles. Journal of Economic Dynamics and Control 34, 1748–1767 (2010)
11. Edmonds, B., Hales, D.: Replication, Replication and Replication: Some Hard Lessons from Model Alignment. Journal of Artificial Societies and Social Simulation 6 (2003), http://jasss.soc.surrey.ac.uk/6/4/11.html
12. Farmer, J., Foley, D.: The economy needs agent-based modelling. Nature 460, 685–686 (2009)
13. Gallegati, M., Richiardi, M.: Agent Based Models in Economics and Complexity. In: Meyers, R. (ed.) Encyclopedia of Complexity and Systems Science, pp. 200–223. Springer Science (2009)
14. Gilbert, N., Troitzsch, K.G.: Simulation for the Social Scientist, 2nd edn. Open University Press, Berkshire (2005)
15. Gilbert, N.: Agent-Based Models. SAGE Publications (2008)
16. Grimm, V., Berger, U., Bastiansen, F., Eliassen, S., Ginot, V., Giske, J., Goss-Custard, J., Grand, T., Heinz, S., Huse, G., Huth, A., Jepsen, J., Jorgensen, C., Mooij, W., Muller, B., Peer, G., Piou, C., Railsback, S., Robbins, A., Robbins, M., Rossmanith, E., Ruger, N., Strand, E., Souissi, S., Stillman, R., Vabo, R., Visser, U., DeAngelis, D.: A standard protocol for describing individual-based and agent-based models. Ecological Modelling 198, 115–126 (2006)
17. Grimm, V., Berger, U., DeAngelis, D.L., Polhill, G., Giske, J., Railsback, S.F.: The ODD protocol: a review and first update. Ecological Modeling 221, 2760–2768 (2010)
18. Hayek, F.A.: Individualism and economic order. University of Chicago Press, Chicago (1948)
19. Holland, J.: Hidden Order: How Adaptation Builds Complexity. Addison-Wesley, Reading (1995)
20. Kaminski, B.: Podejście wieloagentowe do modelowania rynków: metody i zastosowania, Oficyna Wydawnicza SGH (2012)
21. Larman, C.: Iterative and Incremental Development: A Brief History. Computer 36(6), 47–56 (2003)
22. Law, A.: Simulation Modeling and Analysis. McGraw-Hill (2006)
23. Leombruni, R.: Why are economists sceptical about agent-based simulations. Physica A 355, 103–109 (2005)
24. Levy, M.: Agent Based Computational Economics. In: Meyers, R. (ed.) Encyclopedia of Complexity and Systems Science, pp. 92–112. Springer (2009)
25. Macal, C.M., North, M.J.: Tutorial on agent-based modeling and simulation part 2: how to model with agents. In: Perrone, L.F., Wieland, F.P., Liu, J., Lawson, B.G., Nicol, D.M., Fujimoto, R.M. (eds.) Proceedings of the 2006 Winter Simulation Conference (2006)

26. Miller, J.H., Page, S.E.: Complex Adaptive Systems. Princeton University Press (2007)
27. Moss, S.: Agent Based Modeling and Neoclassical Economics: A Critical Perspective. In: Meyers, R. (ed.) Encyclopedia of Complexity and Systems Science, pp. 176–184. Springer (2009)
28. NetLogo: NetLogo BehaviorSpace Guide, (2013), http://ccl.northwestern.edu/netlogo/docs/behaviorspace.html (accessed on May 10, 2013)
29. Object Management Group, OMG Unified Modeling Language (OMG UML), Superstructure. Version 2.4.1 (2011)
30. Oechslein, C., Klügl, F., Herrler, R., Puppe, F.: UML for Behavior-Oriented Multi-Agent Simulations. In: Dunin-Keplicz, B., Nawarecki, E. (eds.) CEEMAS 2001. LNCS (LNAI), vol. 2296, pp. 217–226. Springer, Heidelberg (2002)
31. Olsen, M.: The logic of collective action. Harvard University Press, Cambridge (1965)
32. Palmer, R.G., Arthur, W.B., Holland, J.H., LeBaron, B., Tayler, P.: Artificial economic life: a simple model of a stockmarket. Physica D 75, 264–274 (1994)
33. Philips, A.: Mechanical Models in Economic Dynamics. Economica 17, 283–305 (1950)
34. Poutakidis, D., Winikoff, M., Padgham, L., Zhang, Z.: Debugging and Testing of Multi-Agent Systems using Design Artefacts. In: Bordini, R.H., et al. (eds.) Multi-Agent Programming. Springer (2009)
35. Railsback, S.F., Lytinen, S.L., Jackson, S.K.: Agent-based Simulation Platforms: Review and Development Recommendations. Simulation 82, 609–623 (2006)
36. Richiardi, M.: Agent-based computational economics: a short introduction. The Knowledge Engineering Review 27, 137–149 (2012)
37. Richiardi, M., Leombruni, R., Saam, N., Sonnesa, M.: A Common Protocol for Agent Based Social Simulation. Journal of Artificial Societies and Social Simulation 9 (2006)
38. Riolo, R.L., Cohen, M.D., Axelrod, R.: Evolution of cooperation without reciprocity. Nature 411, 441–443 (2001)
39. Roussopoulos, N., Karagiannis, D.: Conceptual Modeling: Past, Present and the Continuum of the Future. In: Borgida, A.T., Chaudhri, V.K., Giorgini, P., Yu, E.S. (eds.) Conceptual Modeling: Foundations and Applications. LNCS, vol. 5600, pp. 139–152. Springer, Heidelberg (2009)
40. Santos, I.R., Santos, P.R.: Simulation Metamodels for Modeling Output Distribution Parameters. In: Proceedings of the 2007 Winter Simulation Conference, pp. 910–918 (2007)
41. Schelling, T.C.: Micromotives and macrobehavior, New York (1978)
42. Schroeder, R.G.: Operations Management-Decision Making in Operations Function, 4th edn. Mc Graw Hill International Editions, New York (1993)
43. Szufel, P.: O kosztowej efektywnosci procesow edukacyjnych, PhD Dissertation, SGH (2012)
44. Tesfatsion, L.: Agent-Based Computational Economics: Growing Economies From the Bottom Up. Artificial Life 8(1), 55–82 (2002)
45. Tesfatsion, L., Judd, K. (eds.): Handbook of Computational Economics: Agent-Based Computational Economics. North-Holland (2006)
46. Thiele, J.C., Kurth, W., Grimm, V.: RNetLogo: an R package for running and exploring individual-based models implemented in NetLogo. In: Methods in Ecology and Evolution. British Ecological Society (2012); Early Preview

Towards Creating an Evolvable Semantic Platform for Formation of Research Teams

Eduard Babkin, Nikolay Karpov, and Oleg Kozyrev

National Research University Higher School of Economics,
25/12 Bolshaja Pecherskaja Ulitsa, Nizhny Novgorod 603155, Russia
{eababkin,nkarpov,okozyrev}@hse.ru

Abstract. In this paper authors wish to present an approach to information modeling and software design suitable for developing evolvable semantic applications in the domain of research team formation. The novel proposals include specialization of generic paradigm of ontological engineering, specific types of machine-readable RDF ontologies and application of temporal look at information relevant for team formation. In order to validate theoretical approach a software prototype of the evolvable web-based semantic platform InfoPort was developed.

Keywords: teams formation, ontologies, service-oriented design.

1   Introduction

Modern competitive research projects mostly require formation of strong and consistent inter-disciplinary teams [1][2]. In this case the cohesive team of scientific experts shall be combined taking into account competences of each specific performer. The team as a whole shall provide possibility of carrying out the research.

In universities such teams are frequently composed on demand. The issue of team formation, if it is understood as "personalization of the individual's allocation to a group"[3], becomes quite challenging in presence of time pressure, dynamically changed organizational structures and evolving employees skills. To our best knowledge most of university team leaders and grant writers try to solve such issue by *ad hoc* manner, mostly relying upon their intuition and informal inter-personal communications. At the same time the team leaders pessimistically estimate attempts to automate the team formation using information and communication technologies (ICT).

There are several important reasons for such pessimistic attitude. The team formation methods include both formal and human-oriented tasks to accomplish. For example, obviously semantic interoperability should be maintained among the members of the team who have overlapping scientific interests and research qualification. Also personal interconnections and social aspects have great impact, stimulating or declining willingness of team members to be vulnerable to the actions of others on the basis of the expectation that the other members will perform needed actions. The later issue usually is identified as trust management. In [4] Germain mentions that ability,

A. Kobyliński and A. Sobczak (Eds.): BIR 2013, LNBIP 158, pp. 200–213, 2013.

benevolence, and integrity can parsimoniously encompass the concept of trustworthiness, the immediate precursor to trust.

Although several research initiatives and software tools exist for formation of teams in such contexts as manufacturing, collaborative learning, multi-disciplinary research [2][5][6] , the problem of proper conceptualization of the cross-disciplinary domain of team formation and effective information modeling of such complex matters as trustworthiness or competencies still reduces potential benefits of application of information technologies. Most of available software tools exploit traditional database approach and techniques of Human Resource Management (HR). Such approach does not fit well the situation. In presence of dramatic variations in the target domain of research and expected characteristics of the research team end-users wish to get access to evolvable applications. In that case the developers cannot rely upon stable database scheme, predetermined queries and stable application designs.

Because the task of information modeling has great significance for design of evolvable and dynamic applications in general, first of all we suggest to consider the problem of team formation from the information modeling point of view. In that context we applied principles of Semantic web and ontological engineering to provide adequate information models for an evolvable semantic platform in the domain of research team formations with particular interest to the trust management. In order to achieve semantic interoperability relevant well-known ontologies are used to link together different chunks of data. In our research the ontology engineering approach was similar to well-known METHONTOLOGY methodology [7]. Basic RDF inference techniques help to deduce entailments of organizational structure and domains of research interests.

Our principal novel proposal includes application of temporal look at information relevant for team formation. In parallel to traditional semantic repositories which contain only the latest snapshot of information we implemented a particular scheme for historic repository. This feature allows analyzing personal and collective evolution over the time. We found such capability very important for making strategic decisions about feasible directions of advances.

To validate our theoretical approach we designed a prototype of the evolvable web-based semantic platform InfoPort which supports formation of university research teams. The prototype combines four major own modules (data extractor/crawler, import, knowledge engine and web-frontend) and third-party RDF repositories. Paradigm of linked data, service-oriented design and wide application of open standards allow easy extending InfoPort platform and building full-fledged evolvable web-applications for automated or semi-automated formation of research teams.

The rest of the article is structured as follows. Section 2 describes design of principal data models, including overview of historical repository for temporal analysis of research interests. In Section 3 we present design of InfoPort platform and technical information about particular methods and algorithms of data crawling applied in our prototype. In the conclusion we compare our approach to similar researches and define further steps needed to mature the proposed models and software design.

2   Information Modeling of the Discourse Domain

Information modeling and proper world representation play a crucial role in the task of teams formation. Until now in that domain the consensus is not achieved yet in precise definition and conceptualization of the core concepts, including the notion of teams. For example, in [1] J.R. Holenbeck et al. emphasize, that "any researcher doing a meta-analysis might find it difficult to explore the moderating influence of tasks, samples, and contexts because of the lack of consensus on classification systems." In [6] Hodik et al. also support the same statement in terms of lacking in adequate methods of competence management in distributed systems: "there is no common terminology of competency management; the terms 'competency', 'competency class', 'competency instance' and 'profile' are used in several slightly different meanings." For our purposes the following definition of competency [8] seems to be the most adequate: "The notion of competency provides an observable account of concrete human capacities under specific work conditions."

The situation of unstable terminology and confronting view points on team formation processes becomes the key obstacle on the way of exploiting information systems in general, and traditional database technologies with predetermined data schema in particular.

To get rid of repeating reengineering of DB schema in our approach to information modeling we offer to accept the hypothesis of open world and to implement the world representation using the generic concept of "linked data" and technologies of Semantic Web. In this case all information may be represented in the machine-readable form of RDF[1] triples. In the considered scenario RDF allows for extending the informational contents by demand supporting evolvability of our solution.

The second advantage of the proposed approach consists of strong semantic interoperability. Indeed, in the global network large amount of relevant ontologies and vocabularies exist in the form of RDF. Unified representation of heterogeneous information in the form of RDF and ability of SPARQL[2] query language to process federated queries give bold foundations for establishing tight relations between different relevant sources of information and maintain consistence and up-to-date state of information easily.

Selection of the basic semantic technologies determines a methodology for data modeling in our approach. To structure information about researchers, their skills, competences and other relevant facts we apply the method of ontological engineering. From our point of view it is similar to well-known METHONTILOGY methodology [7] which has been recommended by FIPA for the ontology construction task. In our research we also have passed through such development activities as specification, conceptualization, formalization and implementation. On the conceptual level we distinguish four types of ontologies which comprise the information model in the semantic platform, and are described below:

- organizational ontology;
- ontology of scientific areas;
- personal ontology;
- historical ontology.

---

[1] http://www.w3.org/RDF/
[2] http://www.w3.org/TR/rdf-sparql-query/

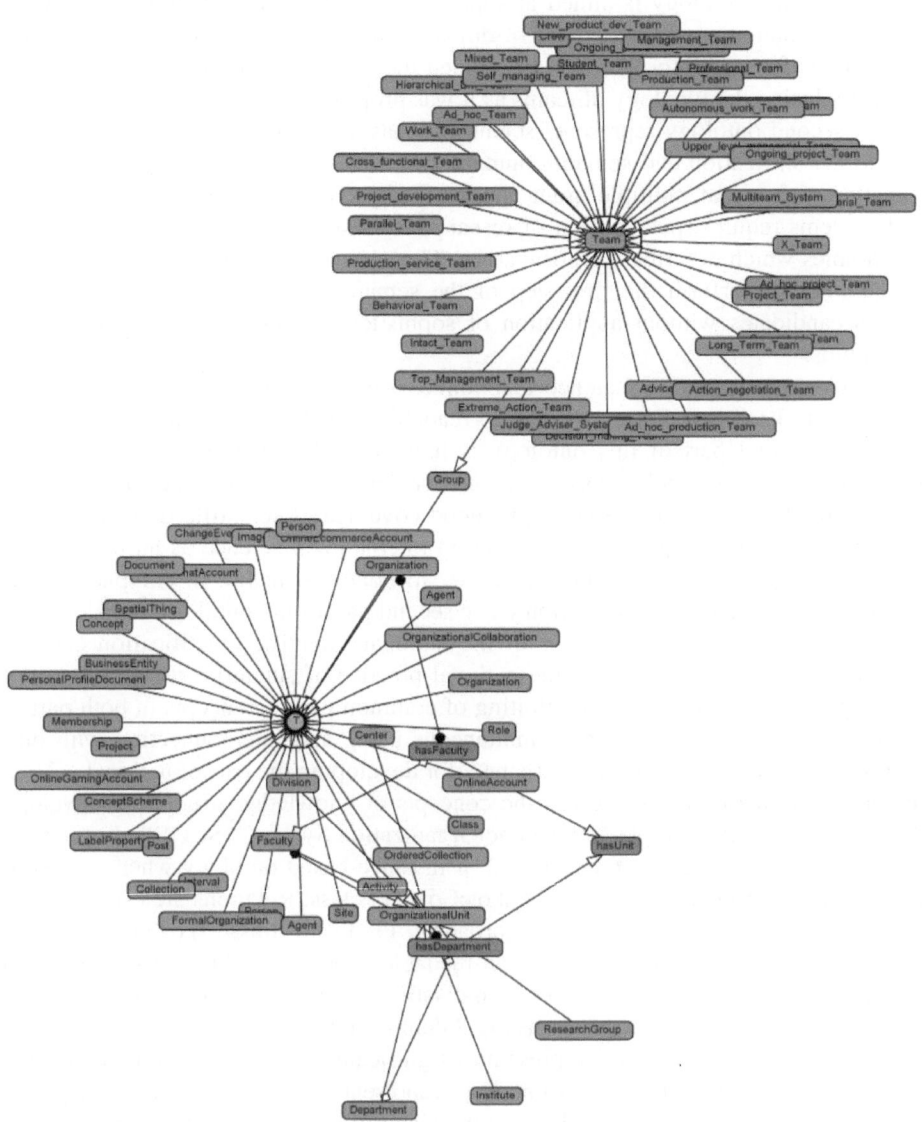

Fig. 1. Organizational ontology

Organizational ontology (Fig.1) contains classes and instances describing an organizational structure of particular research institution. Instances of the ontology represent both stable organizational units like departments or chairs, and *ad hoc* virtual structures like project teams. In order to maintain semantic interoperability we propose to build the organizational ontology on the basis of W3C organization ontology[3]. This ontology is aimed at supporting linked data publishing of organizational information across a number of domains. In order to present more elaborated foundations for teams formation we extended the original W3C organizational ontology introducing the typology of teams as it was proposed in [1].

The second ontology represents scientific areas and brings considerable contribution to the unification and semantic integration of researchers' characteristics. That's a matter of fact that multiple grant application systems, HR components and other ICT-systems require specification of research interests in terms of the limited set of taxonomies which describe scientific areas. This circumstance provides us for a practical ability to perform the first step of the semantic search among corresponding team's candidates without application of sophisticated natural language processing algorithms.

In our research several science taxonomies were considered. Currently two taxonomies are used together as a machine-readable ontology of scientific areas in our project. The first part of this ontology is international UNESCO nomenclature for fields of science and technology[4]. This nomenclature has such attractive features as deep hierarchical structure of concepts, good coverage of scientific domains, several national translations and wide acceptance in international science as an international standard. Also this nomenclature has more affordable structure in comparison with Dewey decimal system classification[5]. The second part of the ontology was developed by our research team on the basis of the national scientific classification called e-library, which is widely used in the national practice of scientific research, multiple grant application systems, etc. Exploiting of common parent concepts in both parts of the ontology may leverage their simultaneous using and interconnecting with other search engines and techniques. That's why for developing the part of national scientific classification we propose to use the concepts of knowledge structuring developed in W3C technology "Simple Knowledge Organization System" (SCOS)[6]. In such case the developed ontology becomes a kind of instance-based ontology where taxonomy topics are represented as instances of skos:Concept class. Relations are established by link types skos:narrower and skos:broader. Predicate links skos:prefLabel and skos:notation are used to define human-readable properties of the instances. In the result the principles of mapping between existing taxonomy and derived ontology of scientific areas may be represented as Fig.2 demonstrates.

The third personal ontology represents a significant part of professional knowledge needed for team formation. This ontology represents an actual snapshot of present person-oriented information available in the result of periodical web crawling through the university portal, results of the articles processing, and results of logical inference which provide for description of competences and skills. In our research we classify information about researchers according the following principal aspects:

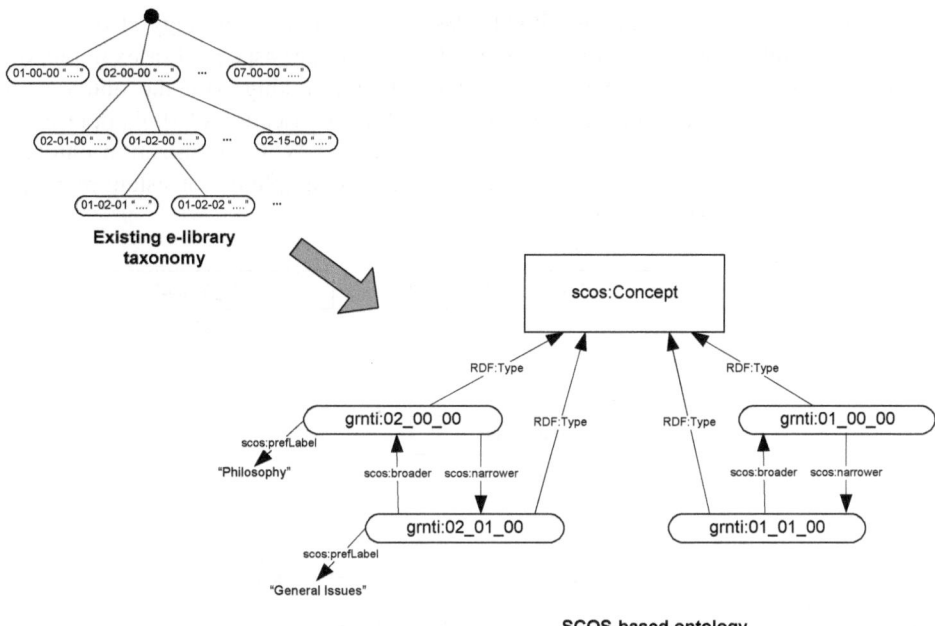

Fig. 2. Principles of mapping between taxonomy and the ontology of scientific areas

   a.   Researcher as a person.
   b.   Researcher as a skillful agent.
   c.   Researcher as a team member.

At some extent the specified aspects reflect the Gero's Function-Behavior-Structure (FBS) Ontology [5] and leverage application of the paradigm of smart design of research community in presence of situatedness. The first aspect of personal ontology describes such traditional and more less stable characteristics as last and first names, education, etc. The second aspect is tightly related to the notion of skills in terms of relevant topics of scientific classification taxonomies and keywords describing interests and skills of the person in free form. The last aspect contains information about participating the person in different kinds of projects or teams, connects personal ontology with the organizational ontology.

In order to consistently represent all three aspects of the person in terms of the same ontology we offer to use major concepts of W3C FOAF (Friend of Friend) vocabulary specification[7]. This specification is aimed at machine –readable representation of reusable information about people, groups, companies and other entities acting as agents in different activities. In this case their relationships become explicitly represented by different types of FOAF concepts from such sections as FOAF Basic (familyName, givenName, firstName), FOAF Personal Info (interest, currentProject, pastProject, etc), FOAF Projects and Groups, and FOAF Documents and Images (image).

---

[7] http://xmlns.com/foaf/spec/20070524.html

In addition to the standardized FOAF classes our personal ontology also contains several new link classes for semantic integration with other aspects. For example, our personal ontology provides class infoport:classify for linking with the ontology of scientific areas and class infoport:freeKeywords for specification of skills in terms of free text keywords. At the same time W3C FOAF and W3C organization ontology have connection via a shared concept foaf:Agent. An example of consistent representation of different aspects is depicted on Fig.3.

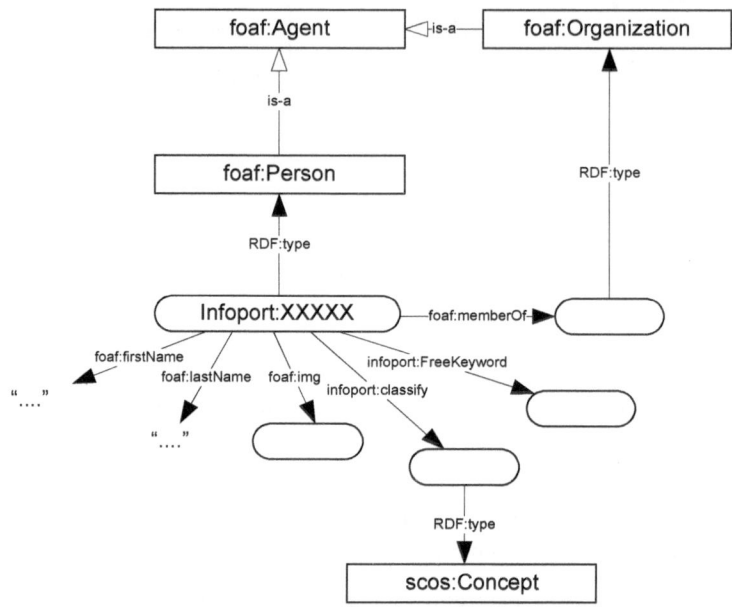

Fig. 3. Classes of personal ontology

The introduction of the fourth element in our approach, the historical ontology, strongly differentiates our work from other known ontology-based approaches to the teams formations. We believe that decision support of such complex task as formation of effective research teams should take into account not only snapshot of present skills and competences, but instead it should be based on the temporal representation and the historic, evolutionary view point.

Temporal representation may be achieved using the paradigm of system's life-cycle. More specifically, in our approach we use the concepts of BORO [9] and principles of temporal modeling proposed in ISO 19526[8]. Temporal aspects of personal information may be represented in the historical ontology using reification of RDF statements as follows (Fig.4).

---

[8] http://www.iso.org/iso/iso_catalogue/catalogue_tc/catalogue_de tail.htm?csnumber=29556

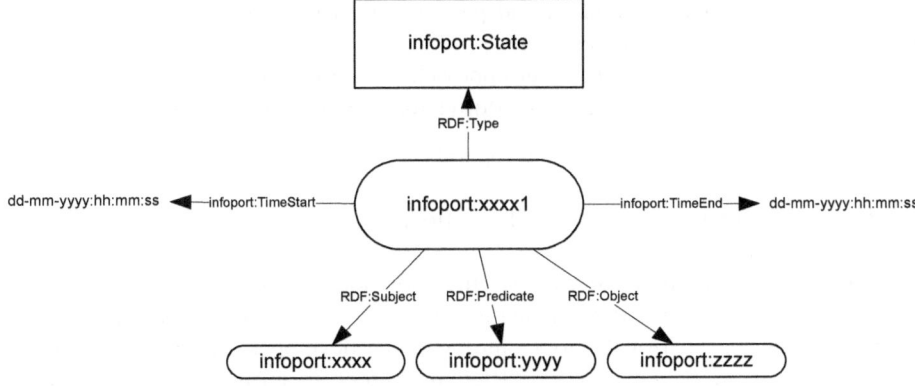

Fig. 4. Structure of the historical repository

Each modification in personal ontology is reflected in the historical ontology via modification of corresponding instances of infoport:State class. Modifications include creating new instances with corresponding values of infoport:TimeStart attribute and attaching attribute infoport:TimeEnd to existing instances. Delete operation is never applied to the historical ontology.

Given complete temporal information from the historical ontology InfoPort platform may provide a team builder with intuitively clear representation of personal evolution in terms of time line view (Fig.5).

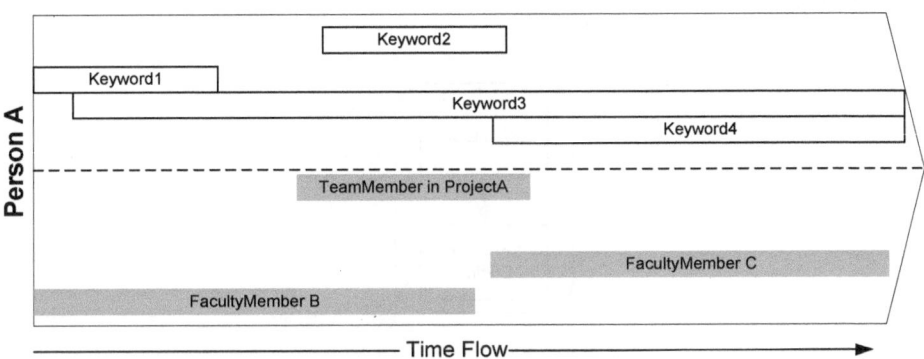

Fig. 5. The timeline of the person

This view combines segments of keywords or topics of science taxonomy together with temporal information about participating in particular research projects or stable organizational structures. Such combination allows for deep analysis of transient or sustainable scientific interests of the person as well as providing the basis for the trust management. Indeed, the temporal view point on the person's research interests has direct connection with the concept of cognition-based trust. In [4] Germain notes that cognition-based trust occurs due to perceptions of competence, reliability, and dependability It is based on reasoning about others' reliability and dependability.

The competence, integrity, ability, and past record of the person being trusted form the rational basis for withholding trust.

Combining all aspects together our approach to information modeling facilitates effective design of evolvable semantic platforms for support of team formation providing:

1) foundations for semantic interoperability;
2) extensibility of information model;
3) temporal representation of information.

Taking a pragmatic point of view we may note that explicit separation of four ontologies allows for flexible implementation strategy. It means that given specifics and update policies for each of the four ontologies the developers can easily choose the most appropriate implementation of RDF repository in terms of performance and representation power of the query language. The available solutions may vary from simple RDF triple stores to quite sophisticated OWL inference engines. Example of such ontology-related implementation strategy is given in the next section.

3   Design of the Platform

Proposed methods of the information modeling were practically applied during design and implementation of the evolvable semantic platform for research team formation called Information Port (InfoPort). High level design of the InfoPort platform is based on principles of Service-Oriented Architecture. The following services are distinguished (Fig.6):

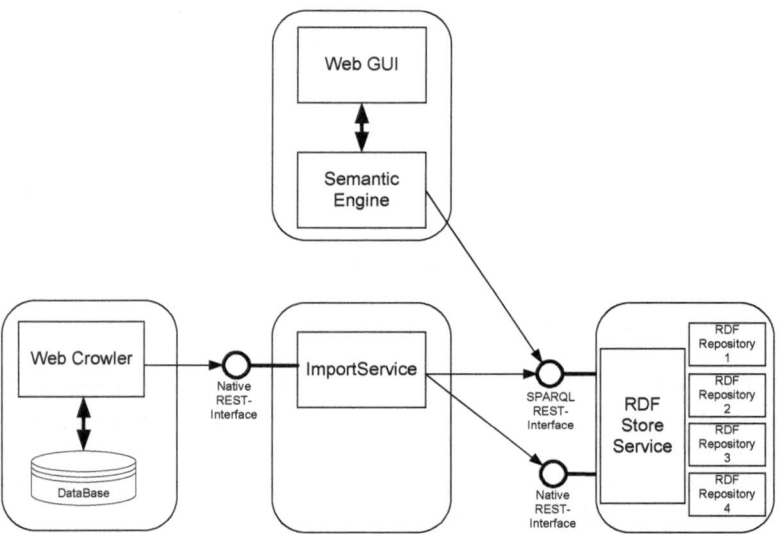

Fig. 6. InfoPort Conceptual Design

- Crawler Service.
- Import Service.
- Web Backend Service.
- RDF Store Service.

Implementation of Crawler Service uses Python[9] programming language and Lxml[10] library for processing HTML. The service is monitoring the information in the website using Hash function within a week period. After changing of information new structured data crawls and extracts from their pages using XML parser. The data represents as RDF triples and stores to the MySQL[11] database. Triples include hierarchical information as it originally is in the source. The first level is an alphabetical ordered list of group of scientist, second is a scientist with his personal interests and papers, and third is papers with its features. This data compose JSON request for native REST interface of ImportService

Implementation of Import and Web Backend services is based on JRuby programming environment and RubyOnRails Framework. During implementation several Ruby libraries for working with RDF were tested like RDF.rb[12], Sparql-client library[13], as well as RDF mappers SPIRA[14], ActiveRdf[15]. Due to performance issues after several experimental mock-ups the final design decision was to refuse using high-level object-mapping libraries (i.e. SPIRA). Instead, the implementation uses low-level SPARQL queries and RDF manipulation methods via native REST-based interface provided by RDF.rb library.

For RDF repository Services two alternatives were tested in our project: OpenRDF Sesame[16] and free version of Allegro Graph 4.0 [17]. Four different kinds of RDF repositories were created for each of four ontologies:

1) Persistent repository for personal ontology with capability of RDFS inference.
2) In-memory repository for e-lib taxonomy with capability of RDFS inference.
3) In-memory repository for organizational ontology with capability of RDFS inference.
4) Persistent plain RDF repository for historical ontology.

InfoPort platform implements communication between services using REST-interfaces and JSON-based encoding. For example, the table below describes the REST interface of the import service.

---

[9] http://www.python.org
[10] http://lxml.de
[11] http://www.mysql.com
[12] http://rdf.rubyforge.org/
[13] https://github.com/ruby-rdf/sparql
[14] https://github.com/datagraph/spira
[15] http://activerdf.org/
[16] http://www.openrdf.org/
[17] http://www.franz.com/agraph/allegrograph/

Table 1. Interface specification for InfoPort Import Service

Method	HTTP	URL	Data Encoding
Create	POST	http://xx.yy.xx.ww/infoport/entities	JSON
Read	GET	http://xx.yy.xx.ww/infoport/entities/:id.json	JSON
Update	PUT	http:// xx.yy.xx.ww/infoport/entities/:id	JSON
Delete	DELETE	http:// xx.yy.xx.ww/infoport/entities/:id	

Currently the InfoPort production environment uses deployment of all components to the same Tomcat server, however distributed configuration is also available due to wide using federated SPARQL queries.

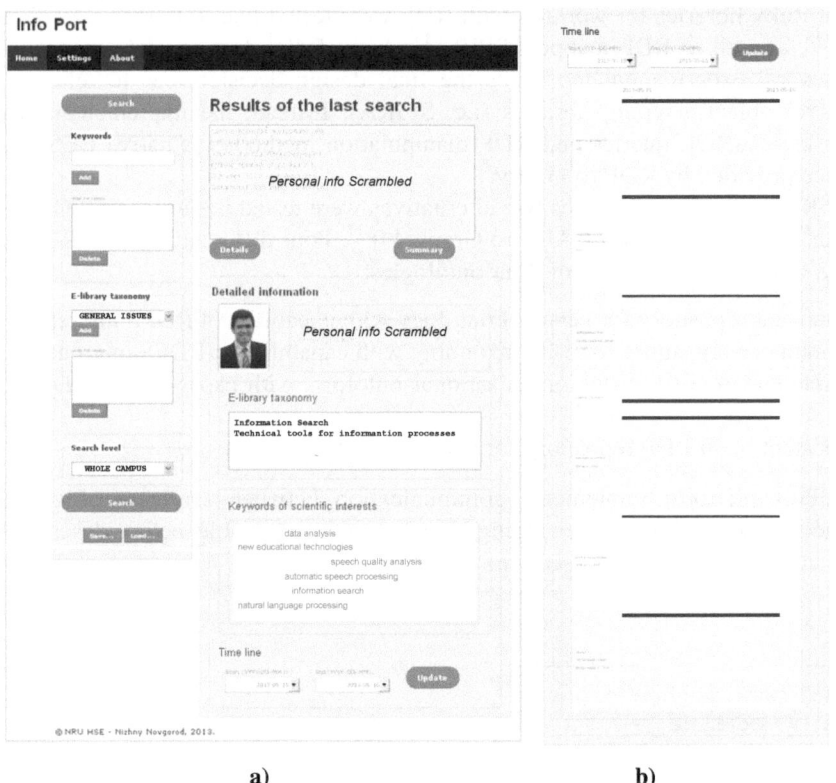

a)   b)

Fig. 7. InfoPort User Interface: a) – front page; b) – enlarged view of personal time line

Experimental setup of InfoPort contains factual information about more than three hundred employees of HSE NRU branch at Nizhny Novgorod. InfoPort updates information every month and temporal part of ontology is modified accordingly.

The multi-service graphical user interface is available for team builders (Fig.7). This interface provides such functions as multi-criterion search, visualization of present keywords in the form of tag cloud, visualization of temporal characteristics of the person in the form of time line.

4   Discussion and Conclusion

In this article we presented a new approach to support of research team formation focusing in information modeling and ICT-support via the evolvable semantic platform. The proposed methods of modeling use the concepts of "linked data" and ontological engineering, supporting the following statement of Christakis and Fowler: "To know who we are, we must understand how we are connected"[10].

Several other approaches also use semantic modeling for teams or group formation and offer using of FOAF vocabulary for building virtual teams and request- based virtual organizations in manufacturing [6][11], Communities of Practice (CoP) oriented towards learning activities [12][13][3]. However those proposals mainly target the domain of collaborative learning and do not take into account intrinsic features of the research teams formation (like specific team types mentioned in [2]).

On the level of information modeling the principal distinction between our approach and other mentioned works mostly deals with modeling the temporal aspect. Such research works in social networking as [14] introduce a similar concept of dynamic co-authorship maps but only partially investigate the temporal aspects of connections between persons and skills.

Machine-readable structured ontologies developed according to our approach laid in the foundation of the semantic service-oriented platform InfoPort. The purpose and functionality of that platform may be compared with e-Cat architecture [6][11] and such systems as ECOLEAD and PANDA which represent prototype implementations of the e-Cat architecture. The e-Cat is an agent-based architecture for the facilitation of members' profiles and competencies in alliances of small and medium enterprises. E-Cat architecture also uses the concept of life cycle, but that concept is applied to modeling the whole virtual organization instead of modeling individual evolution of skills and competences of a researcher as it is done in our approach. Also e-Cat architecture precisely defines the notion of competency and uses graph-oriented structures for their representation which are close to ontologies.

The developed ontologies and software implementation of the InfoPort platform open opportunities for further developing methods and tools for decision support during research teams formation. Several principal research interests form the roadmap for the next steps in our research. Because e-Cat architecture does not provides complete solutions for the problems of automated deducing competencies and ensuring consistency among the shared definitions of competencies we wish to include these issues to the roadmap of our further research. The next target is to develop a comprehensive formal model and practical algorithms for automated team formation based on gathered ontological data. In [15] Ounnass et al propose to use the technique of constraints satisfaction to form the learning groups. In [16] Vokřínek et al. propose to use distributed multi-agent methods of formation of virtual organizations based on contract net and auctions. Their proposals give bold foundations for effective application Multi-agent technologies and multi-agent communication protocols. In our case application of soft–computing paradigm of Kohonen's self-organizing Maps (SOM) allow formation of hierarchical teams.

A promising direction of the research includes integrating own personal ontologies and existing individual-oriented vocabularies and ontologies for competency specification. The later include General User Model Ontology (GUMO)[17] and the former include the Reusable Definition of Competency or Educational Objective (RDCEO) or generic competency schema (GCS)[8]. Such integration will facilitate advanced search capabilities augmented by psychological testing, thorough description of researchers behavior and analysis of competencies gaps. This integration will be a solid basis to cope the problems of strong personality in research teams overviewed in [2]. Inclusion into consideration such aspect will bring us closer to the solution of trust management in the research teams and practical application of the concept of templates for successful virtual teams, as it was described [4].

References

1. Hollenbeck, J.R., Beersma, B., Schouten, M.E.: Beyond team types and taxonomies: A dimensional scaling conceptualization for team description. Academy of Management Review 37(1), 82–106 (2012)
2. Dodson, M.V., Guan, L.L., Fernyhough, M.E., Mir, P.S., Bucci, L., McFarland, D.C., Novakofski, J., et al.: Perspectives on the formation of an interdisciplinary research team (short survey). Biochemical and Biophysical Research Communications 391(2), 1155–1157 (2010)
3. Ounnas, A., Davis, H.C., Millard, D.E.: Semantic Modeling for Group Formation. In: Procs. of Workshop on Personalisation in E-Learning Environments at Individual and Group Level (PING) at the 11th International Conference on User Modeling, UM 2007, Corfu, Greece (2007)
4. Germain, M.-L.: Developing trust in virtual teams. Performance Improvement Quarterly 24(3), 29–54 (2011)
5. Gero, J.S., Kannengiesser, U.: An ontology of situated design teams. Artificial Intelligence for Engineering Design, Analysis and Manufacturing: AIEDAM 21(3), 295–308 (2007)
6. Hodík, J., Vokřínek, J., Bečvář, P.: Support for virtual organisation creation - Partners' profiles and competency management. International Journal of Agent-Oriented Software Engineering 3(2-3), 230–251 (2009)
7. Corcho, O., Fernández-López, M., Gómez-Pérez, A.: Methodologies, tools and languages for building ontologies. Where is their meeting point? Data and Knowledge Engineering 46, 41–64 (2003)
8. García-Barriocanal, E., Sicilia, M.-A., Sánchez-Alonso, S.: Computing with competencies: Modelling organizational capacities. Expert Systems with Applications 39(16), 12310–12318 (2012)

9. Partridge, C.: Business Objects: Re-engineering for Re-use, 2nd edn. The BORO Centre (2005)
10. Christakis, N.A., Fowler, J.: Connected: the surprising power of our social networks and how they shape our lives. Little, Brown and Co., New York (2009)
11. Hodík, J., Vokřínek, J., Bíba, J., Bečvář, P.: Competencies and profiles management for virtual organizations creation. In: Burkhard, H.-D., Lindemann, G., Verbrugge, R., Varga, L.Z. (eds.) CEEMAS 2007. LNCS (LNAI), vol. 4696, pp. 93–102. Springer, Heidelberg (2007)
12. Da Silva, J.L.T., Ribeiro, A.M., Primo, T.T., Viccari, R.M.: A reference profile ontology for communities of practice. International Journal of Metadata, Semantics and Ontologies 7(3), 185–196 (2012)
13. Isotani, S., Inaba, A., Ikeda, M., Mizoguchi, R.: An ontology engineering approach to the realization of theory-driven group formation. International Journal of Computer-Supported Collaborative Learning 4(4), 445–478 (2009)
14. Steffen-Fluhr, N., Collins, R., Passerini, K., Wu, B., Gruzd, A., Zhu, M., Hiltz, R.: Leveraging Social Network Data to Support Faculty Mentoring: Best Practices. In: Women in Engineering Program Advocates Network (WEPAN) National Conference, Columbus, OH, USA (2012)
15. Ounnas, A., Davis, H., Millard, D.: A Framework for Semantic Group Formation. In: Procs. of the 8th IEEE International Conference on Advanced Learning Technologies (ICALT 2008), Santander, Cantabria, Spain, pp. 34–38 (2008)
16. Vokřínek, J., Bíba, J., Hodik, J., Vybíhal, J.: The RBVO formation protocol. International Journal of Agent-Oriented Software Engineering 3(2-3), 135–162 (2009)
17. Heckmann, D., Schwartz, T., Brandherm, B., Schmitz, M., von Wilamowitz-Moellendorff, M.: GUMO – The general user model ontology. In: Ardissono, L., Brna, P., Mitrović, A. (eds.) UM 2005. LNCS (LNAI), vol. 3538, pp. 428–432. Springer, Heidelberg (2005)

The Value of E-Learning to the Lecturer

Ulrike Borchardt and Karsten Weidauer

University of Rostock, Chair of Business Information Systems, 18051 Rostock,
Germany
{ulrike.borchardt,karsten.weidauer2}@uni-rostock.de

Abstract. E-learning is accepted for several years now, however when describing the benefits to be gained the focus usually lies on overall organizations or students of universities. In the context of universities however not only students are of significant relevance, but also the lecturer who is supposed to transfer his work into the operated e-learning platform or application. But which are the benefits perceived by the teaching personnel at universities? Based on the idea of the perceived benefit motivated by the IS success model a case study from the University of Rostock, Germany is presented to illustrate the benefits experienced by the lecturers starting to use an e-learning system for their teaching work. We therewith demonstrate the operationalization of the IS success model as well as illustrate the possible outcomes and value to be gained from evaluating an e-learning system.

Keywords: e-learning, perceived benefit, case study, IS success.

1 Motivation

Broadening the horizon by the means of using different media for lecturing at universities is a common approach, especially relevant in the context of lifelong learning. New media, new target groups and more flexibility for the students are promised and motivate the introduction of e-learning. Though it became clear that e-learning in the narrower sense of pure distance education is not a silver bullet [KES+05], it became an essential part of the learning culture at German universities. However, when having a look at the literature available on the topic it is hardly possible to gain an idea what e-learning means for the content provider, the lecturer. There are studies on the effects for students, for the universities themselves, [BKV09] but what about the professors and staff members who are going from presenting their knowledge in a classroom to entering it into authoring tools and making it durable. They are the content provider of the e-learning process and the ones supposed to deliver good looking, well-structured contents, provide requested feedback on the contents and motivate the students. But what motivates them, how do they experience e-learning and possible benefits?

In this paper we present the findings of a study conducted on teaching personnel and their perceived benefits accompanying the integration of the e-learning

A. Kobyliński and A. Sobczak (Eds.): BIR 2013, LNBIP 158, pp. 214–226, 2013.
© Springer-Verlag Berlin Heidelberg 2013

software ILIAS in the curriculum at the University of Rostock, Germany. The project "Tutorenpool E-Learning" offered lecturers the possibility to be provided with extra training on the authoring part of the software and support by a student assistant for establishing the use of ILIAS within their regular curriculum. To extract the perceptions and motivations of the lecturers we conducted a two parted social empirical study in which we interviewed the participants of the program. The gained results were determined to address the following research questions:

1. Which expectations do lecturers have towards e-learning?
2. What perceived benefits can be gained from the use of e-learning in the regular curriculum at which costs?
3. Where does the lecturer's motivation come from and how does the perceived benefit influence it?

The results and the methodology gained to provide answers to these questions are presented in the following sections. Anyhow, the study had no intention to evaluate the technical platform in use as the decision on using this platform was already made.

The following paper is organized as follows: section 2 holds the fundamentals of our work, followed by the description of the methodology of our work in section 3. The results gained from the study are presented in section 4 and finally section 5 presents the conclusions and implications of the results for our further work.

2   Fundamentals

This section is about to describe the general terms in use for our work as well as the general conditions of the program funding the e-learning activities at the University of Rostock

2.1   E-learning

E-learning as such is a term defined differently within literature [CM11, TLN+04]. Undoubtedly it is connected to the term of software supported learning, however the opinions on whether this includes the interconnected world only (web based training) or should be interpreted in the wider sense of all software supported learning (computer based training) vary [Leh08]. However, for our field of application within the field of learning at universities we focus on web based trainings (WBT) offering the opportunity to learn contents taught at the university using being provided to the student via the Internet.

Nevertheless e-learning has different focuses and therewith can be categorized according to its purpose into content oriented and process oriented forms [KK08]. As such content oriented systems merely support a face to face lecture by distributing or providing the contents, e.g. as slides available for a certain lecture. The process oriented systems however support the whole learning process, from presenting the contents, offering exercise possibilities to the assessing of training success.

Within the field of knowledge management e-learning can be categorized as one of the core knowledge services to be offered by a KMS system according to Maier [Mai07]. And therewith lets us posit e-learning systems as an IS/ KMS to be investigated with the help of the IS Success model [DM03].

2.2   Perceived Benefit

We chose the perceived benefit [THH91] as an approach to measure the success of e-learning based on the IS Success approach introduced by Delone and McLean [DM03]. Usually the question arises whether the success of a certain Information System can be measured in monetary units. This however is difficult in general due to the manifold effects of such a system and its integration in the organization which prevents a direct assignment of made investments. In the field of education and nonprofit organizations an additional issue is that usually no outcome measured in monetary units is provided [Rou10]. Anyhow positive benefits are desirable to make a system successful and keep it running on a high quality level [H$^+$01].

Starting with the assumption that e-learning systems are as such of the character of information systems we chose to evaluate the perceived benefit of the user as indicated in the model of DeLone/McLean, see figure 1.

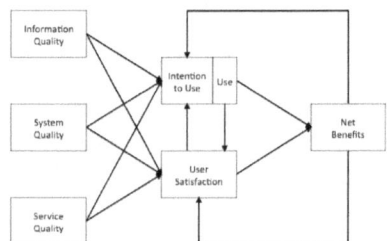

Fig. 1. IS Success model according to [DM03]

This leads to the evaluation categories of information quality, system quality and service quality as a general basis for the perceived benefit. These three were not of concern in our case study because they were already settled by the university (system and service) or are to be provided by the lecturer (information). Accordingly, we focus on the second level: use, intention to use and user satisfaction, neglecting the first dimension since it is not for us to be influenced. How to measure these categories for our application problem or in general is not provided by the model. Anyhow it is indicated by general published studies that this mostly can be done by the use of surveys. The individual items included in a corresponding survey are not provided within the model but are left to be found by researcher himself.

2.3   The Program at the University of Rostock

At the University of Rostock two e-learning related programs, namely Stud.IP and ILIAS, are used as learning management systems for administration, organization and support of lectures in the Internet. Whereas Stud.IP is a content oriented learning management system and fully integrated for content and information provision on the lectures, ILIAS offers the possibilities of a content oriented e-learning system and is as such by now not fully integrated into the curricula since almost all lectures are held offline unsupported by e-learning modules. This should be changed with the help of the program "Tutorenpool E-Learning", which supported interested teaching personnel to apply for financial and educational support to establish new modules in ILIAS. The financial support therefore was given to employ a student assistant. The general idea however was that for the application in the program the outlines as well as the contents of the module to be created were already settled. If approved, the program covered the technical and didactic training of the lecturer, as well as the technical training of the student assistant. Consequently, the team of lecturer and student assistant was supported during the creation of their e-learning module. This covered support for technique, didactics and communication.

The overall goal of the program initiated by a cooperation of the IuK Verbund (Information and communication group) and the ZQS (center for quality management) of the University of Rostock, was to enable the teaching personnel to create further modules in ILIAS on their own initiative. Per term several projects were supported: during the first phase 5 projects per term and later on 10 per term were supported, however it is not possible to take part in the program twice as a lecturer to avoid mere focus on the financial support.

3   Methodology

In this section planning and methodology of the study conducted is described.

3.1   Procedure

To explore the research questions we used an explorative empirical approach containing two stages: a quantitative online questionnaire as well as qualitative interviews. The focus lies on the online questionnaire, the interviews serve as a complement to expand or verify the results of the questionnaire. The quantitative method was used due to the easier operability as well as the better possibilities for comparison of the expected heterogeneous data during interpretation. This way all lecturers could be approached at the same time and directly. The online questionnaire was available for 14 days and had to be composed from the scratch, due to the fact that by literature research no similar surveys from other universities could be found. We chose the online questionnaire as it is independent from time and space and is proven in everyday life of higher education. With regard to the IS Success model, the questionnaire aims at the category of user satisfaction and intention to use. With the help of general literature on the topic a question-naire could be created, however we had to skip extensive pretests on experts due to their availability and the limited time of the project (4 months). For the interview part of the survey 5 lecturers were picked at random, which had to fulfill the criteria of having answered the online questionnaire. They were interviewed with the help of an interview guideline prearranged. After the interview, which was recorded, the results were transcribed before interpretation.

3.2   Stage 1: Questionnaire Design

The basic population of the survey consisted of all teaching personnel that took part in the project "Tutorenpool E-Learning". Since this project has a limited number of participants a term the overall basic population consisted of 34 individuals and accordingly all participants were addressed by the survey instead of choosing a random sample. The notification on the survey was sent via mail and was answered by 50 % of the population; accordingly the basic population of our results in the analysis is 17 and can be considered rather small.

The used questionnaire holds 37 questions including 84 items covering 9 areas of interest. The areas of interest covered were: demographic data, attitude of the lecturer, e-learning culture at the chair/ institute, media competence of the lecturer, module description, acceptance by the students, dedication of the lecturer, expectations of the lecturer and observations of the lecturer. The questionnaire was designed using different question types alternating to avoid automated picking of answers. It consists mostly of closed questions (54%) which were complemented by semiopen (24%) and open (22 %) questions .

Applying Likert scales a four point scale was used to avoid the tendency toward the middle (neutral), and force the participant to build and communicate an opinion. This was accompanied by the answering possibility "refuse to answer" to offer a possibility to skip questions due to the inability to provide an answer. A larger scale was avoided to not confront the participant with too granulated answering possibilities as the classification according to the answer categories remains highly subjective. Moreover, for gathering general tendencies a four point scale is fully sufficient. In addition not all questions covering one field of interest were placed successively in the questionnaire to keep the answering person in the process of active participation. The actual questions and their classification are displayed in table 1.

3.3   Stage 2: Interview Guideline

The interview guideline used for stage 2 of our study should support a relatively free dialogue and is only an approximate guideline consisting of the following 5 questions.

1. What were your reasons for participating in the program "E-learning Tutorenpool ILIAS" ?
2. How were your experiences with the program and the application?

Table 1. Questions in the questionnaire with answer type

Question	Type
Gender	closed
Position	closed
To which part of the university do you belong?	half open
How long is your teaching experience?	open interval
How long have you been involved with e-learning?	open interval
How did you get in touch with the program?	open interval
What were reasons for your participation?	open
Would you have taken part without financial support?	closed
Would you have taken part without technical & didactic training?	closed
Did you continue creating new modules after the end of the program?	closed
If yes - how many	open interval
What purpose serves your module?	half open
Which kind of lecture does your module to support?	half open
How relevant is working with the module for the participating students?	closed
Which incentives do you use to attract students' attentions	open free
Which media are used in the module	closed
Do you still use the module designed/created during the program	closed
If not why	half open
If yes: how long	closed interval
When you are communicating with the students - how fast do you answer?	closed
How much time do you spent on maintenance of the module per week	closed ordinal
How much support from student assistants do you use?	half open
How do you estimate the acceptance of the module by the students?	closed
Did you evaluate your module?	halfopen
-if yes which points relevant for e-learning did you consider?	closed
- if yes which positive/negative feedback did you receive?	open free
Have you improved/reworked your module after the first usage?	closed nominal
- if yes what were your reasons?	open free
Which expectations did you have towards e-learning?	closed
Which of your expectations were fulfilled?	open free
Which additional observations did you make during the module provision?	closed
Working with ILIAS for me is...	closed
Would you recommend the program?	closed nominal

3. Did you perceive any benefits personally or for your work from establishing a module in ILIAS for your lectures?
4. What were your expectations towards the use of ILIAS and were they fulfilled?
5. What motivates you to proceed working with ILIAS, and what are possible drawbacks?

Question 1 and 2 are dedicated to building up a connection between interviewer and interviewee on the topic of the questionnaire. Questions 3 and 4 are directly related to the research questions of this survey and allow for dwelling deeper into the motivation of the lecturer, to find the reasons that motivate or discourage the use of the available e-learning system. By using the critical incident method the interviewer tries to find out how much the positive or negative feedback from the students influences the perceived benefit of the lecturer. Finally, question 5 resembles the third research question on the source of motivation and the effect of the perceived benefit.

4   The Perceived Benefits of the Program "Tutorenpool E-Learning"

This section presents the results gained (questionnaire and interview) and their interpretation for the success of the program and ILIAS per se, as well as the indications on the perceived benefits of IS.

4.1   The Use

Based on the IS Success model of DeLone/McLean as introduced in Section 2, we did not primarily analyze the use of the ILIAS system, however can provide some numbers supporting the general success of establishing the system at the university. In the table 2 the values indicating use from June 2008 and June 2011 are provided, showing the increase in use after the first phase of the "Tutorenpool E-learning".

It becomes obvious that the use increased significantly during this period of time, though the numbers of registered users and active users differ a lot and

Table 2. Usage of ILIAS in 6/2008 and 6/2011

Objects	Amount (2008)	Amount (2011)
registered user	13000	19047
active user	723	5421
categories	106	343
courses	78	415
exercises	33	173
tests(test objects)	33	1248
modules overall	208	1229

irritate in their difference within the different years. The amount of objects however indicates that the variety of e-learning offered is recognized and that ILIAS is more established as full scope e-learning system. This is especially apparent from the establishment of test objects, indicating the support of the full learning process, as well as the establishment of full courses in the system. Both examples illustrate the orientation towards a full e-learning process support by leaving the field of mere content provision and management as generally provided by the mandatory use of Stud.IP. We therewith assume the dimension use of the layer 2 of the IS success model as covered indicating a positive though long termed trend.

4.2   The Perceived Benefits of E-Learning for Teaching Personnel from the Questionnaires

With the help of the questionnaire we wanted to be able to visualize and evaluate the perceived benefits. One approach to gain statements on this was to ask the lecturers for their expectations as predefined items and whether these were fulfilled, since this approach promised more answers than the open question on the benefits. On the expectations towards the usage of e-learning modules in ILIAS following statements were gathered. The statement gaining the most approval was the expectation that by implementing the modules additional practicing possibilities were offered (87.5% fully approved, 6.3% approved). This result was confirmed by the statement on additional immersion possibilities, which essentially means the same and gained 68.8% fully approve and 18.8% approve. In contrast, though still being positive, only 56.3% fully approved the expectation for additional learning possibilities for the students, 31.3% still approved this expectation. Further positive expectations were also directed at the students, namely being able to offer them more flexible studying possibilities (53.3% fully approved, 33.3% approved).

As for their own work only 25% fully approved the expectation that their own time and work expenses lower whereas 34.3% totally disagreed on this point. With regard to their own job security 93.8% (fully disapproved) had no fear that by the establishment of e-learning modules they make themselves redundant. In addition 75% fully approved the expectation that by the established e-learning modules the students have to learn to work self-initiated and independent. Two further statements and the results are shown in table 3 below. As for unexpected issues the result for us this was that lecturers did not expect more frequent and intensive communication with their students (40% fully disapproved, 53.3% disapproved), where we at least expected an equal state to today instead of an assumed sinking communication.

With regard to the real perceived benefit it was planned to use an open question after the aforementioned expectations to let the participants indicate which expectations really came true. Anyway, the bad response rate on open questions confounded that idea. Though it would have been easy to note down the number of the items of the preceding question holding the expectation no evaluable data was gained. Anyhow an overall rating of the perceived benefit was given within

Table 3. Further expectation towards the Ilias modules

Using Ilias is...	fully approve	approve	disapprove	fully disapprove	positive total
easing the lectures	37.5	25	18.8	18.8	37.6
timely design of teaching contents	43.8	50	6.2	0	6.2

the overall question of the impact of the developed e-learning module. There we had several items covering ranges of opposite adjective pairs e.g. useful/ useless and reasonable/meaningless. Here we gained a completely positive perception of the work with the modules, as for the meaningfulness this summed up to a 93.8% positive feedback and for usefulness to 81.3%.

When actually asking for the perceived impact of the establishment of e-learning modules the relevant issues were, that the own abilities with regard to the used technology improved and that colleagues contacted concerning the module and the experiences with it. To only describe the relevant results here we categorized the results according to the percentages gained. Only if more than 66 % fully approved we consider an item highly relevant, up to 33 % mediocre relevant and beneath not relevant. However some positively imagined impacts were not effective: when asked whether a positive evaluation result of the lecture including the created ILIAS module was gained only 5 answers were given and 3 of those stated that it did not. Anyway the evaluation of the lecture and the improvement of the study results were the once with the highest correlation to the positive perceived benefit as indicated by the adjective pairs. This was calculated using correlations coefficients. For these two items these were above 0.5 (Kendall-Tau-b, as well as Spearman Rho). The relevance of this can be questioned due to the small number of answers, thus should be considered for reevaluation.

Nonetheless this does not correlate with the overall positive results gained from the adjectives; at least it is not sufficient to explain to strong positive tendency at the adjective pairs. This only leads to the conclusion, that the suggested items might not be sufficient to describe all reasons responsible for a positive perceived benefit. Since these results could not provide us with further data on the perceived benefits we headed for interviews for further clarification.

4.3   Results of the Interviews

Though the interviews were very few it was possible to reveal some extra facts on the motivation and benefits of the lecturers. As for the initial motivation to work with the application program, the most important remark was that only already motivated colleagues are assumed applying for the program, the basic intrinsic motivation of the participants should consequently be regarded as high. Furthermore most motivation and expectations are directed towards the teaching process. Interviewees see the necessity to adapt to contemporary teaching and experience teaching as service to be improved or at least broadened.

There is the intention to fill gaps in regular teaching, to include a wider media variety, allow for more flexibility in learning and provide contents suitable for different learner stereotypes. Even more positive annotated was that e-learning in the fundamental lectures allows for a shift towards real work on the contents instead of simply doing preparation in the lecture, e.g. reading introductory texts. Consequently to the shift more room for discussion is left in the lectures, which also promises deeper understanding of the contents in the lectures. The e-learning module therewith promised to avoid the mere passive behavior of the students in the lectures accompanied by an e-learning module. Overall it was the aspiration to oneself to provide good didactical profound work that strongly motivated the lecturers to use ILIAS in addition to existing lectures.

As for negative motivation all users indicated high resistance. The usual technical barriers occurring in the first part of the usage usually disappeared rather fast and were no longer reason for frustration. It was stressed ILIAS had much less barriers than experienced with other solutions beforehand. Concerning negative feedback from the students; this usually was not given as long as the e-learning part of a lecture was optional. It seemed as if the students who did not agree with the addition simply ignored it. A steady mandatory integration however gained more resonance, also negative. Anyway it turned out that negative feedback is at least with our interviewees more inspiring and mostly more constructive, for it provides issues to be worked on. However, the claim is also that negative feedback is mostly given after the student failed in the exam, what in general is too late. Anyway the general positive trend in exams results supports the lecturers in proceeding with e-learning.

As for the culture of e-learning in their working environment all participants claimed it being relatively low. Yet, it helps to have colleagues which undergo the same process or have already been there. As for the program the financial aid helped, especially when normally to student assistants could be paid. This also helped coping with the initial work overhead.

4.4   Summary

Though it is difficult to precisely name the components of the perceived benefit as it is not further described how it can be evaluated by the IS success model we found a way to ask participants for their perception. Starting from the point that perception is subjective and everyone forms an expectation towards the usefulness when applying for a certain program on e-learning we were asking for the fulfillment of these expectations. This revealed a generally positive attitude towards the whole program yet concrete benefits for the individual lecture were difficult to be named. Similar holds for the expectations towards e-learning, the participants could not name them concretely and mostly referred to improving themselves and their work by integrating e-learning into their curricula.

One of the shortcomings of our survey is that it only took interested persons into consideration, since the one not willing to engage themselves certainly did not apply for the program "Tutorenpool ILIAS" at all. Consequently the basic population can be expected to have a positive attitude towards the topic of e-learning in general and has accepted that it takes time and effort to establish and maintain e-learning modules. Moreover the experience with the system is only short termed, which asks for long term evaluation with respect to the chances in perception and motivation of the lecturers. Beside the positive attitude of the participants, it is also the case that the focus laid strongly on the lecturing only. How the necessary effort may collide with research or influence the capacities for research was not part of the evaluation. This being an interesting issue was indicated in one of the interviews, where the interviewee stated that the use of ILIAS provided her the freedom to do take a professorship substitute while keeping up her own teaching obligation in Rostock. The positive perceived benefits were based on the lecturers' initial high personal intrinsic motivation and curiosity, something which hardly can be influenced or artificially created by the environment.

5   Conclusions and Further Work

As for the validity of the conducted survey: to provide further insight in the validity of the gained results which are based on a rather small population (34 participants) repetitions of the survey are desirable. These should not only take place at the University of Rostock but also at other universities running other e-learning systems. This would on the one hand further prove the approach to measure the perceived benefit and could on the other hand become a tool to evaluate the benefits of such programs for initiating full e-learning programs at universities. Moreover, some long term evaluation would be suitable, regarding the impact of such a program e.g. 3 years later, having a look on the development and usage of the modules. In addition the comparison to the use of other systems is desirable as to gain different results for the dimensions of layer 2 of the IS Success model [DM03] and consequently allow for comparison.

Considering the value to the teaching personnel, the lecturers, this survey showed that even the rather motivated ones can only provide a tendency of the perceived benefits. The number of applicants for the whole program however shows that especially in the beginning the motivation to start e-learning at all was rather low. Only with massive internal advertisement participants could be motivated to apply for the program. This reveals three issues on the other, non-applying, lecturers; they rather have absolutely no time to take part, are lacking a concept for integrating e-learning into their common teaching or they are simply not motivated to access these systems for their work. The worst thinkable demotivation would be no interest at all, which certainly will hold for some lecturers but an overall survey on this is still missing. We focused for once on the lecturers taking into consideration that in an enterprise, employees mostly should create e-learning modules for their fellow colleagues, considering their motivation comporable. The general possibilities as such have already been explored and published in [BG10], showing the difficulty of using authoring tools as such. This was accompanied throughout this study on the program in which we took part fully realizing the difficulties of didactics when assembling an e-learning module. Accordingly, the results presented here showing the rather long lasting intrinsic motivation of lectures for the use of e-learning provides positive feedback on the perceived benefits. Yet it also reveals that in enterprises "professional" teachers are needed to cope with such systems.

The work presented in this paper is part of our research on the evaluation of KMS systems with the help of the IS Success model or its adaption in the OMIS Success according to Jennex/Olfman [Jen04]. The overall goal of that research is the establishment of a methodological approach to the value-oriented choice of KMS. Anyway to be able to provide such approach, the models for the evaluation of the success of IS/ KMS Systems need adoption, operationalization and further extension within their categories, as was shown in this paper for the user satisfaction. There are very few results published in this field, see e.g. [RS08], and thus the main work for employing this is left to us. Referring also to the knowledge services to be included in a KMS according to [Mai07], learning is one of the central services to be addressed with such a system. Consequently the survey on this special e-learning system fitted the overall general method for evaluation within the field of KMS which should from our point of view be oriented towards the perceived benefit. The general framework for this value-oriented approach was already introduced in [Bor11b], [Bor11a]. With the work presented here we gained further insight into the establishment of surveys to retrieve feedback on the user satisfaction, including the value and efforts of using interviews for that aspect. As presented here these make up a valuable addition at a relatively high cost, so should only be used if no valuable results in form of a questionnaire could be gained.

References

[BG10]   Borchardt, U., Grap, F.: E-Learning Application Support for SME. In: Forbrig, P., Günther, H. (eds.) BIR 2010. LNBIP, vol. 64, pp. 62–72. Springer, Heidelberg (2010)

[BKV09]   Bremer, C., Krömker, D., Voss, S.: Wirtschaftlichkeits-und Wirksamkeitsanalysen sowie Vorgehensmodelle zur Einfuehrung und Umsetzung von e-learning an Hochschulen. In: E-Learning in Hochschule und Weiterbildung: Einsatzchancen und Erfahrungen, Bielefeld, pp. 61–80 (2009)

[Bor11a]   Borchardt, U.: Towards a Value-Oriented KMS Recommendation for SME. In: Liu, K., Filipe, J. (eds.) KMIS 2011 - Proceedings of the 3rd International Conference on Knowledge Management and Information Sharing, Paris, France, October 26-29. SciTePress (2011)

[Bor11b]   Borchardt, U.: Towards Value-Driven Alignment of KMS for SME. In: Abramowicz, W., Maciaszek, L., Węcel, K. (eds.) BIS Workshops 2011 and BIS 2011. LNBIP, vol. 97, pp. 220–231. Springer, Heidelberg (2011)

[CM11]   Clark, R.C., Mayer, R.E.: E-learning and the science of instruction: Proven guidelines for consumers and designers of multimedia learning. Pfeiffer (2011)

[DM03]   Delone, W.H., McLean, E.R.: The DeLone and McLean Model of Information Systems Success: A Ten-Year Update. J. Manage. Inf. Syst. 19, 9–30 (2003) ISSN 0742–1222

[H⁺01]   Maier, R., Hädrich, T.: Modell für die Er folgsmessung von Wissensman-
            agementsystemen. Wirtschaftsinformatik 43(5), 497–509 (2001)
[Jen04]   Jennex, M.E.: Assessing Knowledge Management Success/Effectiveness
            Models. In: 37th Hawaii International Conference on System Sciences,
            HICSS35. IEEE Computer Society (2004)
[KES⁺05]   Kerres, M., Euler, D., Seufert, S., Hasanbegovic, J., Voss, B.: Lehrkompe-
            tenz für eLearning-Innovationen in der Hochschule: Ergebnisse einer ex-
            plorativen Studie zu Massnahmen der Entwicklung von eLehrkompetenz
            (2005)
[KK08]   Keller, K., Krawitz, P.D.R.: Netzbasiertes Lehren und Lernen in Der Be-
            trieblichen Weiterbildung: Eine Fallstudie Am Beispiel Der Telekom. Be-
            triebswirtschaftlicher Verlag Gabler (2008)
[Leh08]   Lehner, F.: Wissensmanagement. Hanser (2008) ISBN 9783446414433
[Mai07]   Maier, R.: Knowledge Management Systems: Information and Communi-
            cation Technologies for Knowledge Management, 3rd edn. Springer, Hei-
            delberg (2007) ISBN 9783540714088
[Rou10]   Roumois, U.H.: Studienbuch Wissensmanagement. In: Grundlagen der
            Wissensarbeit in Wirtschafts-, Non-Profit-und Public-Organisationen 2
            (2010)
[RS08]   Reisberger, T., Smolnik, S.: Modell zur Erfolgsmessung von Social-
            Software-Systemen. System 103(1), 565–577 (2008)
[THH91]   Thompson, R.L., Higgins, C.A., Howell, J.M.: Personal computing: toward
            a conceptual model of utilization. MIS Quarterly, 125–143 (1991)
[TLN⁺04]   Tavangarian, D., Leypold, M.E., Nölting, K., Röser, M., Voigt, D.: Is e-
            learning the Solution for Individual Learning. Electronic Journal of E-
            learning 2(2), 273–280 (2004)

Conversion Method in Comparative Analysis of e-Banking Services in Poland

Witold Chmielarz and Marek Zborowski

Faculty of Management, University of Warsaw,
Szturmowa 1/3 02-678 Warszawa, Poland
{witold.chmielarz,marek.zborowski}@uw.edu.pl
http://www.wz.uw.edu.pl

Abstract. The main objective of this article is to identify the best electronic banking websites from the point of view of an individual client. After a short introduction the authors determined the assumptions for the study. Particular attention is paid to provide conversion method and the way of its practical implementation. Subsequently, they carried out multilateral analyses and presented the conclusions of the study.

Keywords: e-banking services, websites evaluation, conversion method.

1 Introduction

The increase in the number of clients with potential access to account via the Internet is accompanied by a continuous increase of active customers (at least one transaction a month). In Poland, since the end of 2006 till the end of the III quarter of 2012 the number increased by over 7 million users, which is an increase by 164% [6]. Every year the population of new customers using the possibilities offered by the Internet to handle banking transactions is growing. In 2007 more than 700,000 people started to use e-banking services, and in 2012 the number was close to 3 million. Last year we could observe a steady increase of the number of active individual clients, by nearly 12%, from 10.141 million to over 11.364 million people by the end of the year. There are nearly 55% of active users, out of all clients having electronic access to account. The average value of settlements made by individual clients every month increases in 2012 by over 1.67%%, from 6,000 to 6,300 zlotys.

Poland in the European statistics with regard to penetration - compares quite well according to ComScore [5, 7] report it takes the sixth place (52.3%), while the European average is 40%. The largest e-banking penetration is in the Netherlands 66.0%, the lowest in Switzerland (18.8%). France (60%), Finland (56.4%), Sweden (54.2%) are ahead of us, behind are among others: Germany, Spain, Denmark and Norway. The dynamics of the increase of the number of e-banking clients in Poland is still one of the highest on our continent in recent years we note the increase of over one million every year.

The review of the literature [8, 9, 11, 12] shows that e-banking websites may be analysed from the point of view of: usability, interactivity, functionality, visualisation, efficiency, reliability and availability. Most of evaluation methods are

A. Kobyliński and A. Sobczak (Eds.): BIR 2013, LNBIP 158, pp. 227–240, 2013.

traditional scoring methods based on specific criteria sets, evaluated by means of an applied scale. Technical and functional criteria are the most commonly applied. Most of them contain factors which may be evaluated in a very subjective way: text clarity, attractive colours, images and pictures, the speed and intuitiveness of navigation, etc. Moreover, some users do not treat particular criteria sets in an equivalent way. However, on the other hand, there occur frequent problems with determining preferences for particular criteria and the evaluation of relations between them. This part of the work concerns the application of the authors own, though based on the literature, set of criteria for a scoring evaluation and a selection of electronic services of selected banks.

2 Assumptions of the Study

At the beginning of 2013, the authors carried out research on the quality of websites offering electronic access to services of the most popular banks among Polish individual clients on a sample of 84 people, where 73 respondents completed surveys correctly. The participants of the survey were students, aged 22-45, of management and information technology faculties in the University of Warsaw and Vistula University in Warsaw. Among the respondents, 39% were women and 61% men, mainly from Warsaw and surrounding areas. Each of the respondents declared to have at least one electronic access account with one of the banks operating in Poland (15 used e-banking services provided by two banks, 2 people of three banks), thus, in total, the authors examined access to 93 active electronic accounts.

In the surveyed population majority of people held accounts in the banks which are considered to be internet banks (mBank, Toyota Bank, Inteligo PKO BP), or regarded as modern (AliorBank, Millenium), or the largest ones (PKO BP, BZ WBK). This does not correspond to the numbers of electronic access accounts declared by particular banks, however, considering the facts that only the active accounts were described and the fact that the surveyed population is relatively young, the structure of the use of accounts is probably closer to reality than the one presented on the basis of official statistics.

The respondents filled in the tables evaluating e-banking websites of the banks where they had their accounts, performing the analysis and assessment of the obtained results. The tables which they completed were sent by electronic mail. In the second stage, authors implemented the conversion methods. The obtained findings were supplemented with comments.

Criteria applied in this study (as in the previous researches [2]) are divided into three main groups:

- economic - annual nominal interest rate, maintaining an account month/PLN, surcharge for access to electronic channels (including a token, if there is one), a fee for a transfer to a parent bank, fee for a transfer to another bank, interest rate on deposits 10.000 PLN, fee for issuing a card, monthly fee for a card - month/PLN,

– functional - due to large similarity of basic services we only selected non-standard additional services such as: insurance, investment funds, cross-border transfer or foreign currency account,
– technological - the number of surcharge-free ATMs, account access channels (branches, the Internet, Call Centre, mobile phone), security (ID and password, token, SSL protocol, a list of single-use passwords, a list of single-use codes).

Considering the situation of the signs of economic crisis spreading, the authors applied a set of psychological criteria in addition to the criteria used previously in the evaluation of e-banking websites which were discussed above. The psychological criteria included the so-called anti-crisis criteria related to according to the experts cooperating with the authors all those activities, which were to counteract potential impact of the crisis on the banking sphere [4]. This additional group of criteria was also included in the previous evaluation of e-banking websites. The group of the considered anti-crisis measures includes:

– dynamics of interest rates on deposits (reduction, increase, differences in rates, tendencies),
– dynamics of interest rates on credits (reduction, increase, differences in rates, tendencies),
– stability of the policy related to basic fees (the number and the nature of changes),
– stability of the policy related to basic fees (the number and the nature of changes),
– degree of customer confidence (the number of individual clients, its dynamics, how long the bank has been operating in the Polish market),
– the average places occupied in the rankings in the Internet and trade magazines last year.

In the scoring method the authors collected information on selected criteria; they were assigned values according to the assumed scoring scale and the results were analysed in a combined table. For the purposes of the evaluation the authors applied as in previous studies a typical Likert scale. A scoring method was used in situation where criteria were treated equivalently. These calculations were the basis for the conversion method.

In a simple scoring method you need to measure the distance from the maximum value to be obtained (according to the assumed scoring scale). It concerns the value of criterion measure and in the sense of a distance it is the same when we measure the distance from one criterion to another as the other way round. However, we do not define the relations between particular criteria. Implementing a conversion method can be regarded as such a measure. So, apart from the scoring method used to verify the correctness of its applications - the authors applied their own conversion method [2].

3   Conversion Method

Here, we adopt the following assumptions: after constructing the experts table of evaluations of particular criteria for each website, we need to perform the conversion with the established preference vector of the superior level criteria [2, 13]. Next, the authors performs the transformation of the combined scoring table into the preference vector (first converter):

Table 1. The experts table of evaluations of particular criteria for each website

		Websites				
		a_1	a_2	a_3	...	a_m
Criteria 1	f_1	$f_1(a_1)$	...	...	...	...
Criteria 2	f_2	0	...	...	...	...
Criteria 3	f_3	...	0	...	...	...
...	...	...	...	0	...	...
Criteria n	f_n	...	...	...	...	$f_n(a_m)$

The next steps are:

− constructing a matrix of distances from the maximum value for each criterion in every website:
   • establishing the maximum value:

$$P_{i,max} = Max\{f_i(a_j), ..., f_n(a_m)\} \tag{1}$$

$$for \;\; i = 1, ..., n; \;\; and \;\; j = 1, ..., m;$$

   • establishing the matrix of the distances from the maximum value:

$$\delta(f_i(a_j)) = P_{i,max} - f_i(a_j) \tag{2}$$

$$for \;\; i = 1, ..., n \;\; and \;\; j = 1, ..., m;$$

   • calculating the average distance from the maximum value for each criterion,

$$\overline{F}_{i,j} = \frac{\sum_{j=1}^{m}(f_i(a_j))}{m} \tag{3}$$

− as a result of the above operation, constructing a matrix of differences in the distance from the maximum value and the average distance according to criteria,
− for each bank website: constructing conversion matrices - modules of relative distances of particular criteria to remaining criteria (the distance from the same criterion is 0), the obtained distances below the diagonal are the converse of the values over the diagonal:

Table 2. Conversion Matrix

	Criteria				
f_i	$f_{i,j}$	$f_{i+1,j}$	$f_{i+2,j}$	$\ldots$	$f_{n,m}$
$f_{i,j}$	0	$\alpha_{i,j} - \alpha_{i+1,j}$	$f_{i,j} - \alpha_{i+2,j}$	$\ldots$	$\ldots$
$f_{i+1,j}$	$\alpha_{i+1,j} - \alpha_{i,j}$	0	$\ldots$	$\ldots$	$\ldots$
$f_{i+2,j}$	$\alpha_{i+2,j} - \alpha_{i,j}$	$\ldots$	0	$\ldots$	$\ldots$
$\ldots$	$\ldots$	$\ldots$	$\ldots$	$\ldots$	$\ldots$
$f_{n,m}$	$\ldots$	$\ldots$	$\ldots$	$\ldots$	0

- averaging criteria conversion matrices   creating one matrix of average modules of values for all criteria:

$$\overline{A}_{i,j} = \frac{\sum_{i=1,j=1}^{n,m}(\alpha_{i,j} - \alpha_{i+2,j})}{n} \tag{4}$$

- transforming the conversion matrix of criteria into a superior preference matrix (calculating squared matrix, adding up rows, standardization of the obtained preference vector; repeated squaring, adding up rows, standardization of preference vector - repeating this iteration until there are minimum differences in subsequent preference vectors).
- As a result of the above operations we establish a criteria conversion matrix:

Subsequently, the authors performed a transformation of the scores presented by experts on the level of a matrix specifying expert websites evaluations for particular criteria (second converter) [2]. The results have been obtained in an analogical way:

- constructing a matrix of distances from the maximum value for each criterion and each website:
  - establishing the maximum value:

$$P_{i,max} = Max\{f_i(a_j), ..., f_n(a_m)\} \tag{5}$$

$$for \quad i = 1, ..., n \quad and \quad j = 1, ..., m;$$

  - establishing the matrix of distances from the maximum value:

$$\delta(f_i(a_j)) = P_{i,max} - f_i(a_j) \tag{6}$$

$$for \quad i = 1, ..., n \quad and \quad j = 1, ..., m;$$

- calculating the average distance from the maximum value for each website:

$$\overline{F}_i = \frac{\sum_{j=1}^{m} \delta(f_i(a_j))}{m} \tag{7}$$

- constructing a matrix of the differences of deviations from the maximum value and the average distance of the features from the maximum,
- for each criterion: constructing a matrix of transformations (conversions) of the differences of the average distance from the maximum value between the websites, analogically as presented above (the distance for a particular feature in the same website from the same website is 0), values below the diagonal are the converse of the values over the diagonal:

Table 3. Matrix of Transformations for each criterion

f_i		Websites				
	$\alpha_{i,j}$	$\alpha_{i,j+1}$	$\alpha_{i,j+2}$	$\cdots$	$\alpha_{n,m}$	
$\alpha_{i,j}$	0	$\alpha_{i,j} - \alpha_{i,j+1}$	$\alpha_{i,j} - \alpha_{i,j+2}$	$\cdots$	$\cdots$	
$\alpha_{i,j+1}$	$\alpha_{i,j+1} - \alpha_{i,j}$	0	$\cdots$	$\cdots$	$\cdots$	
$\alpha_{i,j+2}$	$\alpha_{i,j+2} - \alpha_{i,j}$	$\cdots$	0	$\cdots$	$\cdots$	
$\cdots$	$\cdots$	$\cdots$	$\cdots$	$\cdots$	$\cdots$	
$\alpha_{n,m}$	$\cdots$	$\cdots$	$\cdots$	$\cdots$	0	

- constructing a module matrix of transformations of the differences of average distance from the maximum value between the websites, for each criterion:

$$\overline{A}_{i,j} = \frac{\sum_{i=1,j=1}^{n,m}(\alpha_{i,j} - \alpha_{i+2,j})}{n} \tag{8}$$

Table 4. A module matrix of transformations of the differences of average distance from the maximum value between the websites, for each criterion

$A_{j,\ldots,m}$		Criteria			
	$f_{i,j}$	$f_{i+1,j}$	$f_{i+2,j}$	$\cdots$	$f_{n,m}$
$f_{i,j}$	0	$\overline{A}_{i,j}$	$\cdots$	$\cdots$	$\cdots$
$f_{i+1,j}$	$-\overline{A}_{i,j}$	0	$\cdots$	$\cdots$	$\cdots$
$f_{i+2,j}$	$\cdots$	$\cdots$	0	$\cdots$	$\cdots$
$\cdots$	$\cdots$	$\cdots$	$\cdots$	$\cdots$	$\cdots$
$f_{n,m}$	$\cdots$	$\cdots$	$\cdots$	$\cdots$	0

- for each module matrix of transformation of the differences of the average distance from the maximum value between the websites, squaring it, adding up rows, standardization of the obtained ranking vector and repeating this operation until the obtained differences between two ranking vectors for each criterion will be minimal.

As a result of the above presented operations we obtain a conversion matrix of websites evaluations $Tf_{m \times 1}$:

- using the obtained vectors to construct a combined ranking matrix returning to the matrix where in its side-heading there are criteria, in the heading names of bank websites by appropriate transfer of the obtained preference vectors for each criterion,
- multiplying the matrix obtained in such a way by the previously calculated preference vector,

$$T' = T_f \otimes T_a \tag{9}$$

- analysing final results and drawing conclusions (note: the lowest distances in this case are the most favourable, comparability adjustments to other methods can be obtained by subtracting these values from 1 and their repeated standardization).

The basis for the creation of the presented method was the assumption that it should be easy to apply. The objective has been reached, which is visible in the number of the advantages presented below. The only disadvantage of the method is the fact that the transformation of the results of the survey is connected with carrying out many complex operations.

The advantages of this method are:

- the ease of application (similar to the realization of a scoring method) which results from the fact that in the survey form there are questions concerning the subjective evaluation of the element,
- in the case of considering a large number of evaluation criteria or alternatives there is no significant increase in the number of questions in the survey,
- the possibility of the application of the method with the participation of people who are not experts in a given field,
- there are no measures, as in the case of e.g. ELECTRE method veto threshold, which may not be fully understandable for the respondent [1],
- the result of the calculations which takes the form of the importance of the evaluations of the examined objects.

A scoring method has been applied to establish relations between clients evaluations of the same websites of particular banks.

4 Comparative Analysis of Internet Access to e-Banking Services by a Scoring Method

To evaluate economical, functional, technological and anti-crisis criteria the authors used a preliminary table presenting bank offers related to internet banking services used by respondents and fees connected with using bank accounts operated via the Internet. This table has been generated on the basis of data obtained from websites of selected banks. On the basis of the surveys the authors created an averaged combined table for the criteria generated by users.

The spread in the respondents evaluations of the analysed banks amounts to nearly 7 percentage points (compared to 5 percentage points in 2010/11, and

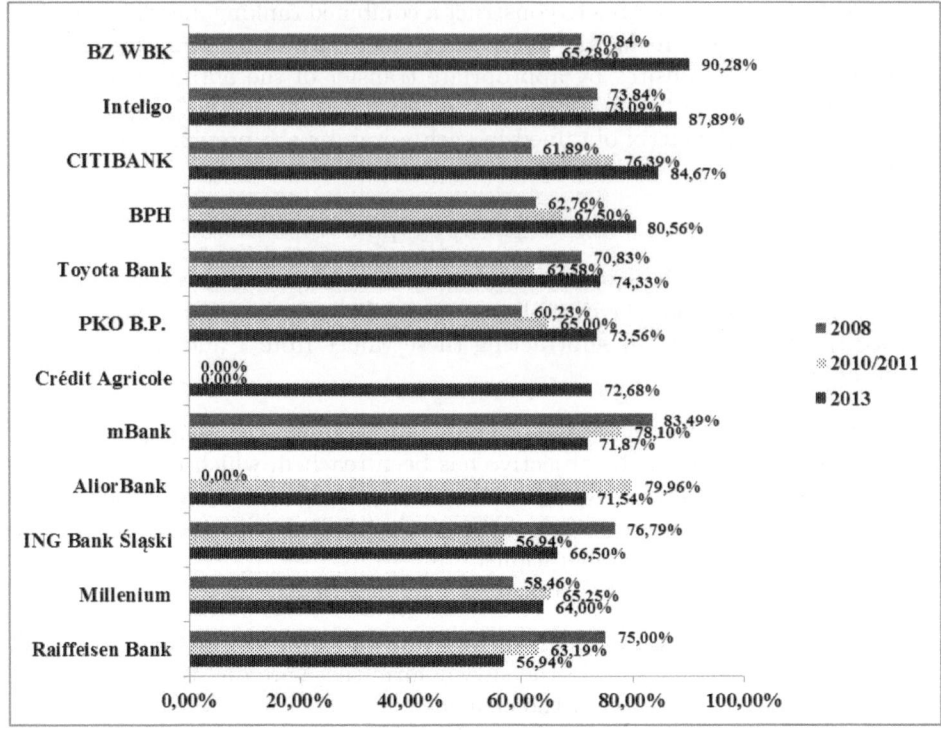

Fig. 1. Comparison of rankings of access to electronic banks for individual clients in the period before and after the crisis (2008, 2010/2011, 2013); Source: the authors own work

2.25 points in 2008), which reflects the growing diversity of evaluations; which confirms the thesis that the period of crisis increased the radicalism of evaluations and heightened expectations concerning the tools used to access an account.

This time the best in the ranking were: BZ WBK (90.28%) and Inteligo (87.89%). Directly behind are: CitiBank and BPH. The low position of mBank (fifth position in the reverse order), came as a surprise because this bank so far occupied leading positions and it was very popular with the analysed group of people (interestingly it received surprisingly low scores for functionality or its behaviour during the crisis 0.5). It is worth mentioning that in the rankings [10] till May 2010 it held the first position.

There occurred a reversal of the situation from two years ago the banks which two years ago fell in the rankings, at present, are trying to make up for the previous losses. Another issue which seems to be characteristic of this study general scores for the quality of the websites increased. It is difficult to compare the present results with the scores before the crisis because due to a number of mergers, the appearance of new players in the market etc., but with the assumption that the group which was examined in the end of 2008 was similar, such a comparison is possible. In 2013 there emerged a new player Credit

Agricole (benefited from the positive opinions of Lucas Bank) and occupied the seventh position. Two years ago Alior Bank moved immediately to the first position. In the last two years the greatest growth in the clients opinions was recorded by BZ WBK (25%) and Inteligo (14%), while the greatest loser is Alior Bank (fall by 8 percentage points) and mBank (6 percentage points). CitiBank (8.28%) and iPKO (8.56%) noted the smallest difference in the respondents opinions. Also, generally, in 2008 clients were more satisfied with online banking services than in 2010/2011 in the previous period in the first ten all banks gained over 70% of the maximum score, in the present ranking only top five. After two years, the situation was reversed again despite higher clients expectations with regard to banks websites.

In the majority of analysed cases there are no obligatory payments for issuing a debit card; transfers to the parent bank are usually free of charge. The level of security can be regarded as satisfactory for clients. Actually, it has not changed from 2008. Based on the compilation, we can conclude that a fee for issuing a card (usually there is no fee for such a service) reached a level which, at present, may satisfy clients needs in 100%. The interest rate on savings accounts is satisfactory (over 88%). Undoubtedly, the worst indicator is an annual nominal interest rate (evaluated by the majority of users as too low 24% of the maximum scores). The fact is that, in response to continually decreasing annual nominal interest rate of the accounts, there appeared savings accounts. The interest rates on deposits reached over 86% of maximum score (Fig. 2). From the factors not listed within the criteria clients paid attention to the lack of possibility to make a cross-border transfer (e.g. SWIFT in Inteligo) or no possibility of fully automatic obtaining a credit via the Internet. In 2008 there were no anti-crisis measures among the criteria; however, if we compare this study with the research carried out in 2010/2011, we have to admit that during the crisis e-banking clients neither noticed any signs of the crisis nor were able to define anti-crisis measures undertaken by the banks, and at present they sometimes suggest criteria to be applied for their evaluation.

5   Comparative Analysis of Internet Access to e-Banking Accounts by Means of a Conversion Method

The applied conversion method produced very interesting results. Due to a large degree of diversification of the users opinions on the electronic services in the same banks, not only averaged and flattened the differences, but also, taking into account the relationship between the maximum and the average values obtained in the calculations, resulted in a significant change of the scores. Previously, a similar effect was achieved using the method of AHP/ANP created by T. Saaty. "Flattening" extreme statements allowed the authors to obtain results closer to the mindset of the most active customers than in the scoring method. Interestingly, the surprisingly low scores assigned to the websites and bank services did not correspond to positive comments provided later by the same clients concerning the same banks (open questions in the survey). The selected, most important opinions of clients are:

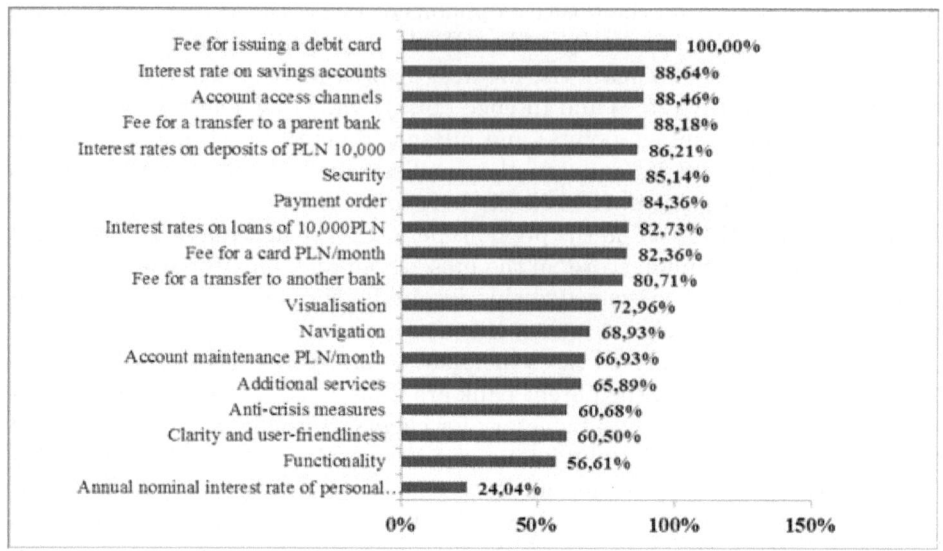

Fig. 2. Ranking of criteria for assessing electronic access to individual accounts in selected banks in Poland in the beginning of 2013; Source: the authors own work

- Millennium - ... *it has bright and clear interface in the same colours as the logo of the bank, it's easy to find proper information, access to regulations, pricing and interest rate tables is easy, ... account security is guaranteed by the standard methods ...both opening and account maintenance are free of charge, the same with transfers between accounts in the bank and beyond, issuing a debit card or activation of the service ... "withdrawals from all ATMs," ... the site is designed in a very clear way and there is user-friendly interface, which makes it transparent, and it is easy to find information which the bank's customer needs ...,*
- Inteligo PKO BP - ... *opening and operating an account is free of charge ... navigation is easy ..., ... issuing the debit card is free of charge, there is a charge for a debit card if the customer does not perform transactions for a total amount of PLN 100 ...,*
- Citibank - ... *taking into consideration the functionality and graphic design of the websites, we can certainly recommend this banks website ... the mobile version of this banks website is clear and user-friendly ... the range of functionality of the site is increasing from year to year, resulting in a positive outlook for the future ...,*
- mBank - ... *the website is clear, easy to use, and navigation is not troublesome, it takes little time to search for relevant information concerning the accounts or bank operations ... the only drawback is the lack of interest on the current account ... almost exemplary visualization of the page, intuitive navigation helps the consumer find the information which he needs , without the necessity to search the site to find the most important items...,*

- Alior Bank - ... *it offers expanded portfolio of services to individual clients, ... the strongest reasons for using the banks services are: high nominal interest rate per annum on an individual account, high interest rates for savings accounts and high interest rates on annual deposits ...,*
- Toyota Bank - ... *the highest interest rate, ... among the drawbacks we can list: high fees mainly for having a debit card, ... this bank deserves special attention because of the high interest rate of account maintenance ... the drawback is the high cost of running the account, if the total amount of the transactions will amount to a minimum of PLN 1000, which is a high value when compared to other banks ...,*
- BZ WBK - ... *For at least seven years, in the bank, little has changed with regard to innovation, functionality, access channels, ... the recent change in the visualization and access to the account via the Internet brought more confusion than positive results ...,*
- PKO BP iPKO - ... *it collects the largest monthly fee for account maintenance, while the fee for a transfer to another bank is comparable with other banks, ... the fee for issuing a debit card and its use is the same as in the other banks, ... the package of additional services offered by PKO BP does not stand out in any way - the bank offers standard services, such as all other banks ..., the website with dominant white color and a variety of font scaling is rather poor with regard to visualization , the functionality may pose some problems for a user - regulations or fees and commissions are difficult to find intuitively ..., ... The site is just poor ...,*
- Raiffeisen Bank - *there are high fees for transfers to a parent bank or to another bank ...*
- BPH - ... *It offers an account with the highest interest rate, the fees for account maintenance are relatively low, and the transfers are free of charge ...,*
- ING Bank lski - ... *very low maintenance costs and comparable, maybe even better, online service; the only thing that it does not offer are free withdrawals from ATMs abroad ...,*
- Credit Agricole - ...*the site is designed in a perfect colour scheme which is associated with banking, and the most important information interacts with the whole, it draws the consumers attention it offers high interest rates, an additional advantage is the most attractive website ... transfers to the parent bank and to other banks are free of charge, but each transfer requires entering one-time SMS password, sending SMSs involves extra cost, which is a considerable disadvantage for customers who need to make a large number of transfers per month; the fee for issuing a debit and the annual card charges do not differ from the other banks ... the website of the bank is not user-friendly and the access to terms and conditions and tables of charges is a bit more difficult due to placing it on the tabs for each account. The colour scheme is not very attractive and it appears to be dominated by the white colour, which may indicate unused space ....*

Perhaps the criticism resulted from an increase in customer awareness, and the fact that in the case of "their" e-banking websites the changes (not always seen

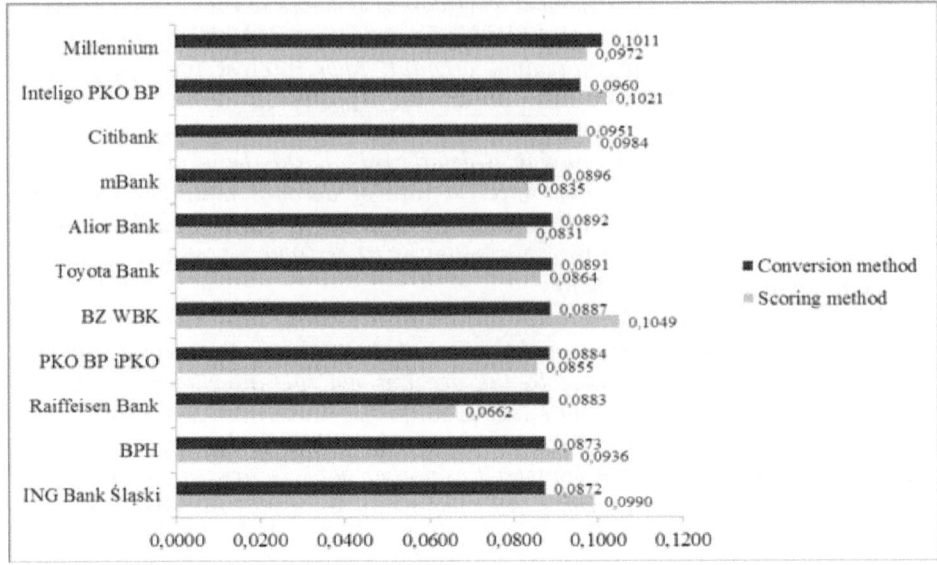

Fig. 3. Comparison of the rankings of selected banks in Poland in the beginning of 2013 by means of the scoring method and the conversion method; Source: the authors own work

as improvements) were too rarely introduced. Also, the results of the ranking have changed, sometimes significantly (see Fig.3, the results were brought to comparability).

Millennium moved to the first place, the bank moved from the fifth position, Inteligo PKO BP SA ranked second, taking the same place as in the previous ranking, and the third place was occupied by Citibank, promoted from the fourth position. The biggest loser in this ranking was ING Bank, which fell from the third position to the eleventh place.

6   Summary

The present analysis has shown that the crisis situation, whose signs are visible in various industries, does not apply to electronic banking. While in 2010/2011 it could be a one-off phenomenon, after four years we may conclude that it starts to be seen as a clear trend. Also, it confirms the changes concerning the banking customers awareness. The choice of the access to an account starts to be a matter of an informed choice, not a chance or habit. The decision is determined both economic and technical conditions. The result is the choices made by clients reflected in the presented study and commented on in the surveys. It is true that some of the opinions indicate - despite the awareness of certain shortcoming of the bank where they hold an account resistance to changes, but it is the first step to move their account to another bank.

Taking into consideration the conducted analyses, we may draw the following conclusions:

- in the minds of users of electronic banking a clear distinction between the virtual banks (electronic access only) and electronic access services of traditional banks lost its importance, and it appears to be a continued trend. It is caused by the following phenomena:
  - virtual and traditional banks try to maximally increase the number of communication channels,
  - it is difficult to separate a virtual bank from a traditional one,
  - e-banking websites of traditional banks are just as technologically advanced and modern as those of virtual banks,
  - we observe lowering of that prices of basic e-banking services in traditional banks, sometimes below the prices of virtual banks,
  - users have higher expectations with regard to the quality of e-services. The averages from the rankings previously relatively constant have become dynamic and fluctuate,
- entering the market (ref.: the case of Alior Bank) and allocating significant resources to a clever advertising campaign does not guarantee an automatic promotion to the top position in the rankings (ref.: Credit Agricole),
- having two accounts in two or more banks to perform various financial transactions is still a rare phenomenon,
- too few clients dynamically respond to changes in banking services market,
- vast majority of active bank customers consider economic criteria to be the most important criteria in the evaluation of electronic access to banking services usually the prices of the most frequently used services. More and more people admit, however, that when selecting a website, to a certain degree, they tend to focus on user-friendliness and intuitiveness as well as the visual attractiveness of the website,
- users of electronic banking services more frequently notice anti-crisis measures of banks and even though they do not influence their choices in any considerable degree, they can note and identify them.

This confirms the authors thesis about the inadequacy and a specific superficiality of standard, unified, quantitative methodologies used for evaluation and selection of e-banking websites. It also points to the need of further studies into constructing multi-dimensional, multi-criteria, hierarchical and multi-faceted system for websites evaluation, with the consideration of additional, more specific information, e.g. customer profile [3].

Nevertheless, despite the problems related to using e-banking services, which the article presents, from year to year we observe that the Internet tends to assume the role of the main (also for an individual client) channel of communication with the bank. Undoubtedly, this development irrevocably changes the expectations, perceptions and habits related to using banking services which users have had so far, and also, simultaneously, it urges the banks to introduce quick changes of the medium which would take into account holders requirements.

References

1. Buchanan, J., Sheppard, P., Lamsade, D.V.: Project ranking using ELECTRE III (January 2013), http://130.217.168.130/departments/staff/jtb/Electwp.pdf
2. Chmielarz, W., Szumski, O., Zborowski, M.: Kompleksowe metody ewaluacji jakości serwisów internetowych, Wydawnictwo Naukowe WZ UW, Warsaw (2011)
3. Chmielarz, W.: Koncepcja ekspertowego systemu oceny i selekcji witryn interne-towych Section 4.2 Chapter 4. Koncepcje zastosowań Systemów ekspertowych. In: Gołuchowski, J., Filipczyk, B. (eds.) Wiedza i Komunikacja w Innowacyjnych Or-ganizacjach. Systemy Ekspertowe - Wczoraj, Dziś, Jutro, Prace Naukowe UE w Katowicach, Wydawnictwo UE w Katowicach, Katowice, pp. 183–190 (2010)
4. Chmielarz, W.: Metody oceny elektronicznych usług bankowych dla klientów indy-widualnych w Polsce. In: Gospodarowicz, A. (ed.) Bankowość Detaliczna - Idee, Modele, Procesy. Prace Naukowe Uniwersytetu Ekonomicznego we Wrocławiu. Wydawnictwo UE we Wrocławiu, Wrocław, vol. (54), ch. 1, pp. 9–26 (2009)
5. http://bank24.blox.pl/2013/03/Bankowosc-internetowa-w-Polsce-i-Europie.html
6. http://www.komputerswiat.pl/nowosci/internet/2013/12/ilu-z-nas-korzysta-z-bankowosci-elektronicznej.aspx (April 2013)
7. http://www.egov.vic.gov.au/focus-on-countries/europe/trends-and-issues-europe/statistics-europe/internet-statistics-europe/comscore-releases-2013 (April 2013)
8. Mateos, M.B., Mera, A.C., Gonzales, F.J., Lopez, O.R.: A new Web assessment index: Spanish universities analysis. Internet Research: Electronic Application and Policy 11(3), 226–234 (2001)
9. Miranda, F.J., Cortes, R., Barriuso, C.: Quantitative Evaluation of e-Banking Web Sites: an Empirical Study of Spanish Banks. The Electronic Journal Information Systems Evaluation 2(9), 73–82, http://www.eiise.com
10. Samcik, M., Ostrowski, M.: W którym banku najlepsze konto, GW, Biznes, Ludzie, Pieniądze, p. 34 (May 24, 2010); Znajdź swój bank, Neewsweek ranking June/July 2010. SMG/KRC auditors^{TM} group Newsweek of 3 October 2010, p. 78 (2010)
11. Sikorski, M.: Usługi on-line. Jakość, interakcje, satysfakcja klienta. PJWSTK, War-saw (2013)
12. Wielki, J.: Modele wpływu przestrzeni elektronicznej na organizacje gospodarcze, Wydawnictwo UE we Wrocławiu, Wrocław (2012)
13. Zborowski, M.: Modelowanie witryn internetowych o profilu ekonomicznym, Uni-versity of Warsaw, Faculty of Management, doctoral dissertation under the super-vision of W. Chmielarz, Warsaw (2013)

Selected Aspects of Information Society Measurement

Michał Goliński

Warsaw School of Economics, Department of Business Informatics,
Al. Niepodległości 162, 02-554 Warszawa, Poland
mgol@sgh.waw.pl

Abstract. The paper presents a brief examination of the use of composite indices in the analysis of information society issues. The problem of measurement is the Achilles heel of the information society research. Despite, or possibly because of this reason, one can find a number of quantitative studies on the topic. In recent years, studies using composite indices are gaining broader media popularity. This paper discusses the basic methodological issues as well as strengths and limitations of such tools. It presents the main pros and cons of using them in information society research.

Keywords: information society, information society measurements, e-metrics, composite indices.

1 Introduction

None of the theories concerning the Information Society (IS) have managed to deal with two fundamental, interconnected and possibly impossible problems: how to define and how to measure it. There is no satisfying and widely accepted definition of the IS [1], [2], [3], [4]. Quoting Webster: „Reviewing these varying definitions of the information society, what becomes clear is that they are either underdeveloped or imprecise or both" [2: 21]. It entails the following problem: it is difficult to decide which characteristics to measure of a practically indefinable notion. One of the most important if not fundamental problem of the IS studies, is defining what and how to measure in order to quantify the extent of IS development. The paper presents a short analysis of selected aspects of the „Grand Challenge" [5], [6], emphasizing the most common measurement tools – composite indices (CI).

2 Measuring the Information Society

The presence of IS issues in public discourse in the last two decades has provoked a rising demand for tools allowing to quantify occurring processes. A number of studies have been carried out aiming to measure different aspects of Information and communication technologies (ICT) and IS.

The main, utilitarian, function of IS quantitative research is:

A. Kobyliński and A. Sobczak (Eds.): BIR 2013, LNBIP 158, pp. 241–253, 2013.
© Springer-Verlag Berlin Heidelberg 2013

- measuring of selected IS characteristics,
- defining the developmental deficits,
- monitoring the occurring processes,
- setting objectives and development priorities,
- underpinning the basis for formulating and implementing development policies,
- assessing progress towards the declared objectives,
- providing arguments in disputes concerning regulatory aspects,
- allowing the benchmarking,
- supporting investment decisions.

The main tools of IS' quantitative description are proper indexes providing information about different aspects of ICT usage in society and economics. They allow to assess the level of IS development in geographical regions, social groups and branches of economy. They are necessary to plan public and commercial projects and investments as well as to assess their implementation. They are an essential part of the creation, implementation and evaluation of policy development [7], [8], [9].

IS indexes are of great importance in IS theory: they measure, monitor and justify. A definitional function is essential. Arranging the threshold values of selected characteristics may be used to determine the critical point when defining the formation of IS – the IS concept critics have called for nearly half a century. According to Webster: „This problem of measurement, and the associated difficulty of stipulating the point on the technological scale at which a society is judged to have entered an information age, is surely central to any acceptable definition of a distinctively new type of society" [2: 11].

It should be noted that construction of such indexes is not without bias. It depends on the author's beliefs, knowledge and intentions. Furthermore, the purpose of the creation of certain tool and its potential recipients are equally important.. Numerical expression of an indicator creates an impression of raw objectivity but its construction is often marked with subjective beliefs and purposes chosen by its author. Thus, it causes that IS indicators are not neutral and are marked with values and judgments. One can say that apart from a common belief about significant and growing importance of ITC usage in the modern world, all other aspects of these issues are being eagerly discussed. There is no consensus as to what are the signs and measures of development and what does IS development mean. These tools show some occurrences rather than explain their character and causes. Thus it is important to identify what and why they indicate. By using these tools one should remember that it is a sort of interpretation of available statistic from the author's point of view.

A comparison of IS indicators from international and historical points of view is very important. Creating proper time series is difficult on the grounds of remaining disputes about the rules of IS statistics and dynamics of the studied field. Developing a universally accepted set of such tools is a complex task. It requires coordination between numerous stakeholders.

Contemporary quantitative IS studies are derived from traditional, state or corporate telecommunications statistics. They concentrated on development of telecommunication infrastructure, marginalizing quality and skipping social aspects. Statistic monitoring of traditional telecommunication was relatively easy. There were a few providers of services (in most countries only monopolistic) and two groups of consumers- private and business subscribers. Analysis of IT was also much easier due to less diverse hardware, dominant mainframe solutions and preliminary stage of convergence. This made it easier to create measures and obtain the necessary data. The emphasis on infrastructure was transferred onto early quantitative IS studies.

IS statistics still focuses on the infrastructure and ability to connect places and people, omitting the qualitative aspects. The focus is, therefore, on the supply side. Following this approach, information on the number of subscribers to the service has become more important than qualitative information about the subscribers i.e. who, for what purpose and to what extent has been using the service. The increasing complexity of the IS and the growing role of the social aspects have been forcing an extensive analysis of the demand and quality aspects. Such information is important in policy formulation and development, however, it is also crucial to the success of business projects. In an increasingly competitive market, only the businesses that will have the best information about the information needs of their potential clients and their use of ICT, will succeed.

Disadvantages of such approach became increasingly apparent. An analysis limited to the technical infrastructure was getting worse in explaining the IS phenomenon. The use of ICT is inextricably linked with the capabilities, skills and motivations of people using these technologies. The role of the information in the society is an economic, social, technological, political and cultural phenomenon [10: 36]. If the research topic is the information society, the sphere of social and human factors cannot be ignored. This growing interdependence of ICT and the social sphere is increasingly forced to include the new monitoring tools not only to access ICT products and services but also their use, barriers and limits of their adoption as well as the effects of their applications.

In the early 1990s quantitative IS studies were rare and pioneering[1]. Currently, there are numerous studies concerning different IS aspects, perhaps even too many. The studies are conducted by national statistics offices, telecommunication market regulators, international organizations (e.g. Eurostat, UN, OECD, ITU, WB), research institutions, universities, non-governmental organizations (e.g. Orbicom, Bridges.org, GISW), commercial companies (e.g. WEF, EIU, Siemens/Nokia) and many other subjects.

The authors of quantitative studies concentrate on different IS aspects, use different research methods, create their own sets of data and measuring tools. IS statistics is a new area. There are still disputes concerning the source data, the indicators and the methodology used as well as interpretation of results. For years numerous attempts have been made to set all its aspects. Up until now, the boundaries of IS statistics have not been established likely due to extraordinary dynamics of studied area – stemming from rapid technological progress, typical to ICT. It is possible that these limitations will never be conclusively defined (Fig. 1).

---

[1] These were not of course first studies of this type. Japanese (Information Flows and Information Index) and American (Machlup and Porat) studies should be pointed out.

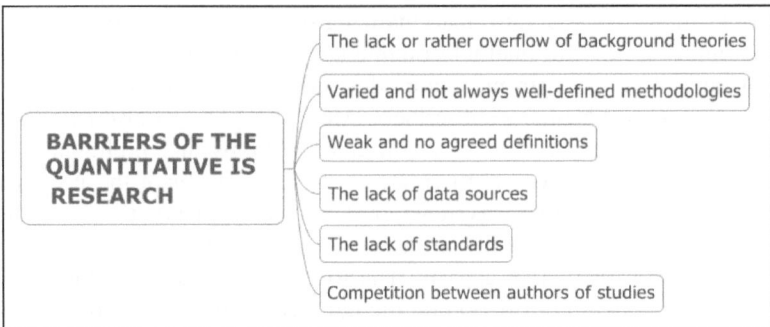

Fig. 1. The main problems of the IS statistic

However, as Menou and Taylor states: "The fact that most of the fundamental drawbacks, such as lack of theoretical background, inadequacy of raw data, superficiality of calculation methods, and dispersion of efforts, to name a few, that have been noted since the inception of social information metrics in the 1960s are still with us is probably the most vexing aspect of the scene." [5].

Statistical monitoring of IS hinders political and economic conditions. Politicians are willing to treat the IS notion as a buzzword useful in the fight for voters.

Media popularity on a subject affects the interpretation of research results and to drawing conclusions of a practical nature aspired from a wide range of people who, in many cases, do not possess the substantive knowledge of the subject. The list of "specialists" in the IS issues increases once the subject becomes part of a public discussion.

The importance and economic potential of the ICT industry impacts the nature and the results of many studies. There are many powerful stakeholders in particular, IT and telecommunications companies may be interested in using the results of such studies as an arguments in lobbying activities, or in the disputes with market regulators. Furthermore, companies willingly become a co-author or a sponsor of such studies.

One of the possible creative models of IS statistics was suggested in 2005 by OECD [11: 12]. It reveals the complex and wide field of possible research difficulties. Complexity is even greater because of rapid nature of the field. It is not possible to set and monitor IS characteristics permanently. Apart from that, one set of indicators to assess areas in different stages of development should not be used at the same time. OECD [11: 13] suggests using their model of e-commerce development and connected with it measurement priorities. This model includes three stages of IS development: e-readiness, e-intensity and e-impact. They have different leading problems and require different methods of measurement.

Monitoring of such a wide and complex field requires the use of many specialist indicators. How many indicators are necessary shows a list of more than 80 basic (not potential!) indicators prepared by Partnership on Measuring ICT for Development [12].

It seems that working on numerous set of indicators is the only responsible way to monitor the complex IS issues. This method is used by most "official" institutions, such as: statistics offices, central government bodies or international organizations (e.g. Eurostat).

Such studies provide essential and thorough information. Their factual value depends mainly on accuracy of the selection process of the indicators and is generally high. Nevertheless, they have a considerable drawback. Many indicators in use are only understandable to the professionals. For others they are too hermetic, difficult and simply boring. Ongoing mediatization of our world has contributed to the popularization of a different research trend – composite indicators. Growing popularity of IS issues forced to create tools that are simple to interpret, can reach wider audience and can be used for marketing purposes and in politics.

3   Composite Indices in Information Society Research

Composite indices enable a simpler interpretation of data acquired from the analysis of socio-economic phenomena in multidimensional variable arrays. They substitute a large set of attributes of objects under study with a single one, i.e. with a synthetic variable. Transition from a multidimensional set of attributes to a single dimensional one is achieved by variable aggregation. It enables us to arrange studied objects according to values of an aggregated variable and also to make comparisons with respect to time and space. What makes the CI so attractive is the fact that they are easy to interpret the audience is presented with impressive rankings showing the development of IS in specific regions. CIs became a subject of interest for the media and the public and this popularity was used by many researchers.

CIs have become an essential part of the contemporary debate concerning social, economic and political problems, and their popularity is still rising. A research conducted in 2005 analyzed over 130 tools of this kind, 80 % of which were created between 1991 and 2005. During the 1970s and the 1980s less than 10 were created every ten years, then the 1990s saw a rise to 40 CIs pro decade, and between the year 2000 and 2004 more than 60 were formed [13: 8]. A research from 2008 analyses almost 180 ICs [14].

Moreover, this trend can be observed in the growing number of studies conducted and the increasing number of authors. The studies are conducted by international organizations, central governments, companies, social organizations, research centres, universities and individual scientists. Finally, the scope of research is also constantly expanding, including virtually all contemporary issues (especially those which are popular nowadays).

The main drivers of a growing popularity of CIs may be explained by the following factors:

- An easier access to statistical data (the Internet).
- Definition of various challenges connected with the global development (IS, corruption, environmental protection, etc.) and their subsequent popularization.
- Relative simplicity of the CIs – the existing methodology (e.g. [15], [16]) enables a correct construction of measurement tools utilised to describe some kind of new/fashionable aspects of the contemporary world. In other words, CIs offer a simple formula for conducting an inventive research.

Many of the CIs have played a vital role in putting some of the researched issues in the centre of public attention, forcing policy-makers to act. Presently, it is difficult to imagine how one could discuss issue of development without the Human Development Index (UN), education levels without the PISA (OECD), issues of corruption without the Corruption Perceptions Index (Transparency International), competitiveness of economies without the World Competitiveness Index (World Economic Forum) or, last but not least, analyse the IS without the help of Networked Readiness Index (also WEF). It seems plausible to put forward a thesis that if the authors would stop at the stage of drafting a large set of indicators and wouldn't continue with the next stage, i.e. aggregation, the popularity of their research would suffer considerably. Moreover, the impact on the public would not have such serious consequences, i.e. people would be less involved and policy-makers responsible for dealing with certain issues wouldn't be forced to act.

One may therefore conclude that CIs have an important political function [17], [18]. They are utilised in order to mobilise the entities which are part of the decision making process and who did not participate in it earlier. According to Porter [17: 11]: "The indicators are objects that are constructed to maximize the aesthetic and exhortative effect of the representation of certain relationships while obscuring others". Table 1 below presents the arguments for and against using composite indices.

Despite the popularity of numerous e-rankings which were created on the basis of CIs, the above-mentioned aspects should make one particularly wary when using CIs in IS analysis. One should bear in mind that the methodology used in creating a CI substantially influences the results and, correspondingly, how countries perform in a ranking. OECD [15: 100 and following] carried out a simulation of changes in the values of Technology Achievement Index (number of countries was limited to 23 first in the original ranking). The differences in the positions of individual countries in the final ranking reached 11 as a result of the various methods of weighting and aggregation.

One can also assume that the IS composite indices are in fact superfluous. If one assumes that the well-being of contemporary societies strongly correlates with the information and the ICT then one also has to assume that the successful countries must have utilised both of these factors effectively. „Wherefore by their fruits ye shall know them"– if they are 'wealthy', they must also have access to information. And in such case one does not need any new tools, since there already exists a measure which has been verified and amended for some 50 years now – the GDP[2]. This risky thesis is made more plausible because of high correlation levels between IS development measured by the ICT Development Index (IDI value) and prosperity measured on the basis of the following values: GDP (Fig. 2) and its main 'opponent' HDI (Fig. 3) in EU countries. The correlation does not mean that there exists any causality relationship, but the problem itself seems to be worth looking into.

---

[2] An intensive debate about GDP drawbacks as a measurement of wealth is omitted.

Table 1. Positive and negative aspects of composite indices

POSITIVE	NEGATIVE
- they synthesize multidimensional reality in a self-explanatory manner	- they simplify an otherwise complex reality too much,
- they are easy to interpret	- an erroneous construction or false interpretation may result in making wrong decisions,
- they reduce the number of single indicators without a substantial loss of input data	
- they provide more data within a short period of time,	- they can induce hasty decisions,
- they contribute to the promotion of researched issues ,	- if during their construction certain areas are ignored wrong decision may be made,
- they make the communication with the public opinion easier and at the same time make people aware of the existence of certain issues,	- the methodology often lacks transparency,
	- in cases when the methodology is revealed, practically all of its elements may undergo a heavy critic,
- they facilitate understanding of these issues to non-experts,	- utilizing the same methodology in evaluation of both developed and developing countries,
- they enable to perform an effective evaluation of complex issues	
- they enable to build impressive and clear rankings and comparisons	- there exist a danger of manipulation by the researchers or by stakeholders interested in a particular issue,
- they enable to evaluate the completion stage of contracts and supranational agreements	- utilizing a methodology which does not take into account the specific features of particular regions, which results in promoting the same states over and over again (e.g. high e-ranking positions of Scandinavian states),
- they inform the policy-makers about the existence of potential development deficits,	
- they support the process of making administrative decisions	- arbitrariness in creating boundaries which determine the category to which a country is assigned (e.g. leaders, runners-up, strugglers),
- they provide a vital source of information for prospective investors	- risk of self-fulfilling prophecy (a negative evaluation of a country may cause a group investors to refrain from their activities and, consequently, make the country's situation even worse).
- they aid the prognosis process	
- they constitute an appealing research tool	

Source: Based on [13: 13-14] and [15: 13-14].

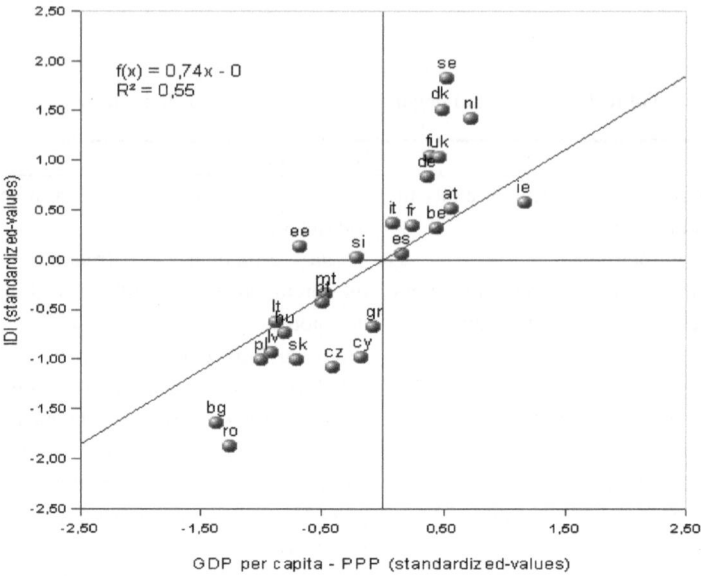

Fig. 2. IS vs. welfare measured by GDP. Data source: [19] and Eurostat

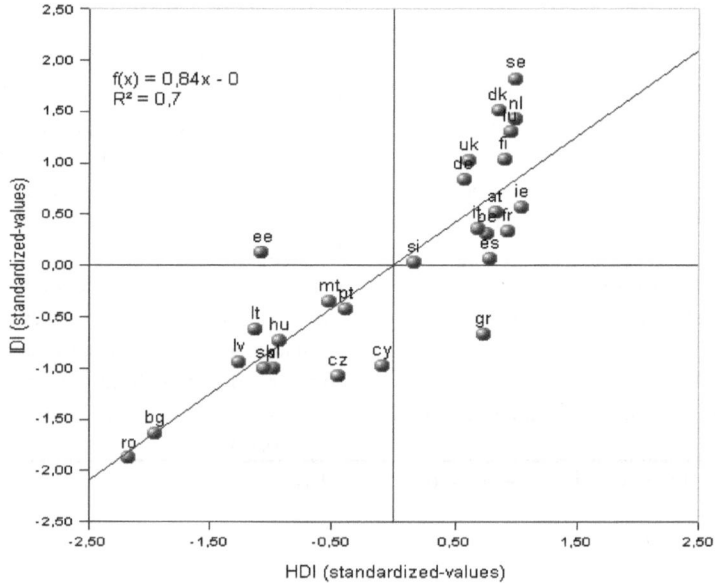

Fig. 3. IS vs. welfare measured by HDI. Data source: [19], [20]

Table 2 presents selected features of 18 IS composite indices, which were analysed by the Author. Research methodology and detailed results are included in [21] and [22]. The Table shows the existence of significant differences between these tools (these differences are present in virtually all aspects of the methodology that was applied). We claim that among these tools one can rank both valuable research, which it is worth to publish and promote (e.g. the ICT Development Index, cf. [8]), as well as those tools in which the marketing aspect dominates over the scientific knowledge (e.g. Networked Readiness Index (cf. [9]).

The CIs creators are almost all those involved in the statistical monitoring of IS, and they are international organizations, commercial firms and individual researchers. Only one but very important group is missing - the official statistical offices. Neither Eurostat nor any of the national offices conduct researches using CIs. This is despite the fact that these organizations collect data concerning IS, which are often used by the CIs creators.

Table 2. Key characteristics of the analyzed CIs

No.	CI	Num. of countries	Sub-indices	2nd.Sub-indices	Partial indic.	Hard indic.	Soft indic.	ICT indic.	Others indic.
1	ISI/IDC	53	4	0	15	13	2	11	4
2	IIDLI/Goliński	29	0	0	7	7	0	7	0
3	ERI/EIU *(est.)	70	6	0	100	50	50	20	80
4	TAI/UNDP	72	4	0	8	8	0	2	6
5	E-GOV RI/UNPAN	182	3	0	8	8	0	6	2
6	NRI/WEF	134	3	3	68	27	41	29	39
7	M/II/ITU	206	3	0	26	20	6	26	0
8	DAI/ITU	178	5	0	8	8	0	6	2
9	IS/Orbicom	183	2	2	10	10	0	8	2
10	NRPI/Goliński	49	4	0	12	0	12	5	7
11	ICT-OI/ITU	183	2	2	10	10	0	8	2
12	DOI/ITU	181	3	0	11	11	0	11	0
13	eE/INSEAD	28	5	0	39	34	5	39	0
14	KEI/WB	140	4	0	12	9	3	3	9
15	IKS/UNPAN	45	3	0	15	14	1	2	13
16	ICT-DI/UNCTAD	180	2	0	8	8	0	6	2
17	CSC/Waverman	50	6	0	28	28	0	28	0
18	IDI/ITU	154	3	0	11	11	0	8	3

A critical analysis of selected research methodologies can be found in [23], [24] or [25]. Some of these tools became quite popular and gained a large group of proponents. An example here may be the Networked Readiness Index by the World Economic Forum or E-Readiness Rankings by Economist Intelligence Unit and IBM Institute for Business Value. However, we believe that this popularity is often undeserved.

Many of the CIs use variables, which are not strictly related to ICT, it is sometimes referred to as the "analog noise" [26: 75]. However, it is necessary and justified by the multidisciplinary nature of IS issues. According to the author, characteristics not directly related to ICT - such as the level of education – can be more decisive for the success in the use of ICT-related opportunities than purely digital characteristics.

Previous quantitative IS studies have focused on three main research areas: ICT infrastructure, its use and indispensable skills. Such elements are presented in most of the IS research, both those that use numerous set of basic indicators as well as those based on composite indices. The possible broader socio-economic relationships have been explored less frequently. This is, at least in part, due to the challenges involved in measuring such interactions.

Less recognized (albeit essential and interesting) is the social and cultural environment conducive to the formation of information society. It seems to be a reasonable argument that, at a certain level of IS development, such issues can be crucial. The social and cultural context of IS is a very broad and complex area. The research object may be a broad spectrum of problems. According to the author, one of the themes of a particular relevance is social capital.

Many empirical studies of IS support the idea that success is determined by infrastructure and education. Informal rules and institutions have not received much attention. An example of the CEE countries has shown that also social and cultural issues can be of crucial importance [27], [28].

4   Conclusions

CIs are the best solutions when it comes to making the public opinion aware of the significance of issues connected with the IS. They do it well and in an impressive manner. However, if someone must make a political or an investment decision (which is often pushed by the policy-makers based on the results of research conducted with the help of CIs) one needs to perform a detailed, multi-criteria analysis of the existing state of affairs by using a set of multiple indicators which enable a thorough analysis of the researched question.

Analysis of CIs used in information society research allows us to formulate the following assessments of this type of measuring tools:

- All analyzed CIs, despite high-sounding titles, explore only selected elements of the IS issues. None of them can aspire to become a comprehensive tool for measuring the information society. This is not a complaint. Defining the universal tool is simply impossible, due to the dynamics and multi-dimensionality of the studied phenomena,
- CIs are affected by the subjective choices done by their creators, virtually at all stages of their design [29: 141]. Thus, all are inherently subjective.
- It seems that in many cases the choice of partial indicators is caused not by the theoretical assumptions but rather by the availability of statistical data.
- The global comparability of some data is questionable. For example, participation in various levels of education - data readily used in IS studies.

- The numerical value of the CI themselves do not have a clear and unequivocal meaning [29: 142], which significantly reduces their value as a tool of analysis and interpretation. Thus CIs do not provide practical findings, needed for decision making.

Despite these objections, one must acknowledge that CIs have several advantages:

- CIs are popular tools of presenting the complex characteristics of the contemporary world in an attractive and accessible way.
- CIs are important complements to the multi-criteria analysis.
- CIs focus on the analysis of IS issues at the highest level of generality. They integrate elements of various economic, social and political characters. This is their essential advantage. Comprehensive analysis of IS issues using large collection of partial indicators is "not for sale" from a marketing point of view.
- The complexity and ambiguity of CI corresponds to the complexity and ambiguity of the IS issues and a character of partial indicator is contrary to the complex and interdependent nature of IS phenomena.

CIs truly fulfil their central role by effectively drawing a public attention to the significance of IS issues. However, for important decision-making (often forced by the publication of research results using CI) one needs to use an in-depth, multi-criteria analysis, using a set of numerous partial indicators - deeply characterizing the investigated phenomenon. The growing diversity of the IS issues and the significant dynamics of the processes that shape them, necessitate the simultaneous use of both groups of tools. This enables both effective and publicly understandable IS analysis.

CIs should be considered as a kind of characteristic point of departure for the policy-makers. They yield arguments and force those with the effective powers to pay attention to the issues connected with IS and to shape policy development properly. Finally, although using these tools to analyse IS often constitutes an attempt to count the uncountable, one cannot dismiss the fact that CIs have played a key role in promoting the importance of IS and the issues connected with it.

References

1. Webster, F.: What Information Society. In: Alberts, D.S., Papp, D.S. (eds.) The Information Age: An Anthology on Its Impact and Consequences, pp. 51–72. University Press of the Pacific, Michigan (1997)
2. Webster, F.: Theories of the Information Society, 3rd edn. Routledge, London (2006)
3. Mullan, P.: Information society: frequently un-asked questions. In: Spiked (2000), http://www.spiked-online.com/Printable/0000000053AA.htm
4. Goliński, M.: Spór o pojęcie społeczeństwa informacyjnego. In: Czarnacka-Chrobot, B., Kobylinski, A., Sobczak, A. (eds.) Ekonomiczne i Społeczne Aspekty Informatyki – Wybrane Zagadnienia, pp. 61–77. SGH, Warszawa (2009)
5. Menou, M.J., Taylor, R.D.: A "Grand Challenge": Measuring Information Societies. In: The Information Society, vol. 22, pp. 261–267. Taylor & Francis Group, Abingdon (2006)

6. Taylor, R.D.: The nature and measurement of information: Two "grand challenges" for the field. Paper Presented at the 16th Biennial Conference of the International Telecommunications Society, Beijing (2006), http://intramis.net/iip_infometrics_papers/ITS2006NatureofInformation.doc

7. Mahan, A.K.: ICT indicators for advocacy. In: Global Information Society Watch 2007, APC, Hivos and ITeM (2007), http://www.giswatch.org/files/pdf/GISW_2007.pdf

8. Goliński, M.: ICT Development Index – nowe narzędzie pomiaru poziomu rozwoju społeczeństwa informacyjnego. In: Babis, H., Buko, J., Czaplewski, R. (eds.) Rynki Przesyłu i Przetwarzania Informacji – Stan obecny i Perspektywy Rozwoju, pp. 53–66. Uniwersytet Szczeciński, Szczecin (2009)

9. Goliński, M.: Networked Readiness Index, czyli siła marketingu. In: Czaplewski, R. (ed.) Rynek Informacji i Komunikacji, pp. 149–169. Uniwersytet Szczeciński, Szczecin (2010)

10. Oleński, J.: Ekonomika informacji: Metody. Polskie Wydawnictwo Ekonomiczne, Warszawa (2003)

11. Guide to Measuring the Information Society – 2009. OECD - Working Party on Indicators for the Information Society (2009), http://www.itu.int/ITU-D/ict/conferences/rio09/material/5-Guide-measuringIS09-E.pdf

12. Revisions and Additions to the Core List of ICT Indicators. UNCTAD - Partnership on Measuring ICT for Development (2009), http://unstats.un.org/unsd/statcom/doc09/BG-ICTIndicators.pdf

13. Bandura, R.: Measuring Country Performance and State Behavior: A Survey of Composite Indices. Office of Development Studies UNDP, New York (2005), http://www.thenewpublicfinance.org/~background/measuring.pdf

14. Bandura, R.: A Survey of Composite Indices Measuring Country Performance: 2008 Update. Office of Development Studies UNDP, New York (2008), http://www.undp.org/developmentstudies/docs/indices_2008_bandura.pdf

15. Handbook on Constructing Composite Indicators - Methodology and User Guide. OECD, Paris (2008)

16. EU - Composite Indicators - An information server on composite indicators and ranking systems (methods, case studies, events), http://composite-indicators.jrc.ec.europa.eu/

17. Porter, T.: Making Serious Measures: Numerical National Rankings, Peer Review and Global Governance (2009), http://www.allacademic.com/meta/p312210_index.html

18. Wesselink, B., et al.: Measurement Beyond GDP. Background paper for the conference Beyond GDP: Measuring progress, true wealth, and the well-being of nations (2007), http://www.beyond-gdp.eu/download/bgdp-bp-mbgdp.pdf

19. Measuring the Information Society - The ICT Development Index. International Telecommunication Union, Geneva (2009)

20. Human Development Report 2007/2008 - Fighting climate change: human solidarity in a divided world. UNDP, Palgrave Macmillan, New York (2008)

21. Goliński, M.: Measuring the Information Society – State of the Art of the "Grand Challenge". International Journal of Digital Information and Wireless Communications (IJDIWC) 1(2), 307–324 (2012)

22. Goliński, M.: Społeczeństwo informacyjne – geneza koncepcji i problematyka pomiaru. SGH, Warszawa (2011)

23. Minges, M.: Evaluation of e-Readiness Indices in Latin America and the Caribbean. United Nation's Economic Commission for Latin America and the Caribbean (ECLAC), Santiago (2005)
24. Grigorovici, D.M., Schement, J.R., Taylor, R.D.: Weighing the intangible: towards a framework for Information Society indices (2002), http://www.smeal.psu.edu/cdt/ebrcpubs/res_papers/2002_14.pdf/at_download/file
25. Jensen, M., Mahan, A.: Towards better measures of global ICT adoption and use. In: Global Information Society Watch 2008. Association for Progressive Communications (APC), Humanist Institute for Development Cooperation (Hivos) and Third World Institute, ITeM (2008), http://www.giswatch.org/gisw2008/pdf/GISW2008.pdf
26. Pena-Lopez, I.: Measuring digital development for policy-making: Models, stages, characteristics and causes. Universitat Oberta de Catalunya, Barcelona (2009)
27. Goliński, M.: Clicking Alone. Social Capital as a Barrier to the Development of Information Society in Countries of Central and Eastern Europe. In: Kommers, P., Isaias, P. (eds.) Proceedings of the IADIS International Conference - E-Society 2011, pp. 181–187. IADIS Press, Avila (2011)
28. Goliński, M.: The Role of Livelong Learning in the Development of Information Society on the Example of Countries of Central and Eastern Europe. In: Kommers, P., Isaias, P. (eds.) Proceedings of the IADIS International Conference - E-Society 2012, pp. 451–456. IADIS Press, Berlin (2012)
29. Booysen, F.: An Overview and Evaluation of Composite Indices of Development. In: Social Indicators Research, vol. 59. Kluwer Academic Publishers, Norwell (2002)

Developing a Data Quality Methodology in Service Oriented Context Using Design Science Approach

Plamen Petkov and Markus Helfert

School of Computing, Dublin City University,
Glasnevin, Dublin 9, Ireland
{ppetkov,markus.helfert}@computing.dcu.ie

Abstract. Service Oriented Architecture (SOA) is a prospective approach, which enables flexible and loose composition of applications whereas data is an integral part of service. However, the more complex SOA develops, the more likely are data quality (DQ) issues to be encountered. Despite the huge number of studies that have been done on SOA, very little has been investigated about the DQ aspect. Our research examines various perspectives of data quality in the flexible service oriented environment. We propose a set of methods that together are able to detect and analyse poor data. The contribution is that we employ different DQ techniques and apply it to SOA. This study is solidly backed by the Design Science (DS) approach for conducting research which suggests collection of techniques for developing and evaluating artifacts and their relevance in Information systems. The accent of this paper is to show how DS approach aid developing Data Quality Methodology in the service oriented context.

Keywords: Design Science Methodology, SOA, Systematic Literature Review.

1   Introduction

Current enterprises need to acknowledge effectively and rapidly to opportunities in todays' global markets. A modern approach for tackle these critical issues are embodied by (web) services that can be easily assembled to form a collection of autonomous and loosely-coupled business processes [1]. Thanks to the key principles that are embedded into SOA foundations such as reusability, interoperability, and standardization, companies can take advantage in numerous ways [2] – reducing the costs of operation and maintenance [3], less time for applying new services [4], more agile service management and many others.

Recent surveys, conducted by different independent organizations [5], prove that the majority of the cited companies using SOA or having SOA project underway report "Web services and Data integration" as main challenge for them. Generally, this issue occurs by the fact that most of the current software is not modularized enough. Service incompatibility could also steam by the fact that many of them are delivered by multiple service providers. Indeed, in more knotty architectures, loosely coupled data can be a source of serious problems that apply to the entire service-

A. Kobyliński and A. Sobczak (Eds.): BIR 2013, LNBIP 158, pp. 254–266, 2013.

oriented environment and in this way make them difficult to handle. Some of the issues that mostly occur within SOA were addressed by [6]. Literature on data quality, on the other hand, provides us with rich selection of methodologies for analyzing, measuring and improvement poor data in different Information systems (IS). However, those methodologies fail short to deliver a comprehensive data assessment especially with respect to the semantic data.

In this paper the objective is to investigate on how to analyze and measure data quality within Service-oriented context by applying the Design Science methodology []. DS is a methodology that proposes a set of analytical techniques and perspectives for conducting research in IS. In order to reach given objective, we propose a DQ approach which is able to detect semantically poor data. More particularly the methodology suggests techniques that will define and assess/measure decayed data. The foundations of this approach follow the Data Quality Management (DQM) [8] model. However, we accentuate on the applicability of the design science approach in producing solutions rather on the solution itself.

The remainder of the paper is organized as follows: Section 2 reviews some of the common data quality methodologies in IS. In this section we also provide with the conceptual requirements that SOA DQ methodology should possess. In section 3 following DS approach, we explain in details the research techniques we used to build /evaluate the solution. Then, in section 4, we present a DQ methodology which will apply to SOA and will facilitate assessing of semantic (business) data quality. Then the paper is completed with some preliminary evaluations and discussions, concluding remarks and outlines the opportunities for future work.

2   Related Work in Data Quality

Literature provides us with many and different Data Quality Methodologies in IS. Before we go any further, it is important to point out that a DQ methodology is a set of methods needed to achieve the goal of detecting poor data. Despite the diverse nature of DQ methodologies, most of them are following certain criteria. The common criteria we have identified from the literature and we are going to use to explore the field in DQ are: 1) data type, 2) information system focus, 3) DQ dimensions, 4) phases and steps. Comparison table 1 below shows an overview of the most common DQ methodologies in IS along the criteria chosen.

The broad difference in focus across methodologies can be recognized at a glance. On the one hand some are more complete but more general; on the other hand others are obviously more focused but not as extensive and flexible. Based on presented DQ methodologies comparison, several conclusions can be made regarding each criterion. Firstly, with respect to data type criterion, most of the methodologies clearly target structured data type. Only [9] and partly [10] supports semi-structural data types in their profiles. Tied with the data, the most supportive IS type by methodologies is monolithic; however few of them concentrate on distributive [11], Data warehouses [12] and even web [9]. With reference to DQ dimensions criterion, most of the methodologies define large number of dimensions. Still metrics reflecting these dimensions remain vaguely explained, i.e. [13] has over 30 dimensions but only 6 metrics. Most importantly, all DQ methodologies consider syntactic accuracy dimension and not the semantic one, at least not explicitly. A phase and steps criterion is the most divisive one. As it can be seen most of the methodologies measure quality of the data using different statistical and data mining methods as well as

Table 1. DQ Methodologies

Author Criteria		Wang 1998 [10]	Jeusfeld et al. 1998 [12]	English 1999 [11]	Lee et al. 2002 [14]	Long and Seko 2005 [15]	Loshin 2004 [13]
Data Type		Structured Semi-structured	Structured	Structured	Structured	Structured Semi-structured	Structured
IS type focus		Monolithic	Data warehouse	Monolithic, Distributed	Monolithic	Web	Monolithic
DQ dimensions		16 dimensions in 4 categories 5 metrics	15 dimensions 5 metrics	categories – inherit and pragmatic, 15 dimensions 8 metrics	14 dimensions 17 metrics	16 dimensions 14 metrics	Over 30 di –mensions in 4 categories 6 metrics
DEFINITION	**Data Analysis**	data consumers, suppliers, manufacturers	supported	supported	supported	supported	supported
	Process Analysis	supported using IP- MAP and UML	n/a	supported	n/a	n/a	supported
	DQ Require-ments	n/a	stakeholders surveys	based on consumers satisfaction	n/a	n/a	n/a
ASSESMENT/MEASURING	**Finding critical areas**	supported	supported	supported	supported	supported	supported
	Measuring quality	surveys	hierarchical Quality assessments	random data samples	question-naires	data gathering Data analysis	objective and subjective

questionnaires and surveys targeting different groups. Furthermore only few methodologies consider DQ requirements analysis step. Only few also take into account process analysis step in the definition stage as mandatory. In addition to definition and analyzing/measuring phases, most methodologies also include improving phase, which considers different techniques for improving data quality as well as methods for evaluating the cost/damage of the data and improvement process. However, order to narrow down the scope of the project and particularly this paper, we do not include the improvement stage in our discussion.

Esteeming form the brief analysis made about current DQ methodologies, the service oriented architecture profile and the problem raised in section 1, we conclude that effective SOA DQ methodology should provide methods and techniques that: 1) support semi-structured data, 2) target Distributive, Cooperative and Web IS types brought together(SOA), 3) clearly defined DQ dimensions along its metrics (with particular focus on semantic accuracy dimension) 4) unambiguously and exact description of definition and assessment phases of data quality process; it has to support data and process analysis as well as method that will objectively detect and measure semantically poor data.

3   Design Science as Research Methodology

This study is conducted by executing the Design Science approach. DS research involves the design of novel or innovative artifacts and the analysis of the use and/or performance of such artifacts to improve and understand the behavior of aspects of Information Systems. Such artifacts include algorithms (e.g. for information retrieval), system design methodologies or languages and etc. We have chosen particularly this approach among the others because it does offer flexibility as well as set of analytical techniques in order to conduct successfully our research. Because our research output is a methodology (set of processes) DS Reference Model suits completely in aiding to developing the artifact. We will build our artifact by using ontology engineering and process modeling techniques to fuse the knowledge obtained from literature and stakeholders. Fig. 1 provides more detailed view of research methodology in the Design Science settings. Furthermore, it demonstrates the relevant techniques and methods selected to accompany the DS process. Also an overview of the expected outputs is presented along with the process. Some of the techniques and outputs have been already conducted and presented in following sections, and the incomplete parts are stated in section 5.

3.1   Identifying the Problem, Motivation, and Research Objectives

Identifying the problem is a crucial step, foundation and starting point of every project. That is why it needs to be precisely and unambiguously defined prior to any further action.

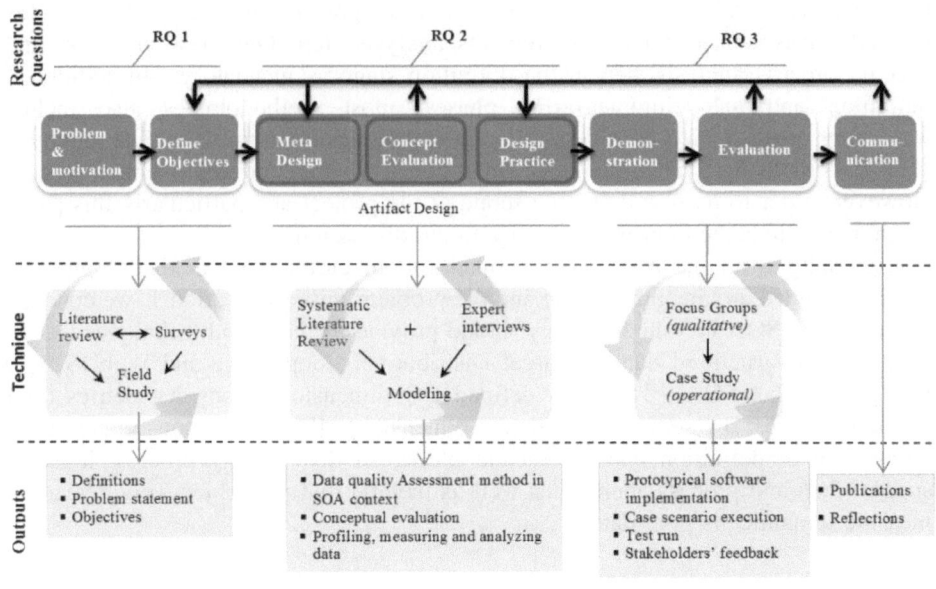

Fig. 1. Overview of the Design Science approach applied to this research

To identify the problem we have referred to the literature. A methodological review of past literature is an essential segment for any research work. The need to uncover what is already known in the body of knowledge should not be underestimated. In the first few months of the project we have mainly examined literature and in more broad context. The target of this examination was to gather as much possible information about problems related with SOA. Then we referred our findings to the domain of Data Quality. Type of literature we have inspected was consisting mainly of periodic issues, reports, journals as well as professional blogs and forums over the Internet. Main keywords that we used to perform searching were "Service Oriented Architectures", "Data Quality", "issues in SOA" and "incorporating poor data in SOA".

Figure 2 depicts the research gap we have identified based on the literature. More specifically, diagram represents two main streams of researches carried out recently - Data Quality stream (red curve) and SOA stream (blue curve). Some key points of prominent studies have been also marked along on each curve. For the purpose of the diagram, two variables are used – time featured on the horizontal axis and number of the revised studies we have investigated, indicated on the vertical axis.

The red curve on the graph clearly indicates that there is a peak of the numbers of findings in Data quality domain during the period of 1996-2002 years. On the other hand, studies in SOA area have been dating from early 2000s and are continuously rising, even at the time of conducting of this research. The increasing trend of SOA studies can be observed on the illustration. However, there is a lack of research addressing data quality in SOA context. The reason for this is the different periods of

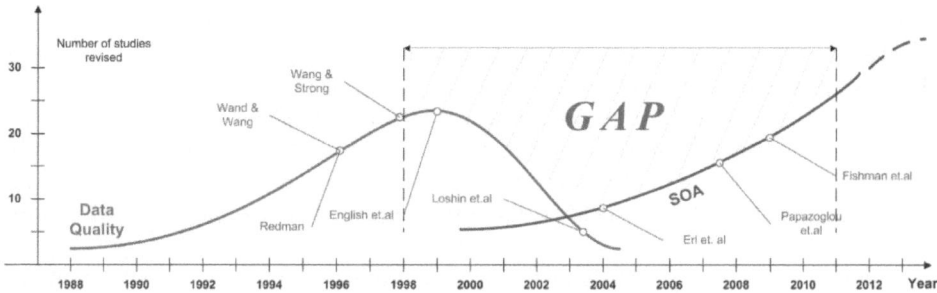

Fig. 2. Literature overview and research gap

time that different information systems have emerged For example, relevant types of IS were monolithic data warehouses partly distributed. SOA is relevantly new type of architecture which combines the features of distributed and cooperative systems involving bunch of new technologies and principles, and because of this, old data quality methodologies had become out-dated and inapplicable. This fact and the nature of the new architecture escalate the need for design of a new kind of Data quality methodology.

Despite our findings in the literature, we have also conducted an independent survey on the data quality issues in Service Oriented Architectures. Targets of this survey were companies who are using SOA or having an SOA project underway. We have surveyed 36 people of which 6 projects manages, 12 business architects and 18 software developers. Questions in the survey were determined based on our findings in the conducted literature review.

Based on the results from the literature and conducted survey, we observed that in complex service oriented architectures data quality problems are persistent and orchestrating the services can be difficult to handle without having awareness of the data. Hence, in section 1 and section 3 we set as the research objective discovering a method that will assess data quality in SOA context.

3.2   Designing and Building the Artifact

In order to construct our process we had to determine few important questions such as "What are the requirements needed for applicable Data Quality assessment in the service-oriented context?" (R1) and "How can Data Quality be measured in a service-oriented context?" R2(fig 1). Following the process oriented reference model, we will answer to these questions using tree main techniques namely, **systematic literature review, collaboration with practitioners** and **information modeling** [14]

The identification of the requirements was done using systematic **literature review** [15] approach on existing DQ literature. In the period of 10 months, we have examined the data quality in the context of SOA in academic and professional literature. It begun with the most cited papers, e.g. Wang [16], English [11], Lee et al [17], Loshin [13], gradually reaching towards other relevant publications and paying particular attention to related special issues and specialist conferences. Closer attention was paid to papers which are focused to Data Quality in SOA, as well as articles, which cover DQ within SOA in parts only, unambiguously accentuating on the keywords such as 'detect' and 'analyse' 'poor data' in 'SOA'. Through that process 30 key articles were identified from which a glossary of DQ and SOA related concepts and definitions were compiled. The collection of literature was performed by searching in Online Public Access Catalogues as well as Open Access Databases and specific subject databases such as Google Scholar, IEEE Xplore, ACM Digital Library, etc.

Collaboration with practitioners. The aim of this phase is similar to the literature review with the exception that practitioners' expertise is used as the source of information for the process. Practitioners are recruited and selected based upon predefined characteristics such as relevant work experience on the domain under investigation. For the purpose of this research, data collected form the practitioners were in form of individual **interviews**. More particularly each interview was as carried out as short **discussion**. The length times of the discussions were approximately 40 min of which 20 min were devoted to familiarizing the expert body with the topic. Five experts' opinions were gathered so far with trend to more as artefact improves over time following DS methodology cycle. Knowledge obtained from discussions was structured in a way of notes and tables in different subtopics. Using this method makes the process of designing the artefact more transparent, unambiguous and clear.

Artifact synthesis/modeling is the stage where we use obtained knowledge form the systematic literature review and discussions with practitioners in a form of methodologies, principles and semantic constraints of concepts to design and develop the artifact. Techniques that are used to model the artifact during the meta-design stage (fig 1) are Ontology Engineering [18] approach and Business Process Modeling Notation (BPMN) [19]The concept of ontology engineering process involves defining terms in the domain and relations among them; defining concepts in the domain (classes); arranging the concepts in a hierarchy (subclass-superclass hierarchy); defining attributes and properties of classes and constraints on their values; After knowledge is structured we use BPMN to describe the kernel process used in our artifact (method for assessing data quality in SOA).

3.3   Demonstration and Evaluation

The aim of the demonstration and evaluation phase of the methodology is to demonstrate that the artefact (DQ method) feasibly works to achieve its objectives (stated in section 3) in at least one context. Additionally, it considers how well developed DQ method support solution to the problem. The utility, quality, and efficacy of the method must be rigorously demonstrated via well-executed evaluation methods. In order to give answer to the third research question "How to evaluate the solution" (RQ3) (fig 1) a combination of qualitative and operational (quantitative) analysis techniques are and will be used. In the initial stage of evaluation we selected as method conducting a survey targeting focus groups. This type of approach suggests qualitative analysis due to stakeholders' subjectivity. A set of questions, based on the categories in the logic model of the artifact, was sent to each of the stakeholders in the group. Questions that were asked reflect the concept criteria that were identified in section 2. This type of evaluation can be referred as 'concept evaluation' and it is essential since it provides valuable feedback about the quality and the relevance of the concept. This allows us to further refine it before been applied and implemented in the real world. To objectively evaluate the research artifact, we have selected a case study method. Case study is an empirical inquiry that investigates a phenomenon within its real-life context. To evaluate the method in quantitative manner we plan to develop a software prototype tool, based on the latter. However, at current stage, due to some limitation (see section 7), we plan apply the in artificial case scenario. Artificial evaluation is unreal in some way or ways according to the three realities [20], such as unreal users, unreal system or unreal problems, but it can be used to prove or disapprove the utility of our artifact before it can be applied in a real-world case scenario.

4   Framework for Execution Quality Predicates in SOA

Following the general perception of DQ cycle and Data Quality Management (DQM) cycle proposed by [8] the following paragraphs present the methodology of defining and detecting semantically inaccurate data in SOA context. The methodology consists of several methods: 1) method for defining data, in term of data profiles, 2) techniques for measuring and execution data quality and 3) Method for analyzing the outputs of measuring and execution. We exclude any methods for improving from this paper. An abstract overview of the latter is depicted on figure 3

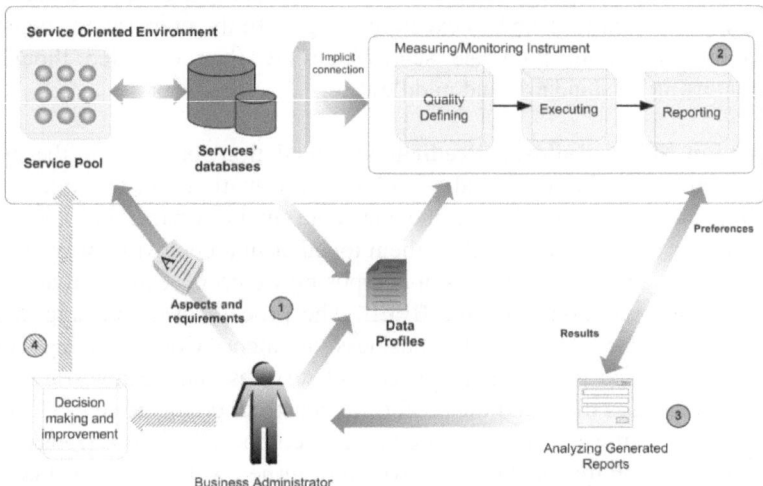

Fig. 3. Overview of the Data quality assessment and analyzing process in SOA

Method: Profiling Data. Data profiling is a process of examining the existing data according to the business requirements and composing data profiles by professional body. Profiling helps to understand anomalies and to assess data quality, but also to discover, register, and assess enterprise metadata [13]. Other benefits of the process of profiling also includes improving data quality, reducing the time for implementation of major projects, and most importantly - improving the understanding of the data. Understanding of the data is vital criterion which lays the foundation of assessing data quality process. The idea of profiling in this paper is to build information profiles of the data used by the services and processes. In order to do so in SOA context, we consider the following characteristics: services involved in the organizational process, data including data types/attributes and data format/structure; processes including the steps and activities in charge of data modification and transformation; and business requirement or condition needed to put the data into context. In Table 2 the contextual data (metadata) captured by the business administrator is classified of who when how and what format. This will serve as an input for the assessment stage and will enable detecting the semantically inaccurate data.

Table 2. Data profiling in SOA

Who	How	What		When
Service	Process	Information Type Entity	Information Elements	Requirement
Service name	Description of the process	Data Object	Data attribute	Condition

Method: Detecting Semantically Inaccurate Data

The method for detecting semantically inaccurate data (measuring) consist of few stages namely i) preparation and ii) execution stages: In the preparation stage profiled data is transformed into predicate sets which are then executed thought SOA environment using its standards and middleware.

i) Preparation Stage. Building Predicates: Foundation for building the predicates which eventually served as data quality arbiter is information profiles composed using the profiling method. Profiled data and metadata about services and processes are used to compose the predicates and tie them together in a contextual way. To bind all these components and aid the process of composing we propose an approach using the business process execution language BPEL. The process of composing starts with selection of a business process by business architect. Corresponding XML file containing the selected process is analyzed and services and variables are extracted. Next the architect uses them and the profiles to construct predicate sets. Then they are stored in repository. Each predicate composed of [returned_value] comparison_operation [expected_value] where [returned_value] is the value delivered by the target service operation (usually fetch function e.g. getOperation()); comparison_operation is any of the following logical operations: '<'(less), '>'(greater), '='equal, '!='(not equal), '<='(less than or equal) '>='(greater than or equal); [expected_value] is expected value. Each predicate has an [linkage] attribute which allows building complex sets of predicates.

ii) Execution Stage. Executing Predicate Sets: In this stage predicates are executed and he result is stored in log files. Generally this process is divided in 4 steps: pre-execution", "reading the predicates and building enquiries", "executing and waiting for service response" and "problem log generating" steps. A key part in this step is to check if any of the service data that have been inquired are used by any process. This will prevent issues where two or more processes are trying to access/modify same data. Next, after the all enquiries have been dispatched, the services generate outputs in accordance with their get operations and input parameters. The generated results are being collected by message aggregator block. Then the final output based on the computed predicate linkage logic operations is stored in practical oriented log file used. Further description of the process will be omitted due to the focus of the paper.

5   Discussions and Preliminary Evaluations

At this stage the research is still in conceptual/implementation level. Following the research methodology presented in section 3 the next step of the research is demonstrate and evaluate our solution. The aim of the demonstration and evaluation phase of the methodology is to show that the artifact we built feasibly works and achieve its objectives (stated in section 2) in at least one context. Additionally, it considers how well developed DQ method support solution to the problem. The utility, quality, and efficacy of the method must be rigorously demonstrated via well-executed evaluation methods.

To evaluate the concept we have chosen a method of conducting expert interviews with stakeholders. They will be asked to provide their professional feedback against the conceptual criteria stated in section 2. Still this method will give us subjective results. To objectively evaluate the methodology we plan to employ a case study method. Case study is an empirical inquiry that investigates a phenomenon within its real-life context.

To evaluate the method in quantitative manner we plan to develop a software prototype tool, based on the latter. Then we will use it to run on specific scenario. Additionally our plans are to conduct a focus group survey to evaluate the operational criteria such as efficiency, effectiveness and usability. Usability in this sense is subjective criteria because it strongly depends on case and purpose the enterprise intends to use the artifact. With respect to efficiency criterion our intentions are to measure the time needed to a business body to achieve the final goal. Here we exclude the technical constraints and delays of the system environment. Using this method we will measure how much human efforts (including profiling data, and building predicate rules) does our solution require in order detecting semantically poor data. Effectiveness criterion, on the other hand, will be measured based on direct output of the execution stage and its ultimate aim is to show detailed report of the errors found.Analysing this report is the phase where the generated result from Execution stage are examined and analysed. This stage can be also referred to the quality monitoring and transformation stage in DQM. Figure 3 portrays the process of assessment and analysing data issues in Service-oriented context, which in its turn, is part of the whole data quality cycle.

In analysing stage (4) a summary reports based on the user preferences and data collected from execution stage are generated. Depends on the business architect intentions and the type of report he wants to create, he can pick form different criteria.

The following Table 1 shows an example of generated problem report involving information about *violated values and the services.* It reports the services that violate the following rule *"Gold-member customers are eligible for free shipping"*

Table 3. User generated problem report including services' information

Service location	Service Name	Ser-vice Id	Service Operation	Input value	Violated value	Entity
url://	CustomerService	2	getCustomerStatus()	6558	'gold'	23
url://	OrderingService	11	getShippingCost()	7458	23**(0)**	563

In this way, examining the generated report could improve business architect's awareness of the services used in the service-oriented environment. Service awareness in that context could be making important decisions about the services that produce the errors by either breaking the contract or replacing it with another which fulfil the functional requirements.

Another example of report could be based on the criteria "violated quality predicate". In this case the report will be generated based on the number of violated predicates. Analysing the most violated rule, could indicate that the problem reported by the service could be not caused by the service but the rule itself. Furthermore this could lead the Business Analytic to examination and redefining the target quality rule. This is very important since the process of analysing is iterative (following Design science approach) and the quality of information depends, de facto, on the quality of the monitoring rules.

6   Conclusion and Further work

Taking into an account the nature of the Service oriented architectures, the importance of data quality is more than obvious. Driven by the gap, that we have identified in the literature about current data quality methodologies, in this paper, we have proposed an approach for analyzing and measuring data quality in Service Oriented Architectures' context. We have presented a methodology that offers a set of methods to the business administrator through which he will be able to capture poor semantic data in particular business context. More in detail, our DQ methodology consist of few methods: method for profiling data, methods for defining and executing data quality within SOA environment and technique for analyzing the results. Ultimately, unlikely to the other DQ methodologies, our approach offers unambiguously and exact description of the process of defining and measuring business data quality in SOA. Most important contribution, however, in this paper is that it presents step by step how the DQ methodology was built using the Design Science approach.

Our samples are currently based and extracted from the literature. Therefore, in future, following Design Science approach, we need to enlarge their scope, by extending the numbers of case scenarios that our methodology will be run on. Another line of future investigation is to go beyond monitoring DQ, and to also consider reactions from the practitioners. Our intuition is that their feedback will provide us with valuable outcome that will contribute to synthesizing and consolidating the process for assessing data quality in service oriented environment.

Acknowledgements. This work was supported by the Irish Research Council (IRC) under the Postgraduate Scholarship Scheme.

References

1. Papazoglou, M., Willem-Jan, V.: Service oriented architectures: approaches, technologies, pp. 389–415 (2007)
2. Bell, E., Michael, M.: Service-oriented architecture: a planning and implementation guide for business and technology. Wiley, Hoboken (2006)
3. Krafzig, D., Banke, K.: Enterprise SOA, service-oriented architecture best practices. Prentice Hall, Upper Saddle River (2004)
4. O'Brien, L., Merson, P., Bass, L.: Quality Attributes for Service-Oriented Architectures. In: SDSOA 2007 Proceedings of the International Workshop on Systems Development in SOA Environments, Washington, DC, USA, p. 3 (2007)
5. Austvold, E.: Service-Oriented Architectures: Survey on Deployment and Plans for the Future, ARM Research Report (2006)
6. Petkov, P., Helfert, M.: Data oriented challenges of service architectures a data quality perspective. In: CompSysTech 2013, pp. 163–170 (2012)
7. Hevner, A.R., March, S.T., Park, J., Ram, S.: Design Science in Information Systems Research. MIS Quarterly 28, 75–106 (2004)
8. Oracle, I.: Understanding Data Quality Management. In : Oracle® Warehouse Builder User's Guide. Oracle Inc. (2008)
9. Eppler, M., Munzenmaier, P.: Measuring information quality in the Web context: A survey of. In: Proceedings of the 7th International Conference on Information Systems, ICIQ (2002)
10. Wang, R.: A product perspective on total data quality management. Comm. ACM, 2–41 (1998)
11. English, L.: Improving Data Warehouse and Business Information Quality. Wiley & Sons (1999)
12. Jeusfeld, M.A., Quix, C., Jarke, M.: Design and analysis of quality information for data warehouses. In: Ling, T.-W., Ram, S., Li Lee, M. (eds.) ER 1998. LNCS, vol. 1507, pp. 349–362. Springer, Heidelberg (1998)
13. Loshin, D.: Enterprise knowledge management: the data quality approach. Morgan Kaufmann (2001)
14. Ostrowski, Ł., Helfert, M., Hossain, F.: A Conceptual Framework for Design Science Research. In: Grabis, J., Kirikova, M. (eds.) BIR 2011. LNBIP, vol. 90, pp. 345–354. Springer, Heidelberg (2011)
15. Keele, D.: Software Engineering Group: Guidelines for Performing Systematic Literature Reviews in Software Engineering (2007)

16. Wang, R.: A product perspective on total data quality management. Communications of the ACM 41(2), 58–65 (1998)
17. Lee, Y.W., Strong, D., Kahn, B.: AIMQ: A methodology for information quality, 2nd edn., vol. 40. Elsevier (December 2002)
18. Mizoguchi, R.: Tutorial on Ontological Engineering, pp. 363–384 (2003)
19. Chinosi, M., Trombetta, A.: BPMN: An introduction to the standard. Computer Standards & Interfaces, 123–134 (2012)
20. Suny, Y., Kantor, P.: Cross-Evaluation: A New Model for Information System Evaluation. Journal of the American Society for Information Science and Technology, 614–662 (2006)

The Willingness to Pay for Information in Digital Marketplaces

Daphne R. Raban and Maya Mazor

Department of Business Administration, 610 Jacobs Building,
University of Haifa, Haifa 31905, Israel
draban@univ.haifa.ac.il, mayamazor@gmail.com

Abstract. While information may carry an intrinsic, objective value, this value is not known before consumption; therefore, it is the perception of its value by the user that determines if and how it will be acquired and applied. This pre-consumption perception is followed by post-consumption experience which may shed more light on the evolution of value perception. A financial markets knowledge game connected to an information shop was the research tool in the present study. Results indicate that the perceived value of information changes over the course of actual usage of information, as evidenced by the tendency to supplement the up-front payment with a voluntary tip and also as indicated by the difference between the very first price bid compared to the average bid. While information was shown to have realistic value, this value may have been difficult to perceive in real time during the game, and thus led to subjective purchasing decisions resulting in less-than-optimal game results. Overall, we demonstrated that given the right incentives and circumstances a vibrant information market arises with pricing practices that are suitable for digital goods. This holds promise for the construction of novel online exchanges for digital goods.

Keywords: value of information, subjective value, experience goods, willingness to pay, digital markets.

1   Introduction

Since the emergence of the Web we are witnessing two concurrent and interdependent processes. One process is the tide of free information online and the other process, linked to the first, is the quest for sustainable business models for information products, such as news, music, film and fiction. A key element of a sound business model is deep understanding of pricing. While there is a body of literature dedicated to information pricing practices such as versioning or bundling, little research attention is given to pricing based on value perceptions, which is the focus of this paper. The quest for the right pricing for information is challenging mainly because of two prominent characteristics: a. the value of information is subjective; b. information is an experience good. We use willingness-to-pay scales to translate subjective and experience perceptions into pricing.

A. Kobyliński and A. Sobczak (Eds.): BIR 2013, LNBIP 158, pp. 267–277, 2013.

The purpose of this work is to investigate the pre- and post- purchase perceived value of information, namely, the subjective and experience-based values. The research is conducted by an experiment where participants solve a financial markets knowledge game with the aid of unique data sources they purchase in an associated information shop powered by the FlexiPrice information pricing software service.

The experiment results indicate that given a certain set of market mechanisms and incentives, a vibrant market for content is generated displaying high subjective and experience values for information as expressed by willingness to pay up-front and to provide supplementary voluntary payment.

2   Theory and Related Work

The quantity of information available today and the freedom to publish that individuals now enjoy have shifted the burden of monitoring the value of information to the user or consumer of information. While information may carry an intrinsic, objective value, this value is not known before consumption; therefore, it is the perception of its value by the user that determines if and how it will be acquired and applied. This pre-consumption perception is followed by post-consumption experience which may shed more light on the evolution of value perception.

2.1   The Value of Information

Information has several unique characteristics which render it difficult to valuate. Information is an unusual good in many aspects - production, distribution, cost, and consumption [18]. Theoretically, there are three ways to assess the value of information: normative, realistic, and subjective [1]. While user utility should be the base for calculating the price of information, utility varies by person and circumstance. Realistic methods are ex post and consequently inappropriate for evaluating information content. This is also referred to as the "inspection paradox" [18].

The value of information may depend on external influences such as market structure or information system affordances, but it is mainly subjective [1], meaning that value perception varies among people and may be affected by the social environment, personal preferences, the passage of time or with the accumulation of experience [11]. Subjective value is formed prior to the acquisition of information. Once information is acquired and used, value perception may change based on the experience of using the information. Based on the current literature review, we are not aware of studies that examined the dynamic nature of the value of information as it is being experienced.

While subjective value is about a priori value assignment, experience value may affect subsequent decisions regarding the purchase of information and thus become part of the user's mind-set for future decisions and formation of subjective value in future events requiring information. The tension between the subjective value before use and the experience value after use raises questions such as: what is known about the value of information before and after consumption and use?

2.2   Experience Goods

Experience goods are items of commerce that can be fully evaluated by the consumer only after purchase and use [8]. Information is an experience good, the full value of which is revealed only after use [16], [18]. Indirect or partial quality cues such as ratings, recommendations or abstract afford limited relief for evaluating experience goods. One must experience information personally in order to form a value judgment of it. Therefore, standard market pricing norms such as are applied when selling printed books, for example, are not uniquely suitable for information. One must pay the full, fixed, price of a book up-front before receiving and reading it. Possibly, the experience gained while reading could make one think the book was a bargain, or, alternatively, that the book was disappointing and not worth its cost. In both cases payment was transferred, cannot be changed, and does not reflect the value of the book to the reader. Experience is inherently personal and thus is different from person to person. This quality makes it similar to the concept of "subjective value".

Voluntary payments can be used as an indication of subjective or experience value, depending on how they are implemented. An example of subjective value is Regner and Barria's study [14] showing that in the case of online music, consumers pay voluntarily and most of the time they pay significantly more than the requested minimum. Experience value relating to satisfaction from answers provided in the Google Answers Q&A site was shown through an analysis of tipping patterns [10]. That research revealed the surprising observation that people are willing to provide supplementary payment (tip) in an anonymized online system even after they have paid the up-front requested price.

In the current web environment where free information is abundantly available and payment is far from the norm as evidenced by the media's struggle to find a business model, it is particularly interesting and challenging to deeply investigate the value of information which is the aim of the present study. We do so by applying an incentive compatible mechanism to extract the willingness to pay for information as well as by providing an opportunity for providing a voluntary payment, tip, after purchase and use of information. Additional research on voluntary payments is described later in section 2.4 on pricing.

2.3   Information Markets

According to Linde and Stock [7] information markets are markets for digital information, including all sorts of digital content: images, films, games, articles etc. These markets are different than markets for non-digital goods especially in the locus of ownership. When a non digital good is purchased, ownership transfers from the seller to the buyer. On the other hand, goods on information markets stay with the seller, buyers usually receive the copy. Often, one side of the market is better informed about the quality of its information goods than the other. The seller knows his product, whereas the buyer cannot assess its quality prior to the purchase and sometimes only partly afterward. The value of information goods can only be judged once the information has been received and experienced.

Raban and Rafaeli [13] created a market for information in simple computer-simulated business games where participants were provided opportunities to buy or sell information. The bidding mechanism was incentive compatible [2]. Results showed that, in agreement with Endowment Effect theory [17], people value information they own significantly more than information not owned by them. The locus of ownership influenced value perceptions despite the fact that information was transferred by copying. The findings indicate that information value perceptions are other than rational. Participants exhibited a strong tendency to purchase but not to sell information even though profit data suggests that the use of information had no objective benefit for profit-making [12].

One type of information markets is digital applications and media markets, such as Apple iTunes store, Nokia Ovi store or Google Play (Android apps) market. There are many applications stores today and each of these stores differs from the other in terms of pricing, billing, presentation and support. Each store even rates the same application in different ways, which could make it difficult for the customer to decide whether or not to purchase a certain application. Yet, all these stores operate in the conventional mode of pricing set by sellers. This research aims to investigate a shift of pricing power somewhat in the direction of consumers.

2.4   Pricing

Pricing information goods is crucial and significant in an information economy. We see that the value of information creates challenges for pricing information products and services. The value is subjective and dynamic and may change upon use. In a broad review of information pricing strategies Chang and Yuan show that pricing more often favors sellers than buyers [3].

Prices for information goods can be formed in several ways. An innovation in static procedures is reverse pricing, where the buyer dictates the price. Such a demand-oriented pricing with a (covert) set minimum price is practiced by eBay, with its "Best Offer" function. Here the buyer may make up to three price offers below the publicly set minimum price. If one of his offers is above the minimum determined by the seller, which is invisible to buyers, he may win the item [7]. Name-Your-Own-Price (NYOP) is another variation of reverse pricing initiated by Priceline [5]. A newer variant of determining prices from the buyers' side is the (open) Pay What You Want. Here the seller foregoes a minimum price and accepts the buyers' price offer without reservation [6] Such offers are more frequent lately, e.g. from music groups such as Radiohead and Nine Inch Nails, who make their music available for download for a certain period of time, merely providing the option of a voluntary payment [7].

In addition, there are dynamic pricing procedures. In these cases the price is determined over the course of the transaction between seller and buyer. Individual price negotiation has been used for a long time. With the advent of the internet and electronic payment services, e-market places have established themselves for business-to-business (B2B) transactions over the past few years. However, the hopes that had originally been nurtured concerning the great economic importance of these trade platforms were disappointed. Individual business-to-consumer (B2C) price negotiations are only gradually emerging [7]. None of the pricing methods mentioned here are based on user experience; they all reflect expectations and subjective value.

2.5   Summary

Information evaluation by users is an intriguing research opportunity. Its direct application in pricing of digital goods promises significant applicative contribution. Prior behavioral research teaches us that value is in the eye of the beholder and can vary depending on the context. Therefore, to inform daily information consumption patterns, the focus of research should be on users' subjective and experience-based evaluation of information [11].

The value assigned to information by the user is of critical importance for information consumption patterns in information markets. It is of high theoretical and applied interest to investigate the relationship between the post-use, experience value of information and the pre-use, subjective value. Using an experiment setup this work attempts to shed light on how individual users perceive the complex concept of the "value of information". We are unaware of prior empirical research on the experience value of information.

3   Research Questions

This work will focus on improving the understanding of voluntary pre and post-experience payments as a value discovery and pricing mechanism.

The research question that we ask is: what is the relation between the subjective and experience value of information in online marketplaces?

The following specific aspects will be explored:

1.   To what extent are people willing to purchase information?
2.   What are the subjective and experience values assigned to sources of information?
3.   Does positive\ negative feedback affect the willingness to pay tip (voluntary payment)?

These questions will be explored by conducting an experiment using the FlexiPrice system [9].

4   Method

We designed an experiment around a financial markets knowledge game.   The multiple choice questions were too difficult to solve based on personal knowledge. Users needed information which we provided through an information shop founded on the FlexiPrice system. All information purchasing bids and post-use tips were logged and analyzed.

4.1   FlexiPrice System Description

FlexiPrice is a software component designed for integration into an online information exchange platform in order to extend it with business capabilities. FlexiPrice allows a seller or a buyer of information to configure a price negotiation method, and assign it to an information item. Once a user chooses to bid on this item, the system displays a negotiation screen. After consumption, the buyer is able to optionally pay the seller an additional gratuity payment [9]. The negotiation method we used is based on the BDM bidding mechanism [2].

Our exchange platform is an information shop where sellers can offer products by assigning pricing to them and wait for a negotiation. In the experiment, the knowledge game players acted as buyers only. We set up the shop with the necessary information.

4.2   Conducting an Experiment via FlexiPrice System

The aim of the experiment is to learn about the subjective and experience value of information. For that purpose we developed an online knowledge game on capital markets directly connected to the FlexiPrice system. The subjective value is represented by the price bids for purchasing information, and the experience value is represented by the tip paid by the player after buying and using information.

The game is composed of 8 multiple choice questions and an information shop that contains information needed to answer the questions. No previous knowledge in the capital market is required. Each participant receives virtual 3,000 NIS (local currency) at the beginning of the game. To answer the questions the player has to look for answers in the shop which contains relevant images, articles, presentations etc. The player can see only brief descriptions of the information in each file. To get full access to a desired file the player has to buy it. If the player found the information useful and relevant, he can give a tip. The system provides the player with feedback about his answers' correctness. The aim of this game is to answer correctly all the questions within limited time. Every question the player answered correctly grants him extra points. If the player answers all the questions right – he gets even more points. The maximum possible score is 118 for players who answered all questions correctly in their first attempt. If the player answered incorrectly, he can re-answer the question after he finishes answering all the questions (if time remains), but it costs him points. At the end of the game, the player who received the most points will get a prize.

As an example, here is one of the questions presented in the game:
As of March 2011 which stock exchanged went up by 260%?

1.   Turkey
2.   Russia
3.   Argentina
4.   USA

After the game, each player was asked to fill a short form with demographic questions, like age, gender, education and some questions about shopping habits on the Web (digital goods and entertainment), and tipping norms for service providers such as waiters, tourist guides, and hairdressers.

4.3   Sample

120 people participated in the experiment, 49% men, 43% women, the rest did not disclose their gender. 82% of the sample was aged up to 50, the rest older or undisclosed. Most participants had little prior knowledge about financial markets,

and fairly low experience with online shopping of information and entertainment. 63% of the sample declared that they usually leave a tip of 9-12% in restaurants. Some participants responded that they leave modest tips to service providers such as hair dressers and tour guides.

5   Results

Table 1 summarizes the descriptive statistics regarding the questions and the purchasing activity.

Table 1. Game activity summary

	Answered Questions	Right Answers	Final Points	Num of Tips per Participant	Final Balance	Num of bought files
Average	11.34	6.72	69.96	2.11	2,677.3	7.87
Median	10.00	8.00	77.00	2.00	2,647.37	8.00
Standard deviation	4.75	2.20	41.19	1.27	211.24	3.45
Min Value	1.00	.00	-84.00	1.00	2,026.85	1.00
Max value	31.00	8.00	118.00	6.00	3,000.00	19.00
N	120	120	120	34	120	99

5.1   Information Purchasing

99 participants purchased files during the game (buyers) and 21 participants decided to play the game without purchasing information (non-buyers). A statistically significant difference was observed between these two sub-groups in the number of correct answers, the final score points earned and in the final account balance. Information buyers had 6.9 correct answers compared to 5.5 for non-buyers (t=-1.95, df=23.085, p=0.06). Buyers earned a total of 76 game score points compared to 39 points earned by non-buyers (t=-3.97, df=118, p<0.01). Obviously, buyers finished the game with less money, 2,608 NIS, as compared to non-buyers who retained the original sum assigned to all players, 3,000 NIS.

In addition, we found a statistically significant correlation of 0.43 (p<0.05) between the number of files bought and the final score points, and a positive correlation of 0.23 (p<0.05) between the number of files bought and the players' age.

There was no statistically significant difference between buyers and non-buyers in the total number of answers submitted during the game, 12.6 and 11 answers, respectively. While the game consisted of 8 questions, the higher mean number of answers indicates that the players were motivated to go back and correct wrong answers in order to win the game.

5.2   Subjective Value of Information

In our experimental setup players submitted several price bids during the game session. The total number of bids submitted by a player ranged between 0-26. Since we expect learning to occur during the game, we consider only the very first price bid submitted by the player to represent his/her true subjective evaluation of information. For this initial price bid values ranged between 20 and 600 NIS, with a mean of 64.72 (N=99), standard deviation=44.94. The mean of all price bids in the game was 70.42.

5.3   Tipping Behavior

34 participants decided to give an extra voluntary payment, tip, for the document they purchased after using it to answer a question (tippers) and did so in 72 transactions. The average tip was 27.19 NIS. 86 participants did not give a tip (non-tippers). A statistically significant difference was observed between these two sub-groups in the number of files purchased and in the final account balance. Tippers bought 8.6 files on average as compared to 5.6 files purchased by non-tippers (t=-4.93, df=117.09, $p<0.01$) and finished the game with 2,563 NIS as compared to 2,722 NIS (t=-2.02, df=116.55, $p<0.05$).

There was no statistically significant difference between tippers and non-tippers in terms of the number of correct answers achieved in the game (7.0 and 6.6 right answers, respectively), however, there was a difference in the final score points earned, 82 and 65, respectively. (t=-2.37, df=93.25, $p<0.05$)

5.4   Participants' Background

The post game questionnaire consisted of seven items relating to prior knowledge, experience and norms: prior knowledge in financial markets (game subject), online shopping habits of digital games, songs, movies, online shopping habits of digital books, papers, newspapers, magazines, tipping in restaurants, tipping the hairdresser, tipping a tour guide, self perception as a tipper.

None of the background variables correlated with the number of files purchased or with actual tipping behavior in the game.

6   Discussion

Most research on information value and pricing focused on refining well-established models such as versioning, personalization, lock-in and so on [16]. These methods tend to focus on the products in order to enhance their value through variety, innovation or bundling. Our approach is to focus on value perceptions of consumers, information users, and to search for ways to translate perception into pricing. The experiment described here is a first attempt of this kind and its outcomes analyzed below lay the foundation for a range of future experiments serving the same purpose.

Looking at Table 1 we observe that players played the financial markets knowledge game enthusiastically, making on average over 11 attempts to answer their 8 given questions, they were correct about 6.72 out of 8 questions (84%), and reached on average about 70 of the possible 118 score points. Interestingly, players selected to purchase files on average about 8 times which means they preferred to play with solid knowledge most of the time. This is in line with the fact that they had abundant budget and were not rated based on any parameter related to their residual budget.

These descriptive statistics present the subjective nature of value perception. While files in our shop proved useful for reaching correct answers, some players preferred to forego the purchasing opportunity. Possibly, this is due to playfulness, playing the game partly for fun and not for pure ambition to succeed. Alternatively, a deeper cause related to value perception or willingness to purchase underlies this behavior and awaits further research.

Information purchasing behavior was somewhat surprising. We assumed that based on the game introduction and instructions (in-class presentation), all players will engage in purchasing files in order to do their best in the game. In fact, 21 participants were "non-buyers" as defined in the Results section. This presented an opportunity to observe the realistic value of information [1], i.e. the contribution of information to succeeding in answering the questions. People who purchased information had significantly more correct answers than players who played casually, based on prior knowledge or luck. Buyers of information scored on average 6.9 correct answers compared to 5.5 for non buyers. Purchasing files improved correctness by 25%, a realistic, objective, value of information in our game.

The positive correlation between information purchasing and the players' age is in line with widely accepted economic knowledge whereby disposable income increases with age leading to reduced sensitivity to price and greater purchasing tendency. No gender, education, or professional differences were observed. The implication here is that content providers who wish to increase their business should find tailored ways to address different age groups.

The subjective value of information exposed in the game was quite high with a minimum of 20 NIS (about 5 U.S. Dollars) and an average of 70.42 NIS (about 18 U.S. Dollars). When given a motivation to buy information (game competition), ample resources (play money) and a sense that the information is likely to be helpful, a lively market emerges with 780 file purchasing transactions and 72 voluntary payment transfers. Approximately 9% of the transactions implemented voluntary payments. The overall impression is that people are not inherently reluctant to purchase and use information. To the contrary, having the opportunity and freedom to purchase information, players happily complied. Possibly, the current structure of information transactions on the web is not conducive to such transactions. The abundance of free information is also likely to inhibit purchasing transactions [15] and will be a topic for future research with similar methodology.

Table 1 suggests an interesting story about tipping. 34 people selected to provide a voluntary payment after the purchasing transaction and the completion of the particular question answering. While a majority of participants preferred not to tip or were indifferent to this option, more than a quarter of the people (38% of information buyers) provided a tip, and did so, on average, twice during the game session. While the numbers may seem modest, this is a striking behavior considering that there are no such norms online and considering that formal payment for the documents had already been processed prior to the voluntary payment option.

People who provided tips in the game bought significantly more files in the information shop than "non-tippers". This provides support to the premise of this experiment that tipping is a way to express value, specifically, the value based on experiencing information, using it to answer a question. The average tip in the game was 27.19 NIS while the average price bid for an information file amounted to 70.42 NIS. Roughly, the tip amounted to 38% of the total average payment, when given. This is very high by any standard. In this way tips play an important part in the economics of information, at least as far as the present experiment is concerned. Merely providing people with an opportunity to "open their hearts and digital purses" resulted in substantial economic activity which could be very meaningful if found in a real market online. For example, when people become accustomed to tipping, they are likely to strategize their initial bids. They may reduce risk by submitting a lower initial bid and later on supplement that with a voluntary *ex post* payment. This, too, is an option for future research.

Interestingly, positive feedback embedded in the game did not lead to more tipping activity. There was no statistically significant difference in number of correct answers between tippers and non-tippers. A possible conclusion is that tipping is an individual inclination rather than a response to positive feedback received after submitting a correct answer.

Lastly, our set of background questions did not predict the players' tipping behavior. This can be interpreted in one of two ways. Tipping behavior online may be so unusual and new that it cannot be well predicted by such background variables. Alternatively, our set-up was not sensitive enough and should be revised in future experiments.

The current study has several limitations. As an experiment its external validity is limited. It does, however, outline a methodology which can easily be refined in order to address the questions more deeply and with other variables. For example, a similar experiment can be run where the shop contains free information files, in addition to the paid items. This would provide a window to the influence of free information on information purchasing behavior. Tipping can be explored in greater depth as can the background predictor variables.

In summary, running an experiment with the financial markets knowledge game taught us that perceived value of information may change over the course of actual usage of information, as evidenced by the tendency to supplement the up-front payment with a voluntary tip and also as indicated by the difference between the very first bid compared to the average bid. While information was shown to have realistic value, this value may have been difficult to perceive in real time during the game, and thus led to subjective purchasing decisions resulting in less-than-optimal game results. Overall, we demonstrated that given the right incentives and circumstances a vibrant information market arises with pricing practices that are suitable for digital goods. This holds promise for the construction of novel online exchanges for digital goods.

The norm in existing markets is that pricing is done by sellers, usually by commercial firms. However, the web, and especially the social web, encourages direct transactions between individual consumers. eBay is the best known example for consumer-to-consumer market. Is it possible generate a customized "eBay for information" [4], an efficient marketplace for intangible, experience goods? Building a pricing mechanism which addresses subjective value in a dynamic ecosystem of a multitude of small transactions of experience goods seems ambitious but the current study may be one small step for future market development.

References

1. Ahituv, N.: Assessing the Value of Information: Problems and Approaches, pp. 314–325 (1989)
2. Becker, G.M., DeGroot, M.H., Marschak, J.: Measuring Utility by a Single-Response Sequential Method. Behavioral Science 9, 226–232 (1964)
3. Chang, W.L., Yuan, S.T.: An Overview of Information Goods Pricing. International Journal of Electronic Business 5, 294–314 (2007)
4. Dushnitsky, G., Klueter, T.: Is there an Ebay for Ideas? Insights from Online Knowledge Marketplaces. European Management Review 8, 17–32 (2011)
5. Hann, I., Terwiesch, C.: Measuring the Frictional Costs of Online Transactions: The Case of a Name-Your-Own-Price Channel. Management Science 49, 1563–1579 (2003)
6. Kim, J.Y., Natter, M., Spann, M.: Pay what You Want: A New Participative Pricing Mechanism. J. Market. 73, 44–58 (2009)
7. Linde, F., Stock, W.G.: Information markets: A strategic guideline for the I-commerce. De Gruyter Saur, Berlin (2011)
8. Nelson, P.: Information and Consumer Behavior. The Journal of Political Economy 78, 311–329 (1970)
9. Raban, D., Geifman, D.: A Theory Based Information Pricing System. In: MCIS 2011 Proceedings, paper 84 (2011)
10. Raban, D.R.: The Incentive Structure in an Online Information Market. Journal of the American Society for Information Science and Technology 59, 2284–2295 (2008)
11. Raban, D.R.: User-Centered Evaluation of Information: A Research Challenge. Internet Research 17, 306–322 (2007)
12. Raban, D.R., Rafaeli, S.: The Effect of Source Nature and Status on the Subjective Value of Information. Journal of the American Society for Information Science and Technology 57, 321–329 (2006)
13. Rafaeli, S., Raban, D.R.: Experimental Investigation of the Subjective Value of Information in Trading. Journal of the Association for Information Systems 4, 119–139 (2003)
14. Regner, T., Barria, J.A.: Do Consumers Pay Voluntarily? The Case of Online Music. Journal of Economic Behavior & Organization 71, 395–406 (2009)
15. Shampanier, K., Mazar, N., Ariely, D.: Zero as a Special Price: The True Value of Free Products. Marketing Science 26, 742 (2007)
16. Shapiro, C., Varian, H.R.: Information rules: A strategic guide to the network economy. Harvard Business School Press, Boston (1999)
17. Thaler, R.H.: Toward a Positive Theory of Consumer Choice. Journal of Economic Behavior and Organization 1, 39–60 (1980)
18. Van Alstyne, M.W.: A Proposal for Valuing Information and Instrumental Goods, pp. 328–345 (1999)

Capabilities and Challenges of Contemporary Service Based Monitoring Systems

Peteris Rudzajs, Marite Kirikova, and Renate Strazdina

Institute of Applied Computer Systems, Riga Technical University, Latvia
{peteris.rudzajs,marite.kirikova,renate.strazdina}@rtu.lv

Abstract. New technology developments have opened opportunities to obtain more data from more sources as well as to handle a larger variety of forms of data. This, in turn, raises the interest in data and information monitoring in different business and engineering contexts. Thus monitoring systems obtain the role of subsystems in contemporary information and knowledge systems. Taking into consideration the quest for agility of business and information systems, the flexibility offered by service systems motivates the consideration of service based monitoring systems. In this paper capabilities and challenges of service based monitoring systems are discussed by considering several issues of analysis.

Keywords: service system, monitoring, monitoring system, semi-structured data, unstructured data, media monitoring.

1 Introduction

The business need for agility requires information systems to be able to sense and analyze the environment of the business system as well as to be aware of the internal situation of the business and information systems. To fulfill this need different types of monitoring systems have to be incorporated inside information systems.

This paper presents a survey of more than 20 different monitoring systems [1–28]. The survey is limited to service based monitoring systems, i.e., monitoring systems that are internally organized as service systems [29–31]. The paper concerns business and application level services as the main constituents of a monitoring system without discussing the details of their architecture and configuration. In literature selection an attention is paid also to so-called media monitoring systems since they handle the highest variety of forms of input data and require advanced data processing facilities, such as natural language processing.

While a large number of research papers on monitoring systems are available, there is a lack of surveys on monitoring systems. The goal of this paper is to partly fill this gap. In the paper the research on service based monitoring systems is discussed in a structured manner by considering the purpose, aspects, and indicators of monitoring, the types of data sources, the internal organization of the monitoring systems, and the parties involved in monitoring data supply, handling, and use.

A. Kobyliński and A. Sobczak (Eds.): BIR 2013, LNBIP 158, pp. 278–289, 2013.

The paper is organized as follows: In Section 2 a motivation of analysis of monitoring systems is discussed. In Section 3 the frame of analysis is introduced and a general view on monitoring system capabilities presented. The results of the survey are discussed in Section 4. Brief conclusions are stated in Section 5.

2   Motivation

In this section we briefly introduce the basic concepts used in the paper and illustrate some of them with data obtained from several repositories of scientific papers.

Monitoring can be defined as a continuous function that obtains and uses data on specific indicators to provide the main stakeholders (human users, company, institution, and others) with indications illustrating the achievement of their objectives [32] (p.540). Effective decision making process is based on the high quality data that are analyzed in a specific period of time. An appropriate monitoring system can positively influence the decision making process by delivering data at the necessary level of detail and by providing the appropriate context for decision making. The choice of measurable indicators is another challenge that is not discussed in the paper. The word "monitoring" is popular in research papers available in such scientific repositories as SCOPUS, SpringerLink, ACM, etc. (Fig. 1).

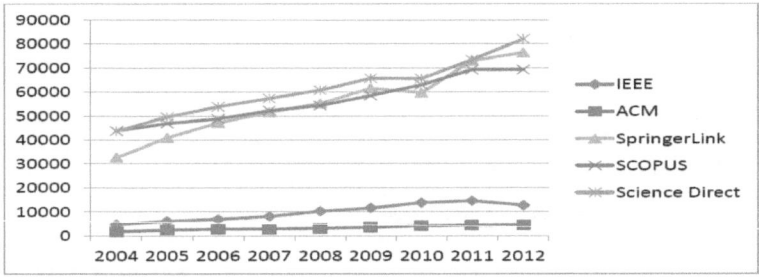

Fig. 1. The use of the word "monitoring" in the papers of IEEE, ACM, SpringerLink, SCOPUS, and Science Direct from year 2004 to year 2012

Fig. 1 shows that the word "monitoring", depending on the size and scope of the repository, features in about 500 to more than 80000 papers per year. Google Scholar shows a very high number of papers, which use the word "monitoring", during 2005 – 2009 (Fig. 2). The number gradually declines towards the number of papers in the repositories reflected in Fig. 1 from 2010 to 2012.

In particular repositories the number of papers featuring the word "monitoring" differs with respect to the research area. For instance, SCOPUS shows a considerable rise in the number of conference papers dealing with monitoring since 2005 in the area of Computer Science, while in other areas there is a small, mostly steady, growth of the number of papers (Fig. 3).

In Figure 3 only conference papers are taken into consideration. In case of all articles, e.g., concerning Computer Science, there are about 500-1500 more papers per year which does not change the tendency exposed by the conference papers. While Computer Science and Engineering prevail in SCOPUS, a different picture is seen in EBSCO (Fig. 4).

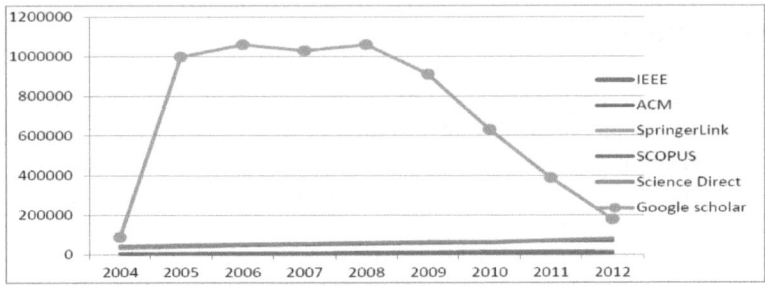

Fig. 2. The use of word "monitoring" in the papers of Google Scholar from year 2004 to year 2012

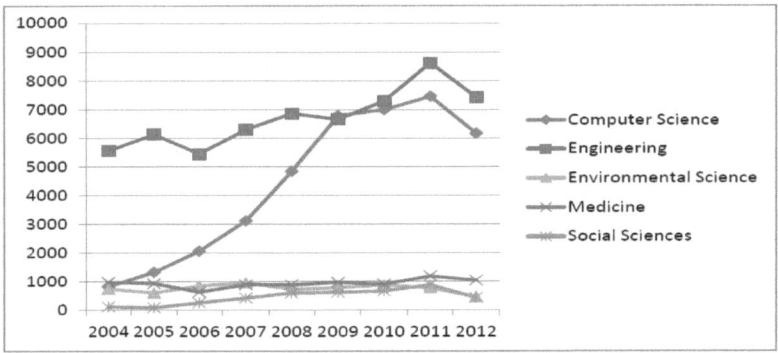

Fig. 3. The use of word "monitoring" in the conference papers of SCOPUS from year 2004 to year 2012

While the absolute number of papers differs per area and per scientific repository, the overall tendency of popularity of the word "monitoring" in scientific papers is obvious.

Taking into consideration that monitoring is a *function* there should be a system that performs it. Therefore a *monitoring system is the system that performs the monitoring function. Monitoring sub-functions such as data acquisition, data handling, and data provision can be considered as services that can be instantiated by various methods.* We consider the monitoring system as a work system: a system in which human participants and/or machines perform work (processes and activities) using information, technology and other resources to produce specific products/services for specific internal and/or external customers [33]. The number of papers that include the words "monitoring system" is shown in Fig. 5.

Comparing Fig. 5 to Fig. 1, we can see that monitoring systems are considered about seven times less than the monitoring per se. This gives the possibility to assume that the need for monitoring systems is still higher than the capacity of provided solutions. As was stated in the introduction, in this paper we focus on monitoring systems that are organized as service systems. *Services* are acts performed for someone else, including providing resources that someone else will use [30]. *A service system* is a work system that produces services for customers [30, 33]. The number of papers that may concern service based monitoring systems, i.e., use the word "service" together with "monitoring system", is considerably smaller than the number of papers that discuss monitoring systems per se (Fig.6). There are around 25% of papers that concern services in the context of monitoring systems (Fig. 6 vs. Fig. 5).

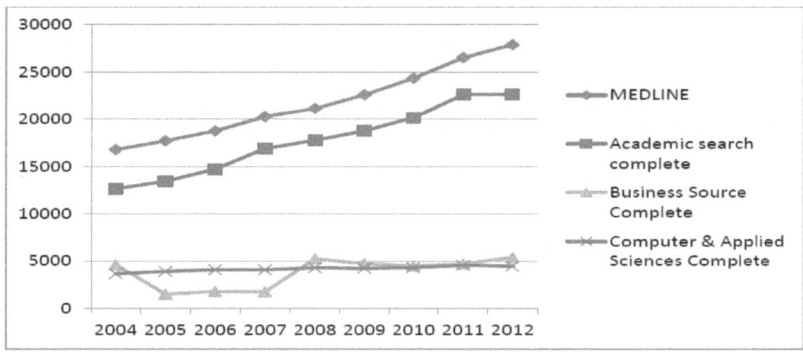

Fig. 4. The use of word "monitoring" in EBSCO academic journals from year 2004 to year 2012

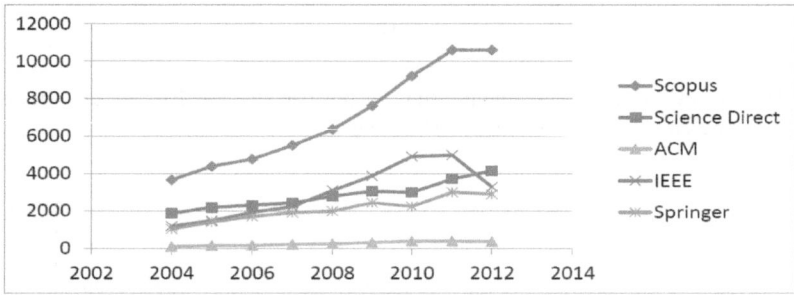

Fig. 5. The use of words "monitoring system" in the papers of IEEE, ACM, SpringerLink, SCOPUS, and Science Direct from year 2004 to year 2012

One of the hot issues in monitoring is a variety of data forms. A new branch of monitoring – so called media monitoring – embraces the highest variety of data forms (semi-structured and unstructured data from news, social media, radio & TV) requiring the use of advanced data processing. The growth in the number of papers in media monitoring is shown in Fig 7. There is not a considerable amount of papers that include the words "monitoring systems" and "media monitoring"; however, there is a number of papers where media monitoring is considered together with services (Fig. 8). The papers on monitoring considered in Sections 3 and 4 belong either to the selection "monitoring systems" and "services" (Fig. 6) or/and "media monitoring" and "services" (Fig. 8).

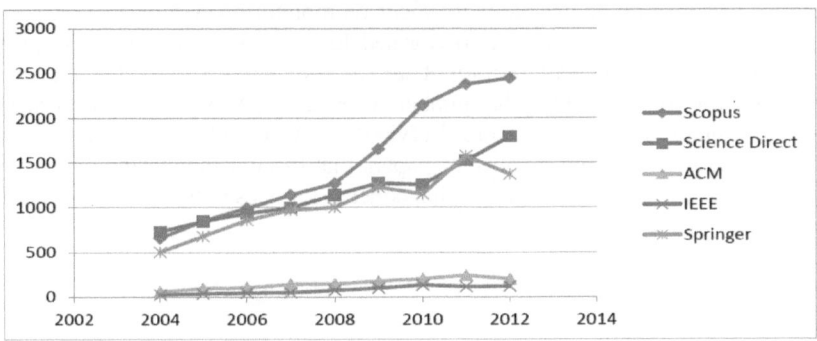

Fig. 6. The use of words "monitoring system" and "services" in the papers of IEEE, ACM, SpringerLink, SCOPUS, and Science Direct from year 2004 to year 2012

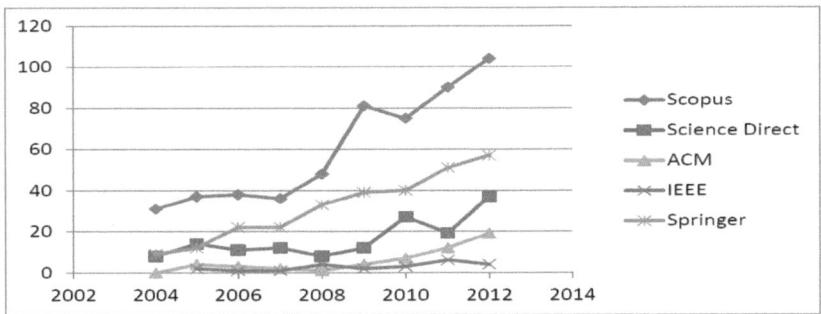

Fig. 7. The use of words "media monitoring" in the papers of IEEE, ACM, SpringerLink, SCOPUS, and Science Direct from year 2004 to year 2012

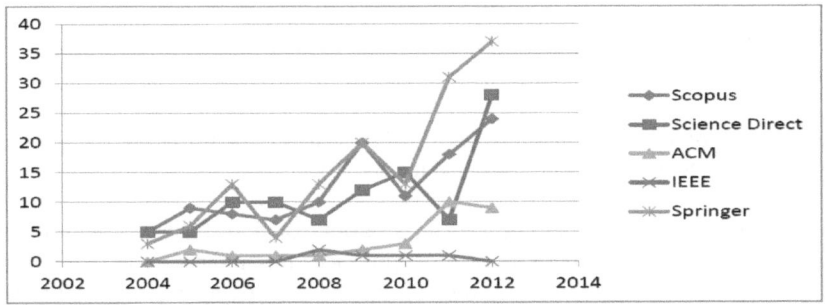

Fig. 8. The use of words "media monitoring" and "service" in the papers of IEEE, ACM, SpringerLink, SCOPUS, and Science Direct from year 2004 to year 2012

3   The Framework of Analysis

To understand the capabilities and challenges of contemporary monitoring systems we considered the following issues of monitoring system analysis:

- *Monitoring Object* (MO) showing the object of monitoring, e.g., business system, climate, technical system, etc.
- *Monitoring Aspects* (MA). This issue concerns the purpose of monitoring, chosen sources of data, and indicators.
- *Type of the Sensor,* where we distinguish between Physical Sensors (PS) and Virtual Sensors (VS) (more details are available, e.g., in [12]).
- *Data Source Format* (DSF) showing the variety of data forms that are used as inputs for monitoring function - these can be numerical data from sensors, data in databases, video files, etc. We specifically distinguish between two types of data, namely:
  - o   *Device or IT system generated data* (obtained from physical or virtual sensors and stored in structured files or databases)
  - o   *Human generated data*
- *Data Rigidity* (DR). This issue is about "machine friendliness" of the data. Here we distinguish between structured, semi-structured, and unstructured data. Usually devices and IT systems provide structured data and human generated data tends to be unstructured, while in some cases it is semi-structured, and in a few cases it is structured.
- *Internal Organization of the Monitoring System* (IOMS) that shows the building blocks and building principles utilized in the internal architecture of the monitoring system.
- *Monitoring Sub-functions* (MS) – basic activities included in the monitoring function, namely: *Data acquisition, Data handling,* and *Data provision.*
- *Monitoring Methods* (MM), i.e., the methods that are used in performing monitoring sub-functions.
- *Involved Agents* (IA) – the software devices, networks, human agents, roles, organizational units and other entities involved in monitoring sub-functions.

The above-presented issues are taken into consideration in the overview of the capabilities of contemporary service based monitoring systems presented in Fig. 9. We can see that the monitoring objects are from a high variety of domains such as IT resource monitoring [1, 15]; mechanical systems monitoring [25, 28]; environmental monitoring [10, 19, 20, 22, 24]; health monitoring [9, 21]; education monitoring [4, 23, 34]; media monitoring [2, 6–8, 11, 14, 16–20, 27]; and other areas such as business activities and process monitoring [3, 13, 26], etc. This lets us conclude that contemporary monitoring systems can be used literally in any area of human interest. This claim is backed by the fact that monitoring systems can handle structured, semi-structured and unstructured data obtained from different data sources, which hold data generated by artificial and human agents; and monitoring systems can handle data so that they can be used by both human and artificial agents.

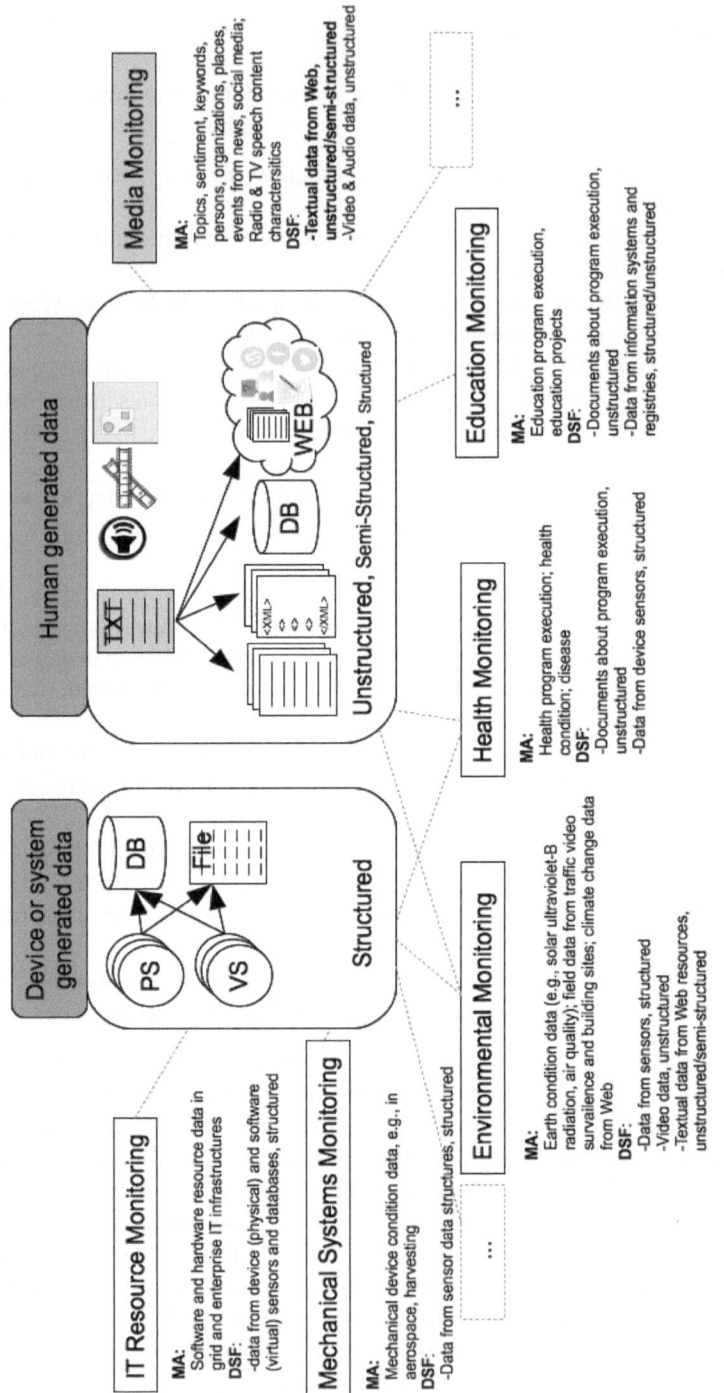

Fig. 9. Capabilities of contemporary service based monitoring systems (MA - Monitoring Aspect; DSF - Data Source Format + Structured/Semi-structured/Unstructured; PS - Physical Sensor; VS - Virtual Sensor)

4   Discussion

In this section, the capabilities and challenges of monitoring systems will be discussed in more detail according to the issues of analysis listed in the previous section. The issues are represented in the first column of Table 1. Some issues are thematically grouped together in one line of the table. In the second column the capabilities of the monitoring systems found in the scientific papers are partly listed. The challenges are discussed in the third column of the table. The lists of capabilities are a bit fuzzy as the papers do not always provide information directly according to all the issues of analysis listed in the previous section. Thus, the completeness of knowledge concerning current monitoring systems is itself one of the challenges in this area of research.

Table 1. Capabilities and challenges of monitoring systems

Issue	Capabilities	Challenges
MO	State of devices in aeronautics [28], state of the soil [24], state of the air [5]; climate changes [19, 20]; environment in construction [10], resources in forestry [25], social media in different areas [14, 16, 18, 27], such as news [8], TV and radio [17], websites and topics [2], crises [11], hotels [7], health programs [9]; state of health [21]; education [4, 23, 34]; business processes [3, 13, 26]; state of the traffic [22], IT systems and applications [25]; state of distributed systems (grids) [1].	While the spectrum of monitoring systems is wide, still the number of papers on monitoring (Fig. 1) is much higher than the number of papers on monitoring systems (Fig. 5), which lets us assume that there are areas not yet supported by monitoring systems.
MA, DSF, and DR	Signals from aeronautics devices [28], forestry devices [25], air condition measurement devices [5], healthcare devices [21], grid devices [1], wireless networks [10], servers and other IT devices [15]; level of UV radiance [24]; video and /or audio data [17, 22]; structured or semi-structured texts [4, 7, 11, 23]; unstructured texts [2, 6–8, 11, 14, 16, 18–20].	The variety of input data is high. Still, most of the challenges are in the area of acquisition of unstructured data, such as text.
PS and VS	Both physical, e.g., [28] and virtual, e.g., [3, 13, 26] sensors are used.	The notion and the types of sensors are rarely discussed. Data acquisition from virtual sensors and fusion of data obtained from different sensors is still a problem to be solved.
IOMS	Modules [28]; JDL fusion framework [28]; function oriented [24]; network of devices [5]; components [9, 22]; multi-agent architecture [22]; layers [1]; distributed computing [10]; mobile computing [25]; SOA [10, 27]; data warehouse [15]; data streaming [2, 8, 24]; portals [19, 20].	The IOMS is discussed from different viewpoints. This hinders comparison of the systems and solution propagation in scientific research.

Table 1. (*continued*)

Issue	Capabilities	Challenges
MS and MM	*Acquisition*: reading data from sensors [5, 9, 10, 21, 22, 24, 25, 28]; reading data from databases (warehouses) [9, 15, 21, 25, 28]; web crawling [19, 20]; data download, etc. [6, 7, 11, 14, 16–20, 27]. *Handling*: Data fusion [2, 6–8, 11, 14, 16–20, 22, 25, 27, 28]; case based reasoning; text analysis; information classification, information contextualization [5, 10, 19, 20, 22, 24]; change identification [15]; text cleansing, keywords based processing, sentiment analysis [7, 19, 20], metadata and semantic data generation [17], surveys, text annotation [18]; language processing and big data integration [14], text mining [11], speech recognition; etc. [2, 6–8, 11, 14, 16–20, 27]. *Provision*: mainly tailored user interfaces [15, 21, 25, 28] etc. or/and portals with search and browsing capabilities . [2, 6–9, 11, 14, 16–20, 27].	The variety of methods used for handling different types of data is high. However, not in all cases the methods used are reported. Even in fewer cases the methods for all three main sub-functions are described. Knowledge on the best combinations of methods in all three sub-functions depending on the internal architecture of the monitoring system is still missing in scientific literature.
IA	*Acquisition*: devices [1, 5, 10, 15, 22, 24, 25, 28], digital data sources [2, 6–8, 11, 14, 16–21, 27]; human agents [4, 9, 23]. *Handling*: human agents [4, 9, 23]. *Provision*: human agents in all cases.	The exact entities handling the data are scarcely discussed in the papers.

Table 1 shows that research in monitoring systems has considerable practical results (in terms of already existing and potential capabilities of monitoring systems). Nevertheless, there are still a number of challenges that are to be met in further research.

5   Conclusions

Monitoring is an important research issue that is discussed in several hundreds of papers yearly. In general, the number of scientific papers continues to grow (except of Google Scholar). In 2012 some data repositories show a small decline in the numbers of the papers; however it is too early to see whether this is the beginning of a permanent decline. The number of papers that concern monitoring systems is about seven times smaller than the number of papers that concern monitoring. This may be interpreted as insufficient amount of research in monitoring systems. Role of services in monitoring system is considered in about 25% of papers on monitoring systems. A small but fast-growing area in monitoring is so-called media monitoring that embraces the challenge of monitoring of unstructured information.

The following are the main capabilities of service based monitoring systems, in general:

- Wide range of application areas.
- Wide range of monitoring aspects.
- Possibility to acquire data from different types of sources.
- Possibility to handle structured, semi-structured, and unstructured data.
- Use of a large variety of components in internal architecture of monitoring systems.
- Wide range of methods supporting acquisition, handling and provision of monitoring data.
- Involvement of human and artificial agents in monitoring activities.

In line with the above-mentioned capabilities there are the following challenges in service based monitoring systems research:

- Incomplete information on current research on monitoring systems (in terms of analysis issues listed in Section 3).
- Much higher number of papers on monitoring than on monitoring systems (this fact may point to the possibility that some domains are not yet properly addressed by research on monitoring systems).
- Handling of semi-structured and unstructured data is still only partly supported.
- Physical and virtual sensors are not fully analyzed and discussed in the papers.
- Internal organization of monitoring systems is incompletely discussed in most of the work on monitoring systems which hinders the comparison of the systems.
- The methods' integration possibilities across the basic monitoring functions are not clearly understood yet.
- The entities handling the monitoring data are scarcely discussed in the papers on monitoring systems.

The papers for this survey were chosen with the purpose to reveal challenges in service based monitoring systems research. Special attention was paid to media monitoring as it reveals new challenges compared to other types of monitoring. This especially applies to the processing of monitoring data and its analysis using natural language processing methods.

While the survey presented in the paper cannot claim absolute completeness, it contributes to the understanding of capabilities and challenges of contemporary service based monitoring systems. It can also be helpful for grounding and positioning further research in the area of monitoring systems.

Acknowledgments. This work has been supported by the European Social Fund within the project "Support for the implementation of doctoral studies at Riga Technical University". It is also partly supported under the framework of the project "New ontology and model transformation driven information technologies and their applications" supported by the National Research program of Latvia in Materialsciences "Development of Novel Multifunctional Materials, Signal Processing and Information Technologies for Competitive Knowledge-Based Products".

References

1. Andreozzi, S., De Bortoli, N., Fantinel, S., Ghiselli, A., Rubini, G.L., Tortone, G., Vistoli, M.C., De Bortoli, N.: GridICE: a monitoring service for Grid systems. Future Generation Computer Systems 21, 559–571 (2005)
2. Best, C.: Web Mining for Open Source Intelligence. In: 2008 12th International Conference Information Visualisation, pp. 321–325 (2008)
3. Buytendijk, F., Flint, D.: How BAM can turn a business into a real-time enterprise. Gartner, AV-15 (2002)
4. Carrizo, L., Sauvageot, C., Bella, N.: Information tools for the preparation and monitoring of education plans (2003)
5. Choi, G., Choi, G.: Design of Service System Framework for Web-based Monitoring and Control of Indoor Air Quality (IAQ) in Subway Stations. In: New Trends in Information and Service Science, pp. 659–663. IEEE (2009)
6. Dai, Y., Kakkonen, T., Sutinen, E.: SoMEST: a model for detecting competitive intelligence from social media. In: Proceedings of the 15th International Academic MindTrek Conference: Envisioning Future Media Environments, MindTrek 2011, pp. 241–248 (2011)
7. Duan, W., Cao, Q., Yu, Y., Levy, S.: Mining Online User-Generated Content: Using Sentiment Analysis Technique to Study Hotel Service Quality. In: 2013 46th Hawaii International Conference on System Sciences, pp. 3119–3128 (2013)
8. Eiken, U.C., Liseth, A.T., Witschel, H.F., Richter, M., Biemann, C.: Ord i dag: Mining norwegian daily newswire. In: Salakoski, T., Ginter, F., Pyysalo, S., Pahikkala, T. (eds.) FinTAL 2006. LNCS (LNAI), vol. 4139, pp. 512–523. Springer, Heidelberg (2006)
9. Görgens, M., Kusek, J.Z.: Making Monitoring and Evaluation systems work: A Capacity Development Toolkit. The World Bank (2009)
10. Hsieh, Y.-M., Hung, Y.-C.: A scalable IT infrastructure for automated monitoring systems based on the distributed computing technique using simple object access protocol Webservices. Automation in Construction 18, 424–433 (2009)
11. Johansson, F., Brynielsson, J., Quijano, M.N.: Estimating Citizen Alertness in Crises Using Social Media Monitoring and Analysis. In: 2012 European Intelligence and Security Informatics Conference, pp. 189–196 (2012)
12. Kabadayi, S.: Pridgen, A., Julien, C.: Virtual Sensors: Abstracting Data from Physical Sensors. In: 2006 International Symposium on a World of Wireless, Mobile and Multimedia Networks (WoWMoM 2006), pp. 587–592 (2006)
13. Kang, B., Kim, D., Kang, S.-H.: Real-time business process monitoring method for prediction of abnormal termination using KNNI-based LOF prediction. Expert Systems with Applications 39, 6061–6068 (2012)
14. Kaschesky, M., Sobkowicz, P., Hernandez Lobato, J.M., Bouchard, G., Archambeau, C., Scharioth, N., Manchin, R., Gschwend, A., Riedl, R.: Bringing Representativeness into Social Media Monitoring and Analysis. In: 2013 46th Hawaii International Conference on System Sciences, pp. 2003–2012 (2013)
15. Krishnamurthy, B.: A Top Down Approach to Enterprise Monitoring Using Change Point Detection. In: 2012 Annual SRII Global Conference, pp. 859–862 (2012)
16. Mackay, H.: Information and the Transformation of Sociology: Interactivity and Social Media Monitoring. tripleC-Cognition, Communication, Co-operation 11, 117–126 (2012)
17. Neto, J., Meinedo, H., Viveiros, M.: A media monitoring solution. In: 2011 IEEE International Conference on Acoustics, Speech and Signal Processing (ICASSP), pp. 1813–1816. IEEE (2011)

18. Paris, C., Wan, S.: Listening to the community: social media monitoring tasks for improving government services. In: Extended Abstracts on Human Factors in Computing Systems, pp. 2095–2100 (2011)
19. Scharl, A., Weichselbraun, A.: An ontology-based architecture for tracking information across interactive electronic environments. In: Proceedings of the 39th Annual Hawaii International Conference on System Sciences (HICSS 2006), pp. 1–9 (2006)
20. Scharl, A., Hubmann-Haidvogel, A., Weichselbraun, A., Lang, H.-P., Sabou, M.: Media Watch on Climate Change – Visual Analytics for Aggregating and Managing Environmental Knowledge from Online Sources. In: 2013 46th Hawaii International Conference on System Sciences, pp. 955–964 (2013)
21. Schikhof, Y., Mulder, I., Choenni, S.: Who will watch (over) me? Humane monitoring in dementia care. International Journal of Human-Computer Studies 68, 410–422 (2010)
22. Vallejo, D.Ã., Albusac, J., Castro-Schez, J.J.J., Glez-Morcillo, C., Jiménez, L., Jime, L.: A multi-agent architecture for supporting distributed normality-based intelligent surveillance. Engineering Applications of Artificial Intelligence 24, 325–340 (2011)
23. Wagner, D., Day, B., James, T.: Monitoring and evaluation of ICT in education projects. In: A Handbook for Developing Countries. infoDev/World Bank, Washington, DC (2005)
24. Wang, X., Gao, W., Slusser, J.R.J.J.R., Davis, J., Olson, B., Janssen, S., Janson, G., Durham, B., Tree, R., Deike, R.: USDA UV-B monitoring system: An application of centralized architecture. Computers and Electronics in Agriculture 64, 326–332 (2008)
25. Westergren, U.H., Wennerholm, E.: Exploring Service System Resources: The Role of Technology. In: 2013 46th Hawaii International Conference on System Sciences, pp. 1317–1326 (2013)
26. Wetzstein, B., Danylevych, O., Leymann, F., Bitsaki, M., Nikolaou, C., Van Den Heuvel, W.-J., Papazoglou, M.P.: Towards Monitoring of Key Performance Indicators Across Partners in Service Networks. In: 1st Workshop on Monitoring Adaptation and Beyond MONA (2009), pp. 7–17. Springer, Heidelberg (2009)
27. Zhou, B., Jia, Y., Liu, C., Zhang, X.: A Distributed Text Mining System for Online Web Textual Data Analysis. In: 2010 International Conference on Cyber-Enabled Distributed Computing and Knowledge Discovery, vol. i, pp. 1–4 (2010)
28. Phillips, P., Diston, D.: A knowledge driven approach to aerospace condition monitoring. Knowledge-Based Systems 24, 915–927 (2011)
29. Spohrer, J., Maglio, P., Bailey, J., Gruhl, D.: Steps Toward a Science of Service Systems. Computer, 71–77 (2007)
30. Alter, S.: Challenges for Service Science. Journal of Information Technology Theory and Application 13, 22–37 (2012)
31. Erl, T.: SOA Principles of Service Design (The Prentice Hall Service-Oriented Computing Series from Thomas Erl). Prentice Hall PTR (2007)
32. United Nations: Toolkit to Combat Trafficking in Persons (2008)
33. Alter, S.: Work System Theory: Overview of Core Concepts, Extensions, and Challenges for the Future. Journal of the Association for Information Systems 14, 72–121 (2013)
34. Rudzajs, P.: Towards Automated Education Demand-Offer Information Monitoring: The System's Architecture. In: Niedrite, L., Strazdina, R., Wangler, B. (eds.) BIR 2011 Workshops. LNBIP, vol. 106, pp. 252–265. Springer, Heidelberg (2012)

Enterprise Utilizing Social Web

Ján Štofa[1], Peter Michalik[2], and Iveta Zolotová[3]

[1,2,3] Dept. of Cybernetics and Artificial Intelligence, Faculty of Electrical Engineering and Informatics, Technical University of Košice, Letná 9, 042 00 Košice, Slovak Republic
{jan.stofa,peter.michalik.2,iveta.zolotova}@tuke.sk

Abstract. This paper considers access to issues of enterprise related to the social web. Justifies the importance of this relationship and compares three ways of interaction. The paper looks on an employee as a risk factor threatening the security of the enterprise and deals options of monitoring and its monitoring instruments. Corporate marketing in relation to the social web can be deal by the support of opinion mining. The paper is an introduction to the security of company integrated in a social web.

Keywords: enterprise, social web, monitoring, corporate marketing, process modeling, security.

1   Introduction

In modern society social networks are incorporated quite naturally. They have become an indispensable part of life for all people. This process of globalization has many controversial issues that have a negative impact on many lives of individuals, philosophy of businesses and ideologies. Social networks represent a huge database. It contains centralized personal information often previously confidential and secret. This globalization causes deanonymization (misidentification) and reduced alertness of users, their mass behavior and uncontrolled sharing personal life. This increases the possibility of access of third part to information of users. Known and unknown forms of attacks become more common because people literally craving for information that could be used to their advantage. It does not look any more at morality and violates the right to privacy more and more.

21st century bring unprecedented opportunities for businesses, how to expand, enhance and promote own business. One such option is the promotion of business through social networking [3]. Small and medium enterprises start to think more and more about establishing a corporate profile on social networks. It is a new level of communication with clients, which takes place based on natural curiosity, spontaneity and directness. Potential customers from social networks are no longer anonymous visitors of corporate web site. They have a name, picture, clearly defined interests, you know about them from where they are, how old they are and so on. Thanks to social networking entrepreneur can easily reach narrowly defined target group, or large masses [4]. Statistics and numbers in relation to social networks and especially Facebook are changing from day to day.

A. Kobyliński and A. Sobczak (Eds.): BIR 2013, LNBIP 158, pp. 290–297, 2013.
© Springer-Verlag Berlin Heidelberg 2013

More important, however, are strategies that are linked with this social network. How to set up a profile, who would be responsible to create an account on Facebook, how to change your URL for Facebook pages, how to upload to Facebook photo album or video online, what "hang" on-line and what rather not, it is important knowledge that should be known by entrepreneur relative to social networks [6].

2   Interaction of Enterprise and Social Web

Interaction of enterprise and social web can be viewed from several perspectives. The first aspect treats the issue of monitoring activities of its own employees in the social web. The second and third aspect treats positive use of social networking to themselves advantage. We mean corporate marketing and personal management in the selection of potential employees. All three mentioned aspects of interaction with enterprise and social web can be developed into processes. Currently for the developing of processes are many variety of modeling tools. These processes should reflect activity of employees and direct enterprise activities in relation to them. Newly created process by using business process modeling tools could facilitate the effective use of strategy of business management and its security components [7].

2.1   Monitoring of Employees' Activities on Social Networks

One of the results of the above mentioned survey conducted by CISCO [2] spoke about frustration of employees by using various workstations and applications. These include restrictions imposed by IT managers on technology cooperation: the lack of integration between applications, incompatible formats (video, data, and voice), restricted range of available instruments of cooperation. More than half of IT managers indicated that inside their company is forbidden to use social networking applications. In some cases, employees take control into their own hands - half of respondents reported that they use prohibited applications once a week. More than half of organizations do not allow the use of social networks or similar applications at work [2].

2.1.1   Monitoring Tools
From the perspective of IT infrastructure are interesting monitoring tools, which do not pursue primarily work ethic, but provide information on the use of systems and software applications in the enterprise. Their aim is to detect the intensity of the work users with monitored systems and applications. Consequently, it is possible to optimize the portfolio of hardware and the number of software licenses [8]. On the market there is several monitoring software. Each software is specific by its features that make it possible to compare and evaluate one another. Studied were the criteria's of this monitoring software: SONAR, Spector CNE Investigator, Spytech NetVizor, SA EAM, Net Spy Pro, Work Examiner Standard, OsMonitor REFOG Employee Monitor, Activity, Monitor StaffCop [9].

Following chart represents results achieved scoreboard of analyzed monitoring software (Fig.1).

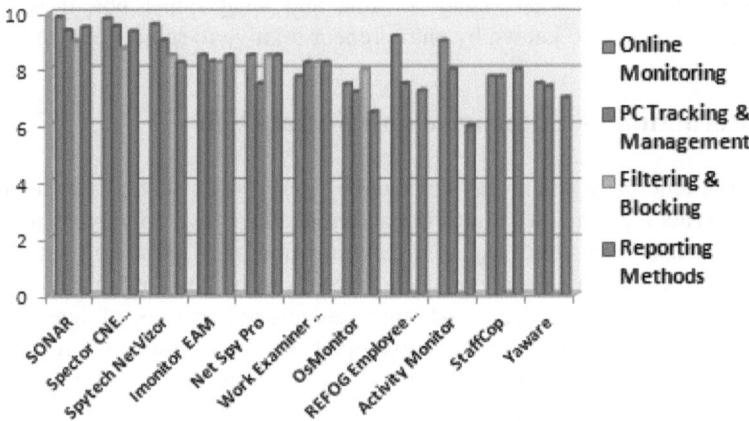

Fig. 1. Scoreboard of analyzed monitoring software [9]

For illustration we show the principle of operation of monitoring software:

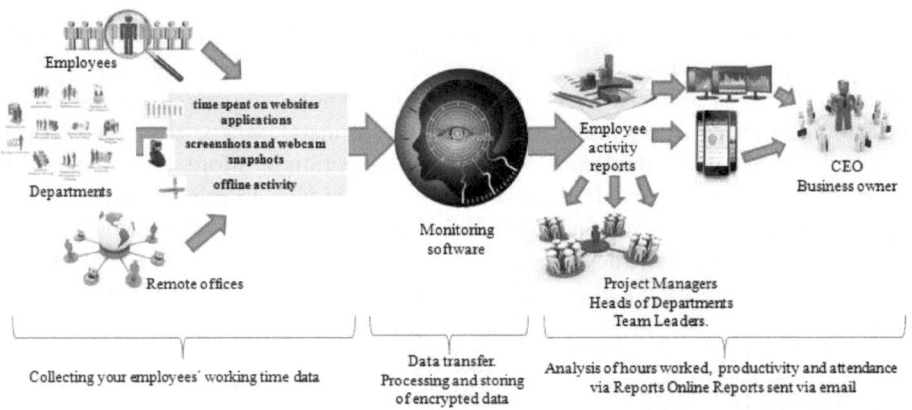

Fig. 2. Principle of operation of monitoring software

Monitoring of employee activity by employer becomes highly debated issue especially for current rapid development of ICT [10]. On one hand stand the employer and its efforts to ensure a smooth and trouble-free operation of the enterprise, so that employees make effective use of your working time and work entrusted funds. On the other hand stand employees seeking to exercise their right to privacy. This discrepancy is partly solved by the Labour Code, which in its regulations define rights and obligations of employers to their employees [11].

The current leader in the forms of exploitation of working hours are mainly tools for instant messaging such as Skype and social networks represented by the particular network Facebook. There are methods called social engineering which through using contacts to specific individuals can elicit sensitive information and passwords. Another risk is caused by employee through his negligence during manipulation with specific assets of enterprise. Reckless activity of employee or intentional threat can cause violation of security of particular enterprise.

Also in this respect we can observe effort of employers to monitor their employees' work activities. Use of outcomes from monitoring tools can help to enterprises in finding cases of failure of one of the employees. Task of monitoring software is to monitor in detail all activities of users of specific computers. In this way it is possible to monitor and evaluate the behavior of the employees on the internet or other communication channels [12].

Recorded information and data can then be viewed or replayed whenever necessary. Based on the information gathered the enterprise is able to develop a detailed analysis. Based on them create different models of processes involving rules of employee behavior on the internet and communication channels.

2.2   Personal Management

In Slovakia, companies look for their new employees in classic way. But for professional "hunters of drain" social networks are first choice how to look for managers [13]. This trend of how to search for new job candidate through social networking is slowly accepted also between our recruiters (HR). Recruitment of potential employees is done through social networks as LinkedIn and Twitter.

On the market appeared a new system of employee evaluation activity. It is basically system that measures Klout score [14] - human activity on social networks. The Klout score can also influence how people will accept for employment. More the person is active in a social network, the higher number on the scale from 1 to 100 can be achieved. So thanks that the man becomes more interesting for the specific company [15]. Behavior and communication style are the most watched aspects of the social networks [16].

2.3   Corporate Marketing

Another positive view of the interaction between enterprise and social networking is usage this opportunity for corporate marketing. Many companies use monitoring discussions about their products and brand in the forum on one of the social networks. Monitoring represents effective tool that helps companies to make an immediate idea in what are people currently interested in. Thanks that the enterprise is able to respond rapidly to customer needs. Enterprise gains rapid feedback, as well as information about competitors. With the issue of obtaining information from social networks it deals classification of opinions (opinion mining, sentiment classification, sentiment analysis).

Opinion mining is a tool designed to identify opinion of an individual contributor or web discussion as a whole, to a certain topic. For this marketing monitoring of online communication has more weight concrete opinion, attitude than a specific author of opinion. Problem that is met in opinion mining is to determine the subjectivity, orientation (polarity) of words and the force of orientation [17].

Effective tool for opinion mining are weighting techniques [18]. For market monitoring seems to be the most effective weighting technique that works on the principle of user relevance when searching in the text. It consists of two parts [19]:

1. TF part, expresses how often the term occurs in the reference document from any database.

$$tf_{i,j} = \frac{n_{i,j}}{\sum_k n_{k,j}} \tag{1}$$

Where $n_{i,j}$ is the number of occurrences of words in a document d_j. Denominator represents the total number of all words in the document d_j, t_j and its length.

2. IDF part, represents the "importance" of the word.

$$idf_i = \log \frac{|D|}{\left|\{j : t_i \in d_j\}\right|} \tag{2}$$

Where $|D|$ is the database size of documents, so the number of documents in which we look for and $\left|\{j : t_i \in d_j\}\right|$ is the number of documents that contain the word i.

The use of this technique makes sense in view of the targeted searches of contributions containing keywords [20]. The social web [21] becomes the most critical marketing environment, because it will become a primary center for most online activities - communication, training, gathering information, shopping, planning, consultancy, etc. [22].

3   Modeling of Security Enterprise Integrated in the Social Web

Social Networking is a new part of life for many people and organizations. From the perspective of security is important to get them under control. Checking the work based on determination of borders and rules would specifically protect anonymity of individuals, their privacy and security. To achieve this goal it is necessary to carry out intensive research. It is important collected information (about networks of communication, what time, with who, about what is communication...) directly from users of various portals.

During our previous research [1] was shown that people neglect or ignore security and privacy of themselves. From the perspective of authors seem to be interesting and useful two solutions - two different approaches to the problem of security of social networks.

On the one hand, this research can be built on previous findings and try to analyze them on the basis of observations of exploitation of the social network to specific users [23]. This means follow these ways: log in, use of applications, use of databases, communication encryption and identification of communication actors, data transmission, search target groups and attacks on software and network resources [24]. On the other hand, it opens the possibility to monitor the communication between actors of social web and specifically focus on pre-defined keywords, which represent threat, as well as the frequency of their occurrence in normal network communications. Through that could be possible to increase the security of any users of different web portals.

Methods and tools for modeling business processes can be functionally used in the modeling of enterprise security as one of the most important strategy business management. If the process of business management wants to be successful, the enterprise cannot forget to threats and direct attacks on its security. It is necessary to pay sufficient attention to the security aspect. Only slightly more than half of surveyed companies have established risk and crisis management in company according to the survey conducted by [25].

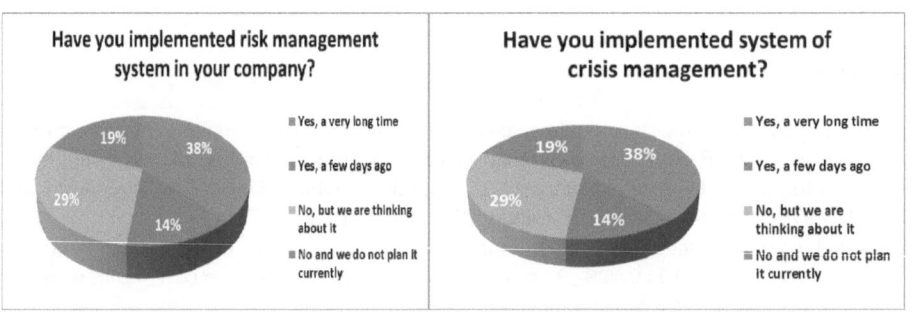

Fig. 3. Results of survey on risk and crisis management in industrial enterprise in Slovakia

Currently in companies is as a new „*helper*" social web, which entails a number of specific security solutions. One of the ways how can enterprises successfully prevent threats and risks arising from the contemporary phenomenon is to apply a process approach also to the level of security management. To apply the process approach to the issue of security management of enterprise we view from our perspective as a highly effective way of dealing with security - prevent threats and risks. It is the place to talk about detection already started up direct or mediated threats to enterprise. There is also possible to count on a process approach solution.

Number of potential threats and risks can be predicted. Although sometimes it is not possible to create a model whose implementation would automatically prevent any threat, there is still a chance to model the process of solving specifically problem, and therefore have a backup method of getting things resolved quickly and thereby avoid chaining attacks, or leakage of personal data and so on.

4   Conclusion

The issue of mutual interaction between the enterprise and the social web is uncharted areas of strategy of business management. With regard to process modeling becomes currently crucial for solving problem of security by using process modeling of relationships between enterprise and virtual world [1]. By integrating process modeling into business management is possible to solve a number of new problem areas arising from ICT progress. Important is to monitor the relationship of social networking with enterprise environments. It is necessary to confront with overall security of enterprise.

Concept security we reasonably elevated to a significant place in the strategy of business management. This issue should be further developed by using analysis of existing models of security evaluation and subsequent modification of the reference model of enterprise security. This reference model of enterprise security is considered as a part of the Security project created for a specific company. Its formation will be in intentions of capturing the behavior of an enterprise during communication with the virtual world.

Acknowledgements. This work presented in this paper was supported by KEGA, under Grant No. 021TUKE-4/2012.

References

1. Štofa, J., et al.: Process modeling as a supporting tool for managing of the enterprise security. In: IEEE 10th Jubilee International Symposium on Applied Machine Intelligence and Informatics, Herľany, January 29-28, pp. 63–67. Óbuda University, Budapest (2012) ISBN 978-1-4577-0195-5, IEEE Catalog Number: CFP1208E-CDR
2. Social networks under control of employees, http://www.cisco.com/web/SK/news/archive/2010/TS_Socialne_siete_pod_kontrolou_zamestnancov_100413.html (cit. November 15, 2011)
3. Social Media Marketing: The Next Generation, http://www.forbes.com/sites/capitalonespark/2012/12/14/social-media-marketing-the-next-generation/ (cit. January 10, 2013)
4. Social media marketing industry report 2012 - how marketers are using SM to grow their businesses, http://www.socialmediaexaminer.com/SocialMediaMarketingIndustryReport2012.pdf (cit. Januray 10, 2013)
5. Facebook Statistics by Country, http://www.socialbakers.com/facebook-statistics/ (cit. January 10, 2013)
6. Entrepreneur on the Internet - Part 1: Company and social networks, http://www.podnikajte.sk/prevadzka-firmy/c/376/category/internet-v-podnikani/article/firma-socialne-siete.xhtml (cit. January 10, 2013)
7. Keeping pace with social media in the workplace, http://www.dlapipershifting landscapes.com/focus/social-media-workplace/ (cit. November 15, 2012)
8. Do you know what your employees do on the web? http://www.itnews.sk/spravy/internet/2012-08-06/c150356-viete-co-robia-zamestnanci-na-webe (cit. November 15, 2012)

9. Monitoring Employee Software Comparisons and Reviews 2013 (2013), `http://`
   `employee-monitoring-software-review.toptenreviews.com/`
10. Workplace Privacy and Employee Monitoring, `https://www.privacyrights.org`
    `/fs/fs7-work.htm` (cit. December 19, 2012)
11. Monitoring of employees by their employer, `http://www.elaw.cz/cs/`
    `pracovni-pravo/739-monitorovanie-zamestnancov-`
    `zamestnavatelom.html` (cit January 10, 2013)
12. Computer Monitoring: Monitoring software for computer monitoring and Internet security,
    `http://pcfix.sk/monitorovanie_bezpecnost_internet_zrychlenie`
    `_servis_pc_programy_download_na_stiahnutie?page=3` (cit. January 10,
    2013)
13. Jobs, `http://www.nytimes.com/2009/05/31/jobs/31recruit.html?_r`
    `=0` (cit. November 20, 2012)
14. Klout, `http://klout.com/home` (cit. November 15, 2012)
15. New phenomenon in the labor market: Klout score increases preferences,
    `http://karierainfo.zoznam.sk/cl/1000160/1327442/Novy-`
    `fenomen-na-trhu-prace-Klout-skore-zvysuje-preferencie` (cit.
    January 10, 2013)
16. Your employer can see your behavior on social networks, `http://www.webmagazin.`
    `sk/biznis/zamestnavatel-si-vie-vystriehnut-vas/84-`
    `clanok.html` (cit. January 7, 2013)
17. Machová, K.: Opinion Analysis from the Social Web Contributions. In: Jędrzejowicz, P.,
    Nguyen, N.T., Hoang, K. (eds.) ICCCI 2011, Part I. LNCS, vol. 6922, pp. 356–365. Springer,
    Heidelberg (2011), Top 10 algorithms in data mining, `http://www.cs.`
    `uvm.edu/~icdm/algorithms/10Algorithms-08.pdf` (cit. January 10, 2013)
18. A study of Information Retrieval weighting schemes for sentiment analysis, `http://`
    `delivery.acm.org/10.1145/1860000/1858822/p1386paltoglou.pdf?`
    `ip=88.212.37.32&acc=OPEN&CFID=264798631&CFTOKEN=93701162&__a`
    `cm__=1359193969_fd4db39c204a3024eccb58517850f23f` (cit. January 5,
    2013)
19. An improved TF-IDF approach for text classification, `http://www.researchgate`
    `.net/publication/225590019_An_improved_TF-`
    `IDF_approach_for_text_classification` (cit. November 15, 2011)
20. Term-weighting approaches in automatic text retrieval, `http://www.cs.odu.edu/~`
    `jbollen/IR04/readings/article1-29-03.pdf` (cit. January 10, 2013)
21. List of social networking websites, `http://en.wikipedia.org/wiki/`
    `List_of_social_networking_websites` (cit. December 15, 2012)
22. The Social Web: Research and Opportunities, `http://www-users.cs.umn.edu/`
    `~echi/papers/2008-IEEE-Computer/socialweb-research.pdf/` (cit.
    January 10, 2013)
23. Stašák, J.: Modeling of business processes with the use of ARIS. Vydavateľstvo Ekonóm,
    Bratislava (2010) ISBN 978-80-225-2971-6
24. Túma, M.: School of practical Marketing. Žilina: SEPI, 1999 a nakladatelství Computer
    Press, a.s. (2006) ISBN 80-251-1200-4
25. Results of survey on risk and crisis management in industrial enterprise in Slovakia,
    `http://www.risk-management.cz/index.php?cat2=1&clanek=1021`
    (cit. May 10, 2013)

Towards Forecasting Demand and Production of Electric Energy in Smart Grids

Agata Filipowska[1], Karol Fabisz[1], Tymoteusz Mateusz Hossa[1],
Michał Mucha[1] and Radosław Hofman[2]

[1] Faculty of Informatics and Electronic Economy, Poznan University of Economics,
Poznan 61-875, Poland
[2] Future Energy Sp. z o.o., ul. 28 czerwca 1956 r. 123/20, 61-544 Poznań, Poland
http://www.kie.ue.poznan.pl, http://www.future-energy.com.pl

Abstract. Recently, the electric energy market undergoes serious changes which impact its future structure. They include also an emergence of smart grid encompassing prosumers, being individual market participants that not only consume, but also produce the electric energy. This imposes a need for a new class of tools (and methods) that will support all market players.

The article presents a solution for managing the energy consumption and production in microgrids. We present challenges of managing such networks as well as functionalities of a system, that enables for e.g. preparation of forecasts, tracing the energy consumption or creation of recommendations for the microgrid prosumers, in order to deal with these challenges.

Keywords: smartgrid, energy management systems, prosumer, energy production, energy consumption.

1 Introduction

Within the last few years, one may notice a rapid changes within many fields of the energy sector. The shift from perceiving electricity as a public good to understanding it as a commodity, which in Europe formally began in Great Britain in 1989 with the revamped Electricity Act [1], continues to advance and spread to other countries [2].

On the other hand, an eco-trend may be observed. This concerns also establishing of international electric energy and greenhouse gas emission certificates' exchange platforms. A political push for environmentally friendly economy resulted in many large renewable energy generation projects, as well as distributed installation of micro-installations in many West and Central European countries, including Germany, Spain, the UK and Czech Republic. For instance in Germany the capacity of energy generation from solar photovoltaic plants has grown from 76 MWp in the year 2000 to over 32 000 MWp in 2012, with an average yearly growth of over 74% [3].

A. Kobyliński and A. Sobczak (Eds.): BIR 2013, LNBIP 158, pp. 298–314, 2013.
© Springer-Verlag Berlin Heidelberg 2013

This caused the emergence of a new class of energy market participants, namely prosumers. Examples include a household fitted with PV panels or a farmhouse equipped with a wind turbine. Since they both produce and consume electric energy, prosumers need to trade energy with the grid in case of both surplus and shortage of the energy.

However, the most significant advancement of all is probably the trend towards the installation of smart metering infrastructures (including the EC activities in this area), which allow for a two-way communication with the meters and automated, remote gathering of real-time energy consumption and production data (what is also a technical challenge with regard to the amount of data).

The future of electric energy market comprises the distributed electricity generation, extensive usage of renewable energy sources, facilitating local energy exchange within quasi-independent microgrids, very efficient load balancing using advanced prediction and energy flow management systems, all set in a legal framework enabling real-time market-determined pricing or dynamic tariffs. Also more accurate balance (long-term effect of management) will reduce the demand for energy, because even today 30% of electricity is lost due to lack of energy balance [10].

Realizing the abovementioned vision, requires a system that may:

- communicate with the smart metering infrastructure, in order to gather data and send commands,
- analyse the data to produce meaningful insights regarding market participants and ways in which they use electricity,
- predict supply (from renewable sources) and demand on the electric energy market,
- facilitate transactions and pricing,
- raise awareness about the energy consumption among users.

This publication examines the problem of designing such a system and presents a proprietary solution developed within the Future Energy Management System project[1].

The paper is structured as follows. Section 2 identifies challenges related to management of energy production and consumption in the smart grid. Section 3 presents the system developed to address these challenges. Section 4 provides description of the related work, showing the insights into the field of the smart grid management systems. The paper is summarised in the conclusions section, that presents the main points of the article.

---

[1] The research results described within the article were achieved within the project: Building a prototype of an innovative system for forecasting the level of consumption and production of electric energy "Future Energy Management System", (Project: UDA-POIG.01.04.00-30-065/10-03, Value: 9.957.022 zł, UE contribution: 5.647.005 zł, period 01.07.2011-31.03.2013), European Funds – for the development of innovative economy (Fundusze Europejskie - dla rozwoju innowacyjnej gospodarki).

2   Management of Microgrids: Challenges

2.1   Definition of the Microgrid

The microgrid is a set of related energy sources, energy consumers and, in some cases, energy storage devices [11]. Each microgrid is connected to the main energy grid, but it should be self-sufficient and work without taking the energy from main electricity grid. The typical microgrid consist of the following elements [12]:

- sources of distributed generation (from renewable sources),
- power inverters,
- control systems,
- connections with the main grid,
- energy storage devices,
- energy consumer devices.

The typical energy sources of distributed generation encompass: biomass energy, geothermal energy, hydropower, ocean energy, wind power and solar photovoltaics [13]. The energy generated from these sources, for example from photovoltaics, must be converted from DC to AC, by using the power inverters. To manage the production and consumption of energy, the microgrid requires an advanced control system to optimize dispatch of energy and to provide load balancing in the microgrid network [14].

The microgrid according to its definition is self-sufficient, but usually it's connected to the main electrical grid, in order to assure a better load balancing in the macrogrid [20]. In microgrids, the energy storage devices are rarely used, because of low efficiency of energy storage technologies. The batteries are used in bungling microgrids, but with an increase in popularity of electric cars, it may end up with using these cars as battery storage devices [15].

The microgrid using the novel smart metering infrastructure is being referred to as smart grid. The rest of the paper, uses these notions as synonims.

Another important concept for the domain of distributed power generation is a prosumer. The prosumers are "professional consumers" or "producer consumers" of electric energy, being in fact also more aware consumers. Referring to the Act on Renewable Energy Sources, a prosumer is a "producer of electricity in micro-installations that is used for his own consumption or for sale (...)" [16].

2.2   Challenges for Microgrids

The microgrids bring a lot of new challenges not known or not so much problematic in the large, typical power grids. Balancing supply and demand in microgrids is much more sophisticated, than in the large grids, mainly because of the law of large numbers, that implies that an average demand of a large number of consumers should be close to expected value [24]. In microgrids, the number of consumers is not always sufficient to expect that the law of large numbers works and therefore, the demand or production forecast may be significantly biased [21].

The load balancing is also more difficult in microgrids in comparison with the typical energy grid. The generation of electricity from for e.g. photovoltaics panels and wind turbines is less predictable [17], than e.g. from the fossil fuel. The efficiency of the renewable energy sources often depends on weather conditions, for example, solar and wind power. The systems for management of smartgrids are therefore forced to make predictions on the basis of weather forecasts, what may additionally increase the forecasts' error [18].

Another challenge, concerns explotation of many advanced technologies to manage and control the network. This factor together with the underdeveloped energy infrastructure often requires a large amount of money from investors [23].

The emergence of microgrids also creates a different structure of the energy network - highly decentralized. The concerns arise, if such a market will be able to act not in the laboratory conditions, but in the real world. The consumers are concerned with the price shocks and power blackouts, experts discuss the minimum legal regulatory level [22]. Another often overlooked challenge is the security of the microgrid (also with regard to personal data from the smart meters). The microgrids should be protected against the data leakage and cypher attacks, which can stop production or even destroy the power stations [19].

2.3   Requirements for the System for the Microgrid Management

The system addressing challenges identified in Section 2.2, that will be able to control and manage the microgrid, should be developed taking into account the following functional requirements:

- generate production and demand forecasts, with the lowest possible error,
- acquire data to improve the forecast models e.g. weather factors data, detailed prosumer data,
- enable management of prosumers, e.g. offerings, recommendations, the overview of energy production/usage,
- support the technical performance management and manage the flow of energy within the microgrid,
- support energy exchange of the microgrid with the macrogrid and manage the energy flow between these grids,
- support communication standards between devices in the microgrid, and between micro and macrogrid, what especially concerns acquisition of data from smart meters,
- support the security standards,
- enable for compliance with the legal requirements (national and European).

The most important feature of the system, from the economical point of view, is generation of low-error forecasts of energy demand, because the bigger the error, the greater the costs associated with the purchase of energy on the market (in the short term). Also, a accurate forecast of energy production in the microgrid is quite important. The knowledge of how much energy we are able to produce and comparing it to the forecasted demand, shows us how much energy we need to buy from the macrogrid, or how much energy we are able to sell [16].

The microgrid management system should also include a module to manage prosumers, in order that collected energy consumption data and detailed data on prosumers, are used also for the advantage of the prosumer. For example a prosumers should be able to list their electrical devices and their usage patterns. Also, the prosumer should be able to describe the specifics of his home, for e.g. type of home insulation (heat losses) or type of home lighting. The main reason for collecting this type of data is generation of forecasts of good quality (even for an individual). Lastly prosumers should provide data about their geographical location, which will allow to match the weather data. Thats why besides of collecting the data on prosumers, it is important to gather data on weather factors which may be useful in generating the energy production predictions.

Another requirement is to provide such a system with specialized mechanisms, which will manage the energy flow, changes in the energy production level like power or voltage, communication with macrogrid in case of excess or deficiency of microgrid production, etc. This kind of system should implement the communication standards between all devices in the microgrid, and between the micro and the macrogrid.

The most discussed issue, is the support of security standards. The microgrid should be protected from outside or internal attacks, which can be devastating to the network stability. In addition to the physical damage of devices, the cyber attacks may aim at the acquisition of users' private data, or data about the operation of the network itself. The security it also essential to meet the legal requirements of setting up a microgrid.

2.4   Scientific and Economical Challenges

The creation of a microgrid management system brings also a number of scientific and economical challenges.

As it was mentioned in Section 2.3, the forecast error is related to costs in monetary terms. If we overestimate the amount of energy needed by the microgrid, we will need to sell the extra energy to the main grid on low prices. On the other hand, if we underestimate the amount of energy, we will need to buy the difference on the high prices (in short term the energy is more expensive than in the longer horizon). The more accurate forecast, the lower costs of acquiring the electric energy (if needed) or higher income from the production.

Forecasting the consumption for small amount of prosumers is also a challenge, mainly because of the large diversity of the power consumption profiles (and the level of uncertainity). For example, for a group of 4-5 prosumers, their consumption is nearly random. Fortunately, with the rising number of prosumers in the microgrid, the forecast error decreases according to the law of large numbers. For example, for a group of 10 prosumers, the forecast error will be on an acceptable level and for a group of 100 prosumers some methods like a linear regression will give an average forecast error at a level of 2-3%. The chance for improvement of forecasting accuracy for small microgrids, is related to obtaining additional information e.g. on habits or appliances the prosumer possess.

One of the biggest problems in the management of microgrids is that the system needs to react to changes in the environment in the real time. This also concerns the accuracy of forecasts that are essential for planning, so that changes made during the system's functioning are as small as possible. Of course, one has to take into account also many periodic fluctuations like day fluctuations, week fluctuations, month fluctuations and seasons fluctuations. That is why, a microgrid management system, should collect additional data about the prosumer from external sources and use this data to provide more accurate forecast.

3   The Concept of a Microgrid Energy Management System

3.1   Market and Legal Background

The Market Potential: from the economical point of view, the potential of microgrids is worth billions of dollars [26]. This estimation takes into account a vast number of interconnected electricity users (households, business clients, etc.), their electricity consumption and value of physical infrastructure (transmission upgrades, automation of substations and distribution, smart grid IT and smart meters) [32]. The annual investment in all kind of RES solutions will rise about four times between now and 2030 [36], from 33$ billion annually in 2012 to 73$ billion by the end of 2020, with 494$ billion in cumulative revenue over that period [35]. Therefore, there will appear a need for designing a new kind of systems. It is expected, that in the next five years, energy operators will expand their investments in home and load management systems and storage technologies [33,25].

In Europe, the microgrid technologies' market is yet underdeveloped, but it is growing rapidly [34]. There are many successful deployments of smart meters and AMI infrastructures in the Western Europe countries (UK, Germany, Spain), but now, the markets of the biggest potential are the ones located in the Central and Eastern Europe (Poland, Slovenia, Slovakia, Czech Republic, Bulgaria) [27]. The value of investment in smart meters in the aforementioned region will reach about 10.3$ billion by 2023 [29]. In other emerging markets from Eurasia, Latin America, Middle East/North Africa, South Africa and South-east Asia, smart meter and AMI infrastructures' market will be worth circa 56$ billion by 2022 [31]. Moreover, the North America Utilities are about to spend over 570$ million by 2016 on home energy management solutions (pilot programs and test deployments) [33]. Even the Brazil, is expected to spend over 27$ billion on total smart grid investments by 2022 [28].

European Regulations: from the legal point of view, all European countries must adopt the EU Renewable Energy Directive, known as "The EU climate and energy 20–20–20 package", until 2020. It is an ambitious plan, that represents an integrated approach to climate and energy policy: reducing green–house gas emissions, achieving sustainable development and ensuring the energy security.

In the context of smart grids, the legislative package includes directives on the promotion of the use of energy from renewable sources. Moreover, the member states have established national targets for raising the share of RES in their energy consumption (e.g. 10% in Malta, 50% in Sweden) to reach an overall 20% renewables goal in EU [37,38,39].

According to the latest multi–annual EU financial framework for the period 2014–2020, the EC decided to propose the creation of a new instrument called "Connecting Europe Facility" (€50 billion total). The main target is to conduct EU investments in transport (€31.7 billion), energy (€9.1 billion) and telecommunications (€9.2 billion) [40]. Moreover, additional €40 billion will be allocated for large–scale deployments of smart grid technologies across the European Union. These investments in key infrastructures can strengthen the Europe's competitiveness, create jobs (forecast of 400 000 places) and promote green energy solutions [41]. Recent studies show that the 20–20–20 policy is mostly affecting and promoting IT/Technical Operations and Engineering/Product Development [42].

Smart Grid Market in Poland: as for now, there is no legal framework supporting emergence and functioning of smart grids in Poland. However, the legislation process is in progress and the appriopriate law is expected to be ready in 2013 [16]. Moreover, to encourage RES micro–producers to become active participants of the energy market, financial support schemes for RES, based on green certificates, feed–in tariffs, subsidies, financial instruments and auction mechanism, are being put in place [43,44]. Moreover, many pilot studies concerning intelligent infrastructure are being carried out. The biggest one is conducted by Energa Operator. The company has already successfully deployed 50 000 smart meters in Kalisz and currently is carrying out research on smart grid system in the Hel Peninsula [45,48].

To provide the quality collaboration between the information and operational technology, within the context of smart energy solutions, new IT systems (e.g. microgrid energy market management) must be introduced (the market is estimated for 8.6$ billion by 2017) [32]. The demand for smart grid products and systems is estimated for about 2000$ billion over the next 20 years. Thus, there appears a great opportunity to create and use solutions, such as the one described within the paper.

3.2   The Microgrid Management System Concept

In comparison to the traditional energy market, there appear few new entities in the microgrid, most of all prosumers and aggregators. All of the market participants should be equipped with tools that enable to carry out the everyday activities, including decision support, local energy trading and the microgrid management (users, devices, loads, efficiency) [47,46]. Moreover, these entities should cooperate with one another or even be provided with a single platform. To address the emerging challenges being faced by the microgrid market participants, we propose the concept of Future Energy Management System (FEMS), that is depicted in the Fig. 1.

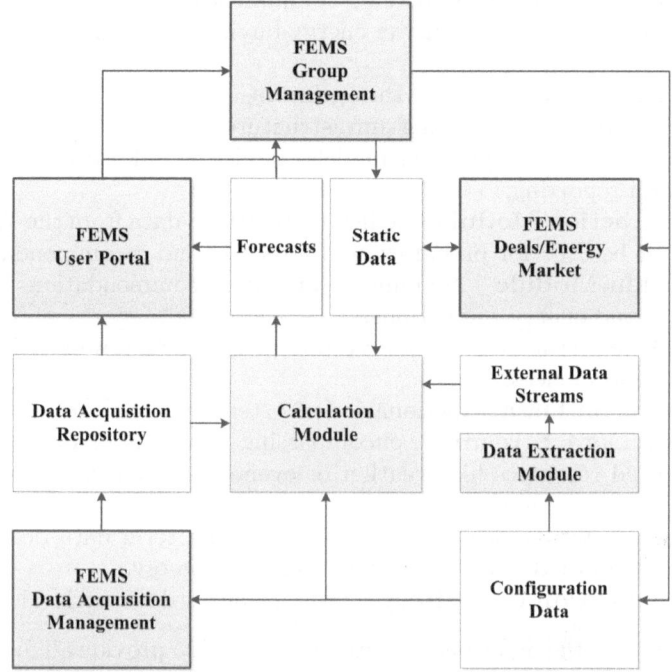

Fig. 1. Future Energy Management System concept

The FEMS system is mainly developed for:

- household administrators of office buildings, apartments, settlements, factories, etc.
- groups of stakeholders e.g. local communities consisting of energy consumers and producers,
- microgeneration administrators and managers.

The architecture of the system is presented in Fig. 1 and encompasses:

- **FEMS User Portal** – being the main user (for all groups of users) tool for managing the energy consumption and production, viewing statistics and tracking personalized recommendations, offering building and electrical energy trading.
- **FEMS Group Management** – the tool prepared for the group administrator that ensures a simple way of managing and analysing energy consumption and production within the whole microgrid subject to management. For instance, the administrator can prepare the energy offers and then send them to the users of the microgrid. Moreover, the tool supports recommendations and communication with users. Finally, it is also responsible for managing permissions and access to the FEMS system and its configuration.

- **FEMS Deals/Energy Market** – component dedicated to energy trading entities, allows the user to answer energy buying/selling inquiries sent by the group administrator.
- **FEMS Data Acquisition Management** – a central tool responsible for the integration with metering infrastructure via two-way communication protocols and data acquisition models. It also handles data measurement, control and reporting.
- **Data Extraction Module** – dedicated to collect data from the Web sources, that might be used for preparation of forecasts and recommendations.
- **Calculation Module** – enabling to prepare recommendations, users' classifications and energy predictions.
- **Static Data** – storage of data describing customers, power delivery points, contracts and devices.
- **Configuration Data** – dictionaries and stereotype definitions.
- **External Data Streams** – encompassing all kinds of data, taken from unstructured resources like weather or events calendar, that are important to energy forecasting methods.
- **Forecasts** – storage of short, medium and long term data describing predicted consumption and production of electric energy.
- **Data Acquisition Repository** – responsible for data retrieval and storage.

We believe, that the described architecture is able to provide all functionalities presented in the Section 3.3.

3.3 FEMS Functionalities

The main functionalities of FEMS encompass inter alia acquisition of data from smart meters, reasoning over the grid model, providing recommendations, forecasting and methods for retrieving information from external sources. Moreover, FEMS aims at developing a service that will strengthen the user engagement in the field of smart consumption within microgrid whilst providing listed below functionalities and intuitive, user-friendly interfaces as the one depicted in Fig. 2.

According to analyses that were carried out, these functionalities include:

1. **Monitoring and comparison of defined key performance indicators of energy consumption** – this functionality implies historic, current and future KPIs tracking and comparing them within the microgrid with regard to location, size, number of household members, etc. The user may therefore not only see his KPIs, but also of users of similar energy profile.
2. **Preparing personalized recommendations of actions towards minimising/maximising energy usage/production** – includes presenting hints, based on the prosumer behaviour, possessed devices, calendar, historical consumption and family model (e.g. "Please check the fridge for repair as it consumes 30 percent more energy than last month."). It also presents recommendations dedicated to microproducers, based mostly on weather conditions and device parameters.

3. **Prosumers profiling** – Includes prosumers' profiling via clustering with regard to static (e.g. user type, household devices, stereotype) and dynamic data (historical consumption). These profiles will be further generalised and used by the forecasting and recommendation methods.
4. **Forecasting energy consumption and production** – Includes preparation of short, medium and long-term consumption forecasts based on data from smart meters and production estimation based on system–external data and unstructured data stream retrieved from the Web. Finally, the outputs will be automatically analysed via recommendation mechanism and personalized hints will be presented to users.

Fig. 2. FEMS interface for defining household devices. Source: FEMS system.

The user (an individual household) in order to benefit from the solution, is obliged to define:

– personal data (indicating the smart meter possessed),
– consumption and production devices and their parameters,
– energy consumption and production schedule,
– description of the building (its features),
– user preferences,
– family model (stereotype).

The abovementioned parameters can be defined as is depicted in Fig. 2. It presents the interface enabling definition of user stereotype by adding devices

to the household with a built-in interactive tool. The users can choose location
and then simply drag & drop devices, set their parameters such as the nominal
power, their number and energy class, etc. This interface allows also to count the
nominal power of all installed devices that might be used for the household energy load forecast or system recommendation methods. By filling in all presented
parameters, the user has an opportunity to save money, improve the awareness
and actively participate in the local microgrid.

The system implementing the described functionalities following the architecture described above was developed and tested within the Future Energy Management System project financed within the frameword of the Polish Innovative
Economy Operational Programme (Zbudowanie prototypu innowacyjnego systemu prognozowania poziomu zużycia i produkcji energii elektrycznej o nazwie
'Future Energy Management System' project: UDA-POIG.01.04.00-30-065/10-
00, project value: 9.957.022 PLN, share of the European Union: 5.647.245 PLN,
therm of the realization: 07.2011-03.2013).

4   Related Work

With the smart metering infrastructure began the dawn of informatization of the
energy sector. Thus, IT companies rushed in, trying to deliver a right product
for different participants of the energy market. Especially those with experience
in development of industrial control systems and analyses of big data.

In Europe, a large part of the development effort is conducted by academics,
who are carrying out research projects with the purpose of fulfilling the vision
of an energy efficient Europe, as set out by the European Union. Some of these
projects, are implemented by start-ups, created by independent entrepreneurs
with the goal of satisfying the new market. Among the software-oriented approaches at utilizing the smart metering infrastructure to provide the maximum
benefit, we can distinguish those which focus on energy savings on the consumer side (supporting the customer), and those which aim at creation of tools
for utilities that allow to run their businesses more efficiently. The latter is addressed mainly by large corporations, which offer solutions for big market players
[4,6,7,8]. These corporations take the former approach usually only for the marketing purposes. Only small companies rely on it for profit, seeing the market
potential [5].

The large scale efforts of big companies are focused on helping utilities control
and maintain the state of the grid, address faults and problems more efficiently,
segment their market better in order to offer more value to their customers, and
lastly, make it easier to fulfil regulatory obligations. There is also a group of
innovative projects for utilities created by smaller companies or academia, as
well as projects catering to new participants of the market, based on innovative
business models. An example can be creating virtual power plants by establishing
clusters of small energy producers [9].

Examples of innovative functionalities offered by ongoing projects are:

- interactive energy use calculators based on manual data input and user-relevant recommendations regarding energy usage – Wattzon[2],
- comparing energy efficiency with the general population and one's neighbors to influence the change of behavior among users by friendly competition – Wattzon, Opower[3],
- communicating with metering infrastructure; support for energy purchasing, contracts, holding accounts; integration of energy management solutions with SCADA systems; integration of customer management with meter data for the purpose of billing – Proximus-IT[4], STC Energy[5], INNSOFT[6], Web2energy[7], ECIX-ORL[8], Opower,
- simulation of energy flow and prices for retail consumers based on statistic methods and stochastic process modelling – resLoadSim[9],
- integration of data visualization and statistics' modules with metering infrastructure – Energy Cap[10], STC Energy.

Other exemplary initiatives in the field, not fully related to functionalities offered by FEMS, are:

- platforms for sharing best practices in executing smart grid initiatives and educating retail consumers to manage their households' energy usage – MeterON[11], EEGI[12], ADDRESS[13], Wattzon,
- efforts to reduce energy needs of buildings by replacing equipment and educating consumers – BEEMUP[14],
- increasing reliance on renewable energy sources and raising awareness about energy usage among consumers – ADDRESS,
- establishing industry standards for smart metering infrastructure, taking into account communication channels and data transfer protocols – OPEN METER[15].

---

[2] www.wattzon.com

[3] www.opower.com

[4] www.proximus-it.pl/b/zarzadzanie-zakupem-energii/0

[5] www.stcenergy.com

[6] www.innsoft.pl

[7] www.web2energy.com

[8] www.eurocim.pl/ecixorl.html

[9] http://ses.jrc.ec.europa.eu/our-models-portfolio

[10] www.nationalenergyconsulting.com/energycap.html

[11] www.meter-on.eu

[12] www.smartgrids.eu/documents/EEGI/EEGI_Implementation_plan_May%202010.pdf

[13] www.addressfp7.org

[14] www.beem-up.eu

[15] www.openmeter.com

5 Conclusions

The microgrid market and technologies that enable to manage microgrids are now highly developed. Despite the challenges posed by the management of small electricity grids, there appear new ideas, advanced management techniques, more accurate forecasting models and better tools to predict the market changes. Fortunately, with the development of the microgrid, the accuracy of forecasting the behavior of the microgrid components is improving. The accuracy of forecasts in the microgrids is extremely important because it's strictly related its functioning costs, what is then further reflected in the profitability of microgrid system as a whole.

The market potential of microgrids, especially in the global context is estimated for billions of dollars of investment (but also of revenue). Also on an European market, namely in the CEE[16] region, a lot of investments are performed e.g. by 2033 smart meters investments will reach about 10.3$ billion in the CEE countries.

Currently developed microgrid management systems are mainly prepared to support the management of large smartgrid networks, which are connected by SCADA class systems. On the other hand, there are many small applications that display data on average energy consumption and recommend environmentally responsible behaviour. There are few systems, which support the small microgrids and these type of grids are currently being developed.

FEMS is a system that fits in this gap of the market, as it supports households and individual clients, and it can be successfully applied to small business entities. FEMS supports the analysis of energy consumption and enables to forecast future consumption, as well as production of the microgeneration. The forecasts are generated based on the historical data, but also data acquired from external sources (i.e. Internet weather forcase, TV programme etc). FEMS also supports the microgrid market transactions to allow the energy trading on the local market, using the neighbourhood of renewable energy resources. One of the important modules is also a recommendation system, that operates on data on prosumers in order to effectively educate them in caring for the environment and saving the energy.

FEMS can be easily extended with additional modules and adapted to a variety of markets in the CEE region, as well as around the world. Using this type of management systems for the microgrid may offer many advantages such as: efficient exploitation of renewable energy sources, reduced emissions of carbon dioxide, protection against blackouts, reduction of cost of energy supply, automated acquisiton of data from smart meters and Internet sources, and many more. This type of systems will soon become present in our everyday life, so at this stage we should support their development, seeing that this kind of systems will provide us with clean and green energy in the cheapest way possible.

---

[16] Central and Eastern Europe countries.

References

1. Simmonds, G.: Regulation of the UK electricity industry: 2002. Centre for the Study of Regulated Industries, Bath (2002)
2. Alsunaidy, A., Green, R.: Electricity Deregulation in OECD (Organization for Economic Cooperation and Development) Countries. Energy 31(6-7), 769–787 (2006)
3. Bundesministerium fur Umwelt, Naturschutz und Reaktorsicherheit, Development of renewable energy sources in Germany in 2012, Berlin (2013), http://www.erneuerbare-energien.de/fileadmin/Daten_EE/Dokumente__PDFs_/20130328_hgp_e_ppt_2012_fin_bf.pdf (accessed May 05, 2013)
4. SAP AG, Energy Data, Smart Meter Analytics Software, HANA In-Memory Computing, SAP, SAP Business Management Software Solutions, Applications and Services, http://www54.sap.com/pc/tech/in-memory-computing-hana/software/smart-meter-analytics/index.html (accessed March 20, 2013)
5. WattzOn, Inc., www.wattzon.com (accessed March 21, 2013)
6. Siemens AG, Infrastructure & Cities Sector, Smart Grid Division, Energy meets Intelligence (2013), http://w3.siemens.com/smartgrid/global/en/products-systems-solutions/Documents/SIEIC_39L_SmartGrid_Update_14s_engl_210x280.pdf (accessed May 05, 2013)
7. Oracle Utilities, Oracle Utilities Smart Grid Gateway (2013), http://www.oracle.com/us/industries/utilities/utilities-smart-grid-ds-323531.pdf (accessed May 05, 2013)
8. IBM Corp., IBM Smart Grid - Solutions - United States, IBM - United States, http://www.ibm.com/smarterplanet/us/en/smart_grid/nextsteps/index.html (accessed April 10, 2013)
9. Fraunhofer Institute, The virtual power plant - stable supply of electricity from renewable energies, Press Release (March 26, 2013), http://www.fraunhofer.de/en/press/research-news/2013/march/the-virtual-power-plant.html (accessed April 12, 2013)
10. Srinivasan, K., Rosenberg, C.: How internet concepts and technologies can help green and smarten the electrical grid. In: Proceedings of the First ACM SIGCOMM Workshop on Green Networking (Green Networking 2010), pp. 35–40. ACM, New York (2010), http://doi.acm.org/10.1145/1851290.1851298 (accessed May 05, 2013)
11. Kaplan, S.M.: Smart grid: modernizing electric power transmission and distribution; energy independence, storage and security; energy independence and security act of 2007 (EISA); improving electrical grid efficiency, communication, reliability, and resiliency; integra. TheCapitol.Net, Alexandria (2009)
12. Olszowiec, P.: Autonomiczne systemy elektroenergetyczne malej mocy. Mikrosieci, Energia Gigawat (7-8) (2009)
13. Ren 21, Renewables 2012 Global status report, Paris (2012), http://www.map.ren21.net (accessed May 05, 2013)
14. Dimeas, A.L., Hatziargyriou, N.D.: Operation of a Multiagent System for Microgrid Control. IEEE Transactions on Power Systems 20(3), 1447–1455 (2005)
15. Markel, T., Kuss, M., Simpson, M.: Value of plug-in vehicle grid support operation. In: Innovative Technologies for an Efficient and Reliable Electricity Supply (CITRES), September 27-29, pp. 325–332 (2010), http://ieeexplore.ieee.org/stamp/stamp.jsp?tp=&arnumber=5619785&isnumber=5619765 (accessed May 05, 2013)

16. Sejm, R.P.: Projekt ustawy o odnawialnych zrodlach energii z dnia 14 grudnia 2012r, http://orka.sejm.gov.pl/Druki7ka.nsf/dok?OpenAgent&7-020-492-2012 (accessed May 05, 2013)

17. Rezaei, E., Afsharnia, S.: Cooperative voltage balancing in islanded microgrid with single-phase loads. In: 2011 International Conference on Electrical and Control Engineering (ICECE), September 16-18, pp. 5804–5808 (2011), http://ieeexplore.ieee.org/stamp/stamp.jsp?tp=&arnumber=6057188& isnumber=6056741 (accessed May 05, 2013)

18. Bando, S., Sasaki, Y., Asano, H., Tagami, S.: Balancing control method of a microgrid with intermittent renewable energy generators and small battery storage. In: 2008 IEEE Power and Energy Society General Meeting - Conversion and Delivery of Electrical Energy in the 21st Century, July 20-24, pp. 1–6 (2008), http://ieeexplore.ieee.org/stamp/stamp.jsp?tp=&arnumber=4596074& isnumber=4595968 (accessed May 05, 2013)

19. Cheung, H., Hamlyn, A., Mander, T., Cungang, Y., Cheung, R.: Strategy and Role-based Model of Security Access Control for Smart Grids Computer Networks. In: IEEE Canada Electrical Power Conference, October 25-26, pp. 423–428 (2007), http://ieeexplore.ieee.org/stamp/stamp.jsp?tp=&arnumber=4520369& isnumber=4520285

20. Li, P., Li, X., Liu, J., Chen, J., Chen, J.: Analysis of acceptable capacity of microgrid connected to the main power grid. In: 4th International Conference on Electric Utility Deregulation and Restructuring and Power Technologies (DRPT), July 6-9, pp. 1799–1802 (2011), http://ieeexplore.ieee.org/stamp/stamp.jsp?tp=&arnumber=5994190& isnumber=5993852 (accessed May 05, 2013)

21. Saad, W., Han, Z., Poor, H.V., Basar, T.: Game-Theoretic Methods for the Smart Grid: An Overview of Microgrid Systems, Demand-Side Management, and Smart Grid Communications. Presented at IEEE Signal Process. Mag., pp. 86–105 (2012)

22. Tao, L., Schwaegerl, C., Narayanan, S., Zhang, J.H.: From laboratory Microgrid to real markets - Challenges and opportunities. In: 2011 IEEE 8th International Conference on Power Electronics and ECCE Asia (ICPE & ECCE), May 30-June 3 (2011), http://ieeexplore.ieee.org/stamp/stamp.jsp?tp=&arnumber=5944600& isnumber=5944368 (accessed May 05, 2013)

23. Colson, C.M., Nehrir, M.H.: A review of challenges to real-time power management of microgrids. In: IEEE Power & Energy Society General Meeting, July 26-30, pp. 1–8 (2009), http://ieeexplore.ieee.org/stamp/stamp.jsp?tp=& arnumber=5275343&isnumber=5260217 (accessed May 05, 2013)

24. Bernoulli, J.: Ars Conjectandi: Usum & Applicationem Praecedentis Doctrinae in Civilibus, Moralibus & Oeconomicis (1713)

25. GlobalData, Press Releases — Smart Grids: Microgrid Market Boom on the Way as Europe and Asia Catch-up to US, http://energy.globaldata.com/pressreleasedetails.aspx?prid=705   (accessed April 18, 2013)

26. GlobalData, Microgrid in Smart Grid - Market Size, Key Issues, Regulations and Outlook to 2020, http://www.researchandmarkets.com/reports/2518946/ microgrid_in_smart_grid_market_size_key (accessed April 18, 2013)

27. Hayes, S., Young, R., Sciortino, M.: The ACEEE 2012 International Energy Efficiency Scorecard, American Council for an Energy-Efficient Economy, http://www.aceee.org/research-report/e12a (accessed April 15, 2013)

28. Northeast Group LLC, Brazil Smart Grid: Market Forecast (2012-2022), Washington (2012), http://www.northeast-group.com/reports/Brazil_Smart_Grid_Market_Forecast_2012-2022_Brochure_Northeast_ Group_LLC.pdf (accessed May 05, 2013)
29. Northeast Group LLC, Central and Eastern Europe Smart Grid: Market Forecast (2013-2023), Washington (2013), http://www.researchandmarkets.com/reports/2556779/central_and_eastern_europe_smart_grid_market (accessed May 05, 2013)
30. Memoori Research, The Smart Grid Business 2012 to 2017, London (2012), http://www.memoori.com/portfolio/the-smart-grid-business-2012-to-2017/ (accessed May 05, 2013)
31. Northeast Group LLC, Emerging Markets Smart Grid: Outlook 2013, Washington (2013), http://www.northeast-group.com/reports/Emerging_Markets_Smart_Grid_Outlook_2013_Northeast_Group.pdf (accessed May 05, 2013)
32. Navigant Research, Smart Grid IT Systems, Boulder, Colorado, US (2012), http://www.navigantresearch.com/research/smart-grid-it-systems (accessed May 05, 2013)
33. IDC Energy Insights, Technology Selection: North America Home Energy Management Spending Forecast, 2011-2016, Framingham, MA, US (2012), http://www.idc-ei.com/getdoc.jsp?containerId=EI236935 (accessed May 05, 2013)
34. Navigant Research, Market Data: Microgrids, Boulder, Colorado, US (2013), http://www.navigantresearch.com/wp-assets/uploads/2013/03/MD-MICRO-13-Executive-Summary.pdf (accessed May 05, 2013)
35. Navigant Research, Smart Grid Technologies, Boulder, Colorado, US (2012), http://www.navigantresearch.com/research/smart-grid-technologies (accessd May 05, 2013)
36. Bloomberg New Energy Finance, Strong growth for renewables expected through to 2030, Bloomberg New Energy Finance, Bloomberg New Energy Finance, http://about.bnef.com/press-releases/strong-growth-for-renewables-expected-through-to-2030/ (accessed May 1, 2013)
37. European Commision, 20–20–20 package, Climate and energy policy of the EU (2012), http://ec.europa.eu/clima/policies/package/index_en.htm (accessed May 05, 2013)
38. Nalco.com, Learn More About Our Air Protection Technologies, http://www.nalcomobotec.com/mb/eu-20-20-20-rule.htm (accessed June 18, 2013)
39. Europedia, The EU "energy-climate" package, http://europedia.moussis.eu/discus/discus-1230747802-321327-28435.tkl (accessed June 18, 2013)
40. European Union, A budget for Europe (2014-2020), Europa.eu, Summaries of EU legislation, http://europa.eu/legislation_summaries/budget/bu0001_en.htm (accessed June 18, 2013)
41. European Commision, Connecting Europe Facility (2012), http://ec.europa.eu/energy/mff/facility/doc/2012/connecting-europe.pdf (accessed May 05, 2013)
42. Emerson Network Power, Business-Critical Continuity EU 20–20–20 Directive, Columbus, OH, US (2013), http://www.emersonnetworkpower.com/en-EMEA/About/NewsRoom/Documents/EU202020-Report.pdf (accessed May 05, 2013)

314   A. Filipowska et al.

43. Green Energy Poland SA, 5. Zielone Certyfikaty mechanizm dzialania, cena, zasady obrotu. Green Energy Poland SA, Inwestycje z nowa energia, http://gepsa.pl/322-2/ (accessed June 18, 2013)
44. Kasnowski, J.: System taryfy gwarantowanej dla fotowoltaiki, Euroinfrastruktura.pl, http://www.euroinfrastructure.eu/finanse-i-prawo/system-taryfy-gwarantowanej-dla-fotowoltaiki/ (accessed June 18, 2013)
45. Smart-Grids.pl, Kalisz pierwszym miastem ze Smart Meteringiem. Smart-Grids.pl, http://www.smart-grids.pl/technologie/749-kalisz-pierwszym-miastem-ze-smart-meteringiem.html (accessed June 18, 2013)
46. Dzikowski, J., Filipowska, A.: Wykorzystanie danych z Internetu w prognozowaniu zachowan prosumentow w mikrosieciach energetycznych, Poznan (2012)
47. Dzikowski, J., Filipowska, A.: Przyczynowo-skutkowy model zmiennosci rynku energii elektrycznej. Zeszyty Naukowe Uniwersytetu Ekonomicznego w Poznaniu, Poznan (2012)
48. Energa Operator S.A., Energa i Instytut Energetyki: Inteligentna siec coraz blizej, http://www.energa-operator.pl/klienci_indywidualni/informacje.xml?id =3357 (accessed June 18, 2013)

Supporting Energy Efficiency Decisions with IT: Initial Experiences from the EnRiMa Project

Martin Henkel[1], Janis Stirna[1], Markus Groissböck[2], and Michael Stadler[2]

[1] Department of Computer and Systems Sciences, Stockholm University,
Forum 100, SE-16440, Kista, Sweden
{martinh,js}@dsv.su.se
[2] Center for Energy and innovative Technologies,
Doberggasse 9, 3681 Hofamt Priel, Austria
{mgroissboeck,mstadler}@cet.or.at

Abstract. IT solutions can aid decision makers in making informed decisions that lower the energy consumption in buildings. However, in order to design and implement an IT solution there are a number of issues that need to be resolved, for example, adequately handling sometimes contradicting goals of the decision makers and integrating the Decision Support System with the existing building IT infrastructure in the form of building management systems. In this paper we report on our initial experiences from implementing a decision support system for the management of energy consumption in public buildings. The experiences are based on our work with the EnRiMa project that aims to develop a state-of art decision support system for lowering the energy consumption and CO_2 emissions of public buildings. We divide our experiences into two areas, namely, business concerns and software architectural, and provide our initial solutions and lessons learned with respect to these areas. Furthermore, we discuss a number of challenges for future work in the area of IT support for energy efficiency.

Keywords: Sustainability, Green IT, Energy Efficiency, Decision Support System.

1 Introduction

Energy efficiency and reduction of CO_2 emissions is one of the main challenges of our society. This paper presents experiences from an ongoing EU funded FP7 project on IT solutions for improving energy efficiency of public buildings - EnRiMa (Energy Efficiency and Risk Management in Public Buildings).

The overall objective of EnRiMa is to develop a decision-support system (DSS) for operators of buildings and spaces of public use. By providing integrated decision support for handling conflicting goals such as cost minimization, meeting energy efficiency, and emission-reduction requirements, the DSS will enable operators to improve building energy efficiency in the most cost-effective manner based on their tolerances for comfort and risk. The DSS will aid the operators' in adjusting on-site

A. Kobyliński and A. Sobczak (Eds.): BIR 2013, LNBIP 158, pp. 315–326, 2013.

generation dispatch, and off-site energy purchases. The DSS will also enable long-term planning aimed at increasing energy efficiency. Specifically analysis of building retrofits and/or expansion of on-site energy systems, in order to meet forthcoming EU targets for reducing CO_2 emissions. Thus the system is aimed at the measurement and improvement phases [1] in a decision process.

The EnRiMa project has been running for 30 months and currently enters the user testing and validation phase of the DSS development. Hence, the objective of this paper is to present the overall business requirements and software architecture of the EnRiMa DSS as well as to discuss a number of emerging challenges pertinent to developing and running IT solutions for energy efficiency. The research findings are based on the requirements engineering and system development work performed in the EnRiMa project. We structure the description of our experiences into two areas - business concerns and software architecture. For each area we discuss the problems we have faced and how we have solved them. In order to make the solutions easier to apply in forthcoming projects, we define a set of *principles* that document the problems and the solutions. We do not claim that these are general or complete principles for building decision support systems in the area of energy efficiency, however we believe that the principles provide important input for projects with similar objectives.

The EnRiMa DSS will contain several novel features that are not present in current solutions proposed by academics or that existing in existing offers from the industry. To start with, existing building management systems, such as the Siemens Desigo system, relies on heuristic rules to optimize the use of installed equipment in order to lower a buildings energy use. The EnRiMa DSS will allow the users to also consider the effects of retrofitted equipment. Furthermore the EnRiMa DSS are capable of using advanced algorithm for handling long-term uncertainties, such as fluctuations in energy prices. This is made possible by a, for the domain of energy efficiency, novel combination of stochastic programing (SP) and a model of the long-term decision options that are available.

The remainder of the paper is organized as follows. Section 2 presents the business perspective of the EnRiMa DSS, that is, what kind of decisions making needs to be done and the types of users making the decisions. Section 3 presents the EnRiMa DSS software architecture, that is, the main software modules that the system consists of. The paper ends with a brief discussion about the challenges for adoption of the DSS.

2   The Business of Energy Efficiency – Decisions, Roles and Requirements

The key function of the DSS shall be to support the decision-maker (a person who actually makes the decisions) to find such decisions that best fits her/his preferences, expressed (usually implicitly) in terms of objectives (often called also outcomes, goals, criteria, indicators) used for evaluation of consequences resulting from implementation of a given set of decisions. The aim of the EnRiMa project is to provide the decisions makers with a DSS that could provide the best possible fundament for taking decisions that reduces the energy consumption in buildings.

Early in the project it was clear that there was several roles that made decisions that influenced the energy consumption; building owner, financial manager, operations manager, outsourced maintenance manager, energy service company, utility company (providing energy), energy consultants, policy makers, as well as energy auditors. Furthermore it was evident that these roles and their respective decisions ranged from short-term day-today decisions, such as how to best manage building's boilers and heat pumps, to more long-term decisions such as investments in alternative technologies. To cope with these different perspectives, the project early on decided to acknowledge them and treat them as equally important. We summarize this way of handling the differences in perspectives in the following simple principle:

Principle 1: Acknowledge that energy efficiency is both concerned with short-term and long-term decisions, thus, let the DSS tackle them both.

Applying the 1st principle to the EnRiMa DSS made us design an operational and a strategic module of the system. The application of the principle thus affected the way the system modeled the decision problem, this model is an important step in supporting decision making [2]. To ensure that these parts were not developed in isolation, we also followed principles for their integration. These principles will be presented later in this paper. In the following two subsections we briefly describe each of these parts.

2.1   Short-Term Operational Planning

The operational DSS module shall assist decisions on how to operate the existing building equipment. For example, this includes controlling a centralized Heating, Ventilation and Air Conditioning (HVAC) system as well as electricity and thermal storages (where available) of a building. The set of objectives includes [3]:

- Minimization of operational costs
- Minimization of environmental impact, in particular the CO_2 emissions
- Diverse indicators of the user comfort based on indoor temperature
- Analysis of the HVAC performance
- Economic dispatch of the dispatchable primary generating units. That is to start and stop or otherwise operate the installed technologies in the most economical way.

Among the parameters for operational planning typically are building facades, materials, and their thermal behavior, external temperature, external humidity, occupancy, internal temperature set-points, energy prices, as well as energy efficiency of installed equipment. In the EnRiMa DSS the given parameters are used on a daily basis to calculate the optimal way of managing the equipment for the next 24 hours. For example, by using weather forecast it is possible to estimate the solar irradiation and adjust the use of heating and cooling equipment accordingly.

2.2   Long-Term Strategic Planning

The strategic DSS module should support making long-term decisions to secure energy supply, minimize energy consumption costs and environmental impacts, and improve existing energy infrastructure. This part enables integration with elements of the operational module, which evaluates the performance of the energy system of the building in real time and triggers long-term decisions on installment of new and decommissioning obsolete technologies, retrofitting, etc. The strategic module takes into account at least the following: long-term evolution of equipment and activities; the long-term evolution of the energy consumption curves; availability of new technologies; as well as depreciation of available equipment. The set of the supported decisions is specific at each building site and typically includes:

- Selection of new devices
- Decommissioning of devices
- Selection of energy sources for electricity and heat generations, as well as for
- Cooling. This includes selecting the appropriate tariffs for buying energy the format/medium in which the energy is bought, for example, cooling can be done by district cooling or by electricity powering a HVAC.
- Financial instruments for coping with uncertainties and risks, such as futures, tariffs and inflation rates.

The following parameters are typically treated as inputs to the strategic DSS: existing building facades, materials and their thermal behavior; options for the building retrofitting; long-term climate parameters, long-term forecasts of prices and availability of energy carriers; long-term forecasts of energy loads/demand at the building; scenarios for changes of regulations affecting building operations; scenarios for changes in the energy markets.

The operational and strategic modules can run in isolation. There are however clear links between them, for example, the day-to day behavior of equipment can affect its long-term use. To strengthen this interconnection we devise the following basic principle:

Principle 2: Find links between the long-term and short term perspectives, and provide a design that supports this link in the DSS.

A concrete example of how this is done in the EnRiMa DSS is the use of profiles to capture equipment's day-to-day performance and feed this into the strategic model. For example, when making a long-term investment in photovoltaic (PV) panels it is interesting to estimate typical long-term parameters such as the evolution of their efficiency and price. However, short-term performance such as how much energy the PVs produce per day is also of interest. To express this short term data the EnRiMa DSS stores *profiles* that represent how much solar irradiation can be expected for each hour in a typical summer day, in a typical winter day etc. This short-term data is the link between the strategic model and the operational model.

Having the DSS handle information on the existing and future equipment both on the strategic and operational level can result in that the decision maker needs to know and enter a lot of information in the system. Manually entering information is cumbersome, and also makes future automation more difficult. In the EnRiMa project we therefore aim to follow a third principle:

Principle 3: As the DSS for energy efficiency handles large set of data, aim to support automation and reduce the manual work.

We follow this principle by providing a set of default values. For example, we will produce valid default profiles that describe the hourly solar irradiation over a year, and likely price development of equipment. This can substantially simplify the process of system configuration for the user, as there are predefined profiles they can choose from.

3   EnRiMa DSS – Internal and External Software Modules

To cater to the need of the decision makers, the EnRiMa DSS is constructed as a web based system where the users can access the DSS using a standard web browser. Internally the software is structured into a set of software modules; this structure constitutes the software's *architecture*. In this section we report on the experiences of creating the software architecture and its implementation. Just as for the business perspective we report on a set of *principles* that are fundamental for the way we build the system. To structure the presentation we divide it into a general overview of the software modules, a discussion about the languages used for the modules, and a presentation of the integration with external software modules.

3.1   General Software Modules

The overall architecture of the EnRiMa DSS follows the common approach of having three principal layers [4]: presentation, domain logic, and data source. In Figure 1 these layers are realized by the user interface (presentation), DSS Engine kernel (domain logic) and database (data source). Figure 1 illustrates the overall EnRiMa DSS architecture using the Unified Modeling Language (UML) component diagram notation [5].

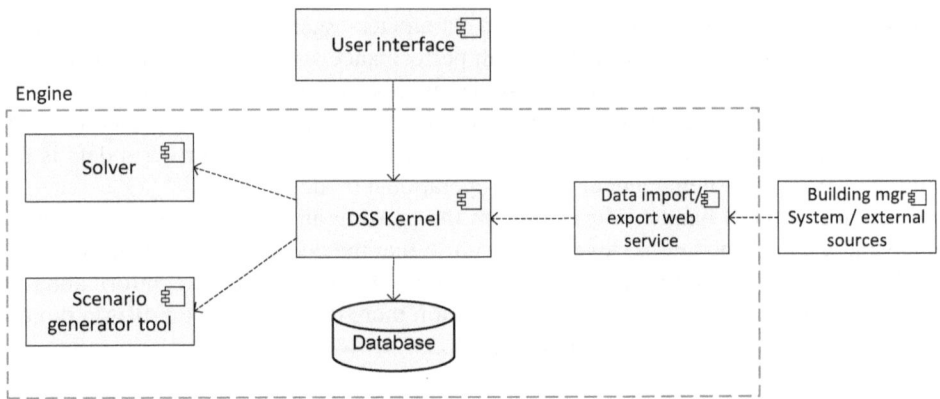

Fig. 1. Overview of the architecture

The role and contents of each part in the architecture are summarized below, a complete description can be found in [6].

The graphical *user interface* (GUI) consists of the modules responsible for the interaction with the user. The user will access the DSS via a Web browser. The user interface consists of regular and custom-made interface elements, such as buttons, tables, tabs etc. To aid in the presentation of these elements the user interface module make use of the Vaadin user interface framework, and a graph tool in the form of Google visualizations. Due to the use of these tools it is possible to create a composite application that combines various user interface elements (see example in figure 2). Currently the GUI of the DSS contains about 40 screens.

The *engine* (shown as a dotted rectangle in figure 1) is the backbone of the DSS, providing services, each through one of the DSS modules, namely the kernel, solver, and scenario generator tool.

The *kernel* is responsible for providing functionality needed to manage the system data and to run the *scenario generator tool* and *solver*. The kernel also supports user handling, access control, and performing queries of the result data. The kernel is interfacing the database via a Java Persistence API (JPA) compliant object-relational mapper (ORM).

The *scenario generator tool* creates a scenario tree representing possible decisions that affect the building management. The scenario tree is based on the configuration values as set by the user via the GUI. The output from the scenario generator is fed into the solver manager that produces the solution that is shown to the user.

The *solver* is responsible for managing the calculations of the optimal use of energy and equipment. Essentially, it extracts the needed information from the database, runs an optimization and puts the result back. Upon request of the user the solver is started by the *kernel*. The time it takes to create a solution varies depending on the input parameters. The current version of the operational module, working with datasets for the next 24 hours, takes about two minutes to execute.

The data *import/export* module manages the import and export of information to external systems. This module is implemented as a web service, making it remotely accessible for external systems. External systems include both the buildings IT infrastructure as such, and external service providers. The building management systems contain information on the buildings, such as current in- and outdoor temperatures. External service providers provide information about weather forecast and energy prices.

The *user interface*, *kernel*, *solver* and *scenario generator tool* are deployed on the same server, while the *database* due to administrative reasons is deployed on a dedicated database server.

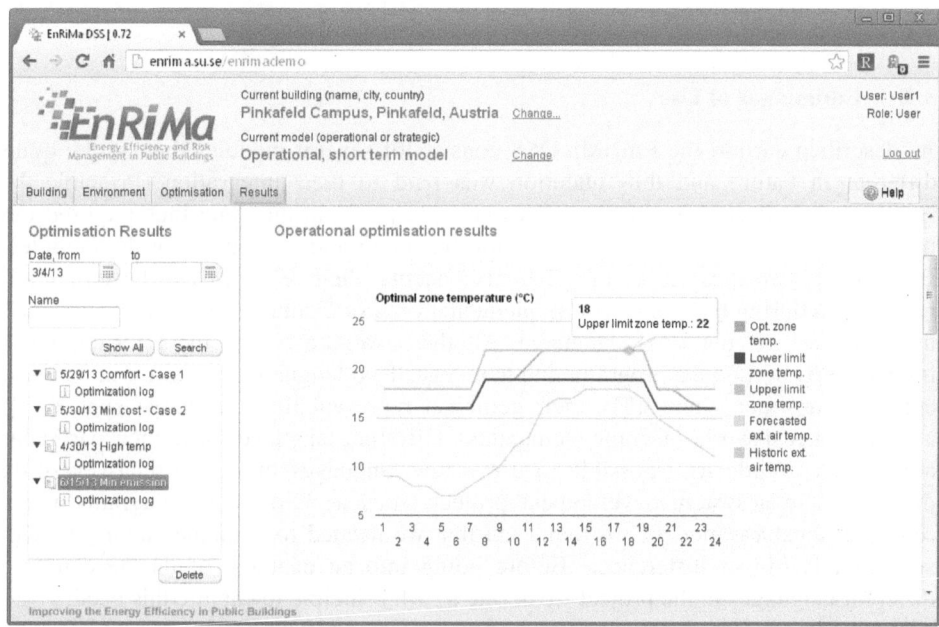

Fig. 2. Screen capture displaying results of running optimizations for the short term operational planning module

As stated earlier the architecture is built on the commonly accepted three layer architecture. Even though the architecture follows common design principles it still contains elements that are special for the EnRiMa project. One of these special elements, or problems, is that the software modules are very different in the way they handle information and their functionality. For example, the GUI manages the data in quite a straight-forward way, i.e. the user creates and updates entities (such as description of existing building equipment) and the corresponding entities are stored in the database. However, the Scenario generator can, based on a few input entities, create thousands of data items to describe the possible scenarios. Likewise, while the GUI request is usually handled in less than a second, running the solver can take from several minutes up to several hours to run. These kinds of differences in the modules create problems in their interconnection. To cater to these problems we describe a forth principle:

Principle 4: Clearly separate the module-internal risks/problems from the inter-module problems in the software architecture.

In essence this principle is useful to highlight that time need to be spent addressing the inter-module module issues. That is, time need to be spent on the module integration. For example, the integration of the kernel with the solver requires that the call from the kernel to the solver is asynchronous; in order to not keep the kernel waiting while the solver is running. Likewise the large amount of data (typically close to 100 000 entities) created by the scenario generator need to be written to the database with highly efficient code.

3.2   Languages of Use

As described earlier, the EnRiMa DSS consists of several modules that can be quite different in nature and thus attention was paid to their integration (Principle 4). However the difference in the modules goes deeper than that, and thus required the project to consider the *languages* used for designing and implementing the modules. By language we mean a set of coherent concepts, their relations and how they are represented during the design and implementation. For example, Figure 1 is expressed using a (part of) the UML language. Another example is that the DSS engine is implemented in the Java programming language. Two languages can differ in the used concepts (abstract syntax [7]), their graphical representations (concrete syntax [7]) and in their real-world meaning (semantics). Different languages have their particular area of use. While it is possible to use a few languages that have relatively little differences in a system development project (such as UML class diagrams and a relational database model), we found out that we needed to combine languages with substantially bigger differences. Before going into an example of the need to use different languages in the project we define a fifth principle to capture this need:

Principle 5: Build on the integration capabilities to leverage the power of different languages.

One of the challenges concerning the use of different languages was the difference in how the optimization problem was expressed in the solver module, compared to how it was expressed in the engine. The task of the solver is to use the huge amount of input data to find an optimal solution or solutions. A language especially equipped to express these kinds of problems is symbolic model specifications [8]. A symbolic model specification contains a mathematical representation of the input data (referred to as parameters), the output data (referred to as decision variables) and mathematical formulas (referred to as constraints) that express the desired optimal solution. An example of the parameters can be found in figure 3. Note that the relationships between parameters are defined using indices, for example the output energy type (EC) is related to a technology (i) and two energy types (k).

i	Energy-generation technology, $i \in \mathcal{I}$.
k	Energy type, $k \in \mathcal{K}$.
l	Type of pollutant, $l \in \mathcal{L}$.
$EC_{i,k,k'}$	Output energy (type k') generated with one unit of input energy (type k) (kWh/kWh).
$AF_i^{p,m,t}$	Availability factor for a technology (kWh/kWh).
$CO_{i,k}^{p,m,t}$	Operation cost (generators) (EUR/kWh).

Fig. 3. A subset of the model specification parameters (from [9])

In figure 4 a small subset of one of the constraints is shown. In essence this constraint calculates the technology operation cost (*CO*) for all types of energy output (*z*) during the optimization period (*DM*). The indices *p*, *m* and *t* refer to the time periods used for the calculation, essentially year (*p*), season (*m*) and hour (*t*).

$$\sum_{m \in \mathcal{M}} DM^{p,m} \cdot \sum_{i \in \mathcal{I}, k \in \mathcal{K}, t \in \mathcal{T}} CO_{i,k}^{p,m,t} \cdot z_{i,k}^{p,m,t}$$

Fig. 4. A small subset of the model specification constraints (from [9])

While the symbolic model specification is an efficient language to express an optimization problem, it is less suited when designing and implementing a graphical user interface. The issue here is that while the model specification contains a list of parameters, a well-structured user interface needs to have the information partitioned, for example to have all fields related to a certain technology on a certain screen. For this purpose languages such as class diagrams and the relational model is better suited as a foundation for the user interface design. A small example of a class diagram covering the same area as the model specification in figure 4 is shown in figure 5.

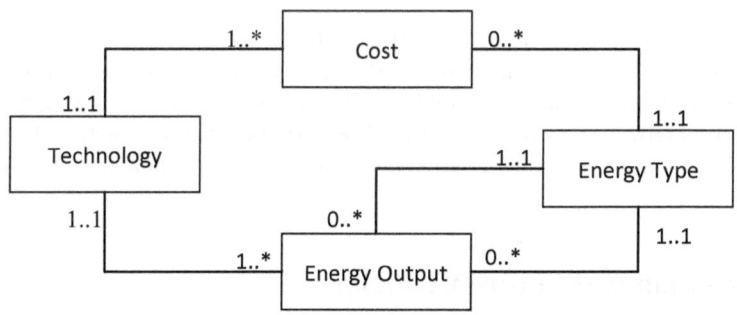

Fig. 5. Simplified UML Class diagram

3.3   Integration Requirements

The EnRiMa DSS should support the integration of both external data sources, such as data coming from building controls systems, and software modules, such as software for running optimizations and presenting results. As the EnRiMa system evolves, it is likely that the data formats that need to be handled will need to be extended, and that the number of systems that would like to make use of the EnRiMa DSS outputs will rise. We thus define the following principle:

Principle 6: A DSS for building energy efficiency cannot be run in isolation, thus look for flexible means for integration.

This principle is reflected in the system, where integrations with external weather forecasting services and building management systems (BMS) are implemented. In order to be easily extended the design of the EnRiMa DSS system considers the following integration requirements:

Protocols. The EnRiMa DSS should make use of well documented and standardized protocols for communication between software modules. For example, for integration purposes the use of Web Service protocols such as SOAP and interface descriptions such as WSDL should be used.

Data import. There are requirements for the EnRiMa DSS to import data from the Honeywell MCR building management system used at one test site, and a Siemens Desigo system used at another. Thus, a requirement on the EnRiMa DSS is that it should be built to be easily extended to allow for the import of different data formats.

Data export. The EnRiMa DSS will have built-in data representations, for example various forms of diagrams. However, there might be a need to further analyze the results from the DSS. In these cases it is important that the system supports export of the resulting data in easily accessible format. Currently the systems at the project test sites supports export of data in the form of Microsoft Excel files. Similar functionality should likely exist in the EnRiMa DSS.

External software modules. There are existing software modules that need to be a part of the EnRiMa DSS. For example the DSS will use solvers and data presentation software. These software modules should be integrated in such a way that a) they do not dictate the internal structure of the EnRiMa DSS, or limit its functionality, and b) that the software modules can be exchanged, for example when the use of a new solver arises.

4   Discussion and Future Challenges

While the presented principles cover some of the aspect the project has ran into, the project continues and we expect to define new problems and solutions. Thus, the list of principles is likely to expand. One area of particular interest is looking at new potential groups of stakeholders. The development process of the DSS has been iterative with active stakeholder involvement. While there is general interest to reducing CO_2 emissions, the main motivating factor for change still is cost reduction. Hence the DSS and similar solutions in this field should take into account the need to consolidate a multitude of stakeholder wishes and objective. Concerning the adoption of the EnRiMa DSS we foresee the following challenges:

- Integration and use of large amounts of data, (e.g. sensor, weather, occupant), information and knowledge. Sensor information is readily available in most modern buildings. E.g. the smart city project in Stockholm will have built in sensors in the newly built houses being about to generating large amounts of data, but at the moment there is no clear vision how this data could be used to reduce the carbon footprint and increase energy efficiency. This requires new theories, algorithms, and approaches for energy efficiency and environmental sustainability.
- User friendly adaptation, customization and evolvement of decisions over time. In a real building usually a diverse group of stakeholders are affected and information provided by them to be taken into account, e.g. market data and trends, technology developments, business strategies of involved actors, environmental considerations, security issues, occupant needs, as well as operator goals. The challenge is to integrate all this data into a model that can be used for decision making.
- Amalgamation of decision making based on mathematical models with business strategy development based for example on conceptual models and balanced scorecards. This would make the strategic decision making more available for people with less experience in DSS, as well as it would stimulate the learning process of the consequences of different decisions.

Furthermore, as demonstrated in section 3, the DSS should be connected to the BMS to import data and to export temperature set points. This requirement is valid for all solutions in this area, i.e. new energy efficiency solutions should be seen as add-ons to the existing BMS. What make this challenging, however, is that many BMS are proprietary systems with limited integration possibilities.

5   Conclusion

In this paper we have presented a prototype DSS for improving energy efficiency in buildings developed in EU supported FP7 project EnRiMa. Furthermore we have presented six high-level principles that reflect our experiences of developing the prototype system. These principles concerns two perspectives - business concerns and software architecture. The business concerns are covered by our recommendation to consider long and short term issues (principle 1), and their integration (principle 2). Furthermore based or the project experiences that a DSS for energy efficiency needs to handle large amounts of data we argued for the use of automatization and default values (principle 3). In the paper we also outlined the software architecture of the system and its constituents in form of software modules. Based on the experiences from the project we pointed towards the importance to tackle the differences in the software modules (principle 4), as well as the need to use different languages (principle 5). A decision support system that is clearly affected by external data sources, such as Building Management Systems in the case of the EnRiMa DDS, also needs to consider flexible means for system integration (principle 6).

The next stage of the project will test the DSS in real life settings, we thus expect to uncover more principles as the project continues.

Acknowledgements. This work has been performed in course of the European project EnRiMa "Energy Efficiency and Risk Management in Public Buildings" and is supported by the European Commission, within the 7th Framework Programme (FP7).

Center for Energy and innovative Technologies (CET) was supported by the Austrian Federal Ministry for Transport, Innovation and Technology through the Building of Tomorrow program as well as by the Theodor Kery Foundation of the province of Burgenland in course of EnRiMa.

We also want to thank the University of Applied Science at Pinkafeld and University of Applied Science at Vienna (ENERGYbase) for their great support of the EnRiMa project. The authors also thank all other EnRiMa partners: University College London, International Institute for Applied Systems Analysis, Universidad Rey Juan Carlos, Minerva Consulting and Communication, SINTEF Group, Tecnalia, and Hidrocantábrico Energía (EDP Group) for their valuable input and support.

References

1. Loos, P., Nebel, W., Marx Gómez, J., Hasan, H., Watson, R.T., vom Brocke, J., Recker, J.: Green IT: a matter of business and information systems engineering? Business & Information Systems Engineering 3(4), 245–252 (2011)
2. Turban, E., Sharda, R., Delen, D., Efraim, T.: Decision support and business intelligence systems. Pearson Education (2007)
3. IIASA, SU, UCL, URJC, SINTEF, CET, HCE, and TECNALIA, Requirement Analysis, EnRiMa Deliverable D4.1, European Commission, FP7 Project Number 260041 (2011)
4. Fowler, M.: Patterns of Enterprise Application Architecture. Addison-Wesley (2003)
5. OMG, OMG Unified Modeling Language (OMG UML), Superstructure, version 2.4.1, Document Number: formal/2012-05-07 (2012), http://www.omg.org
6. SU, IIASA, SINTEF, URJC, and CET. Draft Specification for Services and Tools. EnRiMa Deliverable D5.1, European Commission FP7 Project Number 260041 (2012)
7. OMG, OMG Unified Modeling Language (OMG UML), Infrastructure, version 2.4.1, Document Number: formal/2012-05-06 (2012), http://www.omg.org
8. Geoffrion, A.: Integrated modeling systems. Computer Science in Economics and Management 2, 3–15 (1989)
9. Cano, E., Groissböck, M., Moguerza, J., Stadler, M.: A Strategic Optimisation Model for Energy Systems Planning. IEEE Transactions on Power Systems (submitted, 2013)

Noise Identification in Multivariate Time Series Modelling with Divergence Approach

Ryszard Szupiluk

Warsaw School of Economics, Al. Niepodleglosci 162, 02-554 Warsaw, Poland
rszupi@sgh.waw.pl

Abstract. In this paper we develop ensemble method based on multivariate decompositions taken from blind signal separation techniques. The main idea is to decompose prediction result into constructive and destructive (noises) components. Elimination of the noises from predictions should improve final prediction. One of the key issues in this method is the correct classification and distinction between destructive and constructive components, what provide to random noise detection problem. It can be interpreted in terms of signal similarity, in which the Bose-Einstein divergence can be applied .

Keywords: noise reduction, ensemble methods, noise identification, independent component analysis, divergence function.

1   Introduction

The random noise detection is one of the main task in signal and data processing. The terms: random and noise has wide-ranging physical, epistemological, philosophical and mathematical meaning. Consequently, random noise can be defined, described and analysed in many ways. In the colloquial meaning, the random noise can be treated as unpredictable and undesirable signal generated by source or factors out of our control. In practice, the random noise might be interpreted from two fundamental perspectives: the randomness as some mathematical characteristic, and the noise as an uncontrolled physical factor. Frequent problem concerning noises is the fact that the mathematical definition and interpretation can be far from physical reality, especially when "physical" means economic, social or medical phenomena [15,20].

Such problems can be found in ensemble methods, where latent components are identified using the methods from blind signal separation [16]. The main idea is to decompose prediction result into constructive and destructive components. After identification and elimination the destructive components, final prediction results should be improved. Proposed approach can be treated as ensemble method since it is associated with fact that final result is combination of primary models. The main difference to typical solutions like bagging, boosting or stacked regression we treat prediction errors as noises rather in physical than mathematical sense [3,6,10]. Let's note, that we mean prediction in wide sense as discovering patterns hidden in data and it is not limited to estimation of unknown future variable values. In general, it can be

A. Kobyliński and A. Sobczak (Eds.): BIR 2013, LNBIP 158, pp. 327–334, 2013.
© Springer-Verlag Berlin Heidelberg 2013

interpreted as kind of filtered data regression. However, presentation in prediction context allows to explain method's motivation in easy way.

As mentioned before, the main problem concerns proper components classification, what can be complex task because latent destructive components typically are not pure white noises or, in many cases, we have data without time structure. In such problems noises can be interpreted as signals with destructive impact on prediction, modelling or analysis [18]. Instead of a priori noise identification some kind of comparative signal analysis with some reference pattern (noise or desired pattern) is applied. In such framework the component classification task can be treated as the problem aimed to find similarity (or divergence) between the signals. For this task we present concept based on Bose-Einstein divergence, which can be expressed in convenient form for similarity analysis.

2   Predictors Aggregation

In this section we present the method for models aggregation based on multivariate decomposition of prediction results. Having a few prediction models we treat their results as a multivariate variable with destructive or constructive impact for prediction latent components. The constructive ones are associated with the unknown true value, whereas the destructive components can be present due to many reasons like: missing data, lack of significant variables or not precise parameter estimation. The identification and elimination of destructive components should improve final prediction. For such approach we need to make some assumptions about prediction results, especially how are they generated. The generation model is independent form original prediction models due to the fact that we aggregate information from models of any kind, similarly in the way as generation model is taken in blind signal separation problem.

We assume that after learning various models we have a set of prediction results. We collect particular prediction results $x_i(k)$, $i = 1,...,m$, in one multivariate variable $\mathbf{x}(k) = [x_1(k),...,x_m(k)]^T$. Now we assume that prediction result is a mixture of the m latent components: constructive s_j, $j \in D_1$ and destructive s_i, $i \in D_2$ where $D_1 \cup D_2 = \{1,2,...,m\}$, $D_1 \cap D_2 = \varnothing$ and $D_1 \neq \varnothing$. Next, we assume that the prediction result are the linear combination of latent components

$$\mathbf{x}(k) = \mathbf{A}s(k) = \mathbf{A}[s_1(k),...,s_m(k)]^T ,$$ (1)

where $\mathbf{s}(k) \in R^m$, matrix $\mathbf{A} = [a_{ij}] \in R^{m \times m}$ represents the mixing system. The relation (1) stands for decomposition of prediction results $\mathbf{x}$ into latent components vector $\mathbf{s}$ and mixing matrix $\mathbf{A}$. If the destructive part of the signal is removed (the signals are replaced with zero, $s_i(k)$ for $i \in D_2$) and the constructive components are mixed back, the modified prediction results $\hat{\mathbf{x}}(k)$ will be improved (or filtered):

$$\hat{\mathbf{x}}(k) = \mathbf{A}\hat{s}(k) = \hat{\mathbf{A}}s(k) ,$$ (2)

where $\hat{s}_j(k) = s_j(k)$ for $j \in D_1$, $\hat{s}_j(k) = 0$ for $j \in D_2$, and $\hat{\mathbf{A}} = [\hat{a}_{ij}]$, where $\hat{a}_{ij} = a_{ij}$ for $j \in D_1$, $\hat{a}_{ij} = 0$ for $j \in D_2$.

The most adequate methods to find $\mathbf{A}$ and $\mathbf{s}(k)$ seem to be the blind signal separation techniques (BSS) [4,11] where we try to find unknown signals mixed in unknown system. The BSS methods explore different properties of data like: independence [7,11], decorrelation [4], sparsity [13], non-negativity [12], smoothness [17]. For assumed mutual independence of latent components, as an example of BSS methods leading to $\mathbf{A}$ and $\mathbf{s}$ estimation we can apply independent component analysis (ICA). In ICA approach to BSS, under some conditions, we try to find such matrix $\mathbf{W}$ that for $\mathbf{y} = \mathbf{Wx} = \mathbf{WAs} \approx \mathbf{s}$ we obtain $\mathbf{WA} = \mathbf{PD}$, where $\mathbf{P}$ is a some permutation matrix and $\mathbf{D}$ is a some diagonal matrix [11]. In practice it mean that estimated independent components can be recalled and reordering comparing with original, what is not important in our conception. For practical matrix $\mathbf{A} \approx \mathbf{W}^{-1}$ estimation we can use Natural Gradient Algorithm in the form of

$$\mathbf{W}(k+1) = \mathbf{W}(k) + \mu(k)\left[\mathbf{I} - E\left\{\mathbf{f}(\mathbf{y}(k))\mathbf{y}^T(k)\right\}\right]\mathbf{W}(k) \quad , \tag{3}$$

where $\mathbf{f}(\mathbf{y}) = [f_1(y_1),...,f_n(y_n)]^T$ is a vector of nonlinearities with optimal form of $f_i(y_i) = -\partial \log(p_i(y_i))/\partial y_i$, what can be approximated in many ways [4,11] . Let's us note, that in financial time series case, we use ICA Natural Gradient algorithm based on Extended Generalized Lambda Distribution system [14], due to its flexibility in higher order statistics data modelling.

It should be noted that ICA methods explore spatial relations between data. Therefore, time structure in data, if it exists, is not taken into account in analysis. From this perspective all signals are interpreted in terms of random variables or are assumed (a priori) as white noises. Such assumptions are useful for creation, so called, working ICA model which does not must describe real characteristics of signals. From such perspective the term white noise can introduce ambiguity in practical applications.

3   Destructive Components as Noises – Identification Problem

The key issue in the proposed concept is the classification of the components into destructive or constructive. In case of a small number of models, and thus a small number of basic components, classification of components can be done by the full search. In fact, this means examining the impact of the elimination of basic components and their combination on the final prediction outcome. In case of a larger number of models, examining the impact of all possible combinations of the basic components on the forecasts can be computationally difficult. Therefore, assessment of the component impact must be done based on certain characteristics or derived criteria. One possible approach is to assume that the destructive components are random noises.

To describe the random noise in mathematical way we usually apply the probabilistic approach. The well-known example is the white noise defined IID – as a sequence of independent random variables with identical distribution [8]. In most theoretical and practical considerations of the white noise we observe the application of the Gaussian distribution what is strongly legitimized by the Central Limit Theorem. Therefore, it has a lot of practical implementations especially in the technological problems like signal filtration or system identification [19,20]. Whereas, we have to be aware of the fact that in the technological problems the useful signals are regular and easily recognizable even with some visual inspection, because the deterministic signals strongly dominate the noise components. Thus, the white noise description might be a fine approximation of the signal disruptions, even if they are autocorrelated or coloured noises. If the desired signal differs a lot from the noise the misspecification of the disruption structure does not matter. Moreover, it is very easy to extend the white noise models on the coloured cases [4].

The situation is more complicated if the mathematical description does not reflect the usefulness of the signal. We can observe the problem on the financial markets, where the logarithmic returns are described with stationary stochastic processes [1,15]. In practice it means assumption that the rate of return is generated from the series of identically distributed random variables. Moreover, the variables are uncorrelated or transformed with Box-Jenkins methodology to obtain this property [2]. As a consequence the signal fulfilling the mathematical definition of the white noise might be both disruption (in technological applications) and useful information (in financial time series). We can conclude that the mathematical definition of random noise does not necessarily implicate its positive or negative role in the context of the analyzed problem. The situation complicates, if both the useful and disruption signals reveal similarity. We can observe such situation in case of model aggregation via BSS methods where the constructive and destructive components can be mixture of random and deterministic signals with unknown distributions. Therefore, it is rather impossible to determine in advance what level of randomness can be associated with each component. For this reason, this problem must be considered in terms of the mutual similarity of the signals and the noise rather than their individual characteristics.

4   Bose Einstein Divergence for Signal Similarity Measure

The similarity measure between two nonnegative sequences or patterns can be taken as divergence function [5]. A divergence function $D(y \parallel z)$ between two variables z and y fulfils the following conditions: $D(y \parallel z) \geq 0$ and $D(y \parallel z) = 0$ only if $y = z$. But the triangular inequality $D(y \parallel z) \leq D(y \parallel x) + D(x \parallel z)$ is not a necessary condition for the divergence. Such divergences function are usually used in a manifold of probability distributions but can be also used for general data analysis. The one of the popular divergence is Bose-Einstein divergence, what for vectors $\mathbf{z} = [z_1, z_2, ..., z_L]$ and $\mathbf{y} = [y_1, y_2, ..., y_L]$, id defined as

$$D_{BE}^{\alpha}(\mathbf{y} \parallel \mathbf{z}) = \sum_{i=1}^{L} \left(y_i \ln \frac{(1+\alpha)y_i}{y_i + \alpha z_i} + \alpha z_i \ln \frac{(1+\alpha)z_i}{y_i + \alpha z_i} \right) =$$
$$= y \ln((1+\alpha)y) - y \ln(y + \alpha z) + \alpha z \ln((1+\alpha)z) - \alpha z \ln(y + \alpha z) \qquad (4)$$

where $y_i, z_i \in [0,1]$. This divergence has many interesting properties e.g.

$D_{BE}^{\alpha}(\mathbf{y} \parallel \mathbf{z}) = D_{BE}^{1/\alpha}(\mathbf{y} \Vert \mathbf{z})$ and $D_{BE}^{\alpha \to \infty}(\mathbf{y} \parallel \mathbf{z}) = D_{KL}(\mathbf{y} \Vert \mathbf{z})$, where D_{KL} means Kullback-Leibler divergence. We can see that divergence (4) is asymmetric measure in general, what can be used for signal similarity assessment. For similar signals in some common sense, like random signals derived from the same distributions, we can expect that order of divergence arguments is not important. The opposite situation is for signals witch contain patterns, regularity or trends.

It means, that for random signals v_1, v_2 with the same distributions, the divergence (4), should be symmetric $D_{BE}(v_1 \parallel v_2) = D_{BE}(v_2 \parallel v_1)$. For standardized signals to interval [0,1], similarity effect, can be measured as

$$q = \text{abs}\left(\log \frac{D_{BE}(z \parallel v)}{D_{BE}(v \parallel z)} \right). \qquad (5)$$

The α parameter can be used to control degree of similarity, what can explained as follow. For $\alpha \in (0,1)$ all logarithmic values in (4) are in interval $(0,2)$. In such case, it is possible to express $\ln(x)$ via following Taylor series

$$\ln x = (x-1) - \frac{(x-1)^2}{2} + \ldots + (-1)^{n+1} \frac{(x-1)^n}{n} + \ldots \approx x - 1, \qquad (6)$$

Taking (2) and (6) for $\alpha \in (0,1)$ we obtain

$$D_{BE}^{\alpha}(\mathbf{y} \parallel \mathbf{z}) = \alpha \|\mathbf{y} - \mathbf{x}\|_2^2 + R, \qquad (7)$$

where R means approximation residuals. We can see that R is responsible on asymmetry effect $D_{BE}^{\alpha}(\mathbf{y} \parallel \mathbf{z})$ and α parameter control the sensitivity of similarity measure.

5   Simulation Experiments

In this section we will verify the presented approach on financial data in technical analysis context. Our aim is to find trends or signals which indicate, in advance, a forthcoming main stock value movement. We consider five time series including following stock companies listed on Warsaw Stock Exchange such as BRE (x1), Mostostal Export (x2), Mostostal Zabrze (x3),Rafako (x4), Relpol (x5), see Fig. 1. After ICA decomposition we have independent components presented on the left side of the Fig. 1. Let's us note that according to ICA methods properties we use directly stock values, not their derivatives like return rates or logarithmic return rates what is typical, for instance, in Box-Jenkins methodology.

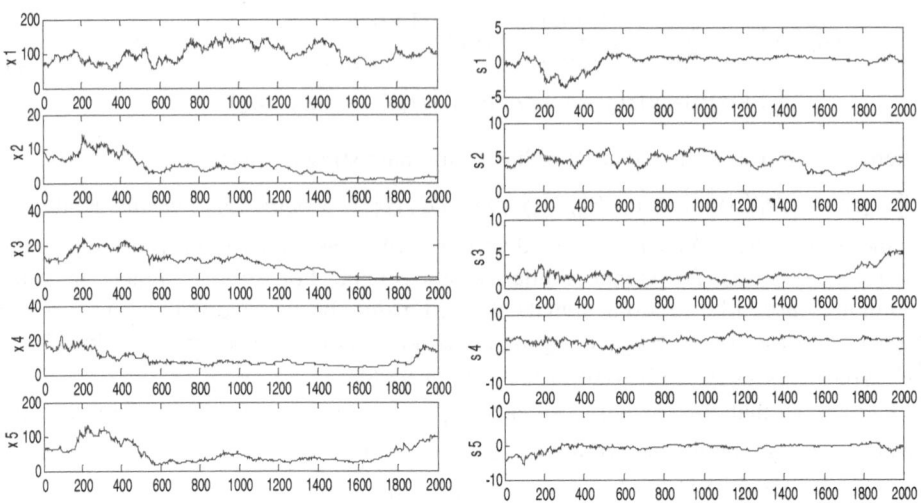

Fig. 1. Stock time series: left column presents original signals x1-x5 , right column presents latent independent components s1-s5

To identify the most noisy signal we compare latent components s1-s5 with reference signal (s6) drawn from Gaussian distribution. Results of the Bose-Einstein divergence between latent components and reference noise are presented in Table 1.

Table 1. Bose-Einstein divergence values for financial latent components

	s1	S2	s3	s4	S5	s6
s1	0	0.0558	0.1299	0.1494	0.1429	0.1218
s2	0.0544	0	0.1552	0.1651	0.1842	0.1656
s3	0.1201	0.1583	0	0.0170	0.0749	0.1065
s4	0.1296	0.1587	0.0168	0	0.1064	0.1473
s5	0.1368	0.1844	0.0825	0.1206	0	0.0594
s6	0.1188	0.1696	0.1171	0.1644	0.0592	0

Table 2. Similarity assessment by q factor

	s1	s2	s3	s4	s5	s6
s1	-	0.0254	0.0784	0.1422	0.0436	0.0249
s2		-	0.0198	0.0395	0.0011	0.0239
s3			-	0.0118	0.0966	0.0949
s4				-	0.1253	0.1039
s5					-	0.0034
s6						-

Signals symmetry measured by q factor is shown in Table 2. This is an important result from investment point of view, since this approach gives an opportunity to predict future direction of the market or to estimate the value at risk, associated with particular stock item. We can see that component s5 is the most similar to the reference noise. Such component can be interpreted as noisy or associated with short term fluctuations.

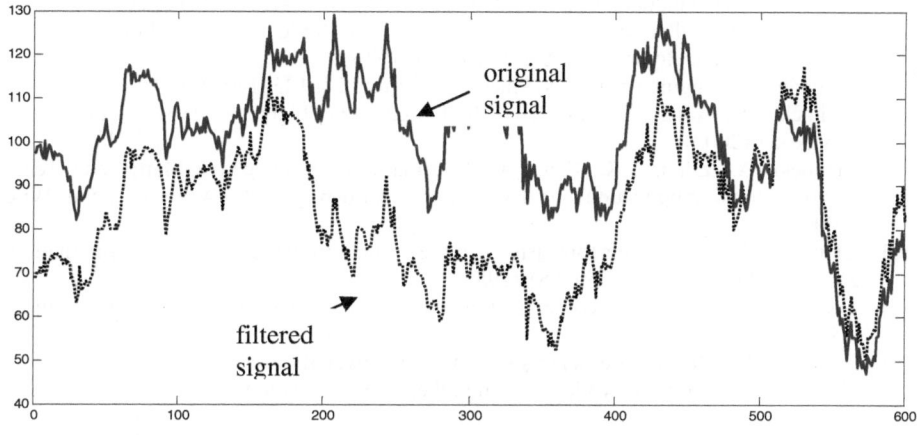

Fig. 2. BRE stock time series

After its elimination and re-combining (mixing) the rest of the latent components we obtain stock signals which are leading the original signals, like presented in Fig. 2 for BRE.

6   Conclusions

This paper presents a divergence based methodology for noisy components identification in multivariate time series analysis. This approach has been applied in the context of predictive models aggregation. The aggregation or ensemble means that final results are mixture of the primary models which, in practice, leads to particular steps such us: models result decomposition into latent components, noisy latent components identification and elimination, and finally mixing back the rest of latent components. The effect of such model combination should result in noise reduction, what, in prediction context, means better model assessment according to different criteria.

The experiment conducted on stock data demonstrated the validity of the proposed solutions and it should be treated as a proof of concept. Nevertheless, the aim was to present novel analytical methodology rather than discuss the results of particular technical application. Additionally, it should be noted, that motivated by interesting properties, we focus on Bose-Einstein divergence and ICA decomposition, but proposed approach gives general framework for different types of decompositions and divergences.

Acknowledgements. The work was funded by the National Science Center in Poland based on decision number DEC-2011/03/B/HS4/05092.

References

[1] Bollerslev, T., Engle, R.F., Nelson, D.: ARCH Models. In: McFadden, D.F., Engle III, R.F. (eds.) The Handbook of Econometrics, vol. IV. North-Holland (1994)

[2] Box, G.E.P., Müller, M.E., Jenkins, G.M.: Time Series Analysis Forecasting and Control, 2nd edn. Holden Day, San Francisco (1976)

[3] Breiman, L.: Bagging predictors. Machine Learning 24, 123–140 (1996)

[4] Cichocki, A., Amari, S.: Adaptive Blind Signal and Image Processing. John Wiley, Chichester (2002)

[5] Cichocki, A., Zdunek, R., Phan, A.-H., Amari, S.: Nonnegative Matrix and Tensor Factorizations: Applications to Exploratory Multi-way Data Analysis. John Wiley (2009)

[6] Clements, T.: Combining forecasts: A review and annotated bibligraphy. International Journal of Forecasting 5, 559–581 (1989)

[7] Comon, P.: Independent component analysis, a new concept? Signal Processing 36 (1994)

[8] Hamilton, J.D.: Time series analysis. Princeton University Press, Princeton (1994)

[9] Haykin, S.: Neural networks: a comprehensive foundation. Macmillan, New York (1994)

[10] Hoeting, J., Madigan, D., Raftery, A., Volinsky, C.: Bayesian model averaging: a tutorial. Statistical Science 14, 382–417 (1999)

[11] Hyvarinen, A., Karhunen, J., Oja, E.: Independent Component Analysis. John Wiley, New York (2001)

[12] Lee, D.D., Seung, H.S.: Learning of the parts of objects by non-negative matrix factorization. Nature 401 (1999)

[13] Li, Y., Cichocki, A., Amari, S.: Sparse component analysis for blind source separation with less sensors than sources. In: Fourth Int. Symp. on ICA and Blind Signal Separation, Nara, Japan, pp. 89–94 (2003)

[14] Karvanen, J., Eriksson, J., Koivunen, V.: Adaptive Score Functions for Maximum Likelihood ICA. VLSI Signal Processing 32, 83–92 (2002)

[15] Shiryaev, A.N.: Essentials of stochastic finance: facts, models, theory. World Scientific, Singapore (1999)

[16] Szupiluk, R., Wojewnik, P., Zabkowski, T.: Model Improvement by the Statistical Decomposition. In: Rutkowski, L., Siekmann, J.H., Tadeusiewicz, R., Zadeh, L.A. (eds.) ICAISC 2004. LNCS (LNAI), vol. 3070, pp. 1199–1204. Springer, Heidelberg (2004)

[17] Szupiluk, R., Wojewnik, P., Ząbkowski, T.: Smooth Component Analysis as Ensemble Method for Prediction Improvement. In: Davies, M.E., James, C.J., Abdallah, S.A., Plumbley, M.D. (eds.) ICA 2007. LNCS, vol. 4666, pp. 277–284. Springer, Heidelberg (2007)

[18] Szupiluk, R., Wojewnik, P., Zabkowski, T.: Noise detection for ensemble methods. In: Rutkowski, L., Scherer, R., Tadeusiewicz, R., Zadeh, L.A., Zurada, J.M. (eds.) ICAISC 2010, Part I. LNCS, vol. 6113, pp. 471–478. Springer, Heidelberg (2010)

[19] Therrien, C.W.: Discrete Random Signals and Statistical Signal Processing. Prentice Hall, New Jersey (1992)

[20] Vaseghi, S.V.: Advanced signal processing and digital noise reduction. John Wiley and Sons, B. G. Teubner, Chichester, Stuttgart (1997)

Author Index